HOUSE OF SLAVES and "DOOR OF NO RETURN"

The Harriet Tubman Series on the African Diaspora

The Harriet Tubman Institute for Research on the Global Migrations of African Peoples

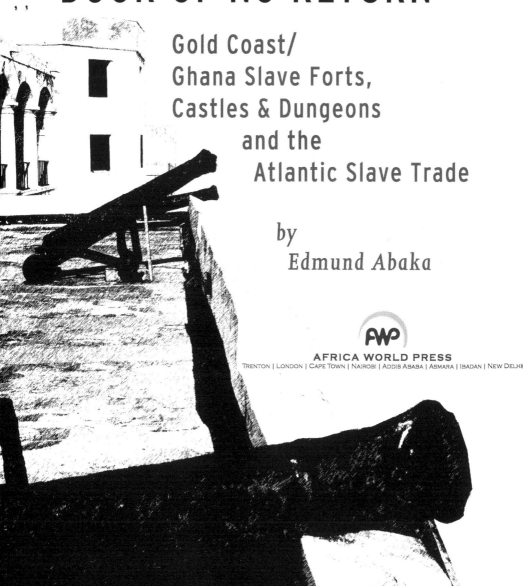

HOUSE OF SLAVES
✛ and ✛
"DOOR OF NO RETURN"

Gold Coast/
Ghana Slave Forts,
Castles & Dungeons
and the
Atlantic Slave Trade

by

Edmund *Abaka*

FWP

AFRICA WORLD PRESS

Trenton | London | Cape Town | Nairobi | Addis Ababa | Asmara | Ibadan | New Delhi

AFRICA WORLD PRESS
541 West Ingham Avenue | Suite B
Trenton, New Jersey 08638

Book and cover design: Saverance Publishing Services

Library of Congress Cataloging-in-Publication Data

"House of slaves and 'door of no return'" : Gold Coast/Ghana slave forts, castles and dungeons and the Atlantic slave trade / Edmund Abaka.
    p. cm.
  Includes bibliographical references and index.
  ISBN 978-1-59221-825-7 (hard cover : alk. paper) -- ISBN 978-1-59221-826-4
(pbk. : alk. paper) 1. Slave trade--Ghana--History. 2. Slave trade--Atlantic Ocean Region--History. 3. Fortification--Ghana. 4. Historic buildings--Ghana. 5. Castles--Ghana. 6. Prisons--Ghana. 7. Slaves--Dwellings--Ghana. 8. Slaves--Ghana--Social conditions. I. Title.
  HT1394.G48A23 2011
  306.3'6209667--dc23
                            2011032533

Harriet Tubman Series

This book is dedicated to

all Africans and African-descended peoples who fought for the
abolition of the inhuman slave trade

as well as

those who visit the slave forts and castles of Ghana every year in
hopes of finding out "that which was not spoken at home."

✛ Contents

✦ List of Illustrations

TABLES

FIGURES

✠ Ode to Cape Coast Castle

WHAT THE CASTLE SAID

I AM at my edge endless like the sea
I cornered by sheer size an adventure of sorrows
And trussed the moaning, uncle tom-tom;
I am bold with legend
I have conquered these gaping shores
With surprise laps of my race

I am my own sea, the jungled drop
I crowd the litanies and the laments
With vain blood;
I laugh at the animal cries women make
I am the necklace of long-irons they ear
The iron-collar crimson with suffering

I am at the very edge myself
I captured the land and its abundant blackness;
The number is fired and numberless
That perished under my watchful eyes;
With my pawns I checkmated the people
Whose resurrection has not yet found the key to life
The formula for counting the dead lies in my belly

I ruined the sea's virginity
When the evening dropped her skirts:
With such delicate arms and gestures
Did love reach me in my deepest dungeons

I am at edge a restless sea
Surinam Jamaica Alabama, Nova Scotia
I echo the owl's surprise-eyes in the glare
The zombie-shuffle of four hundred years

I am surrounded by a colony of bending knees
A people made drunk by lethal fatality
I am the climax
The assay of thumping hearts
I sleep in the silence of scars

The silhouette of a defiled race leaps flaming
But its only a shadow
I remain strong in the darkness of my whitening.

Source: Kwadwo Opoku-Agyeman, *Cape Coast Castle: A Collection of Poems* (Accra: Afram
    Publications, 1996), 47-48. Courtesy of Afram Publications.

✤ Preface

The well-preserved slave forts and castles of West Africa, and more especially those of Ghana, such as Cape Coast and Elmina, constitute some of the most remarkable sites of historical memory that document the Euro-African contact between the fifteenth and nineteenth centuries and the infamous slave trade of the same period. Together with eyewitness accounts (of European officials, ship captains and surgeons, slave merchants and formerly enslaved Africans), old building plans, drawings and photographs, this book is an attempt to capture the essence of both the Euro-African encounter as well as Africa-African diaspora connections (in fact, Pan-Africanism in the true sense of the word), as consummated through the biennial Pan-African Historical Theatre Festival (PANAFEST) and Emancipation (from slavery) commemorations in Ghana.

The slave forts and castles of the Gold Coast (now Ghana) became the focal point of a global commercial network that linked up Africa, Europe, the Americas and Asia. In that sense, globalization far antedated our twenty-first century digital connectivity and brought into contact people from far-flung places who engaged in trade; exchange of ideas, cultural norms, religions; and forged new family relations. West Africans participated in a flourishing trade that involved European governments, accredited European chartered companies, unlicensed and independent merchants, swashbuckling buccaneers and interlopers who profited from their individual enterprise. From that perspective, the slave forts and castles functioned as "Europe in Africa" and the activities of Europeans (mercantilists, slave merchants, soldiers, freebooters and interlopers, missionaries and even colonial officials) in these enclosures highlight political and economic trends and considerations in Europe, together with European rivalry and European wars that were fought, by extension, on the Gold Coast. Power struggles among various European nations reverberated on the Gold Coast as well.

The Gold Coast forts, castles and dungeons were places of torture, violence, brutality and death for countless Africans. Consequently, life was brutish and short for some Africans, whether en-route to the coast or in the slave

Photo 0.0: Seal of Danish Crown Affixed to Exchange/Sale of Forts on the Gold Coast. *Courtesy of National Archives, Kew, England*

Photo 0.1: Inscription in Dutch Reformed Church (atop male dungeon, São Jorge da Mina)

forts, castles and dungeons where the very young or the old and feeble were oftentimes left to die, or died and were thrown into the Atlantic Ocean. This epitomizes the inhumanity that attended the slave trade. The toll on European lives on the coast, while not linked to the inhumanity of the slave trade (due to their privileged position in the trade), was considerable because many of them voluntarily or forcibly lived and worked in the tough climatic conditions on the West African coast between the fifteenth and nineteenth centuries.

While archaeological and architectural descriptions of the slave forts and castles are important, this book goes beyond the structural and the descriptive to link or relink all the continents that interfaced on the African coast due to trade, the slave trade and colonialism. It also links up all facets of the "African family," namely, those who never left the continent and those who were part of the forced migration of over 12 million souls to the New World,[1] not forgetting those who died in the long and arduous march from the interior to the coast of West Africa, in the slave forts and castles along the Gold Coast, as well as those who perished during the dreadful Middle Passage.[2] The views of many of those who worked in the slave forts and castles are no longer available,[3] as are some of the modified architectural plans of the various European hosts who lived in the structures. However, personal accounts by a few occupants, visitors, European governors, factors and castle personnel, merchants, slave ship captains, some enslaved persons and local townspeople, local historians, oral sources and oral traditions provide valuable information that open several windows into life in the slave forts and castles and the mechanics of the Atlantic slave trade as it played out on the West African coast. The accounts help to distinguish new construction from earlier construction and trace modifications, rehabilitations, alterations and changes made to the slave forts and castles by various European powers, albeit not without attendant difficulties of precise dates and, sometimes, origins of materials used. All in all these accounts help to document various important activities and events on the Euro-African frontier.[4]

The lives of Africans and Europeans in the slave forts and castles, the professions represented in these "ships at permanent anchor" – chiefs, emissaries, governors, various administrative officials, chaplains, storekeepers, apothecaries, soldiers, sailors, merchants, carpenters, masons and the enslaved persons – and the trade practices in these fortified enclosures are all important themes worth considering in order to appreciate the role of these slave forts and castles as the linchpin in the slave trade in particular and the Euro-African encounter on the Gold Coast in general. Considering the fact that the forts and castles became the focal points of global mercantile activities, one can examine what manner of architectural edifices these were, and still are, and their role in recapturing historical memory.

What manner of men, women and children lived, loved, worked and died in these forts and castles? What happened in these slave forts and castles – the routine of life, work and conviviality and of death? How were slaves housed, secured, fed, and bartered away or sold (sometimes with a "scented" smile) and what happened to castle slaves when the trade in enslaved Africans was abolished in 1807? What roles did the slave forts, castles and dungeons play in the history of the Gold Coast after the abolition and, later, the suppression of the slave trade? What is the role of the slave forts, castles, and dungeons in the new efforts to connect Africa with its sons and daughters in the diaspora? What is the significance of the forts and castles in European and global history? What do they tell us about European activities on the Gold Coast?

The slave forts and castles provide a poignant look at European systems of government, chartered company activities and administration, architecture, health practices, education and their lasting effects on the Gold Coast in particular, but on Africa in general. These exchanges on the Euro-African frontier on the Gold Coast also affected food, nutrition and cuisine as part of the Columbian exchange. Foods and culinary practices from the other side of the Atlantic were introduced into West Africa and, similarly, African food and foodways followed enslaved Africans into the New World to influence culinary practices in the Americas and the Caribbean. By the same token, what problems emerged on this Euro-African frontier?

The number of major monographs on the Gold Coast forts and castles is comparatively few when viewed against the monumental importance of these structures. The proximity of dungeon, office, residential quarters and "palaver halls" on one hand, existing side by side with dungeon and church on the other, constitute some of the paradoxes that graced the existence of the slave forts and castles of the Gold Coast. Even the names of the forts and castles provide food for thought. The Dutch, for example, called the Apam fort, Lijdzaamheid (Patience), even though they faced local resistance that delayed completion of the fort for an interminably long time.[5] In Elmina the Dutch Reformed Church sat atop the male slave dungeon of São Jorge da Mina with an inscription denoting that God resided only in "this" place (Photo 0.1). In the same vein, Fort Batenstein, despite its name, was a very unprofitable enterprise.[6] Trade in the Butri area of the Gold Coast was pitiful and profits were non-existent. But why call the fort by a name that represented the exact opposite of reality (a profitable as opposed to a very unprofitable enterprise)? In another interesting twist, the Portuguese named their slave forts and castles after patron saints, Jorge, Sebastião and Antonio, not to talk about names of slave ships such as *John the Baptist*.

The book discusses some of the paradoxes inherent in these dimensions of the Afro-European encounter for both the specialist and the general reader who is interested in answers to these questions. As well, it sheds light on several aspects of the history of Ghana in particular and West Africa in general.

Notes

1. Scholars "generally" agree on the figure of 11.2 million people as representing the number of people who landed in the New World. However, recent technological advances have encouraged further revision of the numbers. David Eltis, through the Du Bois data set project, has added almost a million to the number of Africans who landed in the New World. For the debates see Philip D. Curtin, The Atlantic Slave Trade: A Census (Madison: University of Wisconsin Press, 1969); J. E. Inikori, "Measuring the Atlantic Slave Trade: an Assessment of Curtin and Anstey," Journal of African History 17, 2 (1976): 197-223; Paul E. Lovejoy, "The Volume of the Atlantic Slave Trade: A Synthesis," Journal of African History 22, 4 (1982): 473-501. See also David Eltis, "The Volume, Age/Sex Ratios, and the African Impact of the Slave Trade: Some Refinement of Paul Lovejoy's Review of the Literature," Journal of African History 31, 3 (1990): 485-492; and David Eltis and David Richardson, eds., Extending the Frontiers: Essays on the New Transatlantic Slave Trade Database (New Haven, CT: Yale University Press, 2008).

2   See for example, Tom Feelings and John Henrik Clark, The Middle Passage: White Ships/Black Cargo (New York: Dial Books, 1995); Virginia Schomp and S. Pearl Sharp, eds., The Slave Trade and the Middle Passage (New York: Benchmark Books, 2006); Velma Maia Thomas, Lest We Forget: The Passage from Africa to Slavery and Emancipation: A Three-Dimensional Interactive Book with Photographs and Documents from the Black Holocaust Exhibit (New York: Crown, 1997); Estelle Conwill Majozo, Middle Passage: 105 Days (Trenton, NJ.: Africa World Press, June 2003).

3. Thorkild Hansen calls some of the Danes at Christiansborg white devils. See Thorkild Hansen, Coast of Slaves, trans., Kari Dako (Accra: Sub-Saharan Publishers, 2002).

4. See Willem Bosman, A New and Accurate Description of the Coast of Guinea. 4th edn. (New York: Barnes & Noble Inc., 1967); Paul Erdmann Isert, Letters on West Africa and the Slave Trade: Paul Erdmann Isert's Journey to Guinea and the Caribbean Islands in Columbia (1788), trans. from German and ed., Selena Axelrod Winsnes (Oxford: Oxford University Press, 1992); H.W. Daendels, Journal and Correspondence of H.W. Daendels. Governor-General of the Netherlands Settlements on the Coast of Guinea. Part I. November 1815 to January 1817 (Legon: Institute of African Studies, University of Ghana, 1964).

5. See Bosman, A New and Accurate Description of the Coast of Guinea; Kwesi J. Anquandah, Castles and Forts of Ghana, (Paris: Atalante, Paris [for Ghana Monuments Board] 1979).

6. Albert van Dantzig, Forts and Castles of Ghana (Accra: Sedco Publishing Company, 1980), 47; Bosman, A New and Accurate Description of the Coast of Guinea.

7. Louis R. Harlan (Intro.) Up From Slavery (East Rutherford NJ: Viking Penguin, 1985), 2.

✥ Acknowledgments

Originally conceptualized as a project covering the whole Atlantic basin, the research for this book has taken me thus far to Ghana, Senegal, Jamaica, Trinidad and England. Time did not permit trips to Dahomey (Benin), Cape Verde, Madeira, Tunisia and East Africa, especially Tanzania. Those trips have been reserved for another day. This particular project thus focuses on the slave forts, castles and dungeons of the Gold Coast (now Ghana).

If the African saying, "It takes a village to raise a child" is often appropriate for the communal spirit that pervades many parts of the continent even today, then it is important to acknowledge the fact that it had taken the contributions of a "village" indeed to bring the various segments of this project to a fairly successful conclusion. I am very grateful to the staff/guides of both the UNESCO World Heritage sites of Cape Coast and Elmina Castles and the other slave forts in Ghana. I especially single out Mr. Phillip Atta Yawson at Fort Amsterdam (Abandzi/Kormatse). It was a delightful experience to chat with him, given his extensive knowledge of the fort and the history of "Kormantine" [Kormantse] as well as the town of Abandze where the fort is situated. As well, I would like to acknowledge the help of the guides at Fort São Antonio (Axim), Fort São Sebastaio (Shama), Fort Metal Cross (Dixcove), Fort Frederichsburg/Hollandia (Pokesu), and the young men of Akwadae and Butri who took me to the ruins of forts Dorothea and Batenstein.

I also owe a debt of gratitude to the staff of the National Archives, Kew, England, for their help in acquiring site plans of various forts and castles of the Gold Coast and photographs of Christiansborg Castle. As well, I express my appreciation for the assistance of Public Records and Archives Administration Department of Ghana (PRAAD) staff. They have become my constant companions during my annual trips to Ghana. I would like to single out Saana Roland Dok, Senior Records Supervisor in Kumasi, and Felix Nyarko Ampong (former Director of PRAAD, Kumasi, and now Interim Director of PRAAD, Ghana); Bright Owusu, Mr. Ablor (who was a walking encyclopedia of the holdings of PRAAD, Accra, and who is now retired), Auntie Gertrude of PRAAD, Accra, Safohen Kojo Amoasi of PRAAD (Cape Coast) and the staff at PRAAD, Sunyani.

I could not have done all the work without the services of Seth Amankwaa and Samuel Nartey. I thank them for the long hours we spent driving to the forts and castles scattered along the entire coastline of Ghana. We climbed hills, descended valleys and trekked to all of these forts and castles, usually after parking the pickup truck at a safe distance from the buildings. Seth Amankwaa took most of the photographs for this project and Samuel Nartey endured days of driving, sometimes over rugged terrain, especially in the Western Region of Ghana, where we visited Forts *Batenstein*, Dorothea, Metal Cross (Metalen Kruis) and Gross Frederichsborg among others. Messrs. Amankwaa and Nartey often asked what seemed to be very simple questions, but those questions often gave me food for thought and pushed me in directions I had not anticipated. As a result of that encounter, I often pondered how to make the book interesting to the general reader. I am also indebted to Francis Mensah for the use of his pickup truck in Summer 2006.

I would like to thank Sub-Saharan Publishers, Legon, for permission to use photographs of the Danish forts – Fredensborg, Kongensteen, Prindsensteen – all of which are in ruins. They gave me permission to quote *in extenso* from Thorkild Hansen's book, *Coast of Slaves*. Similarly, my sincere thanks to Sedco Publishing for allowing me to use sketches in Albert van Dantzig's *Forts and Castles of Ghana*. The project benefitted from the General Research Support grant from the University of Miami and I am grateful for research support at the University. I thank Luis Vidal of the IT team and Daniel Thompson of the Geography Department for their invaluable help.

I am also indebted to my friends and colleagues who read all or parts of the manuscript. These include, among others, Edward Kissi, Don Spivey, Marten Brienen, David Luis-Brown, Akin Ogundiran and Ezekiel Walker. More especially I am grateful to Marten Brienen whose conversations about, and enthusiasm for, the project made me more determined than ever to get the work done as quickly as possible. Finally, I thank the staff of Africa World Press, especially Kassahun Checole for his commitment to African history and Damola Ifaturoti who worked with me to make this book a reality.

I arrived in Miami in mid-August, 1997, after coordinating a UNESCO/ Social Sciences and Humanities Research Council (SSHRC) institute at York University, for the start of what was to be my first semester at the University of Miami. The staff of the Department of History, Jesus Sanchez Reyes (former Administrative Assistant), Lenny del Granado and Kathryn Harris were instrumental in my transition from graduate student life in Canada to life as a faculty member in the United States. It was often the contributions of individuals who were just doing their job that kept and sustained me since I arrived at the University of Guelph one sunny day on September 2, 1989, to pursue a Master's degree in History. I am forever grateful to a long list of individuals who made it possible for me to do graduate work in Canada for eight years away from family and many childhood friends. I must make special mention of Edward and John Afful, Tony Frimpong and Anthony Eghan, all of Toronto. May all of them be amply rewarded for their generosity and emotional support. Of course, I cannot forget Betty, whom I drove crazy with all the long hours sitting behind my desk trying to get the manuscript ready for publication. George Abakah was a constant research companion and I am eternally grateful for his assistance.

Finally, may this book bring some closure for those who have longed to see the infamous slave forts, castles and dungeons, and to "commune" with their ancestors but have not yet been able to do so. May it bring closure to African-descended people, who, like Booker T. Washington, would note that:

> Of my ancestry I know almost nothing. In the slave quarters, and even later, I heard whispered conversations among the coloured people of the tortures which the slaves, no doubt, my ancestors on my mother's side, suffered in the middle passage of the slave trade while being conveyed from Africa to America. I have been unsuccessful in securing any information that would throw any accurate light upon the history of my family beyond my mother.[7]

May this book help to preserve the collective memory of the ancestors for those who yearn for closure to their storied past from Africa and into the diaspora.

✥ Chapter I

Introduction:
The Gold Coast Slave Forts and Castles as Frontiers of Euro-African Economic and Cultural Encounter c. 1482-1960

Apart from the pyramids of Egypt and Nubia, the obelisks and rock-hewn churches of Ethiopia and the Great Zimbabwe monuments, no other architectural monuments encapsulate African history and, for that matter, African diaspora history, Atlantic history and even global history more than the thirty-three forts, castles and dungeons that dot the 250-mile (320-kilometer) coastline of modern-day Ghana. Grim, forbodden, yet impressive against the skyline, the forts and castles constitute a stark reminder of what some scholars have called the "Black Holocaust."[1] They would long be remembered as the infamous warehouses for the quarantine of enslaved Africans before the forced migration to the Caribbean and the Americas during the four hundred years of the Atlantic Slave Trade. The two preeminent books on the forts and castles in use today - one by the Dutch-Ghanaian historian, Albert van Dantzig, titled *Forts and Castles of Ghana*[2] and the other by the Ghanaian anthropologist, Kwesi J. Ankwandah, titled *Castles and Forts of Ghana*[3] – deal largely with the structures themselves. The same can be said of earlier works, such as A.J. Lawrence's *Trade Castles and Forts*, which represent the first major inventory of the slave forts, castles and dungeons by the Museum and Relics Commission of the Gold Coast. The focus of these works is on the architecture of these forts and castles and their primary function as slave dungeons.[4] However, they do not connect to the Atlantic slave trade and the African diaspora in the way that *House of Slaves* does.

This work goes beyond a description of the architecture of the forts and castles, especially since UNESCO has designated the Cape Coast Castle and São Jorge da Mina at Elmina as World Heritage sites. The slave forts and castles speak to the creation of the African diaspora in Europe, the Americas and the West Indies as well as trade and global linkages among three continents, to wit, globalization, colonization and culture contact (between Africans in the vicinity of the slave forts and castles with those from the hinterland on the one hand and between Africans and Europeans of different nations on the other). At the same time, the forts and castles provide a window into other facets of European activities in Africa, namely, chartered company administration, judicial system, architecture, Christianity and Western education. The castle schools, as they were called, became the vehicle for promoting Western education in West Africa. This early contact explains the preponderant role of West African intellectuals in the struggle against colonialism in the 1940 and 1950s.

The forts and castles also epitomize torture, pain and death on an unimaginable scale of Africans, but also of Europeans (travelers, merchants, company officials, colonial officials, soldiers, freebooters and interlopers). The cumulative impact of this group of Europeans *d'outre mer* can be found in the descendants of Dutch, Danish and Swedish families that live in coastal Ghana today, together with certain food items, crops and even cultural practices.[5]

The slave forts and castles were also sites of European wars as exemplified by the Anglo-Dutch wars of 1642 to1667 that culminated in the seizure of Dutch forts on the West African coast (Senegal, Gambia and the Gold Coast) by English Captains Robert Holmes and Joseph Cubitts and a Dutch counterattack by Admiral de Ruyter that recaptured the forts from the English (with the exception of Cape Coast Castle) in 1664.[6] In this way, the Anglo-Dutch struggle for global supremacy after the Dutch Republic's emergence as a commercial power house in Europe reverberated on the Gold Coast. After the treaty of Breda (1667) restored the captured forts and castles to the respective owners, the English Company of Royal Adventurers complained that it had been hopelessly ruined by the Anglo-Dutch war. This near-bankruptcy accelerated the demise of the company and led to the establishment of a new Company, the Royal African Company on September 27, 1672, to assume control of the British forts and castles on the Gold Coast.[7]

The forts, castles and dungeons that dot the coastline of the Gold Coast were built by European architects and, for a greater part of their history, were occupied by a European mercantile, political and colonial elite. They came from Portugal, Holland, England, Brandenburg-Prussia, Denmark and Sweden and they have left imprints in the sands of time – imprints that have affected every facet of African and African diaspora history.

These forts and castles became centers of global commercial activity – they teemed with gold, ivory and enslaved Africans to be sent to Europe, the Americas, the Caribbean and Asia from the fifteenth until the nineteenth century. The period of the slave trade was indeed an era of globalization and the slave forts, castles and dungeons constituted a linchpin in that global network. Human resources, goods, human cargo, and mail all moved through these forts and castles in a complex web that touched three different continents. The Portuguese, then the Dutch, English, Danes, Swedes and Brandenburgers moved goods from one corner of the world to the other with Africa as the link between the various continents.[8] African, European and, later, North and South American, and Caribbean personnel traveled the globe, many of them passing through Africa in this network of trade goods, enslaved peoples, servants, gold and ivory. If the seventeenth and eighteenth centuries climaxed in the "golden age" of the Dutch Republic, the slave forts, castles and dungeons deserve special mention as a fulcrum that anchored a global commercial system that facilitated Dutch enterprise and ingenuity.[9]

Similarly, there is a strong connection between England and English development, the slave trade and the slave forts, castles and dungeons of West Africa in general and the Gold Coast in particular.[10] The British Empire also encompassed extensive holdings with Africa as a focal point of trade and the forts and castles played an important role in the growth and development of Great Britain through trade in commodities and in enslaved Africans.

The English coin, the guinea, with an elephant embossed on one side of the coin, encapsulates one major dimension of the English commercial venture in the forts, castles and dungeons of the Gold Coast.[11] In 1673, the Royal African Company minted 50,000 guinea coins bearing the company's stamp or imprint. The importance of the slave fort and castle in this long durée of British history lies in the fact that when Britain colonized parts of West Africa in the 1880s the former slave castle, Cape Coast Castle, continued to be the seat of the colonial administration in the Gold Coast. And down to the time of Ghana's independence in 1957, the British governor-general resided in the Christiansborg Castle in Accra. It has remained the seat of the government of Ghana until now. The government of Ghana is scheduled to move into a brand new presidential palace (built partly with funds from the government of India), probably sometime in 2012, and to turn the Christiansborg Castle into a site of historical memory.

The slave forts, castles and dungeons embody untold torture, suffering and death—a Black Holocaust.[12] Adu Boahen calls the slave trade "an unpardonable crime, a crime unmitigated by any extenuating circumstance."[13] From the perspective of Africa and the African diaspora, the slave trade symbolized humanity's inhumanity toward its own kind and the slave forts, castles and dungeons of the Gold Coast played a central role as the holding pens for the enslaved prior to the journey to the New World.

SLAVE ROUTES FROM THE GOLD COAST HINTERLAND TO THE VARIOUS FORTS AND CASTLES OF THE GOLD COAST

Five major slave trade routes emanating from inside and outside of the Gold Coast emptied their human "cargo" into these slave forts, castles and dungeons. The westernmost slave route started from the Bouna-Bonduku region in present-day Côte d'Ivoire and entered the Gold Coast through Sampa before reaching Kumasi and then bifurcating to many of the slave forts and castles at Benyin, Axim, Elmina or Anomabu (Map 1.1).[14] Another route started at Wa in modern Ghana and passed through Bole, Banda and Bono Manso and joined the principal slave center, Kumasi, and thence to the slave forts, castles and dungeons along the coast of Ghana.[15] From the region beyond Jenne and Ouagadougou in what is now Burkina Faso, the central slave route passed through Daboya, Buipe, Kintampo and then to Kumasi.[16] From Kumasi, the main entrepôt of the slave routes through the Gold Coast, the enslaved went to Assini, Benyin, Takoradi, Sekondi or Cape Coast via Assin Manso.[17] The fourth major slave route started from beyond Sansane Mango in modern Togo and passed through Yendi, Salaga, Atebubu to Kumasi; one route branched off from Atebubu, through Kete Krachi to Abomey in Dahomey and also bifurcated through Akwamu to Ada and Keta. Yet another route from Hausaland passed through Salaga to Kumasi and linked up with Atebubu, Kete Krachi and as far as Abomey in Dahomey.[18]

From the perspective of the slave routes, Kumasi was a major entrepôt from which the enslaved were marched down to the slave forts, castles and dungeons at Assinie, Benyin, Axim, Dixcove, Sekondi, Komenda, Elmina, Cape Coast, Anomabu, Kormantin/Abandzi, Osu, Nungua, Teshie, Keta and the many other forts along the then Gold Coast. How many Africans died during the process of enslavement – wars, raids, and kidnappings? How many died during the months of arduous and forced marches from regions far beyond the Gold Coast to the slave forts, castles and dungeons along the coast? How many died in the forts and castles awaiting shipment to the New World? How many died in revolts in the environs of the forts and castles or in these "ships at permanent anchor?" How many were starved to death in the condemned cells of the various slave forts, castles and dungeons? The condemned cells of São Jorge da Mina with the trademark skull and crossbones symbolize the fate that awaited the enslaved individuals who were considered "recalcitrant" or troublemakers. How many died after they came

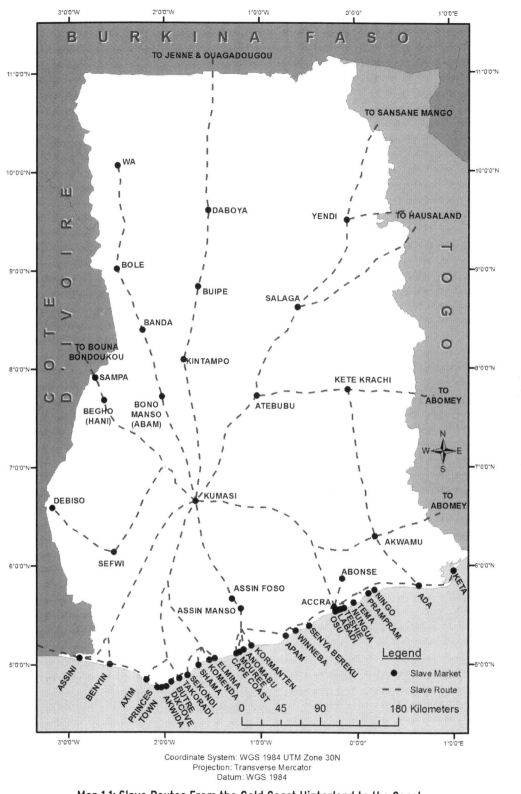

Coordinate System: WGS 1984 UTM Zone 30N
Projection: Transverse Mercator
Datum: WGS 1984

Map 1.1: Slave Routes From the Gold Coast Hinterland to the Coast

Map drawn by Daniel Thompson, Courtesy of Sub-Saharan Publishers – Akosua Perbi, *A History of Indigenous Slavery in Ghana From the 15th to the 19th Century*, (Legon, Accra: Sub-Saharan Publishers, 2004), xviii.

out of the "doors of no return" to face the prospect of final departure from the land of their birth and into the unknown? Scholars are still grappling with the totality of the forced migration from Africa.[19] There is still a whole lot of data to be collected on the African side of the trade.

Table 1.1: Annual Departures of the Trans-Atlantic Trade in the 1780s

COUNTRY	NUMBER
Senegambia	2,200
Sierra Leone	2,000
Grain and Ivory Coasts	4,000
Gold Coast	10,000
Slave Coast to Benin	12,500
Niger Delta to the Cameroons	22,000
Total	52,700

Source: A.G. Hopkins, *An Economic History of West Africa* (New York: Columbia University Press, 1973), 102.

Table 1.2: West Africa Slave Departures, c. 1640-1800 (approx. totals)

REGION	TOTAL	APPROX PERCENTAGE
Western Coast	910,000	23
Gold Coast and Akan interior	730,000	18
Bight of Benin	1,510,000	38
Bight of Biafra	850,000	21
West Africa	4,000,000	100

Source: Paul E. Lovejoy, *Transformations in Slavery: A History of Slavery in Africa* (Cambridge: Cambridge University Press, 3rd ed., 2011) Culled from Patrick Manning, "The Slave Trade in the Bight of Benin, 1640-1890." In *The Uncommon Market: Essays in the Economic History of the Atlantic Slave Trade*, ed. H. A. Gemery and J. S. Hogendorn (New York: Academic Press, 1979), 117; Johannes Postma, "The Origin of African Slaves: the Dutch Activities on the Guinea Coast, 1675-1795." In S. L. Engerman and E. D. Genovese (eds.), *Race and Slavery in the Western Hemisphere: Quantitative Studies* (Princeton: Princeton University Press, 1975), 49.

The figures in Tables 1.1 and 1.2 and the quotation below are designed to show that a considerable number of enslaved Africans were shipped from the Gold Coast during the slave trade, especially from the last decade of the seventeenth century to the early decades of the nineteenth century. In 1647, Jan van delwell, the Dutch Director-General at Elmina Castle noted: "so many ships and yachts of foreign nations have appeared on the Gold Coast with commissions from the crowns of France, England, Denmark and Sweden. Various of them have their principal trade based on the slave trade."[20]

Similarly, English trader William Smith was struck by the number of enslaved peoples on the Gold Coast and wondered aloud thus: "why this is called the Gold Coast I know not."[21] Smith was intimating that the region should be appropriately called the Slave Coast instead of the Gold Coast on account of the large number of enslaved Africans sent from this region to the New World, as opposed to the amount of gold exported to the New World. Ships left Europe with trade goods to exchange for enslaved Africans, taking four months or so to reach Cape Three Points, the southernmost tip of the Gold Coast. In 1725, a ship hoping to purchase 500 enslaved Africans on the Gold Coast listed items of exchange for the enslaved Africans (Table 1.3):

Table 1.3: Shipload of Items for the Exchange of 500 Enslaved Africans (Projected)

Cowries	20,000 lbs
Coarse German Linen	1,500 pieces
Cotton Lengths, 30 yards white	100 pieces
Cotton Lengths, 30 yards blue	50 pieces
Cotton Lengths, 15 yards white	250 pieces
Cotton Lengths, calico with large flowers	150 pieces
Cotton Lengths, striped	130 pieces
Firearms	200
Copper or Brass basins from 3lb. to 8 lb.	600 lb.
Gunpowder for small arms	1,000 lb.
Iron bars	1,006 lb.
Coral	50
Dutch pipes, best stores, 5 boxes	50
Beads and glass toys of different colors	-

Source: Rosemary Cave, *Gold Coast Forts* (London: Thomas Nelson & Sons, 1900), 31.

INHUMANITY OF DUNGEONS IN SLAVE FORTS AND CASTLES

Due to the active prosecution of the slave trade in the Gold Coast, these forts, castles and dungeons, also came to symbolize one of the greatest acts of inhumanity, cruelty and death. They represent the cruelest sites of collective memory for African-descended people in the diaspora. From 1989 when I took a group of American Peace Corps volunteers undergoing training at the University of Cape Coast to the São Jorge da Mina Castle, up until May 2008 when I was at the same castle with a group of University of

Miami students, I often witnessed the emotions of diaspora Africans who come face to face with the very embodiment of the sufferings endured by their ancestors during the slave trade. Their reactions to the sometimes gut-wrenching accounts of the tour guides concerning the degradation and deprivation, cruelty and inhumanity against the enslaved Africans, especially women, in the fortified enclosures encapsulate how they feel about the slave forts and castles of Ghana and how that collective memory of the African diaspora should be preserved.[22]

Various groups, individuals and prominent leaders come to the slave forts, Castles and dungeons and other sites of historical memory (Nelson Mandela, Bill Clinton and George W. Bush visited the *Maison des Esclaves* on Gorée Island, while President Barack Obama visited Cape Coast Castle) with different sensibilities and interests. So do the guides who conduct the tours. After joining different tours numerous times, I can rightly assert that this is a fair assessment even though some people have complained about the account of a particular tour guide who emphasized the predatory activities of European officials in the castles on enslaved African women.

The remnants of the instruments of torture of the enslaved peoples - from the cannon balls and chains for recalcitrant females who rebuffed the sexual advances of officials and soldiers, to the condemned cells (with the trademark skull and cross-bones at São Jorge da Mina), the iron stakes in the concrete or cement floor for chaining the enslaved, especially in Fort William at Anomabu (Photo 1.1), and shackles (for ankles, wrists and necks) - are all vividly displayed in these forts and castles and speak to a horrendous dimension of the trade in human beings.

The flood of emotions one encounters, especially from some diaspora Africans who come face to face with these stark reminders of the inhuman slave trade, keeps the collective memory of the diaspora alive in the forts and castles. How do people of the African diaspora, especially African Americans, react or respond to the dungeons in the slave forts and castles? The one word that aptly captures the moment is: sobering. For many African Americans, the slave forts and castles represent nothing short of sacred ground, and making the pilgrimage from the other side of the Atlantic to the motherland and to the infamous slave forts, castles and dungeons is a "necessary act of self realization," for the "spirits of the diaspora are tied to these historic structures."[23] The slave forts, castles and dungeons were graveyards and torture chambers for the ancestors and must be left as is, that is untouched rather than whitewashed, even if the latter is for preservation purposes. Visiting such sites, some argued, "physically allows African Americans to pay their respect to their enslaved ancestors by grieving over

Photo 1.1: Fort William, Anomabu – Iron Stakes in the Floor for Chaining the Enslaved

their suffering and rejoicing in their strength of survival."[24] Therefore, these "sacred sites" should be "restored and preserved" but not whitewashed.

However, this ran counter to the vision of some of the officials of the Central Region Development Commission (CEDECOM) who had initiated a restoration and commercialization of Cape Coast and Elmina project designed to spur the engine of development in the Central Region of Ghana. This broad regional integrated development program envisioned the Cape Coast Castle and São Jorge da Mina Castle as tourism centers that would help to bring visitors to Cape Coast and Elmina. Under this program, the government of Ghana, in conjunction with the United States International Agency for Development, (USAID) and the United Nations Development Program (UNDP) funded the restoration project.[25] Cognizance should be taken of the fact that even before Ghana became independent in 1957, the Monuments and Relics Commission of the Gold Coast had undertaken restoration and preservation work on the forts and castles. That is the context in which B. H. O'Neil and A.W. Lawrence took an inventory and reported on the state of the slave forts and castles.[26]

The 1991-1996 Ghanaian initiative to memorialize the slavery experience by restoring two of the three slave castles and dungeons in Ghana provoked strong reactions from some members of the African diaspora who felt that the two historic sites that embody the African diaspora experience were being commodified, contaminated, as well as distorted. This certainly was the view of Imakhüs Vienna Robinson (who changed her name to Imakhüs Nzingah Okofu) who posed this question in a letter published in newspapers and magazines (such as *Africa Link* and *New African*) as an article: Is the Blackman's History Being Whitewashed?"[27] Robinson argued that African American history was being

> " 'whitewashed' by the very European-Americans who enslaved Africans," and that "whitewashing" the structures was designed to "mask the evils of slavery."[28]

Similarly, Afrikadzata Defu described the project as "'tele-guided falsification' in the name of preservation for the promotion of tourism."[29]

Imakhüs Robinson's 1987 visit to the dungeons of Cape Coast Castle is instructive in capturing how diaspora Africans feel when they enter the cavernous walls of the slave cells. From my numerous visits to the slave forts and castles between 1989 and 2008, I can testify to the fact that while the reactions of people vary, it is quite a memorable experience to be in the dungeons. According to Imakhüs Robinson,

> As I stood transfixed in the Women's Dungeon, I could feel and smell the presence of our Ancestors. From the dark, damp corners of that hell-hole, I heard the whimpering and crying of tormented Mothers and Sisters being held in inhumane bondage, never knowing what each new day ... would bring. Strange white men that kept coming in to look at them, feeling them, examining their private parts as if they were some kind of animals; removing them for their own sick pleasures, while awaiting the Devil ships that would take them into a four hundred year long hell.[30]

In this sense, Imakhüs Robinson's view of the slave dungeons may not be too far off from the view reflected in Richard Wright's *Black Power: A Record of Reactions in the Land of Pathos*. Wright perceived in the slave dungeons

> a tiny pear-shaped tear that formed on the cheek of some black-woman torn away from her children, a tear that gleams here still, caught in the feeble rays of the dungeon's light – a shy tear that vanishes at the sound of approaching footsteps, but reappears when all is quiet, a tear that was hastily brushed off when her arm was grabbed and she was led toward those narrow, dank steps that guided her to the tunnel that directed her feet to the waiting ship that would bear her across the heaving mist-shrouded Atlantic.[31]

LIFE IN THE FORTS, CASTLES AND DUNGEONS FOR THE ENSLAVED AND EUROPEANS

The main dungeon of Cape Coast Castle, unlike those of any other slave fort or castle, was built underground and could hold over five hundred enslaved persons and up to a thousand enslaved Africans at any particular time. Fort William at Anomabu was specifically built with a view to holding enslaved Africans and was one of a kind – a gigantic holding cell for the enslaved. Into the dungeons of these forts and castles poured human beings who were treated as mere chattel or property devoid of the rights we take for granted – to eat when one wants, to move about or walk around, to love and be loved, to cry when one wants to, and laugh when one feels like it. Many enslaved Africans died from the shock of the experience; others succumbed to malnutrition, starvation, torture and death and were dumped in the Atlantic Ocean, which lapped the walls of many of the forts and castles. Above all, however, many survived the ordeal and arrived in the New World.[32]

Upon arriving on the Gold Coast in 1471, the Portuguese participated in a coastwise trade, transporting enslaved Africans and goods from Benin to other parts of West Africa, especially the Gold Coast. Many of these enslaved Africans were brought to São Jorge da Mina Castle in exchange for gold and were used in carrying goods from the Gold Coast interior and beyond to the coast and vice versa (Photo 1.2).[33] These enslaved Africans were the "carrier corps" of the early European trade on the Gold Coast. Before long, the Portuguese had become the major carriers of enslaved Africans to Brazil and other places in the New World to meet the demand for labor in the sugar, coffee and cotton plantations and mines of the Caribbean, Central and South America. The cultural heritage of Bahia, Brazil, is in part a by-product of Portuguese slave trading activities on the Gold Coast, São Tomé and later, Congo and Angola. Thus, a steady stream of enslaved Africans passed through the slave forts, castles and dungeons of the Gold Coast, transported by the Portuguese and later Dutch, English, Danish, Prussian merchants, government officials and interlopers from various European nations. These Africans became the anchor of certain cultural norms, musical styles,[34] language patterns (such as that of the Gullah of South Carolina),[35] and religious practices (such as santéria, candomblé, abakuá)[36] and even Islam[37] in the Black Atlantic.[38] In many parts of the Americas, Amerindian, European and African cultures have mixed to some extent and fewer and fewer people can claim to exemplify European cultures in the real sense of the term.

The slave forts and castles also speak to European mortality in Africa in the period of the slave trade and beyond. The Dutch cemetery at Elmina, doubtless established several decades later after the construction of São Jorge da Mina (an earlier cemetery was closer to the castle), together with other smaller European cemeteries in coastal Ghana, represent a grim reminder of the toll the European commercial enterprise exacted on European personnel during this period. The sheer size of the Dutch cemetery at Elmina, coupled with the epitaphs of various European officials in the slave forts and castles (such as Bosman at Fort São Antonio, Captain George Maclean (Cape Coast Castle) or Lambert Jacob van Tets (São Jorge da Mina) and others buried beneath the forts and castle walls with no plaque or tombstone indicating their presence on the site, serve as a poignant reminder of the death toll on Europeans.[39] In fact, the courtyard of Cape Coast Castle is described as one gigantic graveyard.[40] Extant records or whatever is left of those records as per a burial register (dated 1824-1895) in the possession of Rev Elliott, the priest-in-charge of Christ Church, Cape Coast, in 1944, show that other Europeans were buried in the castle, including the son of Governor Archibald Dalzel who wrote the famous *History of Dahomey*[41] while working in the Cape Coast Castle (Photos 1.3 and 1.4).

Photo 1.2: São Jorge da Mina

Photo 1.3: Tombs of European officials buried in slave forts and castles
(top) Willem Bosman, Fort São Antonio   (bottom) Capt. George Maclean, Cape Coast Castle

Photo 1.4: Dutch Cemetery in Elmina outside of São Jorge

Table 1.4: Governors of São Jorge da Mina

1482 - 1484	Diego de Azambuja
1485 - 1486	Alvaro Vaz Pestana
1487 - 1489?	João Fogaça
1489 - ?	Alvaro Mascarenhas
? - 1493	Dr. Fernando Pereira
1495 - 1499	Lopo Soares de Albergaria
1499 - 1502	Fernão Lopes Correia
1502?	Nuno Vaz de Castelo Branco
1503 - 1504	Diego Lopes de Sequeira
1504 - 1505	António de Miranda de Azevedo
1505 - ?	D. Martinho da Silva
1508? - 1509	Bobadilha
1509 - 1511?	Manuel de Goios
1511? - 1513	Afonso Caldeira
1514 - 1516	Nuno Vaz
1516 - 1519	Fernão Lopes Correia
1519 - 1522	Duarte Pacheco Pereira
1522 - 1524	D. Afonso de Albuquerque
1524 - 1525	Joao de Barros
1526 - 1529	João Vaz de Almada
1529 - 1532	Estevão da Gama
1532 - 1536	António Lópes Pereira
1536 - 1540	D. Manuel de Albuquerque
1540 - 1543	António de Miranda
1543 - 1545	António de Brito
1546 - 1548	D. Martim de Castro
1548 - 1550	Lopo de Sousa Coutinho
1550 - 1552	Diogo Soares de Albergaria
1552 - 1556	Rui de Melo
1556 - 1558	Afonso Gonçalves Botafogo
1558 - 1562	Ruy Gomes de Azevedo
1562 - 1564	Manuel Mesquita de Perestrello
1564 - 1567	Martim Afonso
1567 - 1570	Francisco de Barros de Paiva
1570 - 1573	António de Sá
1573?	Martim Afonso
1574?	Mendo da Mota
1574 - 1579	?
1579 - 1583	Vasco Fernandes Pimentel
1583 - 1586	João Rodrigues Peçanha
1586 - 1594?	João Roiz Coutinho
1596 - 1608	D. Cristóvão de Melo
1608 - 1613	D. Duarte de Lima

1613	João de Castro
1613 - 1616	Pero da Silva
1616 - 1623	Manuel da Cunha e Teive
1623 - 1626?	D. Francisco Sotomaior
1626? - 1629	João de Sera de Morais
1630 - 1631	governorship vacant
1632 - 1634	D. Pedro de Mascarenhas
1634	Frei Duarte Borges
1634 - 1637	André da Rocha Magalhães

Source: John Vogt, *Portuguese Rule on the Gold Coast 1469-1682* (Athens: The University of Georgia Press, 1979), 214-215.

The turnover of Portuguese governors, due often to death, but also sometimes to recall back to Lisbon, open a window into the mortality rate of Europeans in the slave forts and castles (Table 1.4).

Life was indeed brutish and short for governor, factor, merchant, chaplain, soldier, sailor and interloper alike. Out of two hundred English troops who landed on the Gold Coast in February 1782, for example, only sixty remained alive after six months.[42] The average life span of many European officials in the Gold Coast – Portuguese, Dutch, Danish governors and factors – was usually two to four years. While some lived longer, many succumbed to the grim reaper within a year of their arrival on the Gold Coast or after two to three years on the coast. Aside from this, capital punishment for soldiers also provides a window into an aspect of European life in the forts and castles. For example,

> In 1782, at Moure Fort, near Cape Coast, a Private of the Independent Companies[43] was, by his Captain's order, blown from the muzzle of one of the guns.
>
> In that year also, at the Island of Goree, the Commandant ordered a serjeant of the African Corps, who was charged with mutiny, to receive 800 lashes. The Serjeant died shortly afterwards. The Commandant was tried for murder and hanged.[44]

For many Europeans, especially soldiers, life was shortened through excessive drinking, especially on,

> punch, a liquor made of brandy, water, lime juice and sugar, which make together an unwholesome mixture ... It is incredible how many are consumed by this damnable liquor ... which is not only confined to the soldierly, but some of the principal people are so bigoted to it that I really believe for all the time I was on the coast that at least one of their agents, and factors innumerable, died yearly.[45]

EUROPEAN TRADING AND DEFENSE

The infamous role of the forts, castles and dungeons in the slave trade has obscured other dimensions of their role in West African history. The forts and castles were initially constructed as lodges, defensible trading posts and miniature forts for various European trading "factors" on the Gold Coast in the late fifteenth and early sixteenth centuries. They were used to store European trade goods for sale on the Gold Coast as well as for African trade goods purchased on the Gold Coast. West African export commodities of the early phase of Euro-African trade included wax, hides, wood, gum, pepper, ivory and gold. Most of the West African gold was exported through the Gold Coast. In the late fifteenth and early sixteenth centuries Europeans, most especially the Portuguese, carried about £100,000 worth of gold a year to Europe.[46] By the mid-sixteenth century, English and French interlopers cut into the Portuguese monopoly, carrying about £500,000 worth of gold to Europe.[47] The Dutch would do the same thing a century later.

Some of the slave forts and castles served as repair depots for ships sailing off the West African coast to Europe, the Americas, the Caribbean, the Far East and Asia, as in the case of Fort Batenstein at Butri. The forts and castles also served as places where sailors stopped to replenish dwindling stocks of food, water and other provisions and even got some needed rest.[48] Representatives of various chartered companies such as the Company of Royal Adventurers Trading to Africa, the Royal African Company, the Dutch West India Company, the Brandenburg Africa Company, among several others, operated out of these forts and castles, storing trade goods, and later, human beings for the Atlantic slave trade.[49]

The work of the Company of Royal Adventurers, the Royal African Company and the Committee of Merchants, all British chartered companies on the Gold Coast, provided a blueprint for running the colonial administrations that were set up after the abolition of the slave trade and the British takeover of the Gold Coast.[50] The British used this blueprint to maximum effect in the 1880s, when the scramble for African colonies resulted in the creation of British colonies and settlements. Contrary to the argument that the experience of the British in India provided the first major template for the Indirect Rule system of British colonial administration in Africa, the forts and castle administration of the slave trade period provided a valuable administrative road map that helped the British in governing their African colonies from the 1880s until the 1960s.[51]

The architectural style of the forts and castles had an impact on architecture in the coastal cities of the Gold Coast. In the late fifteenth century, the Portuguese constructed São Jorge da Mina along the lines of European medieval castles and started a practice that revolutionized the construction of European forts and castles in the Gold Coast - the double enclosure defensive system.[52] It also affected architecture in the towns and cities where the castles were situated. Houses built for African mistresses of Europeans in the immediate vicinity of the forts and castles copied the European architectural style of burnt bricks and that style gradually diffused into the neighborhoods and towns that grew exponentially in the "shadow" of the forts and castles. Merchants, influential persons and well-to-do people in the coastal towns and cities (such as Abandzi, Anomabo, Cape Coast and Elmina) began to build houses that were patterned in some way after the forts, castles and nearby European-built houses for African mistresses and their children. Houses in the immediate vicinity of São Jorge da Mina Castle and dating from that period are at present being renovated to preserve them due to their historical significance.[53]

From the end of the Thirty Years' War (1648) to the end the slave trade in 1807, the forts and castles assumed the role of permanent European defensive fortifications on the Gold Coast, surrounded by gun/canon emplacements, together with sentinel posts and even moats (in the case of Elmina) against both local and foreign enemies (Photo 1.5 and 1.6).

Some Africans encountered Europeans in these forts and castles as slave merchants, castle slaves, laborers, artisans, soldiers, cooks and servants. The forts and castles became "warehouses" for other Africans (commoners and even some princes) who passed through their walls through the "Door of No Return" and then on to the next leg of the Middle Passage to the Caribbean and the Americas.[54] European officials, soldiers, missionaries and African merchants, chiefs, artisans, prisoners of war, free people and castle slaves met in these enclosures to do business (buy and sell), usually in the palaver halls, to share stories, to pray, to enjoy themselves, to decide cases, to plead cases, to exchange presents, even to love, voluntarily or forcibly. In this case, the forts and castles became an important frontier of Euro-African encounter.

A NEW "CLASS" OF AFRICANS

Ghanaian families with Dutch, Danish, Swedish and English last names abound in coastal cities in Ghana today.[55] Born of European men and African women, these children were provided with Western education in the slave forts and castles and often lived in brick or European-style houses near the European stations or in the towns where the forts and castles were situated. The Danes started a school at Christiansborg Castle for mulatto children in 1722,[56] while the Brandenburgers did the same at Pokeso. The castle school system marked the beginning of western education on the Gold Coast. This

Photo 1.5: Moat – São Jorge da Mina (Elmina)

Photo 1.6: Raviola and other defensive positions – Fort Coenraadsburg

was continued by missionaries almost a century later. It was the missionaries who introduced the school system into various coastal communities. The graduates of the castle school, the children of European officials and African women, grew to become an important mercantile elite during the colonial period and have continued to be influential families in Accra, Cape Coast, Elmina and other places. In this way, the significance of the slave forts and castles goes beyond the four hundred years of the slave trade.

Even *asafo* companies, traditional military groups comprised of young men in the coastal towns and cities, were influenced by this European inroad into African society. In Elmina and Cape Coast, a specific *asafo* company was, and still is, called *abrofommba* – literally the children of white men. A number of them are lighter skinned; they celebrate their European descent and heritage and are recognized as such by others.[57]

What was the role of the forts and castles in the development of a new class of people along the West African littoral? This new class, children of European fathers and African mothers, became the beneficiaries of education and inherited an economic status that enabled them to constitute themselves into a "new elite." In this context, what was the nature of social life in the shadows of the forts and castles? Did sexual liaisons between European men and African women in the shadow of the forts and castles endanger the European colonial enterprise in any way? What was the status of these African women who enjoyed the company of European consorts and the advantage of "insider trading" and preferential treatment in their communities – in the immediate vicinity of the forts and castles?

THE CASTLE AS HEADQUARTERS OF EUROPEAN COLONIAL ENTERPRISE

After 1807 the forts and castles became the means of gaining direct access to raw materials – rubber, groundnuts, gum, indigo, cotton – from the interior of the Gold Coast as the demand for raw materials for the industrial revolution in Europe became more and more acute.[58] African merchants and, later, African merchant princes, interacted with Europeans in these enclosures, buying goods on credit, selling them and paying back their creditors.[59] The forts and castles became the headquarters of various European chartered companies that traded in raw materials on the West African coast. For example, the British used Cape Coast Castle, and later, Christiansborg Castle as their headquarters, while the French were based on Gorée Island in Senegal. Thus West Africa was drawn once more, in the nineteenth and twentieth centuries, into the global economy of industrialization and the need for raw materials to feed factories, markets for manufactured goods and places of investment of profit from the industrial process.[60]

During the period of European informal and formal control (from the 1840s to 1880s) European powers – English, French – used some of the forts and castles as command headquarters, residence for governors and deputy governors, barracks for soldiers, and churches for religious services. The forts and castles served as seats of government of colonial administrations in some West African countries. The British used Cape Coast Castle as the colonial headquarters until 1874 when they moved the capital to another Castle, Christiansborg, in Accra. Provincial and District Commissioners and other colonial officials continued to use the slave forts and castles as offices. The third-storey apartments of Cape Coast Castle, which formerly housed the governor, were initially occupied by the African police magistrate. The magistrate held court in the adjacent room. A decade later, the governor's former residence was used by the local Education Department and the newly formed Broadcasting Department. The northern portion of the third storey of the castle served as living quarters as well as a church for colonial chaplains but later became Cape Coast Town Council offices and offices for other government departments.[61]

The storey below the governor's residence, the second storey, was used as living quarters for commissioned officers of the Gold Coast regiment and the basement rooms served as living quarters for non-commissioned officers of the regiment.[62] Later, this second storey housed a post office, the local treasury and the customs office. It also contained the school rooms, hospital, the judicial assessor's quarters and the police station.[63] Troops were quartered under the ramparts of the castle, on the southern side, and the same space was later converted into a prison.[64] São Jorge da Mina served as police barracks, prison, hospital (sanitorium), offices and living quarters of the district commissioner and Public Works Department officials and even a jailer's quarters.[65] Several rest houses were also created in the forts and castles for European and other government officials who travelled to the various provinces on colonial assignment or official duties.

These "ships at permanent anchor," as one scholar calls the forts and castles, also became European enclaves and centers of Western education, Christianity, and the colonial administration on the West African coast. Out of their doors emerged the first batch of African teachers, pastors, catechists and, in general, the African educated elite who led the nationalist struggle against colonialism in the late nineteenth and early twentieth centuries. Philip Quacoe, the first African ordained as an Anglican priest by the Church of England, was appointed missionary, pastor and headmaster of the Cape Coast Castle School for the children of European and African parentage.[66]

British colonial officials in the Gold Coast made use of the various forts and castles as district and provincial headquarters. As a result, the forts and castles laid the foundation for the high premium placed on education in the coastal towns and cities of the Gold Coast. It is not surprising that at independence Ghana and West Africa had the largest number of Western-educated individuals (merchants, lawyers, doctors) on any part of the African coast. These Western-educated individuals were at the forefront of the struggle for independence and included J.E. Casely Hayford, T. Hutton Mills, Dr. H.C. Bankole-Bright, Chief Oluwa, H. Van Hein, Herbert Macauley and others.[67]

During the colonial period, São Jorge da Mina Castle served as a training center and base for the Gold Coast/Hausa Constabulary, a frontier police (trained by British and Irish military officers) that later became, first, the core of the colonial army, then the West African Frontier Force, and the precursor to the Ghana army. The frontier force was set up by the British to police the fluctuating and permeable frontiers between the British colony of the Gold Coast and the German colony of Togo on the one hand, and the French colonies of Côte d'Ivoire and then Upper Volta (now Burkina Faso) and the Gold Coast on the other. It was also to maintain law and order in the Gold Coast. The Hausa Constabulary was instrumental in the British defeat and pacification of Asante in 1874 and 1896.[68] From 1900 onward, São Jorge da Mina castle became a guest house for European (largely British) officials on the Gold Coast – surveyors, health inspectors and administrators – as well as other visitors traveling through the Gold Coast colony. Fort William at Anomabu, Fort Metal Cross (Metalen Kruis) at Dixcove and the Cape Coast Castle all served similar functions – as guest or rest houses for colonial and other officials.[69]

In 1948, the British colonial administration used São Jorge da Mina castle as a training depot for what eventually became the Ghana Police Force (Photo 1.8). They made modifications to the structure, especially in the Castle compound itself to provide "obstacle course" training to police recruits.

In the 1970s, São Jorge da Mina functioned as a high school (Edinaman Secondary School) for the local Elmina community and the nearby towns. Students from the University of Cape Coast went on teaching practicum to the school until it was moved out of the castle in the early 1990s. Other forts and castles have served as leprosarium (Elmina), prisons (Anomabu, Winneba and Accra - Ussher Fort and James Fort), rest houses (Apam and Dixcove), post offices (Dixcove, Axim and Shama), among several other uses. Christiansborg Castle has continued to be the seat of the Ghana government to date. A presidential palace is being built so that the awkward

Photo 1.7: Fort Coenraadsburg – Living Quarters of Non-Commissioned Officers of Dutch Military unit responsible for defense of São Jorge da Mina.

scenario of running a nation from a slave castle can be expunged from the history of Ghana. Christiansborg Castle has been an illogical dimension of Ghana's history for almost half a century and more so at a time when Ghana is urging people of African descent to "return" home.

São Jorge da Mina and Cape Coast castles are at present United Nations Educational Scientific and Cultural Organization (UNESCO) World Heritage sites. Hundreds of visitors – primary school students, high school students, professionals, interested community members and, more important, people of African descent, college students and some city officials from the United States, Europe and the Caribbean - visit the former "Doors of No Return" every year. However, the slave forts and castles do not have the same significance for some Ghanaians as they have for diaspora Africans. First, over five hundred years of Gold Coast/Ghana history is represented in the forts and castles – storehouses, slave dungeons, headquarters of European chartered companies and later colonial administrations, colonial offices, barracks for soldiers and policemen, hospitals and leprosarium, post offices, rest houses and in the case of Elmina, a school. Closer to our time, District Assemblies and some Regional Houses of Chiefs have used some of the rooms in the former slave forts and castles as offices. Some African Americans who have visited the slave forts and castles see a disconnect between the diaspora perspective of these infamous structures and the perspective of their Ghanaian brothers and sisters. They (the diaspora) come to Ghana in search of their roots and to reconnect with the dungeons and slave forts and castles that spewed their ancestors across the Atlantic. They are surprised that Ghanaians do not have the same revulsion for the structures and the Europeans who occupied them. But the main issue underlying the two perspectives is embedded in different historical experiences and even educational experiences. After all, the slave trade, until recently, was not a very important topic in the school curriculum in Ghana. It is, however, instructive that of the 17,091 people who visited Elmina Castle in 1993, 67 percent were Ghanaians, 12.5 percent were Europeans and 12.3 percent were North Americans. Of course, many of the people in this last group were African Americans.[70] What do the numbers mean if this many Ghanaians are now visiting the slave forts and castles? Some African Americans have relocated to Ghana and others have lived in the country for extended periods of time and continue to do so. Some have found the peace of mind they needed for their "restless souls," but others have been disappointed that the experience had not been the homecoming they expected. Life was more difficult than they anticipated and they felt alienated and out of place.[71]

Photo 1.8: Police Recruits at São Jorge da Mina
Courtesy of National Archives, Kew, England

CONCLUSION AND OUTLINE OF THE BOOK

During the slave trade, the forts and castles were the living presence of the inhuman slave trade. Into the deep and pulsating bowels were thrust "masses of humanity" after long treks from the interior – forest or savanna regions. Out of the gated portals of the forts and castles, European slave traders, officials of merchant and chartered companies, and various European government officials ventured out to trade in human cargo, execute warrants, enforce orders in a complex relationship that was part of the machinery of the Atlantic trade – a vast network of individuals and groups (official, semiofficial, layperson, privateer, brigand, civilian, soldier, European, African, slave, semifree and unfree) who constituted cogs in the vast machinery that made the Atlantic slave trade a reality. Consequently, the forts and castles became the focus of a global commercial relationship between Europeans and Africans. In some cases, small African communities grew into towns and villages in the shadow of the forts – due to the availability of several types of jobs as well as profits to be made from trade and the provision of services to the occupants of the forts and castles. Seaside towns like Cape Coast, Elmina, Abandzi and Axim all grew exponentially due to the European presence and the attendant trade that went on between Africans and Europeans.

At the same time, the forts and castles became the seats of temporal power due to the guns and garrisons that they harbored. Consequently, fort and castle officials became arbiters in local disputes. Concomitantly, the forts and castles became sites of contestation and extension of European rivalry in the eighteenth and nineteenth centuries. Wars in the European arena spilled over to the Gold Coast and often culminated in the siege or seizure of forts or castles of rival powers, often enduring bombardment or shelling from ships at sea and assault from the landward side, sometimes utilizing local allies on the Gold Coast. The struggle between the Dutch and the Portuguese over Elmina Castle, the English and the Dutch over Fort Amsterdam and several other examples speak to this phenomenon.

The forts and castles served as important "frontiers" for the exchange of goods, ideas, technology, and a way of life. What was life on this frontier like for Africans as soldiers, servants, cooks, castle slaves, preachers, teachers, and for European officials, merchants and soldiers? No dioramas, fragments of ships or pictures surpass the impression that is made by the forts and castles along the coast of the former Gold Coast, now Ghana, on anyone who enters their gated portals. Their sheer magnitude and impregnability, differences in architectural styles, location and uses, speak volumes about the notorious slave trade in particular, and the European presence in general.

In the end, the slave forts and castles represent a crucial link in a trifecta of major historical epochs in global history: European expansion in Africa, the Atlantic slave trade and Gold Coast history. The slave forts and castles, as the linchpin of this trifecta, have affected global history in a way that has not been recognized for their monumental importance in as far as they contributed to pull Africa into the global political economy.

Methodologically, this study combines a rigorous historical approach with architectural history as well as accounts (contemporaneous and reported) of individuals who were on hand at the time of the forts and castles. It uses an amalgam of sources: freedom narratives by former enslaved peoples, accounts by local people and local historians, African merchants, archival material (European traders and European governors' accounts – journals, memoirs, correspondence to various European capitals, military dispatches from the Gold Coast and adjoining region), architectural drawings (initial plans and changes made during the high point of European rivalry in the late seventeenth century), writings of various European slave traders who traded with or visited the forts and castles, European military and naval officers who were received at the forts and castles, travel literature and secondary literature dealing with the forts and castles. This book uses text and photographs to construct an intricate web that links up the role of the European forts and castles as the launching pads for Atlantic commerce, the slave trade, globalization, western education, Christianity and Euro-African intercultural activities as frontier experience par excellence to flesh out the role of the Gold Coast slave forts and castles in the European encounter with Africa as well as in the Atlantic slave trade. Above all, it seeks to extend the boundaries of Atlantic studies to include the forts and castles that served as "ships at permanent anchor" on the shores of the Gold Coast (Ghana).

Chapter 1 situates the forts and castles in the discourse on global, Atlantic, African and African diaspora history. It delineates the different roles of the forts and castles as sites of Euro-African encounter epitomized by commercial dealings, the Atlantic slave trade and the African diaspora it spawned, colonization and independence.

Chapter 2 emphasizes the long shadow cast on Africa and the world at large by the large number of enslaved Africans who were dispersed to different continents and who have made significant impact on world culture, cuisine, religion, education, to mention a few. The writings of some of these former enslaved Africans shed significant light on their places of origin, the slavery experience and life in the New World. The narratives of Olaudah Equiano,[72] Ottobah Cuaguano[73] and Mahommah Gardo Baquaqua,[74] provide excellent examples. These accounts help us to stand on the diaspora side of the Atlantic and cast a searchlight on the continent, a method Paul Lovejoy has eloquently argued for. In the process, we learn about practices and events that had long been discontinued or forgotten. In short, the chapter links the various facets of the Atlantic slave trade using the slave forts and castles of the Gold Coast as the linch-pin of that commercial network and more important, it helps us to reframe discourses about the Atlantic basin.

Chapter 3 focuses on the Portuguese period and situates the Portuguese presence in the context of globalization and wars between various European powers for supremacy.

Chapter 4 discusses the Dutch role in ousting the Portuguese and asserting themselves as the largest European trading nation on the Gold Coast and underlines their work in the context of the Atlantic slave trade and the workers of that trade.

Chapter 5 looks at the English contribution to European activities on the Gold Coast, especially during and after the slave trade and as part of a global network. It also delineates briefly British colonial activities during the period of European colonization to discuss the role of the slave forts and castles in that enterprise. Cape Coast Castle played a very important role in the Atlantic economy and the chapter highlights this role.

The activities of the Danes and the Brandenburgers (who were late arrivals on the Gold Coast and who departed from the coast earlier than the dominant Dutch and British), constitute the essence of chapters 6 and 7. How these European fort and castle construction activities are tied into the larger picture of the slave trade and the African diaspora is the underlying motif of the two chapters.

Chapter 8 looks at the Pan-African activities of our time and shows how these have become avenues for re-linking diaspora Africans and those on the continent, using PANAFEST and Emancipation commemorative activities in Ghana as windows into activities surrounding the "return" of the diaspora to Africa. In this case, the slave forts and castles, once the site of the rupture, have now become the sites of return and reunification. Thus, the story of the slave forts and castles have come full circle to link up Africa and the African diaspora.

Notes

1. Maulana Karenga defines the "Holocaust of enslavement" as a holocaust that expresses itself as: a morally monstrous destruction of human life (involving millions of people and whole peoples); a morally monstrous destruction of human culture (cities, towns, art, literature etc.); and a morally monstrous destruction of human possibility (aspiration, freedom, dignity and solidar-

ity). See Maulana Karenga, *Introduction to Black Studies*. 3rd edn. (Los Angeles: University of Sankore Press, 2002), 134-135.

2. Albert van Dantzig, *Forts and Castles of Ghana* (Accra: Sedco Publishing,1980).

3. Kwesi J. Ankwandah *Castles and Forts of Ghana* (Paris: Atalante, [for Ghana Monuments Board] 1979).

4. See A. W. Lawrence, *Trade Castles and Forts of West Africa* (London: Jonathan Cape, 1963).

5. Dutch names like Vroom, de Graaf, van Dyke and van Ess; English names like Bannerman and Byrd, and Danish names like Quist, Reindorf, and Svanekjer, speak to the existence of Euro-African families in coastal Ghana.

6 See Public Records and Archives Administration (Hereafter, PRAAD) ADM 3/1/337, Ancient Castles and Forts in the Central Province. Upkeep of. J.J. Crooks, *Records Relating to the Gold Coast Settlements From 1750-1874*, new ed. (London: Frank Cass, 1973), 2-3.

7. W. Walton Claridge, *A History of the Gold Coast and Ashanti From the Earliest Times to the Commencement of the Twentieth Century* (London: Frank Cass, 1964), 108-119. For a history of Royal African Company see K. G. Davies, *The Royal African Company* (London, 1957).

8. For a diagrammatic and pictorial representation see James Walvin, *Atlas of Slavery* (Edinburgh Gate: Pearson-Longman 2006), 68-69, 73-80.

9. For the Dutch commercial activities see C. R. Boxer, *The Dutch Seaborne Empire 1600-1800* (London, 1965). See also Ernst van den Boogart and Pieter Emmer, "The Dutch Participation in the Atlantic Slave Trade, 1596-1650." In *The Uncommon Market: Essays in the Economic History of the Atlantic Slave Trade*, ed. H. Gemery and Jan Hogendorn (New York: Academic Press, 1979), 353-375; Ernst van den Boogart, "The Trade Between Western Africa and the Atlantic World, 1600-90. Estimates of Trends in Composition and Value," *Journal of African History* 33 (1992): 369-385; Johannes Menne Postma, *The Dutch in the Atlantic Slave Trade 1600-1815* (Cambridge: Cambridge University Press, 1990); Albert van Dantzig, *The Dutch and the Guinea Coast 1674-1742. A Collection of Documents from the State Archive at the Hague* (Accra: Ghana Academy of Arts and Sciences, 1978).

10. For a generalized view on this contribution see Eric Williams, *Capitalism and Slavery. With a New Introduction by Colin A. Palmer* (Chapel Hill: University of North Carolina Press, 1994). See also Margaret Makepeace (ed.), *Trade on the Guinea Coast 1657-1666. The Correspondence of the English East India Company*. (Madison: African Studies Program, University of Wisconsin-Madison. African Primary Texts, 4).

11. The crest of the Company of Merchants Trading to Africa was an "armed Elephant with a Tower and Castle Proper and St. George's Flag Displayed." Crooks, *Records Relating to the Gold Coast Settlements from 1750-1874*; Rosemary Cave, *Gold Coast Forts* (London: Thomas Nelson & Sons, 1900), 28.

12. For the term Black Holocaust, See Maulana Karenga, *Introduction to Black Studies*. 134-135.

13. A. Adu Boahen, *Topics in West African History* (London: Longmans, 1986) (repr.).

14. For slave routes through the Gold Coast see Akosua Adoma Perbi, *A History of Indigenous Slavery in Ghana From the 15th Century to the 19th Century* (Accra: Sub-Saharan Publishers, 2004), 40.

15. Ibid., 40.

16. Ibid.

17. Ibid.

18. Ibid., 40-41.

19. The literature is vast, but see for example, Philip D. Curtin, *The Atlantic Slave Trade: A Census*. (Madison: University of Wisconsin Press, 1969); Philip Curtin, *The Rise and Fall of the Plantation Complex: Essays in Atlantic History*, 1st ed. (Cambridge: Cambridge University Press); Patrick Manning (ed.), *Slave Trades, 1500-1800* (Aldershot, Hampshire: Varorium, 1966); Herbert S. Klein, *The Atlantic Slave Trade* (Cambridge: Cambridge University Press, 1999); Paul E. Lovejoy, *Transformations in Slavery. A History of Slavery in Africa* (Cambridge: Cambridge University Press, 2001); David Eltis, "The Volume and Structure of the Transatlantic Slave Trade: A Reassessment," 3rd Series, 58, 1 (2001): 17-24; David Eltis and David Richardson (eds.), Introduction to *Extending the Frontiers: Essays on the New Transatlantic Slave Trade Database* (New Haven, CT: Yale University Press, 2008).

20. Furley Collection, University of Ghana, Legon, cited in Akosua Perbi, "The Relationship Between the Domestic Slave Trade and the External Slave Trade in Pre-Colonial Ghana," *Research Review* 8, 1 (1992), 67.

21. William Smith, *A New Voyage to Guinea* (London: Frank Cass, 1967), 138.

22. While there were sexual encounters between Europeans in the castles and the female enslaved Africans, the extent of rape of enslaved Africans by castle officials as narrated by tour guides appear to be disputed as unbalanced due to the absence of historical evidence. This statement is, however, not to discount the incidence of rape in the slave forts and castles.

23. Report of the Proceedings of the Conference on Preservation of Elmina and Cape Coast Castles and Fort St. Jago in the Central Region Held in Cape Coast Castle May 11-12, 1994, 3, in Edward M. Bruner, "Tourism in Ghana: The Representation of Slavery and the Return of the Black Diaspora," *American Anthropologist* 98, 2 (1996): 291.

24. Brempong Osei-Tutu, "The African-American Factor in the Commodification of Ghana's Slave Castles," *Transactions of the Historical Society of Ghana* 6 (2002), 123.

25 Ibid., 116; Vera Hyatt, *Ghana: The Chronicle of a Museum Development Project in the Central Region* (Washington, D.C.: The Smithsonian Institution, 1997); Anthony Hyland, "Monuments Conservation Practice in Ghana: Issues of Policy and Management," *Journal of Architectural Conservation*, 2 (1995), 45-62.

26. See Lawrence, *Trade Castles and Forts of West Africa*.

27. Bruner, "Tourism in Ghana," 294.

28. Osei-Tutu, "African American Factor in the Commodification of Ghana's Slave Castles," 117-118; Afrikadzata Deku, "The Truth About Castles in Ghana and Africa," *Ghanaian Weekly Spectator*, May 8 (1993), 5, and May 15 (1993), 14.

29. Osei-Tutu, "African-American Factor in the Commodification of Ghana's Slavery," 118.

30. Bruner, Tourism in Ghana," 294.

31. Richard Wright, *Black Power: A Record of Reactions In a Land of Pathos* (New York: Harper, 1954), 341-342.

32. The numbers game focused on the number of enslaved Africans who arrived in the New World. Philip D. Curtin's path-breaking work, which estimated that 8.5 million enslaved Africans arrived in the New World has been challenged on several fronts. However, the number he estimated, has been revised upward, albeit slightly, by other scholars. See for example, Curtin, *The Atlantic Slave Trade*; Roger Anstey, *The Atlantic Slave Trade and British Abolition, 1760-1810* (Atlantic Highlands, NJ: Humanities Press); J.E. Inikori, "Measuring the Atlantic Slave Trade: an Assessment of Curtin and Anstey," *Journal of African History* 17, 2 (1976): 197-223; J.E. Inikori, Measuring the Atlantic Slave Trade: A Rejoinder, *Journal of African History* 17, 4 (1976): 607-627; Paul E. Lovejoy, "The Volume of the Atlantic Slave Trade: A Synthesis," *Journal of African History* 23, 4 (1982): 473-501; David Eltis, "The Volume and Structure of the Transatlantic Slave Trade: A Reassessment," *William and Mary Quarterly*, 3rd Series, 58, 1 (2001): 17-46.

33. See John L. Vogt, "The Early São Tomé-Príncipé Slave Trade with Mina, 1500-1540," *International Journal of African Historical Studies* 6, 3 (1973): 453-467; John Grace, *Domestic Slavery in West Africa: With Reference to the Sierra Leone Protectorate* (New York: Barnes and Noble, 1975); Timothy F. Garrard, *Akan Gold Weights and the Gold Trade* (London: Longman, 1980).

34. Maurice Peress, *Dvorák to Duke Ellington. A Conductor Explores America's Music and its African Roots* (New York: Oxford University Press, 2004); Samuel A. Floyd Jr., *The Power of Black Music. Interpreting its History from Africa to the United States* (New York: O.U.P., 1996); Charley Gerard, *Jazz in Black and White. Race, Culture, and Identity in the Jazz Community* (Wesport, Conn.: Praeger, 1998); Saadi A. Simawe, *Black Orpheus: Music in African American Fiction From the Harlem Renaissance to Toni Morrison* (New York: Garland Publishing Inc., 2000).

35. William S. Pollitzer, *The Gullah People and Their African Heritage* (Athens: University of Georgia Press, 1999); James J. Kilpatrick, "So it Don't Make no Never Mind With Dialects, *Chicago Sun-Times*, January 30, 2000.

36. Miguel Barnet, "La Regla de Ocha: The Religious System of Santeria," in Margarite Férnandez Olmos and Elizabeth Paravisini-Gilbert (eds.), *Sacred Possessions: Vodou, Santéria, Obeah, and the Caribbean* (New Brunswick, N.J.: Rutgers University Press, 1977); Migene González-Wippler, *Santeria. The Religion* (St. Paul, Minn.: Llewellyn Publications, 1999). For abakuá, see Eugenio Matibag, *Afro-Cuban Religious Experience: Cultural Reflections in Narrative* (Gainesville: University Press of Florida, 1996); Ivor Miller, *Voice of the Leopard.* Mississippi: University Press of

Mississippi, 2008; idem, "Cuba Abakuá Chants: Examining New Evidence for the African Diaspora," *African Studies Review* 48, 1 (April 2005), 23-58.

37. Michael Gomez, *Black Crescent: The Experience and Legacy of African Muslims in the Americas*. Cambridge, New York: Cambridge University Press, 2005; Allan D. Austin, *African Muslims in Antebellum America: Transatlantic Stories and Spiritual Struggles* (New York: Routledge, 1997); Joao José Reis, *Slave Rebellion in Brazil: The Muslim Uprising of 1835 in Bahia* (Baltimore: The University of Johns Hopkins Press, 1993).

38. For the Black Atlantic see Paul Gilroy, *The Black Atlantic. Modernity and Double Consciousness* (Cambridge, Mass.: Harvard University Press, 1993).

39 Willem Bosman is reportedly buried at Fort São Antonio at Axim ; Captain George Maclean and his wife, Letitia Landon, are buried at the forecourt of the Cape Coast Castle.

40. ADM 23/1/337.

41 Archibald Dalzel, *The History of Dahomy, an Inland Kingdom of Africa: Compiled from Authentic Memoirs by Archibald Dalzel* (London: Frank Cass, 1967, repr.).

42 Crooks, *Records Relating to the Gold Coast Settlements* vi-vii..

43. Two companies of English troops disembarked at Cape Coast in February 1782.

44. Crooks, *Records Relating to the Gold Coast Settlements*, vii.

45. Crooks, *Records Relating to the Gold Coast Settlements*. 8. This is Bosman's account of what he saw of the Europeans in the various forts and castles on the Gold Coast, but he has been described by other Europeans as a partial observer.

46. Richard Bean, "A Note on the Relative Importance of Slaves and Gold on West African Exports," *Journal of African History* 15, 3 (1974): 351; K.Y. Daaku, *Trade and Politics on the Gold Coast 1600-1720* (Oxford: Oxford University Press, 1970), 8; Harvey M. Feinberg, "Elmina, Ghana: A History of Its Development and Relationship with the Dutch in the Eighteenth Century, " Ph.D. Dissertation, Boston University, 1969, 5.

47. See for example, Thomas Astley (ed.), *A New General Collection of Voyages and Travels* (London, 1968), 142, 147; Bean, "A Note of the Relative Importance of Slaves and Gold," 352.

48. Feinberg, "Elmina, Ghana," 4.

49 See Davies, *The Royal African Company*. For the Dutch, see for example, Albert van Dantzig, comp. and trans., *The Dutch and the Guinea Coast 1674-1742: A Collection of Documents from the State Archives at the Hague* (Accra: GAAS, 1978); Crooks, *Records Relating to the Gold Coast Settlements*; Paul Erdmann Issert, *Journey to Guinea and the Caribbean Islands in Columbia* (1788), trans. & ed. from German by Selena Winsnes. (Oxford: Oxford University Press, 1992).

50. See Eveline C. Martin, *The British West African Settlements 1750-1821: A Study in Local Administration* (London: Longmans, Green, 1927).

51. Lord Lugard's blueprint for colonial administration is detailed in his book, *The Dual Mandate for Tropical Africa* (London: Frank Cass, 1965).

52. For the European forts and castles, forts at Shama and Axim followed this system and the Dutch adapted it to some of their forts.

53. These houses date from the time of the Portuguese in Elmina and are now historical sites that are being restored with the help of the government of Ghana, UNESCO and the European Union.

54. New video featuring an African Prince.

55. See Michael R. Doortmont and Natalie Everts, "Vrouwen, familie en eigendom op de Goudkust. Afrikaanse en Europese systemen van erfrecht in Elmina, 1760-1860" in Geld & Goed. *Jaarboek voor Vrouwengeschiedenis* 17 (Amsterdam: Stichting beheer IISG 1997), 114-130. ['Women, Family and Property on the Gold Coast. African Women and European Systems of Inheritance in Elmina, 1760-1860'].

56. Georg Nørregård, *Danish Settlements in West Africa 1658- 1850*, trans. Sigurd Mammen (Boston: Boston University Press, 1966), vi.

57. For *asafo* see A.E.A. Asiamah, *The Mass Factor in Rural Politics: The Case of the Asafo Revolution in Kwahu Political History* (Accra: Ghana Universities Press, 2000); Stanley Shaloff, "The Cape Coast Asafo Company Riot of 1932," *International Journal of African Historical Studies* 7, 4 (1974): 591-607; Jarle Simensen, "Rural Mass Action in the Context of Anti-Colonial Protest: The Asafo Movement of Akim Abuakwa, Ghana," *Canadian Journal of African Studies* 8, 1 (1974): 25-41; Ansu K. Datta and R. Porter, "The Asafo System in a Historical Perspective," *Journal of African History* 12, 2 (1971): 279-297; John Kwadwo Osei-Tutu. *The Asafoi (Socio-Military Groups) in the History and Politics of Accra (Ghana) From the 17th to the 20th Century*. Africa Series No. 3 (Trondheim: Norwegian University of Science and Technology, 2000).

58. For a rationale for the colonization of Africa see, for example, Albert Adu Boahen, *African Perspectives on Colonialism* (Baltimore: Johns Hopkins University Press, 1987). Chapt. 2.

59. These merchant princes include Swanzy, John Konny based at Komenda and John Kabes at Pokesu.

60. The literature on the reasons for the European colonization of Africa is vast. Suffice it to say that the following provide a good overview of the subject, see Boahen, *African Perspectives on Colonialism*.

61. ADM 23/1/341. Maintenance of Ancient Castles.

62. Ibid..

63. Ibid.

64. Ibid.

65. Ibid.

66. See F. L. Bartels, "Philip Quacoe 1741-1816," *Transactions of the Historical Society of Ghana* (1952-1955): 153-177.

67. J.B. Webster and A. A. Boahen with H.O. Idowu, *The Growth of African Civilisation. The Revolutionary Years: West Africa since 1800* (London: Longmans), 306-311. See

also I.S Ephson, *Gallery of Gold Coast Celebrities 1632-1958.Vol. I* (Accra: Ilen Publications, 1969).

68. See Report of Captain La Trobe Lonsdale of His Mission to Coomasie, Salagha, Yendi &c., October 1881 to February 1882; Parliamentary Papers, 1882, XLVI, C. 3386, enclosure 2 in # 42, Samuel Rowe to Earl of Kimberley, 10 May, 1882; Edmund Abaka, "Traders, Slaves and Soldiers": The Hausa Diaspora in Ghana (Gold Coast and Asante in the Nineteenth and Early Twentieth Centuries," in Toyin Falola and Aribidesi Usman (ed.), *Movements, Borders, and Identities in Africa* (Rochester, NY: Rochester University Press, 2009), 185-199.

69. ADM 23/1/341. Maintenance of Ancient Castles.

70. Bruner, "Tourism in Ghana," 290.

71. Some of the most famous African Americans who relocated to Ghana or lived in Ghana for an extended period of time included W.E.B. Du Bois and Maya Angelou. See Maya Angelou, *All God's Children Need Traveling Shoes* (New York: Vintage Books, 1986); Eddy L. Harris, *Native Stranger: A Black American's Journey Into the Heart of Africa* (New York: Vintage Books, 1992), Saidiya V. Hartman, *Lose Your Mother: A Journey Along the Atlantic Slave Route* (New York: Farrar, Straus & Giroux, 2007).

72. Robert J. Allison (ed. and intro.), *An Interesting Narrative of the Life of Olaudah Equiano Written by Himself.* Ed. & Intro., Robert J. Allison (Boston: Bedford/St. Martin's, 1995).

73. Ottobah Cuguano, *Thoughts and Sentiments on the Evil and Wicked Traffic of Slavery and Commerce of the Human Species* (London, 1787).

74. Robin Law and Paul E. Lovejoy (eds.), *The Biography of Mahommah Gardo Baquaqua. His Passage from Slavery to Freedom in Africa and America* (Princeton, NJ: Markus Weiner Publishers, 2003).

✠ Chapter 2

The Long Shadow of the Enslaved: From Africa into the Diaspora

A very prominent "photographic display" in the Cape Coast Castle museum exudes the aura of "who is who" in African Diaspora history. From one corner, W.E.B. Du Bois stares majestically into the distance seeming to ponder strategies for countering what he characterized as the double-consciousness that African Americans faced in the United States.[1] From another section, Frederick Douglass appears to wax poetic in his arguments that a back-to-Africa movement is not a solution to the problems of racism and lack of recognition African Americans received in the United States. In the same tableau, the steely stare of Malcolm X epitomizes his radicalism and internationalism and underscores his message about the harsh realities of being African American in the 1950s and 1960s (Photo 2.1).[2] His features speak to his emergence as a radical voice on African American and African affairs. At the same, he also symbolizes the tentative attempts by the civil rights movement to take a more proactive stance on the liberation struggles that had engulfed the African continent in the 1950s and 1960s while at the same time trying to come to terms with its responses to the Vietnam war.[3] In the same picture mentioned above, a somber and pensive Dr. Martin Luther King Jr. gazes into the future and appears to be recalling his days in Ghana as a guest of then Prime Minister Dr. Kwame Nkrumah at the 1957 independence celebrations. After his visit to Ghana, Dr. King often regaled his Atlanta congregation with the sense of euphoria that engulfed Ghana's declaration of independence from Britain. He noted that, as the people shouted freedom, freedom, "I could hear that old Negro spiritual once more crying out: 'Free at last, free at last, Great God Almighty, I'm free at last'. ... And everywhere we turned, we could hear it ringing out from the housetops ... 'Freedom! Freedom!'"[4] Malcolm X was not at the independence celebrations in Ghana but he visited Africa and the Middle East during this period when African Americans were searching for a way to support liberation struggles in Africa. He returned from his trips with a different perspective of the African American struggle. Unfortunately, he did not live long enough to chart a new course for the struggle.

Dr. King attended the independence celebrations in Ghana in solidarity with the linkages and networks that were developing between the civil rights movement and the decolonization struggle in Africa. Du Bois, invited by Dr. Nkrumah to attend the 1957 independence festivities, could not go to Ghana because the U.S. government refused to grant him a visa. Marcus Mosiah Garvey never visited any African country, but far more than Martin Delaney, Paul Cuffe and others before him, he single-mindedly pushed the idea of "Africa for Africans," and championed a back-to-Africa agenda that caught the imagination of many African-descended people in North America, the Caribbean, and South America.[5]

What is the significance of this photographic display? What has it got to do with the trade in enslaved Africans and the African diaspora? The display in question represents a poetic depiction of the significance of the Gold Coast/Ghana slave forts, castles and dungeons in African diaspora history. It is as if the "doyens" of African diaspora history, in their different ways, are asserting with panache at Cape Coast Castle that "the journey into the diaspora started from "here, and that to understand this history in its fullest extent one needs to start from the African continent, as opposed to the often truncated beginning of the long and traumatic journey across the Atlantic."[6] Thus, finally, in one fell swoop, some of the major players in the struggles of people of African descent for dignity, civil and human rights, in the context of the photographic display in the Cape Coast Castle, have united the main points of the African world – North America, the Caribbean and Africa at the very point of departure of various enslaved peoples from the continent. In essence, the common threads that bind people of African descent together had all come together symbolically at the Cape Coast Castle, the starting point of the fateful journey to the New World.

HOW THE ENSLAVED BONDED ON THE GOLD COAST/GHANA BEFORE DEPARTURE TO THE NEW WORLD

The point in the preceding paragraph sums up the essence of this work titled *House of Slaves and Door of No Return*, designed to chronicle the missing link in the story that began in Africa and ended in the New World: the slave fort

Photo 2.1: Photo of (clockwise from top left) Marcus Garvey, Malcolm X, W.E.B. Du Bois, Joseph Jenkins Roberts, and Dr. Martin Luther King Jr. at Cape Coast Castle

or castle experience. In this story, both the long trek of the enslaved from the interior to the slave forts, castles and dungeons on the coast, the slave fort or castle experience itself and the Middle Passage are all highlighted, and rightly so, in order to delineate both the horrific nature and the totality of the experience of enslavement. The ordeal of the Middle Passage began beyond the slave forts and castles dotted along the West African coast. Similarly, the bonding of persons from the same ethnicity or from different ethnicities who did not understand each other's verbal language started here in the slave forts and castles, but even then, the process had already been under way before the enslaved reached the shores of "Guinea." Confined together from one day to three months or even more, sign language or some other forms of communication became the basis of a lingua franca that enabled the enslaved to get acquainted. The nods and grunts and arm movements in the confines of the slave forts and castles started a process that continued on slave ships. The rudiments of new communities and lines of communication, however loose the terms may be used, had begun before the slave fort and castle experience. House of Slaves, therefore, calls for an expansive definition of the Middle Passage to include the slave fort and castle experience because these structures were, in principle, slave "ships at permanent anchor."[7] This assertion is cognizant of the fact that the term is often associated with the trip aboard ship across the Atlantic.

During the period of the slave trade, the slave forts and castles constituted the first major assembly point that enabled enslaved persons from different ethnic groups, and even different states and kingdoms to meet in close quarters. As a result, "communities" were not "formed" in the New World but rather on the African coast. While Michael A. Gomez has argued that the enslaved formed bonds on ships en route to the New World, I argue that the process started earlier during transit from the interior (which could take days or weeks) and, more especially, in the slave forts, castles and dungeons where the enslaved were herded together in the musty dungeons, as hapless "passengers" on the "ships at permanent anchor."[8]

By the time the enslaved were loaded onto ships to commence the Middle Passage, close association had already resulted in some form of familiarity, however limited and perfunctory. Therefore, the frequency of revolts during the Middle Passage can be attributed to the slave forts and castle experience, which had enabled people who had been in close proximity for weeks and months to establish some measure, albeit small, of comfort with others.

Yet it is important not to overstate this point.[9] If it has now been recognized that there was a high degree of revolts on board slave ships, the seeds were sown in that period in the slave forts and castles. The condemned cells of various forts and castles were designed to deter revolts by the enslaved

Africans but they [the cells] certainly did not. While not minimizing the nature of the enslavement ordeal and the difficulties the enslaved faced, one should also not underestimate the tenacity of the human spirit under very trying circumstances.

African diaspora history embodies the totality of the black experience – beginning with the location of the ancestors of the enslaved peoples on the African continent (their experiences and institutions), and following them to all the corners of the world. For a very long time African American history, as taught in classrooms and appeared in books, started with enslaved Africans in the United States and the world the enslaved made. For some people, 1619 marks the most significant period for the appearance of African Americans in the United States. For others, African Americans were here in the Americas before the arrival of Christopher Columbus.[10] And for many others, the history of African Americans, and the African diaspora for that matter, begins with the Atlantic slave trade. Since the 1980s however, this has begun to change.

African diaspora history as a discipline argues for an understanding of Africa and African institutions (especially of precolonial Africa) as a *sine qua non* for a better understanding of the societies and institutions enslaved Africans created and recreated in the New World. When slave institutions are discussed with a thorough knowledge of the African background – religion, ethnicity, sexuality, family patterns, political systems, and naming systems a more meaningful discussion of the African diaspora emerges. Scholars such as Colin Palmer, Robin Kelley, Robin Horton, Paul Lovejoy, Michael Gomez and James Sweet, among others, have increasingly called for this approach in the field of African diaspora studies.[11]

The important contributions people of African descent made to various societies, as bonded persons, free persons and active members of communities where they reside, have been finally acknowledged in several works. This project reinforces the argument that the beginnings of African American history (and African diaspora history) are anchored in Africa from whence enslaved Africans were taken and dispersed around the world. As a result, African diaspora history should be studied and taught with a strong African anchor (especially precolonial African history) to facilitate a better historical understanding of the nuances of the cultural experience.[12] The same argument suffices for Atlantic studies, which often creates the impression that Atlantic discourses often encompass Europe and the Americas and leaves off the African experience as integral to understanding the Atlantic experience

House of Slaves also makes the important point that the slave forts and castles and the infamous "doors of no return" marked the point of total rupture, separation and departure from Africa between 1441 (when the

Portuguese took a party of ten Africans to Portugal) down to the late 1880s (when slavery was eventually abolished in Brazil). Like ritual performance in a rite-of-passage ceremony, passage through the "door of no return" violently tore slaves from one state of being and ushered them into another state via the dreaded Middle Passage. Since 1999 history has gone full circle and the "door of no return" has become the "door of return"; the rupture that occurred through the door of no return has been replaced with a ritual homecoming through the same door. This ritual homecoming has become part of the biennial commemoration of Emancipation from Slavery and the Pan-African Historical Theatre Festival (PANAFEST) that brings together people from the continent and people of African descent in the diaspora to participate in events designed to reconnect various branches of the "African family." Following the success of the experimental PANAFEST in 1991, the first official PANAFEST was held in 1992 in Cape Coast and Elmina. The festival is centered on the historical and cultural connections among Africans in the world. Events that highlight the festival include, among others, a reenactment of the slave trade (the capture and sale of Africans), tours of Cape Coast and São Jorge da Mina Castle dungeons, a durbar of chiefs (in Cape Coast and other places), musical performances (by artists from Africa and the diaspora) and a visual arts exhibition.

PANAFEST and the commemoration of Emancipation from Slavery, which was added later, play on the connections between Africans on the continent and in the diaspora that fueled the desire of Paul Cuffe and Martin Delaney and others to push for a return to Africa.[13] The same relationship fueled W.E.B. Du Bois, Marcus Garvey and other doyens of the African diaspora in North America, the Caribbean and Europe to fight against racism and injustice and fight for equal rights for people of color in the 1920s through the 1950s.[14] In the aftermath of independence in the 1960s, some Africans in the diaspora, largely from the United States, settled in Ghana.[15] In the 1990s and onward, the connection between Africans and the African diaspora have often been seen through the prism of the Atlantic slave trade.[16]

RETURN OF REMAINS OF ENSLAVED AFRICANS

In 1999, the remains of two former enslaved Africans – Mr. Samuel Carson from New York, and Madam Crystal from Jamaica – were brought back to Ghana by relatives and friends to be interred.[17] There is very little information about Madam Crystal but Lady Minion, who accompanied Madam Crystal's remains to Ghana, indicated she had promised "her ancestor" that she would bring "her [Madam Crystal's] bones" to the motherland to lie with her ancestors.[18] Mr. Sonny Carson, an African-American nationalist and activist from New York petitioned the U.S. government in 1998 for permission to rebury his great-great-uncle, Samuel Carson, in the land of his fathers. Samuel Carson reportedly escaped from South Carolina after the Denmark Vesey rebellion and subsequently served in the U.S. Navy.[19] Long after the death of Samuel Carson, Sonny Carson wanted his great-great-uncle to return to the land of his ancestors.

The caskets containing the remains of the two African-descended ancestors were flown to Ghana from New York and Kingston, Jamaica and taken to the Accra International Conference Center. After a day of national mourning, the caskets were conveyed by road to Anomabu, one of the major slave ports of the Gold Coast. From Anomabu, the caskets were conveyed to Cape Coast Castle in a trip reminiscent of the actual journey of enslaved Africans between Cape Coast Castle and the European ships on the high seas. Surf boats were used during the Atlantic slave trade to ferry enslaved Africans from the slave forts, castles and dungeons to the ships anchored far out to sea because of the rough surf and the absence of natural harbors along the Gold Coast. In this reenactment of the trip between the slave castle and the European ship anchored off the coast, surf boats or canoes were used for the "return" or reverse trip from the high seas to the Cape Coast Castle.

About fifty meters out at sea from the Cape Coast Castle the two caskets were transferred from the two fishing boats onto the shoulders of eight to ten stalwart men who carried them ashore from the sea, and through the "door of no return," in a "homecoming" into the courtyard of Cape Coast Castle. This symbolic action of returning the remains of two African-descended people through the door of no return was designed to break the myth of "no return" and to demonstrate the present reality that where there was once no hope of return, there is now a warm homecoming for Africans of the diaspora. Pronouncements of Ghanaian state officials clearly articulated this new desire. Since the symbolic breaking of the myth of "no return," many Africans in the diaspora return to Ghana every year for PANAFEST and the commemorative activities that mark Emancipation from slavery. During these times as well as at other times, African-descended peoples visit some of the slave forts and castles as a means of coming to terms with the violent past of their ancestors. Wreaths from many institutions and organizations in North America and Europe can now be found in the slave dungeons of Elmina and Cape Coast Castles (Photo 2.2).

THE IMPREGNABLE FORTS, CASTLES AND DUNGEONS

An important site or edifice of historical memory, the slave fort or castle stands as a forlorn link between the African continent and various parts of the world to which Africans were forcibly sent during the period of the Atlantic and Indian Ocean slave trade. The grim, impregnable (albeit in varying degrees), and forbodden structures, often whitewashed in recent times in part due to various restoration projects in Ghana in particular, constitute the link in the chain that connects Africa to the diaspora, though whitewashing the structures had come under fierce criticism by African Americans who felt that the grim reality of the fort and castle experience was being diluted in the process.[20] These structures constituted a linchpin in the journey of enslaved Africans from the continent to the New World.[21]

The slave fort or castle of Ghana has centuries of history in its damp, musty, haunting dungeons. Imakhüs Vienna Robinson notes that painting the dungeons would obliterate "the musty, lingering smell of time and of Black male bodies, the lingering feel of the spirit of these ancestors who had been forcibly removed from their 'Mother' land."[22] Concerning the state of the male dungeon in Cape Coast Castle before the restoration projects, Saidiya Hartman writes that

> Human waste covered the floor of the dungeon. To the naked eye it looked like soot. After the last group of captives had been deported, the holding cells were closed but never cleaned out. For a century and a half after the abolition of the slave trade, the waste remained. To control the stench and the pestilence, the floor had been covered with sand and lime. In 1972, a team of archaeologists excavated the dungeon and cleared away eighteen inches of dirt and waste. They identified the topmost layer of the floor as the compressed remains of captives – feces, blood, and exfoliated skin.[23]

From several visits to the dungeons and the accounts of several others, one feels as if the souls of those who were imprisoned in the dungeons are still hovering around, albeit silently, in the same dungeons. In this sense, I contend that the enslaved indeed have left their shadows in the dungeons.[24] This feeling of the presence of unseen shadows[25] is accentuated by a face-to-face encounter with the door of no return, through which one gazes at the sea (though by now receded from the walls of the forts and castles). Looking out through the door of no return at Cape Coast Castle or São Jorge da Mina, one sees that "only the swell of the ocean is still not diminished; even on calm days, the waves roll on to the coast. Thus the ocean lies before the white fort like a surfeited beast of prey that only bares its teeth but is too lazy to rise."[26]

Thorkild Hansen's description of the location of Christiansborg Castle in Accra mirrors the location of other castles and forts along the coast of

Photo 2.2: Wreaths left in São Jorge da Mina by U.S. Educational Institutions, City and County Officials

IN MEMORY OF OUR ANCESTORS
FROM: LA, CA 2007 PIGRIMAGE TOUR
TO GHANA

Ghana. He writes about the Danish period in Gold Coast/Ghana history and in the Atlantic slave trade thus: "We once had a fort in Africa. It is still there, erected on a low promontory of rock, where the coastline extends a foot into the ocean. The oft-whitewashed walls are visible among the palms."[27] Into the cavernous halls of these slave forts and castles marched a constant flow of men, women and children who became links in the chain that became the Atlantic slave trade from Africa to the New World for over four hundred years.[28] As Hansen notes,

> Like a long caterpillar the procession emerged from the forest and wound its way across the grass of the savannah. The men and the women were on the whole in their best years, tall and well-formed with long slim limbs, broad noses, small ears and short wooly hair ... the long procession finally reached the village Osu under the palms behind the white fort. The prisoners were escorted into a fenced compound ... men and women had all bodily hair removed and then smeared with palm oil to make it difficult for the purchasers to assess their age, the decisive factor in estimating their value. ... The long caterpillar once more moved, creeping towards the gate with Christian VII's initials.[29]

In this way, the slave coffle entered the castle, no longer visible to the outside world until a slave ship arrived to take them to the New World (Photo 2.3). It is worthy of note that the coffle might have traveled anywhere from a hundred miles (or probably up to two hundred or more miles), sometimes across different ecological zones. Embedded in this experience was a culture shock stemming from seeing different people speaking different languages.[30]

Though the description above is specific to Christiansborg Castle (Photos 2.4, 2.5, 2.6), the author might as well have been describing the procession into São Jorge da Mina or Cape Coast Castle, Fort William (Anomabu), Fort São Sebastião (Shama), Fort São Antonio (Axim) or Fort Patience (Apam). Thus from farther inland, the enslaved were marched in a long procession to the forts and castles. The use of neck irons, leg irons, wooden yokes and other accoutrements, some of which can be found on display in the forts and castles, indicates that some of the newly captured people would often try to escape, hence the need to restrain them as much as possible.

HOW THE ENSLAVED WERE OBTAINED

It is worthy of note that the enslaved persons had been obtained in various ways. Some of the enslaved, in all likelihood most of them, were

Map 2.1: The African Diaspora Showing Where Enslaved Africans Went
Courtesy: Joseph E. Harris, Professor Emeritus, Howard University. Map drawn by Daniel Thompson, University of Miami.

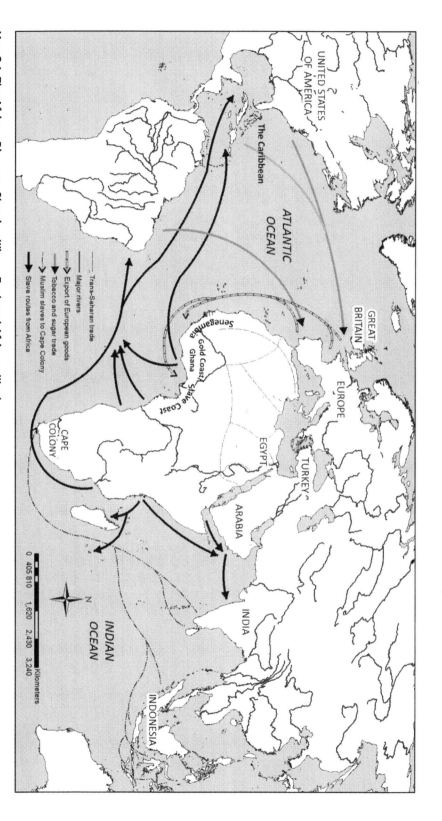

obtained through warfare (prisoners taken in wars of expansion fought by various kingdoms of the Gold Coast and beyond the Gold Coast) in the late seventeenth century through the early decades of the nineteenth century. Venture Smith notes in his *Narrative of Venture Smith* that

> The army of the enemy was large, I should suppose consisting of about six thousand men. Their leader was called Baukarre. After destroying the old Prince [his father], they decamped and immediately marched toward the sea, lying to the west, taking with them myself and the women prisoners. In the march a scouting party was detached from the main army. To the leader of this party I was made waiter, having to carry his gun, & c. ... The enemy had remarkable success in destroying the [country] wherever they went.
>   ... Having come to the next [tribe], the enemy laid siege and immediately took men, women, children, flocks and all their valuable effects. They then went on to the next district which was contiguous to the sea, called in Africa, Anamaboo. ... All of us were then put into the castle, and kept for a market.[31]

Thus, Venture Smith was captured when an enemy army overran his homeland in the 1730s and spent time in Fort William at Anomabu before he was transported to the United States. John Hawkins, an English privateer who voyaged to Cape Verde in search of a cargo of enslaved Africans, reported that on his third voyage to the Island,

> There came to us a Negro sent down from a King oppressed by other Kings his neighbors desiring our aid, with a promise that as many negroes as by these wars might be obtained as well of his part as ours should be at our pleasure whereupon we concluded to give aid, and sent 120 of our men which the 15th of January assaulted a town of negroes of our Allies' adversaries ... and put the inhabitants to flight where we took 250 persons men, women, and children and by our friend the king of our side there were taken 600 prisoners whereof we hoped to have had our choice: but the Negro (in which nation is seldom or never found truth) meant nothing less, for that night he removed his camp and prisoners, so that we might feign to content us with those few which we had gotten ourselves.[32]

Hawkins' account also demonstrates the use of war as a method of securing enslaved persons, though his explanation that the king did not give him the honor of choosing from the king's captives because truth is seldom found in that nation is part of the arrogance of the early travelers and missionaries in Africa in their description of Africans and their way of life. Africans were

Photo 2.3: Slave Coffle, Western Sudan, 1879-81 (image Buel-01) from www.slaveryimages.org; compiled by Jerome Handler and Michael Tuite, and sponsored by the Virginia Foundation for the Humanities and the University of Virginia Library.

Photo 2.4: Christiansborg Castle – enslaved hustled onto slave ships from beach on side of the castle. Courtesy Sub-Saharan Publishers – Svalesen, *Slave Ship Fredensborg*, 212.

Photo 2.5: Entrance to Slave Dungeon, Christiansborg Castle

Courtesy of Sub-Saharan Publishers – Leif Svalesen, *The Slave Ship Fredensborg*, Trans. Pat Shaw and Selena Winsnes. Accra: Sub-Saharan Publishers, 2000, 215.

often portrayed as unfaithful, unreliable and untrustworthy on account of being savages and uncivilized. This was part of the spurious justification, in some cases, for enslaving Africans.

Many other enslaved Africans were "stolen" and innocent of any crime, or they were kidnapped during slave raids.[33] Olaudah Equiano was captured when he was left at home after his parents and the older people of his village went to the farm.[34] The same can be said of Cinque or Singbe Pierre of the *Amistad* fame.[35] Some Africans were also sold after committing heinous crimes while others, for other casual reasons, were acquired by Europeans. In this case, the criminal justice system was subverted by some people in authority toward benefitting from the sale of countrymen who had committed crimes. Toward the end of the slave trade, pawns or debtors were also sold into slavery even though a pawn was not a slave, and could not be legally sold.[36] In some of these cases, environmental reasons (including lack of rainfall or drought) are given for the poverty of certain families leading to the pawnship of family members as a matter of survival or life and death.[37] It is also realistic to argue that some of the enslaved were born to enslaved parents who were part of the domestic slavery system in Africa.[38]

Commercial bargaining for enslaved Africans began in the forts and castles with a physician thoroughly examining the enslaved to ascertain their physical fitness and to ensure that there were no "blemishes" and no hidden deformities that would make them unsuitable for the tasks of the plantation complex. Thus, right from the slave forts, castles and dungeons, the slave dealers and slave traders engaged in a process of getting the best of each other through hard bargaining as each party tried to maximize his gain in haggling over the price of slaves.[39]

BRANDING THE ENSLAVED

The enslaved were branded soon after purchase (Photo 2.7). Where several European merchants had purchased enslaved Africans, branding the enslaved immediately after purchase helped European traders to distinguish between their enslaved Africans. Branding was done "with the help of some long-shafted iron stamps that were made glowing hot on a charcoal fire."[40] Usually, the slaves were branded with the initials of the company or individual merchant who had purchased them. Thorkild Hansen quotes the Moravian scholar, Georg Andreas Oldenthorpe (1777), who arrived on the Island of St. Thomas in May 1761, as describing the process of branding thus:

> initially a piece of oiled paper was put on the place where the
> slave was to be branded, but that was in the West Indies; in Guinea

Photo 2.6: Christiansborg Castle courtyard
Courtesy of Sub-Saharan Publishers – Svalesen, *Slave Ship Fredensborg*, p. 214.

[West Africa] one often just smeared the place with some palm oil before the red-hot iron was pressed to the skin. The result was that the scar came to stand with clear, easily legible contours.[41]

Branding could be done on the right breast, left breast, right arm or left arm. Paul Erdman Isert, chief physician in the Danish settlement of Christiansborg, notes that after the enslaved were purchased by the factors of the slave forts, they were housed and guarded, and that in the baracoons, the purchased "were set aside for branding with a hot iron on the breast or the shoulder with the identifying iron mark of the Company or individual purchaser."[42] Isert claims that the Dutch tried to avoid branding by selling entire cargoes to single proprietors where feasible but when they had to, "the operation was performed carefully with pieces of silver wire, heated just enough to blister without burning skin."[43] Isert's description of the Danish branding of the enslaved at the Christiansborg Castle should be taken with a healthy dose of skepticism.

LIVING CONDITIONS OF THE ENSLAVED

After branding, the enslaved Africans were shepherded into dungeons, holding cells and the "so-called slave boxes, some vaulted stone chambers below the eastern bastions of the fort [Christiansborg]."[44] H.C. Monrad, who was at Christiansborg Castle, noted in 1822 that after branding, slaves in the Danish fort

spend the night on wooden pallets, one above the other, in the dark vaults where only a little air can enter through a square hole in the iron-bound door that is reinforced with iron bars ... the heat increased through the many people and the odours of that which one at times must excrete and which is collected in big basins, cause an abominable stench that in the morning, when the doors are opened, spreads over the whole fort and contaminates the air ...[45]

Monrad's eyewitness account aptly describes the living conditions of the enslaved in the dungeons of the various forts and castles along the Gold Coast (Photos 2.8, 2.9. 2.10). The damp/dank floors of Cape Coast Castle, São Jorge da Mina, and the Anomabu, Apam, Axim and Sekondi forts, to mention a few, all served the same purpose. With only shafts for air vents and pans of convenience for nature's call, the stench would undoubtedly have been overpowering. Sometimes, the enslaved were too weak after the long march from the interior to summon enough energy to move from one part of the slave dungeon to "the place of convenience" at the other end of

Photo 2.7: Branding irons
Courtesy of Sub-Saharan Publishers – *The Slave Ship Fredensborg,* p. 99.

Photo 2.8: Slave dungeon (male) – Cape Coast Castle

Photo 2.9: Slave dungeon – Anomabu Fort

Photo 2.10: Slave dungeon – Elmina Castle

the dungeon. In such instances, nature took its course and human beings, excrement and urine co-mingled on the dungeon floor. As one tour guide at Elmina Castle explained in 2004, feacal material was removed from the dungeon floors of Cape Coast and Elmina Castles when restoration commenced to preserve the two castles as UNESCO World Heritage sites.[46] This was in 1972 when the dungeons of Cape Coast Castle were excavated after they had been closed for over a century after the abolition of the slave trade.[47]

The dungeon experience in the slave forts and castles approximated the experience in the "floating tombs" or ships during the Middle Passage. It is therefore not surprising that bacterial infections led to dysentery, diarrhoea and other epidemic outbreaks in the slave forts and castles and preceded similar outbreaks during the passage across the Atlantic. The one big difference in the experience was that the slave forts and castles were "ships at permanent anchor," unlike the ships of the Atlantic voyages that dropped anchor only when the wind was very still or when they docked at a port. Not only were the experiences similar but in reality, part of a seamless process of moving enslaved Africans from the interior to the coast to await transportation to the New World. This is the context in which the Middle Passage experience should encompass the time spent in the slave forts and castles.

All the slave forts and castles have condemned cells for the enslaved persons who were considered recalcitrant and rebellious. As symbolized by the skull and cross-bones that mark out the condemned cell at São Jorge da Mina, the enslaved persons who entered the condemned cells never came out but died in their cells (Photo 2.11). As well, any enslaved persons who died in the slave forts and castles due to diseases like smallpox or to malnutrition and distress were thrown into the sea, which was then very close to the structures. One nineteenth-century observer noted that "Were the Atlantic ocean dried up today, one could trace the pathway between the slave coast of Africa and America by a scattered roadway of human bones."[48] In this case, I add for emphasis, that the pathway of human bones extended to the Gold Coast slave forts, castles and dungeons, especially those that were closest to the Atlantic Ocean.

With very little or no air to breathe, and with very little or no food at all in these cells, life was gradually and slowly squeezed out of the "damned" enslaved in the dark and musty interiors of these tiny death cells. According to the curator of the *Maison des Esclaves* on Gorée Island, when Nelson Mandela visited the infamous house after his release from prison in 1994, he went into the tiny condemned cell of that infamous structure. A few minutes later, he emerged from that enclosure, his eyes red with tears.[49] It can be surmised that Mandela's experience on Robben Island certainly made him appreciate, more than anyone else, the excruciating experience the "troublesome and recalcitrant" slaves went through in the tiny condemned cells of the slave forts and castles.[50]

Photo 2.11: Condemned cell – São Jorge da Mina

Frank Gray noted after a tour of Cape Coast Castle that

> In the Cape Coast Castle the visitor is taken to the dungeons and then to the tunnel, damp and dark, relieved only by its healthy sea smell from the gates at the bottom of the tunnel giving immediate access to the foreshore on which the sea breaks. Here were the slaves driven so that they might be hustled into the surf boats and the holds of the ships for a life of servitude. And from this scene we immediately returned to the offices housed within the castle of modern administration and British freedom.[51]

In the last sentence of the above quotation is embedded the contradictions of the slavery experience – servitude side by side with "modern administration and British freedom" as per Cape Coast Castle or the Dutch Reformed Church and the church services that were held right above the male dungeon at São Jorge da Mina.

SLAVE SHIPS AND THE "FINAL JOURNEY"

In the solid bastions of the dungeons of the various slave forts and castles, the enslaved awaited the arrival of ships to take them across the Atlantic Ocean to the "land of no return" (Photo 2.12). Sometimes, several ships anchored "in the roads" by the time a coffle of enslaved Africans arrived at the forts and castles. At other times, the enslaved stayed in the dungeons for months before a slave ship arrived to carry them off to the New World. Attoborah Kweku Enu, popularly known as Ottobah Cugoano, who was enslaved in the Gold Coast, notes that "When a vessel arrived to conduct us away to the ship, it was a most horrible scene: there was nothing to hear but rattling of chains, smacking of whips, and groans and cries of fellow men."[52] The final rupture in the contact with Africa occurred at this time when the enslaved saw their country for the last time. In essence, the "last goodbye" was a traumatic and heart-wrenching experience. Form this point onward the enslaved entered a period of "social death"[53] or the "Damned of Dante's inferno."[54]

It is worthy of note that "packing" the enslaved in the slave dungeons of the forts and castles to await the arrival of slave ships was not radically different from the "tight" packing of the enslaved that occurred during the Middle Passage trip across the Atlantic. It is therefore important to underline the fact that the conditions of the dreaded Middle Passage were very much present in the slave dungeons of the slave forts and castles. Paul Erdman Isert, who traveled on a slave ship (as a physician) from the Gold Coast destined for the Caribbean and Denmark, gives a vivid account of the condi-

Photo 2.12: Reconstruction of the Slave Ship Fredensborg
Courtesy: Sub-Saharan Publishers – *The Slave Ship Fredensborg*, 172.

tions on the ships that compare, in some way, with the conditions in the slave dungeons in the forts and castles on the coast. He notes that

> A slave ship is equipped amidships with a strong, high [traverse] wooden partition called the bulwark whose side facing forward must be extremely smooth, without any open groves in which the slaves might get a fingerhold. On top of this wall there are as many small cannons and guns as there is room for, and these are kept loaded at all times and are shot off every evening in order to keep the slaves in a state of fear. There is always a man on watch near these, who must pay meticulous attention to the movement of the blacks. In the stern section on the other side of the bulwark, all women and children are kept, while the men are kept on the forward side of the bulwark where they can neither see the women nor join them. The men are always chained together, hand and foot, in pairs. Moreover, along the row in which they sit on the deck, a strong chain is drawn between their feet so that they cannot stand up without permission, nor can they move from the spot except when they come up on deck in the mornings and are locked in the hold in the evenings.[55]

The slave forts and castles with their thick walls, small slits in the dungeon walls to admit some air as well as light, the leg irons, as well as other paraphernalia, and the gun emplacements atop the structures compare favorably to slave ships on the Atlantic.

The fear of revolts caused slave ship owners to invest in extra manpower, swivel guns and cannons. When Isert left the Gold Coast to return to Denmark (October 7, 1786), he boarded a slave ship that legally held 200 people but carried 452 enslaved Africans packed into the hold of the ship. It had a crew of thirty-six Europeans and the enslaved were brought up to the deck every other day for exercise and fresh air.[56] On such occasions ships' crews kept close watch to prevent the enslaved Africans from jumping into the ocean and taking their own lives.

The point here is not to minimize the horrific nature of the Atlantic Passage ordeal. Rather, it is to argue that the Middle Passage experience should be extended to include the ordeal in the slave forts and castles before the actual journey to the New World. The slave forts, castles and dungeons were indeed part of the middle leg of the entire journey, spanning the trek from the interior to the coast (the first leg), the time in the various slave forts and dungeons (second leg) and the Middle Passage (third leg). The journey from the various arrival destinations in the New World to the place of engagement in the Americas or the Caribbean constitutes the fourth and final leg of the incredible journey. In all discussions of this journey, the slave fort and castle experience, which lasted anywhere from three days to three months, is not highlighted. Iron pegs in the floor of Fort William at Anomabu mirror the chaining of enslaved Africans on ships. Cape Coast Castle housed its enslaved Africans in underground dungeons and thus the enslaved were brought up to the courtyard for exercises and fresh air periodically, which again mirrors a similar practice on board slave ships. In short the slave forts and castles constitute an important cog in the slavery experience, but are all but neglected by scholars.

UPKEEP OF FORTS AND CASTLES

Who were the people responsible for the upkeep of the slave forts and castles, of the slaves, of all *palavers* in the slave forts and castles, of all commerce, and the security of the "ships at permanent anchor"? Various European governors, chaplains, soldiers, merchants, castle slaves (Africans) and artisans (Africans) all worked to keep the slave forts and castles functioning like well-oiled machines. Sometimes castle personnel had to contend with the predations of rival European powers. For example, the Portuguese ensconced at Elmina had to contend with the Dutch who, after an initial failure to seize the castle in 1596, finally succeeded in taking Elmina Castle and dislodging the Portuguese in 1637. There is also the case of the Akwamu leader, Asameni, who took over the Christiansborg Castle from the Danes.[57] It is not surprising that most of the guns in the slave forts and castles point out to sea from whence rival European powers were likely to appear (Photo 2.13). There were also instances where villages or towns in the vicinity of a fort or castle were shelled by the guns of the fort in reprisals, often for supporting rival factions against their European allies or for supporting a local faction against the fort or castle.[58] Villages and towns were shelled on these occasions as a lesson to the local people. At other times, towns and villages near the forts were shelled by European ships anchored off the coast, as in the case of the English shelling of Winneba after Henry Meredith, the British governor of the fort, was murdered by the local people.[59] It was a point that was often made, and often well-taken, for at the end of the day "we have the Maxim gun and they have not," to quote Hilaire Belloc's oft-quoted statement to explain the eventual defeat of African societies by European powers during the scramble for colonies of the 1880s.[60]

Thorkild Hansen has asserted that

> The slaves do not cast any shadow in history. They can be likened to the damned in Dante's inferno, they are themselves a people of black shadows. A stranger has to step down into the underworld

> to follow them on their wanderings, that contrary to Dante's,
> lead from paradise to hell. ... The slaves are silent, they could not
> write. Still, now and then we make out a phrase, catch a phrase.
> Their owners spoke for them, through them they were trans-
> ferred to history, as they were transferred to the West Indies.[61]

There is no denying the fact that the enslaved, from the journey in the interior to the slave forts and castles on the coast, kept no written records. Unlike Hansen, however, I contend that the enslaved did cast very long shadows in history, especially in the diaspora, and in fact, some went on to leave very rich and detailed accounts that have helped scholars to appreciate and understand the ordeal of the enslaved; their rich cultural and political activities; and their contribution to society even under very trying conditions. The fact that the enslaved in the end cast a very long shadow over history, I would argue, explains the current interest in various facets of the Atlantic, Indian Ocean, and Saharan-Mediterranean slave trades.[62] It is for the same reason that UNESCO designated São Jorge da Mina and Cape Castles as world heritage sites at par with other historic monuments in the history of humankind (see earlier Photos 1.2 and 2.13).

Certainly, the enslaved have cast a long shadow over African-American, Caribbean, and Latin American history, among several others.[63] The annual "pilgrimages" of many diaspora Africans to Ghana have as their focal point the slave forts and castles, the most indelible mark, the most impregnable edifice, the most outstanding historical artifact and sites of historical memory of the infamous Atlantic slave trade. The slave forts, castles and dungeons signified the final break between enslaved Africans and the continent they called home. Once the enslaved disappeared into the cavernous halls of the forts and castles, "the slow march of social death" had begun.[64] In the case of the enslaved Africans who eventually entered Cape Coast castle, the process of separation began at Assin Manso (a sleepy little town on the Cape Coast-Kumasi road) where the slaves were given their final bath in the "*Ndonko Nsuo*" or *Slave River* before the last leg of the march to Cape Coast Castle (Photo 2.14). Any enslaved who entered the Slave River for a bath eventually ended up in Cape Coast Castle and those who did not take a bath in the river were left behind to die either because they were too weak to continue the journey or were considered too old or infirm.[65]

Furthermore, contrary to Hansen's position that the enslaved left no records, some of them did leave records, albeit at a later date, in the New World and not at the point of embarkation in the Gold Coast. The works of Olaudah Equiano (or Gustavus Vassa), Ottogbah Coguano (Attobora Kweku Enu), Jacobus Eliza Capittein, Omar Ibn Saïd, among several others, have

Photo 2.13: Cape Coast Castle Showing a platform Mounted with Guns Facing the Atlantic Ocean

enabled scholars to "stand in the diaspora" and cast a "searching research glance" back at the continent, often with very illuminating results.[66]

Through the "Gates of No Return" at Cape Coast, Elmina, Anomabu, Apam, Axim, Shama, and Christiansborg forts and castles, the enslaved saw their continent for the final time as they were marched to the boats to begin the transfer to the ships that would take them to their fate in the New World. Today, in the small coves near the slave forts and castles, fishermen ply their trade – setting off for fishing trips, pulling in their nets, mending their nets and preparing to set out to sea once more. This certainly is a routine of life that seems incongruous against the walls of the various forts and castles.

The magisterial work of A. W. Lawrence, K. J. Anquandah and the Dutch-Ghanaian historian Albert van Dantzig, together with other smaller works such as Rosemary Cave's *Gold Coast Forts*, focus more on the architecture of the forts and castles. My work seeks to move beyond architectural history to connect the slave forts and castles to the Atlantic slave trade and the Atlantic diaspora. It seeks to locate the slave forts and castles in the larger story of the Middle Passage, intimating that the story of life in the slave dungeons is a missing link in the totality of the Atlantic story. As this chapter has described, the enslaved were tightly packed into the slave dungeons, brutalized, sometimes chained and sparsely fed. The conditions are, to a limited extent, reminiscent of aspects of the Atlantic Passage and so I argue that the slave fort and castle experience should be seen as the first leg of what became the Middle Passage. *House of Slaves* also continues the history of the slave forts and castles through the colonial period and right into the very present.

These dimensions of the history of the Ghana slave forts and castles are not adequately discussed in the few works that deal with the topic. These elements are often left out of the very intriguing and riveting history of the slave forts and castles. In this sense, *House of Slaves* fulfils a recommendation of the May 1994 conference organized at Cape Coast Castle by the Ghana National Commission On Culture: all the different epochs and powers should be presented in the history of the slave forts and castles, but that "the area symbolizing the slave trade should be given reverential treatment."[67] This is what this project has attempted to do here – tell the slave forts and castles and the diaspora story but also link the structures to the longer durée of Ghana's history.

House of Slaves also connects African history to the reconquista, and the Portuguese effort to drive Muslims out of Europe and other places like North Africa. The Portuguese built São Jorge da Mina along the lines of fifteenth-century European castles and the plan of two inner courtyards became the standard for all the later European fortifications on the Gold Coast. Finally

Photo 2.14: Slave River - Enslaved given last bath before final march to Cape Coast Castle.

the project is designed to help African descended people make some sense of the totality of the story of their forebears, for the work of the historian has meaning for the present. Where did this story begin? How can we relive, retell and understand this very complex story? Any effort designed to place in context some of the several layers of the story of the African diaspora is welcome and, hopefully, this work peels off one layer and shines a small beam of light on a neglected aspect of the African diaspora experience.

Notes

1. See W.E.B. Du Bois, *The Souls of Black Folk* ed. with an introduction by David W. Blight and Robert Gooding-Williams (Boston: Bedford/St. Martins, 1997). See also David Levering Lewis, *W.E.B. Du Bois. Biography of a Race 1869-1919* (New York: Henry Holt & Co., 1993).

2. George Breitman (ed.), *Malcolm X Speaks* (New York: Pathfinder Press, 1989), 79-88, 166-176; Malcolm X, *The Autobiography of Malcolm X* (New York: Grove Press, 1965).

3. Kevin K. Gaines, *American Africans in Ghana: Black Expatriates and the Civil Rights Era* (Chapel Hill: The University of North Carolina Press, 2006).

4. Ibid., 83-84.

5. See Amy Jacques Garvey (ed.), *The Philosophy and Opinions of Marcus Garvey*, repr. (New York: Humanities Press, 1968). For the back- to-Africa movement see, for example, Martin R. Delaney, *The Condition, Elevation and Destiny of the Colored People of the United States*, repr. (New York: Arno Press, 1968); Martin R. Delaney, *Official Report of the Niger Valley Exploring Party* (New York, 1861); Dorothy Sterling, *The Making of an Afro-American: Martin Robinson Delaney, 1812-1885* (Garden City, New York: Doubleday, 1971); Edwin S. Redkey, *Black Exodus: Black Nationalism and Back-to-Africa Movements, 1890-1910* (New Haven, CT: Yale University Press, 1969). See also, Alexander Crummell, *The Relations and Duties on the Free Colored Men in Americas to Africa* (Hartford, CT., 1861).

6. Any serious attempt to understand the African Diaspora entails a serious effort to understand the "ideology of Africa," that is, to understand issues of gender, sexuality, ethnicity, religion, family and other themes from an African perspective rather than imposing a Western ideological framework on African issues. See Colin Palmer, "The African Diaspora," *The Black Scholar* 30, 3-4 (2000): 56-59; James Sweet, "Teaching the Modern African Diaspora: A Case Study of the Atlantic Slave Trade," *Radical History Review* 77 (2000), 106-122; Robin D.G. Kelley, "How the West Was One: On the Uses and Limitations of Diaspora," *The Black Scholar* 30 (Fall 2000-Winter 2001): 31-35.

7. The term is adapted from Albert van Dantzig, *Forts and Castles of Ghana*.

8. See Michael A. Gomez, *Exchanging Our Country Marks: The Transformation of African Identities in the Colonial and Antebellum South* (Chapel Hill: The University of North Carolina Press, 1998).

9. Ibid., See also Okon Edet Uya, "The Middle Passage and Personality Change Among Diaspora Africans." In *Global Dimensions of the African Diaspora*, 2nd ed. Joseph E. Harris (Washington, DC: Howard University Press, 1988), 83-98. See also Joseph Miller, *Way of Death: Merchant Capitalism and the Angolan Slave Trade 1730-1830* (Madison: The University of Wisconsin Press, 1988).

10. Ivan van Sertima, *They Came Before Columbus: The African Presence in Ancient America* (New York: Random House, 1976); Lerone Bennett, *Before The Mayflower: A History of Black America* (Chicago: Johnson Pub. Co., 1969).

11. See Palmer, "The African Diaspora," 56-59; Sweet, "Teaching the Modern African Diaspora: A Case Study of the Atlantic Slave Trade," 106-122; Robin D.G. Kelley, "How the West Was One," 31-35.

12. There is no denying that some scholars are doing just that. At the 32nd National Congress on Black Studies Conference in Atlanta (March 19-22, 2008) Professor Molefe Asante, on a panel discussing African American identity, suggested strongly that scholars dealing with African diaspora issues and teaching Africa and African diaspora issues would be better served studying and understanding African culture first and foremost, before they can be very effective in getting the younger generation to understand this history. It is worthy of note that Afrocentrists have long understood the centrality of Africa in their analyses, even if they sometimes go overboard with their insistence but do not provide adequate documentation due to the paucity of sources for very early periods in African History. For Afrocentricity, see Molefe Kete Asante, *Kemet, Afrocentricity and Knowledge* (Trenton, NJ: Africa World Press, 1990); Asante, *In their Faces: Situating Alternatives to Afrocentrism*. This book is a response to John Miller, ed., *Alternatives to Afro-centrism?* (Washington, D.C.: Manhattan Institute, 1994).

13. For the work of Paul Cuffe and Martin Delaney, see for example Delaney, *The Condition, Elevation and Destiny of the Colored People of the United States*, and *Official Report of the Niger Valley Exploring Party*; Sterling, *The Making of an Afro-American*; Redkey, *Black Exodus*. See also Crummell, *The Relations and Duties on the Free Colored Men in Americas to Africa*.

14. For the Philosophy and Opinions of Marcus Garvey see Amy Jacques Garvey, *The Philosophy and Opinions of Marcus Garvey*; Du Bois, *The Souls of Black Folk*; Du Bois, *Dark Water: Voices from Within The Veil*; Du Bois, *Dusk of Dawn: An Essay Toward and Autobiography of a Race Concept*, (New York: Harcourt, Brace, 1940); W.E.B. Du Bois, *The Autobiography of W. E. B. Du Bois: A Soliloquy on Viewing of My Life From the Last Decades of Its First Century* (New York: International, 1968). See also Manning Marable, "W.E.B. Du Bois and the Struggle Against Racism," *Black Scholar* 16 (May-June, 1985): 443-44, 46-47.

15 See Gaines, *American Africans in Ghana*; Maya Angelou, *All God's Children Need Traveling Shoes* (New York: Vintage Books, 1991), 18-22.

16. The theme for PANAFEST 1999 was "Uniting the African Family: Youth and the Agenda for a New Millennium," and that of the 2001 celebration was "Bridging the Technological Divide."

17. The place of origin of the two former slaves was identified through the painstaking work of archaeologists in Jamaica and the United States. Funerary artifact found in their graves helped archaeologists and historians to piece together evidence used to locate the places of origin of the two former enslaved Africans. The scholars concluded that the two ancestors likely came from the Gold Coast. It was on that basis that Samuel Carson and Madam Crystal were reburied in Ghana in 1999. Today, DNA is widely used in this project of tracing places of origins of people of African descent in the diaspora.

18. This was Lady Minion's response to a journalist who wanted to know why she went to all the trouble to bring the remains of Madam Crystal to Ghana for burial.

19. See Bayo Holsey, *Routes of Remembrance: Refashioning the Slave Trade in Ghana* (Chicago: University of Chicago Press, 2008), 164.

20. The forts and castles were certainly not whitewashed at the time of their construction by Europeans. While huge and easy to spot on the shoreline, a white coating would have accentuated their presence to other rival powers, even though they were already difficult to miss. However, the restoration projects of the 1990s and the attendant whitewashing or painting of some forts and castles evoked emotional responses from some African Americans who decried the "desecration of the tombs of their ancestors." For the fierce opposition to whitewashing the structures, see, for example, Imakhüs Vienna Robinson, "Is the Black Man's History Being White Washed?" in a newspaper article that Edward M. Bruner cites in "Tourism in Ghana: The Representation of Slavery and the Return of the Black Diaspora," *American Anthropologist* 98, 2 (1996): 291-294.

21. Map 2.1 represents the African diaspora.

22. Bruner, "Tourism in Ghana," 294.

23. Saidiya V. Hartman, *Lose Your Mother. A Journey Along the Atlantic Slave Route* (New York: Farrar, Straus and Giroux, 2007), 115.

24 A tour of the slave forts and castles of Ghana is always a "special" event. One certainly feels that one is on "hallowed ground" during such tours. This emerges out of an uneasy feeling that the souls of the departed had remained behind, especially since a large number of enslaved Africans perished in the dungeons and did not make the journey across the Atlantic.

25. Many visitors to the dungeons have spoken about this feeling of some "unseen presence" in the dungeons of the slave castles of Ghana. I have asked different people over several years and get basically the same response each time I pose the question.

26. Thorkild Hansen, *Coast of Slaves*, trans. Kari Dako (Accra: Sub-Saharan Publishers, 2002), 24. However, Hansen could as well have been describing the scene at Cape Coast Castle and São Jorge da Mina at Elmina.

27. Ibid., 19.

28. See Phillip Curtin, *The Atlantic Slave Trade. A Census* (Madison: University of Wisconsin Press, 1969).

29 Hansen, *Coast of Slaves*, 25-26.

30. Gomez, *Exchanging Our Country Marks*, 155; Patrick Manning, *Slavery and African Life*, 58, 62, 64-72; Albert van Dantzig, *The Dutch and the Guinea Coast, 1674-1742*.

31. *A Narrative of the Life and Adventures of Venture Smith, a Native of Africa, but Resident Above Sixty years in the United States of America. Related by Himself* (New London, CT: Printed in 1798). Reprinted in AD 1835, and published by a Descendant of Venture. Revised and Republished in 1896 (Middletown, CT: J.S. Stewart, 1897), 10-12. See also Koelle's informants for a discussion of methods by which people were enslaved, in S.W. Koelle, *Polygotta Africana, or a Comparative Vocabulary of Nearly 300 Words and Phrases in More Than 100 Distinct African languages* (London, 1854), 13. Joseph Miller, *Way of Death: Merchant Capitalism and the Angolan Slave Trade* (Madison: University of Wisconsin Press, 1988).

32. P.E.H. Hair (ed.), *John Hawkins in Guinea 1567-1568* (Leipzig: Institut für Afrikanistik, Universität Leipzig, 2000), 64.

33. The story of Cinque and the *Amistad* captures the practice of kidnapping as a source for acquiring enslaved persons. Olaudah Equiano also narrates his account in his *Interesting Narrative of the Life of Olaudah Equiano Written by Himself*, ed. & intro., Robert J. Allison (Boston: Bedford/St. Martin's, 1995).

34. Ibid.

35. For the Amistad story see Marcus Rediker, *The Slave Ship. A Human History* (New York: Penguin Books, 2007).

36. For pawnship in Africa see Toyin Falola and Paul E. Lovejoy (eds.), *Pawnship in Africa. Debt Bondage in Historical Perspectives* (Boulder: Westview Press, 1994).

37. Joseph Miller in *Way of Death* gives prominence to the environmental factors in the enslavement of Africans.

38. Paul Erdman Isert, *Letters on West Africa and the Slave* Trade, 175. Eleventh Letter, Christianstad on St. Croix in Columbia, 12 March, 1787.

39. Haggling over prices has always been an integral part of the commercial system in the Gold Coast.

40. Hansen, *Coast of Slaves*, 32.

41. Ibid.

42. Isidor Paiewonsky, *Eyewitness Accounts of Slavery in the Danish West Indies* (New York: Fordham University Press, 1989), 12.

43. Ibid.

44 Hansen, *Coast of Slaves*, 29.

45. Ibid.

46. Point made by tour guide during a tour of the Elmina Castle by students of the University of Miami who were in Ghana for a Study Abroad program in early June 2004.

47. See Hartman, Lose Your Mother, 115.

48. Paiewonsky, Eyewitness to Slavery, 45.

49. This information was provided by Mr. Boubacar Sr. the curator of the Maison des Esclaves in 2002 when the author visited Gorée Island during a West African Research Association conference in Dakar.

50. Guides at the Elmina castle usually ask visitors to the Castle to spend a few minutes in the condemned cell and the cell for recalcitrant European soldiers in order to get a sense of the nature of the two different experiences.

51. Frank Gray, My Two African Journeys (London: Methuen, 1928), 143-144.

52. Ottobah Cuguano, Thoughts and Sentiments on the Evil and Wicked Traffic of Slavery and Commerce of the Human Species (London, 1787).

53. For the concept of slavery and social death see Orlando Patterson, Slavery and Social Death: A Comparative Study (Cambridge, MA: Harvard University Press, 1982).

54. Hansen, Coast of Slaves, 16.

55. Isert, Letters on West Africa and the Slave Trade, 177, Eleventh Letter, Christiansstad on St. Croix in Columbia 12 March 1787.

56. Ibid., 175, 177.

57. For Asameni, see Ephson, I.S. Gallery of Gold Coast Celebrities, 1632-1958, Vol, I (Accra: Ilen Publications, 1969), 3-4.

58. Van Dantzig, comp and trans., The Dutch and the Guinea Coast 1674-1742.

59. I. S. Ephson, Ancient Forts and Castles of the Gold Coast (Accra: Ilen Publications, 1971).

60 See J.B. Webster and A. A. Boahen with H.O. Idowu, The Growth of African Civilisation. The Revolutionary Years: West Africa Since 1800 (London: Longmans, 1967), 242.

61. Hansen, Coast of Slaves. 16.

62. See, for example, J.O. Hunwick, "African Slaves in The Mediterranean World: A Neglected Aspect of the African Diaspora," in Global Dimensions of the African Diaspora. 2nd edn., Joseph E. Harris ed. (Washington D.C.: Howard University Press, 1993), 289-324; Colin Palmer, "Afro-Mexican Culture and Consciousness During the Sixteenth and Seventeenth Century," in ibid., 125-136.

63. Allison Blakely, "The Negro in Imperial Russia: A Preliminary Sketch," The Journal of Negro History 61, 4 (October 1976), 351-361; Allison Blakely, Russia and the Negro: Blacks in Russian History and Thought (Washington D.C.: Howard University Press, 1986); Cheryl Johnson-Odim, "Review of Allison Blakely, Russia and the Negro: Blacks in Russian History and Thought," in African Studies Review 34, 3 (December 1991): 123-124; Olaudah Equiano, The Interesting Narrative of the Life of Olaudah Equiano.

64. Orlando Patterson describes enslavement as "social death." For more on this see his *Slavery and Social Death: A Comparative Study* (Cambridge, Mass.: Harvard University Press, 1982).

65. The Slave River at Assin Manso is at present a popular destination for African-descended peoples who visit Ghana and the slave forts and castles. Some have argued that a memorial to slavery should be erected at the site to make it a place of annual pilgrimage by the African diaspora.

66. "Autobiography of Omar ibn Said, Slave in North Carolina, 1831," *American Historical Review* 30 (1924): 787-795; Venture Smith, *A Narrative of the Life and Adventures of Venture, A Native of Africa, but Resident above Sixty Years in the United States of America, Related by Himself* (New London, 1835); Ottobah Cuguano, *Thoughts and Sentiments on the Evil and Wicked Traffic of Slavery and Commerce of the Human Species;* Olaudah Equiano, *Interesting Narrative.* See also, Charles H. Nichols, *Many Thousands Gone: The Ex-Slaves Account of Their Bondage and Freedom* (Leyden, 1963); Robin Law and Paul E. Lovejoy (eds.), *The Biography of Mahommah Gardo Baquaqua: His Passage From Slavery to Freedom in Africa and America* (Princeton, NJ: Markus Weiner, 2003).

67. Bruner, "Tourism in Ghana," 294.

✢ Chapter 3

Portuguese Global Trade, Slave Forts, Castles and Dungeons on the Gold Coast and the Atlantic Slave Trade

Portugal, the first European nation to establish a permanent foothold or military base on the West African coast (some 3,000 sea miles from the home country), sought to monopolize the lucrative trade on the Gold Coast and keep other European nations out of the region. The Portuguese period covered 150 years and during this time, a castle (São Jorge da Mina in 1482), several forts (São Antonio in 1515; São Sebastião in 1553), and in 1576 a lodge (in Accra) were built on the Gold Coast. Trade in gold and ivory flourished and was later expanded to include trade in enslaved Africans for use initially in West Africa, and also in the Portuguese New World possessions such as Brazil. After repeated failures, the Dutch finally captured the Portuguese headquarters of São Jorge da Mina in 1637 and used it as a bridgehead to dislodge the Portuguese from their Gold Coast possessions, especially at Shama and Axim.

The 150 years of Portuguese presence left a lasting legacy of Christianity (albeit in a diluted form). Portuguese loan words such as fetish, *palaver*, *krataa* [paper], *asopatser* [shoes], *piccin* or *piccaninny* [baby], *abrobe* [pineapple] and several others are still in use along the coastal region of the Gold Coast.[1] In fact, a kind of "African Portuguese" developed along the coast and became the "lingua franca" of Africans in their commercial dealings with Europeans on this Euro-African frontier. As well, the Portuguese introduced a few new crops into the Portuguese enclaves on the Gold Coast. The Portuguese (European) presence did have some negative consequences that are often ignored. The Portuguese participation in the carrying trade, transferring indigenous

West African cloth from the producing areas like Benin to the Gold Coast, disrupted the carrying trade and the trade in cloth. Eventually, this African enterprise was taken over by the Portuguese and other Europeans using boats bigger and faster than the West African canoes. The cumulative impact of this was that certain indigenous or local industries such as the local cloth industries were abandoned or lost forever as cheap and more attractive European and Asian goods were imported into West Africa.[2]

EUROPEANS AND WEST AFRICA:
THE PRE-PORTUGUESE PERIOD

European interest in Africa dated back to the Middle Ages, even if very little was known about the continent, especially its interior, at that time. The Roman Empire, at the height of its power, extended its sway along Africa's Mediterranean coastline through conquest and trade, but the interior of Africa remained relatively untouched by any European military, exploratory and mercantile activity. The desire to learn more about the interior occasioned Emperor Nero's expedition into the Nubian Desert but the expedition brought back news that the region beyond the Sahara was covered by impenetrable swamps.[3] Herodotus, it is reported, traveled up the Nile but could not advance beyond the first cataract, and thus went no further than Aswan.[4] In essence, Europeans had some knowledge about North Africa but the interior of the continent was *terra incognita*, thus resulting in fantastic tales about the people who lived in these unknown parts of Africa including stories about people having tails or even heads of lions.[5]

Claudius Ptolemaus, who spent some time in Alexandria around AD 140, utilized information from merchants to map out the African interior beyond the Mediterranean coastline. He reportedly showed that not only did the River Nile enter the sea beyond what he called the "Mountains of the Moon," a geographical feature farther than what is now the Madagascar Republic, but that the River Niger traversed Africa from Ethiopia in the east to Senegal in the west.[6] The egregious nature of the errors in these assertions sums up the nature of European knowledge about the African interior at the time. More accurate information was a couple of centuries away.

Knowledge about the African interior and the inhabitants began to proliferate after the Arab invasions of Egypt in AD 639-642 and their subsequent advance across North Africa over the next one hundred-or-so years. The Arab invasions, coupled with the use of the camel, the ship of the desert, gradually led to the spread of verifiable information about the African hinterland.[7] This was initially the preserve of Arab geographers, scholars and travelers who were able to travel to the region as a network of trade routes were gradually opened up, linking the Mediterranean region with the Western Sudan.[8]

Two major transformative forces had far-reaching implications for Africa from the eighth century onward. Trade (international) and religion (Islam and Christianity) transformed European perception and knowledge of Africa and its peoples. Down to the eighteenth century, trade and religion supplied a steady stream of information to interested and inquisitive minds about Africa. International trade and religious influence (spread of Christianity) attended first, the Muslim Arab presence in North Africa and, later, the European presence on the West African coast. European presence eventually led to the construction of the numerous trade and slave forts and castles that dot the coastline of modern day Ghana. Other slave forts were built in other African countries such as the Gambia, Senegal, Dahomey (now Benin), Tunisia, and Tanzania. The initial operational imperative of the European presence, international trade in commodities, was later eclipsed by the "mother of all international trades," the Atlantic slave trade.

The Arab invasion of North Africa and the subsequent Islamization of some of the Berbers both produced as well as attracted travelers whose voyages provided information about the interior of Africa. Ibn Haukal, a tenth-century Baghdad native, and Ibn Batuta, born to a Berber family in Algiers, visited the empires of the Western Sudan – Ghana and Mali. In 1355 Ibn Batuta detailed his travels in Africa in a series of lectures in Granada.[9] Similarly, Leo Africanus, described as a Moor from a Granada family, settled in Fez and visited Songhai Empire, Bornu and the Hausa States - all in what is now West Africa.[10] All the same, cartographers' early attempts at African maps, mostly based on travelers accounts, got the details of Africa's geography, especially location and direction of rivers, largely wrong.

The trans-Saharan trade, an international trade that made manufactured products of the Mediterranean world (including North Africa) and Europe available to the forest zone of West Africa in exchange for gold, kola nuts, ivory and slaves, among several other commodities, gradually contributed to the dissemination of information about the interior of Africa. Goods such as bangles, items of clothing, ostrich feathers, leather sandals and leather saddles were sent from North Africa to the Western Sudan between the seventh and the eighteenth centuries.[11] The preeminence of the Western Sudan was rooted in the economic exploitation of the forest zone to the south, specifically the large quantities of gold that traveled from the forest zone via the trans-Saharan trade routes to the Mediterranean world and Europe.[12] This gold traffic became more pronounced during the era of the Western Sudanese empires of Ghana, Mali and Songhai between the seventh and sixteenth centuries.

The impression of the fabled *el dorado* in the Western Sudan was communicated to the outside world through the colorful descriptions of the Western Sudanese rulers and their courts by the Muslim and Arab merchants, travelers and writers, who were contemporaneous in those countries. For example, Ibn Batuta, Ibn Hawqal, Al Fazari and Al Omari, all of whom wrote about the empires of the Western Sudan, traveled through the region.[13] And more especially, the picture of the Sudanese *el dorado* was given credence by the pilgrimage of Mansa Musa to Mecca in 1324-1325. The pilgrimage, the most elaborate of its time in the number of servants and the volume of materials for the trip, advertised the gold of the Western Sudan to the European world. Subsequently, Mali appeared on two European maps of the period, the Mappa Mundi of Angelino Dulcert and the Catalan map drawn by Abraham Crisques for Charles V in 1375.[14] The map identified commercial centers like Timbuktu, Taghaza and Sijilmasa on the caravan routes from North Africa to the Western Sudan. [15] One of these maps portrayed Mansa Musa as the "'Lord of the Negroes of Guinea,' sitting enthroned in the midst of his kingdom" and holding an orb of gold.[16]

European knowledge of the interior of Africa and its fabled mines remained at best impressionistic and hazy throughout the early fourteenth century. The European impression of Africa was one of an exotic land with strange-looking creatures and humans. For one thing, Europeans could not, and did not, utilize many of the Arabic sources that the early Muslim travelers compiled. For another, only a few European merchants from Italy, the Iberian Peninsula and France reportedly participated in the trans-Saharan trade during the early phase of the trade, especially when Maghrebian kingdoms and merchant princes, holding monopoly positions in the trans-Saharan trade, created a middleman's cordon that prevented European rivals from penetrating the interior. Thus, only one or two Europeans such as Anselme d'Isalguier, a Toulouse merchant (lived in Gao between 1405 and 1413), and a Genoese merchant who got to Tuat in 1447 broke this cordon at an early date.[17]

European merchants tried to find the source of the famous gold of Guinea (from which the English coin of the same name was minted in 1662) in the fifteenth century. After a few false starts, Prince Henry the Navigator of Portugal, who had distinguished himself at the Portuguese capture of Ceuta on the Moroccan coast, turned his attention to the gold of Guinea. He was determined to seek the gold fields by way of the sea, rather than the desert.[18] But Henry the Navigator was not the first to recognize the significance of the sea in the "battle for Guinea"[19] if earlier accounts and records are to be believed. Herodotus reportedly mentioned Phoenician sailors as circumnavigating Africa in about 600 BC, and the Carthaginian Hanno probably explored the Atlantic coast as far as the Rio de Oro in about 480 BC.[20] Also,

Pliny reported that a Carthaginian admiral had sailed down the West African coast in 450 BC.[21] While European knowledge of the interior was sketchy and impressionistic, it is worthy of note that the northern coastline of Africa has been in contact with Europe across the Mediterranean for a long time dating to Greco-Roman times. And it was from this frontier that the Portuguese exploration of Western Africa was undertaken in the fifteenth century.

THE PORTUGUESE AND SUSTAINED AFRICAN EXPLORATION

The first major European drive to establish sustained contact with Africa began with Prince Henry and the Portuguese voyages of discovery in the fifteenth century. Economic, military and religious motives undergirded the Portuguese drive down the African coast and, eventually, to India. First, the Portuguese wanted to get to the source of the West African *el dorado* and enslaved Africans by outflanking their traditional enemies, the Muslims, who controlled the trade across the Sahara.[22] Second, they were interested in finding a sea route to India to participate in the rich trade in spices. In the military sphere, the Portuguese hoped to find the legendary Christian king of Ethiopia, Prester John, with whom they hoped to forge a military alliance to attack the Muslims in the rear (that is, in the south as opposed to a frontal attack in North Africa). In a sense, this was to be another phase of the reconquista – taking the war to the Muslims who controlled the northern part of the African continent.[23]

The major problem Henry and his sailors faced was the fear of the unknown and the dangers of the sea at a time when stories were bandied about of an Atlantic Ocean inhabited by sea monsters and unimaginable terrors. Yet the lure of gold and glory proved irresistible and the Portuguese braved the unknown oceans.[24] After repeated failures to get past Cape Bojador, Gil Eanes sailed past the Cape in 1414, and two years later the Portuguese constructed a trade fort at Arguin (the earliest such fortified station on the Western African coast). Thus began a phase in West African history that would alter the political economy of the region forever and transform the region into a "shopping mart of Europe."[25] In 1421 Antão Gonçalves reached the *Rio de Ouro* (river of gold, probably the Senegal or the Gambia River),[26] and in early 1430 Nuno Tristão passed Cape Blanco and arrived at Arguin where he captured a party of fourteen inhabitants of the island.[27] One immediate result of these early voyages was that a party of ten Africans was sent to Portugal in 1441, and in 1444, that is, soon after reaching Cape Verde, about two hundred enslaved Africans were sent to Portugal. This marks the beginning of a long period of African presence in Europe. The number soon climbed to seven hundred or eight hundred a year and this constituted the foundation of the Portuguese African slave trade.[28] This "opening salvo" of the slave trade set the tone for the frenetic trading in slaves for the next four hundred-or-so-years that followed this initial effort, and long after the Portuguese had been dislodged by the Dutch on the Gold Coast, the trade continued unabated.

The Portuguese persevered in the voyages of discovery and in 1445 Dinnis Dias sailed past the mouth of the Senegal River and continued past Cape Verde. After the death of his mentor, Prince Henry in 1460, Pedro de Sintra sailed along the Sierra Leonean coast in 1462.[29] At this early date, the Portuguese exchanged European goods for gold, ivory and indigo from the people they encountered on the West African coast. They captured and also purchased small numbers of enslaved Africans who were shipped to Portugal.

The Portuguese arrived off Elmina, believed to be originally called Anomee,[30] in 1471 (in an expedition led by Juan de Santarem and Pedro d'Escobar), and sailed past Fernando Po and the Bight of Biafra in 1473.[31] The Portuguese finally achieved a major objective when Vasco da Gama sailed around the Cape of Good Hope in 1497 to the eastern seaboard of Africa (where the Portuguese encountered the Swahili City States) and thence to India.

THE PORTUGUESE ON THE GOLD COAST AND PLANS TO BUILD SÃO JORGE DA MINA

The arrival of the Portuguese on the coast of what is now modern Ghana resulted in the construction of what would become the largest European structure outside of Europe at the time, the Castle of São Jorge da Mina. But more important, it started a process of global commercial activities and culture contact that we now call globalization. Portuguese merchants traded goods from Europe to West Africa, East Africa and Asia.

In December 1481, a Portuguese expedition of ten caravels and two transports carrying ready-dressed stones for the "foundation all the way up to the tiles for the roof," arrived at Elmina to build a fortress and a church. João de Barros writes that

> The King [John II of Portugal], considering, as a wise man, the great profit and good health, which his subjects would receive in body and soul, and also how his merchandise, and the affairs of his honour, estate, and service would be properly secured, if he were to possess in those parts of Mina a fortress of his own ...[32]

resolved to build a fortress at Elmina contrary to the opinions of his advisers. Upon arrival at Elmina in 1482, the expedition of five hundred Portuguese officers and soldiers and one hundred masons led by Don Diego d'Azambuja

Photo 3.1: Drawbridge - Elmina Castle

erected a cross and sang the first mass on the Gold Coast. The Portuguese requested for land to build a fort but the Elmina monarch asserted that it was better for the Portuguese to come and go as merchants rather than settle among the people. After initially refusing to grant the request, the Elmina monarch, Kwamena Ansa (referred to in some European texts as *Caramança*), eventually acceded to the request and the Portuguese lost no time in constructing the fort, erecting the tower that stands today just beyond the drawbridge at the main entrance to the castle, and the entire first storey in twenty-one days (Photos 3.1 and 3.2).[33] This initial structure was a two-storey rectangular block containing a courtyard with a brick-lined cistern underneath it.[34]

Why did the Portuguese choose Elmina as the site of the fortress? Three main reasons are adduced: a sizable African population that raised the prospective of lucrative trade; the site for the castle was a rocky peninsula surrounded on two sides by the sea and a third by the Benya Lagoon and hence provided safe anchorage to ships. And as a result, the castle could be approached only by land on the western side. Finally, the site afforded quarriable stone for constructing the fortress.[35] Substantial material was carried directly from Portugal to Elmina, the rocky peninsula chosen for the fortified station, because the site provided stones for construction purposes.

ELMINA AND THE PORTUGUESE

The people of Elmina on the West African coast were participants in an international trading system that involved exchange of products from different parts of Africa, South and Southeast Asia and Europe. As Harvey Feinberg notes, Elmina was an important trading center in the Gold Coast. The people were linked up with the West African interior through different trade networks. During the fifteenth century, Mande traders linked up with Elmina in the trans-Saharan trade network. Through this network, gold and other forest products were sent to the western Sudanese cities of Jenne, Timbuktu and others.[36] Gradually, from the fifteenth century until the eighteenth century, Elmina and other coastal towns underwent a reorientation away from the northern trade in favor of trade with Europeans at the coast and, for that matter, integration into a European-centered economic system.

Not long after their arrival in the fifteenth century, the Portuguese began to play a very important role in the coastwise trade, exchanging goods with Benin merchants to the east of Elmina. Similarly, the Portuguese were involved in a brisk trade in enslaved Africans between São Tomé-Principé and Sao Jorge da Mina.[37] This trade, as shown in table 3.1, yielded a large number of enslaved Africans who were used in carrying gold, ivory and other trade goods from the interior to Mina for exchange with the Europeans.

Photo 3.2: Coat of arms – main entrance into courtyard of São Jorge da Mina

Table 3.1: Early São Tomé-Principé Slave Trade with Mina, 1500-1540

1504-1507	183 SLAVES PER YEAR (AVERAGE)		
1508-1510	NO AVAILABLE DATA		
1511-1513	199 SLAVES PER YEAR (AVERAGE)		
1514-1516	NO AVAILABLE DATA		
1517-1519	331 SLAVES PER YEAR (AVERAGE)		
1520-1522	433 SLAVES PER YEAR (AVERAGE)		
1523-1525	NO AVAILABLE DATA		

1526:	SLAVES	CORIS	
Corpo Santo	80	10,772	(II, maço 131, doc. 157, 19 Feb.)
São Miguel	122	10,737	(II, maço 132, doc.41, 15 March)
Santiago	102	-	(II, maço 132, doc. 122, 2 April)
?	43	8,938	(II, maço 134, doc. 103,13 July)
São Pedro	79	15,130	(II, maço 135, doc. 51, 18 August)
São Miguel	103	8,020	(II, maço 136, doc. 71, 10 October)
Santa Cruz de Mayo	50	-	(II, maço 137, doc. 107, 28 Nov.)
São Cristovao	70	7,330	(II, maço 138, 32, 25 December)
Totals	649	60,927	

1527:	SLAVES	CORIS	
?	80	9,303	(II, maço 138, doc. 104, 10 Jan.)
Esperanza	72	-	(II, maço 139, doc. 145, 11 March)
São Pedro	80	5,593	(II, maço 140, doc. 135, 2 May)
Totals	232	14,896	

1528	NO AVAILABLE DATA		
1529	506 SLAVES (ESTIMATED)		
1530	552 SLAVES		
1531	300 SLAVES		

1532:	SLAVES	CORIS	
Misericordia	83	-	(II, maço 173, doc. 136, 11 Feb.)
Santo Antonio	65	3,743	(II, maço 176, doc. 56, 17 June)
Santo Antonio	80	6,272	(II, maço 178, doc. 9, 23 August)
?	73	3,028	(II, maço 179, doc. 10,22 Sept.)
?	80	1,442	(II, maço 180, doc. 3,9 November)
Misericordia	109	(slaves revolted)	(II, maço 181, doc. 78, 21 Feb.)
Totals	490	14,485	

1533:	SLAVES	CORIS	
Santo António	114	13,909	(II, maço 181, doc. 31 4 Feb.)
Corpo Santo	76	8,065	(II, maço 182, doc. 25, 2 April)

Santa Maria	120	6,988	(II, maço 183, doc. 109, 15 June)
?	95	1,774	(II, maço 184, doc. 71, 5 August)
?	80	3,224	(II, maço 185, doc. 109, 10 Oct.)
Santa António	78	-	(II, maço 186, doc 160, 19 Nov.)
Totals	563	33,960	
1534:	SLAVES	CORIS	
Santo António	79	6,201	(II, maço 187, doc. 90, 14 Feb.)
Santo António	92	16,184	(II, maço 189, doc. 79, 8 May)
?	79	2,592	(II, maço 192, doc. 84, 29 July)
	85	1,816	(II, maço 195, doc. 109, 24 Oct.)
Totals	335	27,793	
1535:	SLAVES	CORIS	
São Francisco	101	15,298	(II, maço 197, doc. 17, 6 Jan.)
São Vicente	100	-	(III, maço 12, doc. 84, 28 Feb.)
Santa Maria do Cabo	97	3,000	(II, maço 200, doc. 127, 17 May)
São Cristovão	80	-	(II, maço 202, doc. 133, ? Aug.)
São Cristovão	120	3,543	(III, maço 12, doc. 103, 20 Nov.)
	80	17,000	
Totals	579	38,841	(II, maço 205, doc. 21, 21 Dec.)
1536 (INCOMPLETE):	SLAVES	CORIS	
Espirito Novo	31	-	(II, maço 206, doc. 75, 8 March)

Coris (cowries) or shells were the third most important item of trade. On the Benin coast cowries were bought by slave traders and taken to São Tomé where the Portuguese Factor would count, weigh and dispatch them to Mina in sealed boxes.

Source: John L. Vogt, "The Early Sao Tome-Principe Slave Trade with Mina, 1500-1540," *The International Journal of African Historical Studies* 6, 3 (1973): 464-465.

Table 3.1 covers the Portuguese trade between Sao Tomé-Principé and Elmina for the forty-year period between 1500 and 1540. Table 3.2 similarly deals with the coastwise trade in enslaved Africans who were shipped from Benin and the islands of São Tomé and Principé to São Jorge da Mina. While the number of enslaved Africans are averaged out for half of the period the table provides specific details of the number of enslaved Africans carried on each coastwise voyage, together with details of the ships involved, including the name of the captain and the pilot. Also see Table 3.3.

Table 3.2: Movement of Slave Ships Carrying Enslaved Africans Between the Coast of Benin, the Island of Sao Tomé and São Jorge da Mina During the Sixteenth Century

Date	Ship	Captain	Pilot	Provenance	Delivered São Jorge da Mina Esclaves	Source A.N.T.T
?.05.1515	un caravelon	Luis Alvarez		Principé	48	cc I,4,102
?.08.1515	navire du roi	Luis Alvarez		Benin	40	cc I, 4,102
25.05.1516	Sam Pedro	Luis Alvarez		Principe	48	cc II,64,154
17.01.1519	Santa Maria a Nova	-	Johamdo Porto	S. Tomé	70	cc II,79,67
14.03.1519	Santa Maria a Nova	-	Johamdo Porto	S. Tomé	40	
8.08.1519	S. André		Joham Rodriguez	S. Tomé	80	cc II,84.1
1.12.1519	Santa Maria a Nova	L. Alvarez	Jorge Gonçalvez	S. Tomé	60	cc II,86,30
10.01.1520	Santa Maria		Joao Dias	S. Tomé	92	cc II,87,2
29.10.1525	Todolos Santos		Francisco Sergeliano	S. Tomé	106	ccII,129,134
19.02.1526	Corpo Santo		Jorge Martins	S. Tomé	80	ccII,131,157
15.03.1526	San Miguel		Fernao Dos Naos	S. Tomé	122	ccII, 132,41
02.04.1526	Sam Pedro		Martins	S. Tomé	102	ccII,132,122
13.07.1526	Santa Cruz de Mayo		Bartolameu Fernandez	S. Tomé	43	ccII,134,102
18.08.1526	Sam Pedro		Martins Fernandez	S. Tomé	79	ccII,135,51
25.09.1526	Sam Miguel		Fernao dos Naos	S. Tomé	126	ccII,136,17
10.10.1526	Sam Miguel		Fernao dos Naos	S. Tomé	103	ccII,136,71
28.11.1526	Santa Cruz De Mayo		Duarte Luis	S. Tomé	50	ccII,137,107
25.12.1526	Conceiçao		Alfonso Alvarez	S. Tomé	70	ccII,138,32
10.01.1527	Nossa Senhora Da Luz		Pero Anes	S. Tomé	80	ccII,138,104
11.03.1527	Sperança		Diogo	S. Tomé	72	ccII,139,145
02.05.1527	Sam Pedro		Martino Fernandez	S. Tomé	80	ccII,140,135

		Cristovao Careiro	Fernam Carvalho			
11.02.1532	Miséricordia	Cristovao Careiro	Fernam Carvalho	S. Tomé	83	ccII,173,136
14.05.1532	Le Caravelon	Pero Anes	Pero Anes	S. Tomé	95	ccII,175,52b
17.06.1532	S. Antonio de Sezymbra	Fernas Carvalho		S. Tomé	65	ccII,176,56b
02.08.1532	Caravelon S. Antonio	Joao Gomes	Antonio Gomes		80	ccII,178,9
22.09.1532	-	-	-	S. Tomé	63	ccII,179,10
09.11.1532	-	-	-	S. Tomé	80	ccII,180,3
04.02.1533	S. Antonio Gomes	Joao Gomes	Antonio	S. Tomé	114	ccII,181,31
21.02.1533	Miséricordia (1)	Cristovao Careyro	Borlameu Gomes	S. Tomé		ccII,181,78
02.04.1533	Caravelon Corpo Santo	Joao Gomes	Antonio Gomes	S. Tomé	76	ccII,182,25
15.05.1533	Caravelon S.	Joao Gomes	Antonio Gomes	S. Tomé	120	ccII,183,109
15.08.1533	Caravelon S.	Joao Gomes	Antonio Gomes	S. Tomé	95	ccII,184,71
10.10.1533	Santa Maria	-	Duarte Luis	S. Tomé	80	ccII,185,109
19.10.1533	Caravelon S.	Joao Gomes	Antonio Gomes	S. Tomé	78	ccII,186,60
14.02.1534		-	Pedro Gomes		79	ccII,187,90
08.05.1534		Joao Gomes	-	S. Tomé	92	ccII,189,79
7.1534	San Antonio	Pedro Anes	Pedro Anes	S. Tomé	79	ccII,192,84
10.1534	Conceiçao Flamenga	Joam Gomes	Pedro Anes	S. Tomé	85	ccII,195,09
1.1535	S. Francisco	Joam Gomes	Pedro Anes	S. Tomé	101	ccII,197,17
2.1535	S. Vincente	Gaspar Vaz	Pedro Anes	S. Tomé	100	ccIII,12,34
5.1535	S. Maria do	Duarte Luis	Duarte Luis	S. Tomé	97	ccII,200,127
7.1535	S. Cristovao	Pero da Costa		S. Tomé	78	ccII,202,133
11.1535	S. Cristovao	Pero da Costa	Fernam das	S. Tomé	120	ccIII,12,103
12.1535	S. Cristovao	Joan Luys	Bastiam Alvarez	S. Tomé	80	ccII,205,21
3.1536	S. Cristovao	Pero da Costa		S. Tomé	100	ccII,206,75

ANTT refers to the Arquivo Nacional de Torre do Tombo.

Source: J.B. Ballong-Wen-Mewuda, "Le Commerce Portugais Des Esclaves Enter La Cote de L'Actuel Nigéria et Celle du Ghana Moderne Aux VXe et XVIe Siecles." In *De La Traite À L'Esclavage. Actes Colloque International Sue la Traite de Noirs*, édités par Serge Daget, Tome I: V–XVIIIe Siècles (Nantes, 1985): 139–142.

Table 3.3: Yearly Totals of Slave Traffic in the Islands: Enslaved Africans Delivered to São Jorge da Mina Between 1515 and 1536

Year/Period	Number of Enslaved Africans	Number of Voyages
1515	88	2
1516	48	1
1519	250	4
1520	92	1
1526	775	9
1527	232	3
12/6/1528-1/2/1529	2,060	3
1532	446	6
1533	643	7
1534	335	4
1535	576	6
1536	97	1
Total	**5,768**	**48**

Source: J.B. Ballong-Wen-Mewuda, "Le Commerce Portugais Des Esclaves Enter La Cote de L'Actuel Nigéria et Celle du Ghana Moderne Aux VXe et XVIe Siecles," in De La Traite À L'Esclavage. Actes Colloque International Sue la Traite de Noirs, édités par Serge Daget, Tome I: Vᵉ-XVIIIᵉ Siècles (Nantes, 1985): 139-142.

In the last decades of the fifteenth century, Elmina was plugged into the Atlantic Ocean trade and exchanged products from various parts of Africa, Asia and Europe. Feinberg notes that by 1700, while Elmina's participation in the northern trade to the savanna region and the coastwise trade had declined in volume, the expanding Atlantic trade in gold, ivory and slaves was on the ascendancy, due to the expansion of the plantation complex from the Mediterranean region to the Caribbean and the Americas.[38] This is the context in which the Portuguese constructed the castle of São Jorge da Mina, ten years before Columbus' first voyage to the Americas. After 1637, the Dutch (the Dutch West India Company) who occupied the Elmina Castle, became the most important players in both Elmina history and the trans-Atlantic slave trade. The relationship between Elmina and the Portuguese on the one hand, and between Elmina and the Dutch on the other, represents case studies of similar Euro-African economic and cultural encounters on the "frontier" in the port towns of the Gold Coast: Axim, Sekondi, Elmina, Cape Coast, Kormantine/Abandzi, Anomabu, Apam, Winneba and Accra among several others. Elmina, more than any of these port towns, however, became notable for the large number of people of mixed ancestry who lived on the Gold Coast. A similar phenomenon existed in other places like Cape

Coast and Accra. It is not for nothing that one of the Asafo companies in coastal Ghana is known as *Abrofo mba*, literally the children of white people.[39]

The Portuguese traded in gold with the people of Elmina. The gold supply was largely obtained through gold washing or panning from the rivers and other interior mines where rudimentary versions of modern "deep-shaft mining" were in use at the time.[40] A gold mining belt stretched from Elmina along the western shores to Komenda, Abrobi, Kafodzidzi and other auriferous districts.[41] There seems to have been no shortage of gold in the region of Elmina (from the perspective of the Portuguese in Elmina and the surrounding regions) as most ornaments and personal adornments of the people were, and are still, made of gold.

Along the Guinea coast, the Portuguese encountered people who were interested in European metals. Iron smelting was an old industry in Africa, and was especially important in the manufacture of agricultural implements, weapons of war and other items. However, smelted quantities barely met local needs. Consequently, the Portuguese sent shiploads of "brass pots and basins, monstrous bracelets of solid brass or copper to be melted down and re-cast according to local requirements … hatchets and knives, beads and wine and many other novelties."[42] These commodities were of interest to both the local people as well as their trading partners in the interior. One strand of evidence of the volume of these early exchanges is borne out by the fact that Portuguese records show that "in 1502 a single ship carried 125 lb weight of gold to Portugal and Portuguese gold exports back home amounted to about twelve such shiploads every year"[43] (see Table 3.4)

By the time European currencies were backed by gold in the fifteenth century, West Africa was the largest supplier of gold through North Africa to the Mediterranean region. The first Portuguese transactions in exchange for gold occurred possibly near the mouth of the Pra River and since the transaction was right at the coast, the Portuguese thought the goldfields were near the coast and called this place *Mina de Ouro* or the gold mine. Other accounts record that the trade itself was concentrated "on a place the Portuguese called *Aldea das Duas Partes*, the 'Village of Two Parts,' situated at the mouth of a little river, or rather lagoon, the Benya, near one of the best natural harbors on the coast,"[44] and believed by some to be Edina and Eguafo.

Table 3.4: Annual Gold Receipts of São Jorge and São Antonio (Axim), 1482-1560

Year	Marks	Ounces	Drams	Grains	
1482-1486	no data available				
1487	982	0	0	0	(estimate)
1488	982	0	0	0	(est.)
1489	982	0	0	0	(est)
1490-93					n.a.
1494	2,820	0	0	0	(est.)
1495	2,820	0	0	0	(est.)
1496	2,820	0	0	0	(est.)
1497	1,617	0	0	0	(est.)
1498	1,617	0	0	0	(est.)
1499	1,617	0	0	0	(est.)
1500	1,617	0	0	0	(est.)
1501	1,220	5	0	0	(est.)
1502-3					n.a.
1504	1,910	3	0	0	(average)
1505	1,910	3	0	0	(avg.)
1506	1,910	3	0	0	(avg.)
1507-10					n.a.
1511	1,400	0	0	0	(avg.)
1512	2,255	4	2	?	
1513	1,805	6	0	0	(avg.)
1514	1,761	5	0	0	(avg.)
1515-16					n.a.
1517	1,846	2	4	4	
1518	1,868	5	0	44	
1519	2,001	5	0	0	
1520	2,025	0	5	37	
1521	1,867	5	7	9	[2187 5 7 8]
1522					
1523	1,308	4	7	19	[1760 0 0]
1524	1,237	3	3	53	[1310 0 0]
1525	897	0	0	0	
1526	1,079	1	4	37	[1310 0 0]
1527					n.a.
1528	971	3	1	33	
1529	972	4	0	7	
1530	654	4	1	69	[1405 3 1 45]
1531	925	7	1	47	
1532	2,960	7	7	35	
1533	1,580	0	0	0	(est.)

Year	Marks	Ounces	Drams	Grains	
1534	1,184	2	3	47	
1535-39					n.a.
1540	1,447	7	2	56	
1541-42					n.a.
1543	1,520	6	7	32	
1544	616	7	7	30	
1545	1,671	2	7	11	(est.)
1546-48					n.a.
1549	733	1	0	59	
1550	674	6	3	28	
1551	922	0	6	64	
1552	537	4	2	26	
1553	414	5	7	15	
1554					n.a.
1555	1,645	1	7	30	
1556	1,056	3	1	60	
1557-59					n.a.
1560	625	7	0	46	
1561	630	1	3	24	
1562-71					n.a.
1572 (incomp.)	146	0	1	36	

Source: John Vogt, Portuguese Rule on the Gold Coast 1469-1682 (Athens: The University of Georgia Press, 1979). Appendix C, 218-219.

Table 3.5: Portuguese Daily Trade at Elmina, 1529-1530

Date	Folio No.	Lambeis	Manilas	Slaves	Pezos of Gold recv.	Daily Gold Receipts
			1529			
10-VI	23	16	405	14	265	13-4-3-36
19-VI	23v	28	870	9	271	25-7-7-49
21-VI	24	14	1,555	3	53	15-6-5-56
26-VI	24v	22	2,610	-	-	36-7-7-28
5-VII	25	14	1,210	-	-	15-8-4-1
8-VII	25v	11	1,055	-	-	12-2-6-10
15-VII	26	1	295	-	-	3-4-7-21
20-VII	26	11	2,260	31	587	36-3-9-0
26-VII	26v	9	1,205	14	268	19-1-1-5
30-VII	27	6	2,895	7	139	24-7-7-3
3-VIII	27v	6	290	-	-	4-5-5-36
6-VIII	28	5	320	-	-	5-4-2-0

Date	Folio No.	Lambeis	Manilas	Slaves	Pezos of Gold recv.	Daily Gold Receipts
21-VIII	28	17	1,305	2	34	18-2-2-36
28-VIII	29	38	2,350	-	-	50-1-5-56
10-IX	29v	17	965	27	511	40-6-2-7
11-IX	30	6	1,005	13	250	15-8-1-2
13-IX	30v	12	995	4	80	13-6-0-0
16-IX	31	3	240	6	114	6-0-5-0
22-IX	31v	3	665	6	106	11-0-3-39
28-IX	32	8	2,250	-	-	18-5-2-31
5-X	32v	6	870	1	18	8-5-2-31
11-X	33	16	730	-	-	10-6-2-31
18-X	33v	8	445	-	-	12-6-5-68
30-X	34	5	2,815	49	961	46-0-4-1
20-XI	34v	1	7,085	1	20	42-3-2-32
26-XI	35	6	3,725	-	-	20-7-6-29
9-XI	35v	3	2,910	10	199	29-8-3-59
13-XII	36v	1	105	55	1100	31-4-2-52
18-XII	37v	12	1,9255	1	14	200-1-4-23
1530						
24-I	38v	41	2,535	3	50	51-7-4-36
28-I	39	13	4,225	34	689	63-8-1-21
10-II	40	31	1,450	14	69	55-5-5-20
22-II	41v	16	-	41	801	34-1-3-50
28-II	42v	8	95	6	111	13-0-5-56
12-III	43v	34	120	3	48	24-7-4-24
26-III	44	13	-	41	809	32-3-2-33
20-IV	44v	41	1,560	53	1014	65-0-6-60
30-IV	45	8	2,400	14	265	35-4-1-4
9-V	46	15	2,490	14	278	38-2-3-0
21-V	47	22	3,635	2	37	42-4-2-71
30-V	37v	31	525	43	847	52-3-4-24
14-VI	48v	22	7,085	6	110	83-0-0-23
30-VI	49v	50	980	4	72	28-4-4-59
18-VII	50v	54	60	69	1389	72-6-5-1
23-VIII	52	69	2,520	-	-	66-2-2-0
31-VIII	52v	35	3,820	-	-	59-1-0-0
15-IX	53v	26	6,175	-	-	62-8-0-25
30-IX	54	63	5,060	63	1318	123-0-6-46
15-X	55	25	10,235	-	-	66-4-1-68
31-X	55v	34	830	5	76	78-3-5-21
20-XI	56	46	2,505	3	57	45-6-5-68
30-XI	57	23	1,305	-	-	23-3-1-20

Date	Folio No.	Lambeis	Manilas	Slaves	Pezos of Gold recv.	Daily Gold Receipts
17-XII	57v	52	4,160	-	-	62-7-2-47
31-XII	58	47	5,855	61	1253	123-3-1-10

Lambeis are narrow strips of colored cloth.

Manilas are bracelets or anklets of metal that served as currency in the Gold Coast until the early twentieth century.

Source: Daily trade at Sao Jorge da Mina during the factorship of Goncalo de Campos, May, 1529-August 1531 (A.T.T., Nucleo Antigo, no. 722) in John Vogt, "Portuguese Gold Trade: An Account Ledger From Elmina, 1529-1531", *Transactions of the Historical Society of Ghana* 14, 2 (June 1973): 99-100.

Table 3.5 shows Portuguese trade as per an account ledger from 1529 to 1930 and is a good illustration of the nature of exports and imports to the Gold Coast. Over the one-and- a-half years in question (from June 1529 to December 1530), 732 enslaved Africans were purchased by the Portuguese on the Gold Coast.

By the early fifteenth century, the Portuguese were involved in slave trading in West Africa, moving enslaved persons from Benin to Elmina, and from São Tomé-Principé to Elmina, in exchange for gold and ivory with merchants who utilized the enslaved persons as porters in the long-distance trade between the interior and the coast. At a time when horses and donkeys could not thrive in the forested region of West Africa and mechanized transport was not available, porterage was one of the most important means of conveying goods over long distances from the interior to the coast, especially in areas where water transport was not available. Early Portuguese trade also connected Elmina with Arguin. For example, in 1518 a Portuguese merchant on the Gold Coast wrote to Arguin for "a delivery of forty or fifty slaves, preferably all male and the best youths available,"[45] and between 1535 and 1550, a "great caravan of Negroes," according to a pilot (of a boat) began to arrive in areas where the Portuguese lived and traded.[46] This is the context of Portuguese-African exchanges in which construction of the largest castle in Africa, São Jorge da Mina, was started in 1482.

SÃO JORGE DA MINA

Compared to its predecessor, the trade fort at Arguin, *São Jorge da Mina* was a humongous structure. In fact, it remains to date the largest slave castle in Africa. Against the advice of his courtiers, the king of Portugal gave instructions to build this castle in what was considered an isolated region far from

Portugal to be easily resupplied or reinforced by soldiers. The reticence of the Portuguese nobility in the construction of Elmina Castle was predicated on the fact that many European interlopers were beginning to trade in West Africa after rumors of enormous profits at Elmina trickled to other European countries. The precarious nature of the Portuguese monopoly at Elmina was demonstrated by the fact that in 1479 the Portuguese seized both French and Spanish fleets for trading at Elmina.[47]

King John II persisted over the advice of his nobles and the construction of São Jorge da Mina gave Portugal a huge tactical and strategic advantage over its rivals. The castle enabled the Portuguese to station a large military and naval force on the West African coast to protect its monopoly over the gold trade in the region and to sink, capture and confiscate ships and cargo in the vicinity of Elmina.[48] To protect its seaborne trade all the way from Elmina to Assinie, the Portuguese constructed other forts at Shama (São Sebastião 1558) and at Axim (São Antonio 1515). The construction of São Jorge da Mina, and other forts along the coast, for example in Accra, had significant implications for the Portuguese enterprise on the Gold Coast. First, the internal trade at Elmina and the surrounding region and other places along the coast were reoriented toward the castle and forts because of the ready demand for local products – gold, ivory and several others. Second, the Castle also opened new avenues of trade for the local people. As a city unto itself, São Jorge da Mina needed food for its occupants and while most of the needs of the castle were initially supplied directly from Portugal, local merchants increasingly began to supply some of the food needs of the castle's occupants – especially soldiers and the large army of castle slaves and artisans who worked there.[49] Timber and wood for construction and renovation as well as for ship repairs (masts, sails, etc.) were also supplied locally, together with seashells and palm oil to make the "cement" for construction.[50] The castle contained enormous storerooms where goods could be stored awaiting the arrival of ships from Portugal (Photo 3.3).

The Portuguese were thus engaged in continuous trading throughout the year. They bought and stored goods to await the arrival of ships as opposed to trading only when Portuguese ships arrived from Europe. Similarly, goods from Portugal could be off-loaded and kept in the cavernous storehouses of the castle rather than traded directly from the ships. This made for a quick turnaround of shipping and Portuguese ships could be loaded for the return journey in a matter of weeks as opposed to months. This was of tremendous significance for mortality rates of Portuguese personnel at Elmina. At least the quick turnaround time for Portuguese ships meant less deaths on the dreaded West African coastline compared to ships of interlopers that sometimes spent months on the coast before returning to

Photo 3.3: Storerooms – Elmina Castle

Europe. A huge reservoir supplied water for the needs of São Jorge da Mina (Photo 3.4) but more important, it supplied ships that needed to replenish their water supply. Thus under the protection of the guns of the castle, Portuguese ships could undertake all of these activities – off-load/load goods, repair masts/sails, replenish food and water supply – and commence the return trip to Portugal in a fairly short time.[51]

It is worthy of note that even with the construction of the castle and the presence of a Portuguese military and naval force, other European countries continued to trade on the Gold Coast. Therefore in order to guarantee the monopoly of Portuguese trade, in April 1557 the governor at Elmina Castle requested that "the king of Portugal should send a fleet every year for protection against foreign ships who 'glutted the whole coast with many goods of all kinds,' taking half of the available gold in return."[52]

THE ARCHITECTURE OF SÃO JORGE DA MINA

Many scholars note that São Jorge da Mina was, in actuality, a pre-fabricated castle shipped from Portugal in sections with each stone numbered; the pieces were later put together. A.W. Lawrence disagrees with this assertion. He maintains that while materials were imported in bulk from Europe, the Portuguese imported only small quantities of ready- cut stone for São Jorge da Mina. As well some of the bricks for the construction of the castle came as ballast for ships.[53] In short the Portuguese quickly built Sao Jorge da Mina, but not as a prefabricated fort. Due to the existence of the Bastion de France some scholars argue that São Jorge da Mina might have started life as a fort built in 1381 by French adventurers from Dieppe.[54] While Lawrence regarded it (the bastion) as a gun platform of a late Portuguese date, Colin Flight disagrees. He notes that the French Battery "forms an irregular polygonal salient at the north corner of the service yard, close by the mouth of the river. Two of the faces lie within the line of the wall, and three outside."[55] Consequently, Flight avers, "it would take an exceptionally incompetent engineer to lay out a battery with every face wrongly aligned."[56] He suggests that the regularity in the length and orientation of the outer faces of the battery suggests that the structure was built at different times. He leans toward the view that the French Battery started out as a symmetrical structure and ended up as a distorted hexagon built as a reservoir to receive rain water from the roofs of the castle and dispense the water to ships.[57] However, there is very little evidence to support this.

Flight maintains that São Jorge da Mina's real history started in 1481 with the arrival of the Azambuja-led expedition and materials just as William the Conqueror had "shipped forts" to England to build castles in the elev-

Photo 3.4: Water Reservoir or Cistern - Elmina Castle

enth century.[58] The task of building the Castle started with the 1481 expedition led by Don Diego d'Azambuja. The expedition arrived in three ships with five hundred soldiers, one hundred masons, a hundred carpenters, a quantity of cut stones, tiles, bricks and doors. When these materials landed at Elmina, the Portuguese requested permission to build a fort.[59] After initial reluctance by the ruler of Elmina, Caramansa [Kwamena Ansah] permission was finally given to build the fortress.[60]

Soldiers and craftsmen were used in the construction of the fortress. Rock was quarried from a rocky promontory where the castle was eventually constructed. However, the area was considered sacred to the people of Elmina and the Portuguese workers were attacked for desecrating a sacred place. This initial setback delayed construction of the fortress but the Portuguese compromised by giving generous gifts to the king and his elders, building a shrine to pacify the sacred spirits of the area and defusing a very tense situation. After this gesture, work on the fort quickly resumed and "within three weeks the tower was erected and stands today just below the drawbridge at the main entrance."[61] Large quantities of red brick from Portugal were used to "provide the finishing touches to such structures as door and window arches or rib-vaults" linking the small courtyard with the big one on the east side of the main structure.[62] The exposed red bricks of the old Portuguese chapel in the middle of the courtyard is a testament to this.

Soon after the fortified base had been quickly built, the fleet returned to Portugal leaving behind Don Diego d'Azambuja and a garrison of sixty men to protect the just- completed castle. The original tower was soon found to be too small to protect the flourishing trade in gold and, not long afterward, enslaved Africans. Consequently, the fort was strengthened and the Portuguese discouraged early English adventurers from trading near the fort on pain of being made galley slaves (a form of impressment).[63] The Portuguese made every attempt to sink or capture all intruder ships that appeared on the Gold Coast.

Local wooded forests not far from the coast provided the wood needs of the Portuguese construction crews.[64] The forests near the mouth of the Pra River at Shama also supplied timber and firewood to the Portuguese. In fact, in some of the forts and castles, a few of the huge beams from Europe can still be found, though many have been replaced (Photo 3.5). Such beams from Europe were used on ships during the trans-Atlantic journey to the Gold Coast. Mortar, plaster, rafters and beams were initially imported, but later, seashells and palm oil became very important as a source of mortar and plaster and were obtained in the vicinity of Elmina.[65]

Photo 3.5: Beams – São Jorge da Mina: believed to be original material from Europe

Keeping in mind their strategic and defensive concerns, the Portuguese initially built Sao Jorge da Mina as a "structure with a purely vertical towers of a 'keep,' with relatively thin towers and curtain walls, but this was later modified to slightly taper towards the top, so that it could withstand withering canon fire."[66] Years later, the initial structure was modified to be able to carry heavier cannon for the defense of the Castle[67] (Photo 3.6)

As Figure 3.1 demonstrates, São Jorge da Mina was enlarged several times from the time the Portuguese constructed it in 1482 to the time of the English take-over of all Dutch possessions on the Gold Coast in 1872. It probably started life as a high square building with towers on the corners, around a central courtyard – the smallest of the three courtyards of the modern castle – much in the same style as the Tower of London. Of the original corner-towers only the round tower on the north-east, and the half-octagonal tower on the south-west are still in existence; the latter was probably originally round too, as can be seen in the small, odd-shaped and dark room in the mezzanine floor above the main entrance. On the north-west and south-east were probably at first square towers, but nothing remains of these. At a very early stage the north-western bastion tower must have been replaced by a huge bastion known in the Dutch days as the *Generaelen Battery* because of its proximity to the Director-General's quarters. This bastion pointing towards the land, provides another indication that the Portuguese expected an attack using sophisticated arms from that side.[68]

There is a prevailing belief that the breach of the walls of Constantinople by Muslim cannon-fire in 1453 was still fresh in the memory of the Christian world, and consequently, the Portuguese appeared to be gearing up for a similar attack, possibly from the Muslim world on this Christian outpost far out on the West African coast. As a result the castle was sufficiently defended by enough firepower to withstand such an attack.[69]

Van Dantzig believes that the bastion Generaelen Battery "and other bastions defending the extensions of the castle on the seaside, together with the 'French Bastion' were part of an initial and separate fortification designed to protect the entrance into the Benya River" and thus could have been designed to deal with French threat to the Portuguese position on the coast in the mid-sixteenth century.[70]

On account both of its position and design, São Jorge da Mina was an important fortress of its time. The location and more especially the design of the castle – the double enclosure defense system – was conceptualized to be a formidable redoubt against enemies and interlopers alike. This is evidenced by the fact that, expecting an attack by land from the local people or the Moors and by sea from rival European powers, two batteries on the seaward side of the castle carried six guns each while another six-gun

Photo 3.6: São Jorge da Mina – modified to carry heavier cannon

battery covered the landward side. On the side facing the River Benya and a hill beyond it, where, in Portuguese strategic thinking, not much could be expected by way of an attack, two small pieces of ordnance were sited.[71] The seaward side was protected by a shorter wall (compared to the wall on the landward side) but strengthened by the French bastion which could provide substantial withering fire toward any attacker from the sea. In short, the very high walls on the landward side supplemented the weaker ordnance on that side of the building.

The Portuguese provided for additional defenses to the castle by constructing a deep ditch which almost surrounded the entire structure[72] (Photo 3.7). However, the ditch also served another practical function: sea water was allowed to drain into the section of the ditch nearer the sea so that small boats could come up to the castle wall to offload or load goods. The extra precaution of a deep ditch and a drawbridge straddling the western access to the castle was very important because the governor's quarters was on this side of the castle.

The castle could be entered via two gates on the eastern or western side (Photo 3.8). The main entrance, the western gate, was furnished with a drawbridge that faces Don Diego d'Azambuja's original stone tower and the governor's quarters, while the eastern gate was near what was then the Customs House. This door was used primarily as a passageway way for carrying goods in and out of the castle.[73]

While a Portuguese church – with four rows of Portuguese red brick visibly showing – still remains in São Jorge da Mina (Photo 3.9), the Portuguese initially built a little chapel (around 1555) on Iago Hill, overlooking the castle from across the Benya River. This little chapel dedicated to St. Iago was later converted into a well-fortified stronghold between 1555 and 1558, when a small watchtower and a stone wall, complete with a gate in it, were added to the structure. The chapel was further strengthened when the Portuguese dug a deep ditch around it (as they had done at São Jorge da Mina) and added several guns to the defenses. The guns were aimed directly across the neck of the peninsula on which the castle stands.[74] This would protect the approach to the building on Iago Hill as well as help repel any landward attack on the chapel and on the castle. After the 1596 Dutch attack on Elmina, the church was demolished and a new one reconstructed in the courtyard of São Jorge da Mina at the seaward end of the Great Court.[75]

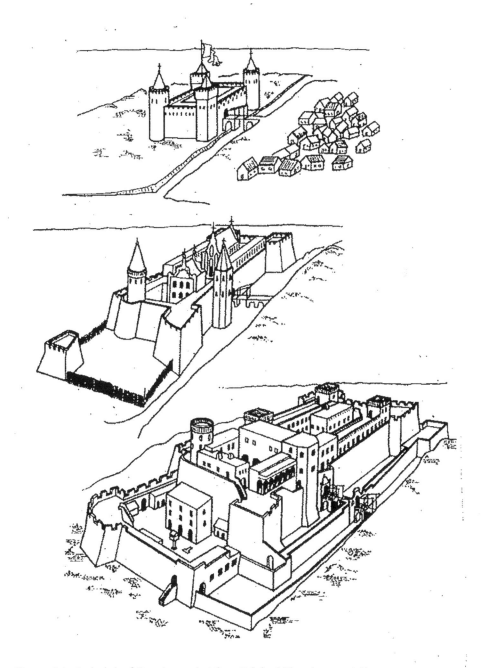

Figure 3.1 : A sketch of Sao Jorge da Mina: Original Structure and Changes over the Centuries

Source: Albert van Dantzig, *Forts and Castles of Ghana*. Accra: Sedco Publishing, 1980, 4.
Courtesy: Sedco Publishing.

Photo 3.7: Ditch - Front Part of São Jorge da Mina

Photo 3.8: Front Gate – São Jorge da Mina with Drawbridge

Photo 3.9: Portuguese Chapel – São Jorge da Mina

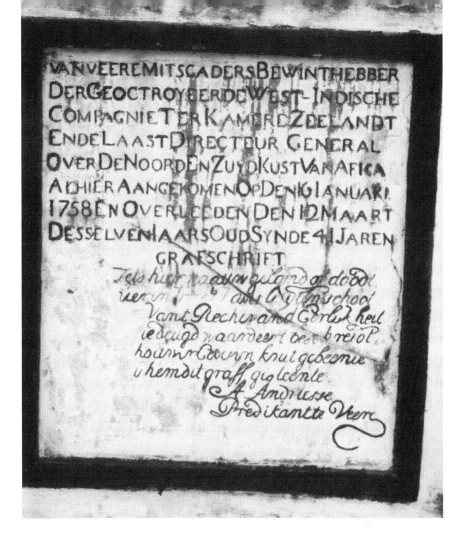

VAN VEERE MITSGADERS BEWINTHEBBER
DER GEOCTROYEERDE WEST-INDISCHE
COMPAGNIE TER KAMERE ZEELANDT
ENDE LAAST DIRECTEUR GENERAL
OVER DE NOORD EN ZUYD KUST VAN AFICA
A DHIER AANGEKOMEN OP DEN 16 IANUARI
1758 EN OVERLEEDEN DEN 12 MAART
DESSELVEN IAARS OUD SYNDE 41 JAREN
GRAFSCHRIFT

Photo 3.10: Portuguese Officials and Personnel Buried at São Jorge da Mina

The fort or castle as a "ship at permanent anchor" was a self-sufficient entity with its own staff: administrative (including clerical), security, pastoral (or evangelical), artisanal, service (servants and slaves), and domestic personnel (Photo 3.10). The European colonial establishments of the nineteenth century (both colonial administration, chartered companies and even missionaries) all utilized an administrative system that had already been tried and tested in the various forts and castles by crown officials and earlier chartered companies of the Dutch, French, and Brandenburgers, albeit with modification, to suit particular purposes.[76]

There was a distinct hierarchy of officials with clearly designated duties and responsibilities. The rank and functions of these officials corresponded to the type of accommodation offered to Europeans in the forts and castles as well as the perquisites given to them. At the time of the construction of these forts and castles (fifteenth century), authority was organized along the lines of the feudal system with a feudal governor in charge and subordinate officials reporting to him.[77]

When the Portuguese King John II formed the Guinea Company in 1500, he granted it sole right to trade on the West African coast in return for a payment of a hundred pieces of gold. Consequently, King John directed that the castle be further fortified and well-provisioned. The King reserved for himself the sole right to appoint the governor and the principal officers of this Portuguese station on the Gold Coast, each of whom served for a period of about three years. The captain or governor, drawing an annual salary of 800 milreis (about £10,800) had ten servants to take care of his needs. He had wide judicial powers and could try cases at São Jorge da Mina and at Fort São Antonio involving both Africans and Portuguese. In many instances, his sentences were final. It was only in cases involving an African king, chief or a senior Portuguese official who had been sentenced to death or the loss of a hand that an appeal could be made to the Portuguese crown in Lisbon.[78] The governor was also in charge of defense of the castle. He was to maintain a supply of guns, cross bows and shields for the defense of the castle and could draw money from the castle's gold reserves to pay for defense.[79]

Apart from the Governor, there were a number of other officials such as the *viedor* or chief factor, the *padre* or chaplain, the King's *Procurador* or judge, the officer commanding the garrison and the company's chief clerk, all of whom resided in the castle. The Portuguese officials received one percent of the year's profit after expenses were deducted. In April 1529, for example, they received bonuses (in unequal proportions) after the castle ledger recorded a profit.[80]

The chief factor was the second most important official in the castle. He worked with four personal employees and two highly-paid clerks, who served as book keepers. The chief factor or factor managed the warehouse for which he was paid 150 milreis (about £1,500).[81] The third most important official was the surgeon whose responsibility covered the health needs of the administrative personnel and the garrison. He was assisted in his work by a barber, a male nurse and an apothecary. The barber bled the patients and the apothecary dispensed medicines.[82] Given the level of mortality and the periodic outbreak of diseases in the Portuguese establishment at Elmina, the medical unit was often tasked to breaking point.

There was a superintendent of provisions; a senior official in charge of all the food supply needed by the castle personnel; and a master baker, who worked with four Portuguese women to bake bread for the castle residents. Each resident received four rolls of bread a day, together with a daily flagon of wine, and each month they were supplied with a pot of olive oil, two pots of vinegar and a pot of honey.[83] The arrangement remained in effect from 1529 to 1607 and probably till 1637. The catering department also employed up to six women for domestic chores. Meat, especially chicken, could be purchased only from local people who brought chickens to the castle. This was supplemented with cattle imported from São Tomé. Each animal was killed and shared in the governor's presence and none was sold to the people of Elmina.[84]

The vicar and three chaplains were responsible for the spiritual life of the castle and said daily mass for the soul of Prince Henry the Navigator. The priests were to organize a school to teach village boys how to read and write and thus get them to serve in the choir. The Portuguese king offered rewards to officials (such as the captain and the priests) for training choir boys or converting people to Christianity.[85]

The soldiers, barber-surgeon and other lesser officials did not have quarters in the Castle. Rather, they lived in Elmina town beneath the walls of the castle and reported daily for work. The post garrison was paid in gold from the trading chest after a quarterly muster and inspection.[86] The garrison was largely composed of criminals who were banished from Portugal for life to live whatever was left of their lives in that far-away frontier outpost on the Gold Coast. Not surprisingly discipline was poor and the Portuguese were hated by the local people for their high-handedness in all the coastal port towns under Portuguese sway.[87] In spite of this, some sort of order was maintained, for twice a year – in April and September – a fleet of four or five ships arrived from Portugal with fresh supplies of merchandise and criminals to augment the garrison. The fleet returned home with the profits of the trade.[88] On the whole, however, security was generally lax "except when there were ships in the roads, when the sentries in helm and breastplate and armed with heavy halberds might have been seen pacing up and down the ramparts."[89] After the Dutch attack of 1596, the Portuguese made further changes to the defenses of São Jorge. They strengthened and enlarged the west bastion and located a gun port in the inner gateway to defend the main entrance to the castle.[90]

São Jorge da Mina was garrisoned by sixty Portuguese soldiers and the castle was organized as a royal stronghold. Apart from the garrison, the Portuguese recruited and drilled the "Mina Blacks" into an affective fighting force that could be called upon to fight on behalf of the Portuguese whenever the need arose.[91] Eric Tylleman notes that "at this place [Kingdom of Fetu] is the largest negro settlement to be found along the whole coast, which is called Ampenny. Several thousand men can be had from here for war, all with guns and well trained."[92]

MAJOR TRADE ITEMS

Fifty-two Portuguese citizens, employed and paid by the Portuguese crown, lived in São Jorge da Mina (accorded the status of a city by the Portuguese crown) in 1529. This Portuguese colony of Mina was linked up with the overland gold trade that the Akan carried on with North African and European markets. The Wangara from the upper reaches of the River Niger were purveyors of the gold through Mina and Bighu on the edge of the forest to the savanna and thence to the termini of the trans-Saharan trade.[93] The gold trade became the immediate focus of the Portuguese who eventually succeeded in linking their maritime trade routes to the overland trade routes and diverted the gold through Mina to Europe. They achieved their monopoly position in the gold trade by offering goods that enticed the gold producers to trade with only the Portuguese. A *Regimento da Mina* was drawn up in Lisbon and regulated the entire commercial system on the Gold Coast.[94] Four major items of trade offered by the Portuguese were metal ware (including brass chamber pots, gold pans and, in earlier decades, brass bells, sheets of copper, small copper boxes, weights for weighing gold, lead crosses, axes and knives) cloth, enslaved Africans and other miscellaneous items. Metal ware accounted for fifty per cent of the sales at São Jorge da Mina. The Portuguese offered, in addition to the metal products aforementioned, brass manilas (about 0.60 kilograms each), small shaving bowls and varieties of cooking pots.[95]

The second major item of exchange was cloth. One important type of cloth, the *lambeis,* was a narrow strip of colored cloth; the other type consisted of Moroccan burnouses called *algeravais.*[96] In addition, the Portuguese offered red capes, caps and unfinished finely-woven cloth that could be dyed to replicate local patterns.[97] Given the tradition of cloth trade in the region, the Portuguese invested the supervision of the cloth trade in the hands of the Mina factor who inspected all consignments of cloth upon arrival; he was required to return all damaged cloth back to Portugal. As well, he checked the stock every four months and kept any damaged cloth to prevent private trading [in cloth] by Portuguese residents of São Jorge da Mina.[98] The price of cloth was fixed in Lisbon and though the factor could sell cloth at 20 percent above the fixed price, he was not allowed to sell cloth below that price under any circumstance.[99]

The third major item of exchange in 1529 was enslaved Africans. The Portuguese, soon after their arrival, tapped into the coastwise trade and began to purchase enslaved Africans from Arguin, São Tomé, Benin and other places bound for the Gold Coast. This is exemplified by Eustache de la Fosse who purchased enslaved Africans on the Grain Coast (the region of what is now Liberia and Sierra Leone) for the gold trade at Shama.[100] More important, the Portuguese purchased enslaved Africans from São Tomé at a price of about 40-50 manillas per person,[101] and sent a ship every six weeks to the island for the enslaved, paying the crew in slaves at a rate of 900 *reis*[102] per month and one slave (valued at four *milreis*)[103] as the cost of subsistence.[104] An estimated 506 enslaved Africans were sent to São Jorge da Mina in 1529; 552 were sent in 1530 and 300 in 1531. These enslaved Africans were shipped by Georg Erbert and Association who held a monopolistic contract to supply about 500 enslaved Africans a year beginning in 1529. The company was to ship the enslaved Africans aboard royal Portuguese vessels.[105] It is also worthy of note that enslaved Africans were also obtained "on the adjacent mainland from the Niger Delta to south of the Congo estuary."[106] Tables 1.3 and 3.3, as already indicated, dealing with Portuguese daily trade at Elmina and with the São Tomé and Principé slave trade with Mina, illustrate this early trade.

Able-bodied, young, enslaved people were utilized in porterage and in the mines but old men and women were rejected for such work with the gold merchants. Rather, many of such men and women were used as castle slaves (responsible for cleaning work in the castle) and some of the finest female slaves were taken as "temporary" wives by the Portuguese, though temporary in this case was a nebulous term since the Europeans did not, of necessity, return to Europe after a couple of months or even years.[107] Out of the slaves acquired via São Tomé, the Portuguese sent the "best slaves" to Elmina. A third of the consignment of enslaved Africans from São Tomé was selected to work at Elmina. Most of the rest were sent to Portugal and those considered to be in poor shape were sold to sugar planters on São Tomé.[108]

The fourth category of items, the miscellaneous category, was one that featured coris (beads),wooden chests, belts and purses.

FORT SÃO SEBASTIÃO - SHAMA

Fort São Sebastião (St. Sebastian) was built at Shama by the Portuguese in about 1505 on a "bank of gravelly conglomerate, between the beach on the south and east and a deeply eroded stream-bed to the west"[109](Photo 3.11) São Sebastião did not turn out to be anywhere near as important economically as the Castle at Elmina. Its slave supply was also not as profitable as in other places. Instead, Fort São Sebastião was built at Shama as part of a defensive system to maintain Portuguese monopoly on the eastern coastline of the Gold Coast and keep other European powers and merchants, especially the French, out of the area. More important, however, was the fact that it provided São Jorge da Mina with timber, provisions and firewood on account of its location near the River Pra.

Shama was associated with the gold trade in earlier times but there is no evidence that the Portuguese obtained much gold from Shama. In aggregate terms not much trade occurred at Shama and the fort fell into decay, especially after it was bombarded by the Dutch. In 1554 the Portuguese were embroiled in a dispute with the people of Shama "over a man they had stolen," notes Claridge. As a result of the dispute, the Portuguese were very nearly driven out of the town, half of which they had already destroyed with their guns.[110] One of the major features of Fort Sebastião, that is visibly clear to anyone, is a long tier of semicircular steps leading to the courtyard. One half of that courtyard is taken up by a post office.

According to a Portuguese chart of 1630, the fort was composed of a "bastion, two-single-storeyed buildings with pitched roofs, and a two-storeyed tower on the inland side"[111] (Fig. 3.2) On the upper floor were three gun ports, interspersed with small-arm slits. J. Barbot had sketched it in 1679 to be "a low bastioned enclosure, apparently narrow towards the sea, with a couple of single-storeyed gabled buildings within (stretching inland) ..."[112] Barbot added that the fort was roughly the size of Fort Batenstein at Butri, being slightly longer in length; it mounted only eight guns and had pretty convenient lodgings.[113] The fort was stronger on the landward side pointing to a Portuguese concern for security from the people of Shama due to disputes.

Photo 3.11: Fort São Sebastião

The Dutch took the fort in 1642 and altered it in 1648, building a rectangular battery in the middle of the structure but due to the use of mud instead of mortar, the fort was almost leveled to the ground by the English bombardment of 1664.

FORT SÃO ANTONIO, AXIM

São Antonio was a Portuguese fort until 1660 when it was captured by the Dutch who had earlier seized Elmina Castle in 1637. The Dutch launched an unsuccessful attack on São Antonio in 1641 and when they attacked again in 1642, the Portuguese withdrew from the fort just before the Dutch bombardment began. In 1664 the English Captain Holmes attacked it and left it in ruins as part of the expedition that captured nearly all the Dutch forts on the Gold Coast. However, Admiral de Ruyter shortly took back all the forts the English captain had taken from the Dutch. In this way, the European fortified positions on the Gold Coast were embroiled in the Anglo-Dutch War of 1664-1666. In 1872, the English bought Fort São Antonio from the Dutch. It was in fairly good condition at the time and the English later added offices, a rest house and a prison.[114] *São Antonio* was restored to its Dutch form in 1957 and some of the rooms were used as local council offices. In the 1970s, the Axim post office was located in the fort.

Fort São Antonio at Axim (1515) was the second of the three major Portuguese fortified positions on the Gold Coast – the triad designed to enforce trade monopoly over the eastern part of the Gold Coast from Elmina to Assinie, especially over the gold fields in the western part of the Gold Coast. The Portuguese fort at Axim was probably begun at another location closer to the mouth of the Ankobra river but due to the indefensible location and continual harassment by the local people they abandoned that initial site. The present location is a defensible promontory which consists of "a triangular mass of hard rock, which then stood perhaps thirty feet higher than the adjacent ground on the east and dropped steeply, though not abruptly, to the sea"[115](Photo 3.12)

The fort thus stands on a small but high rock in the sea, which formed the rounded head of a peninsula. This limited rocky outcrop resulted in a small triangular fort that followed the contours of the cape on which it stood. It was open to attack on the land side and, as a result, the landward side was strengthened with breastworks. The Portuguese constructed a rock-cut ditch which was over eight-foot deep. As well, they built a drawbridge and covered the approach to the bridge with several guns.[116] The drawbridge and gun emplacements near the bridge mirror the defensive system the Portuguese had put in place in Elmina. In addition to the ditch and

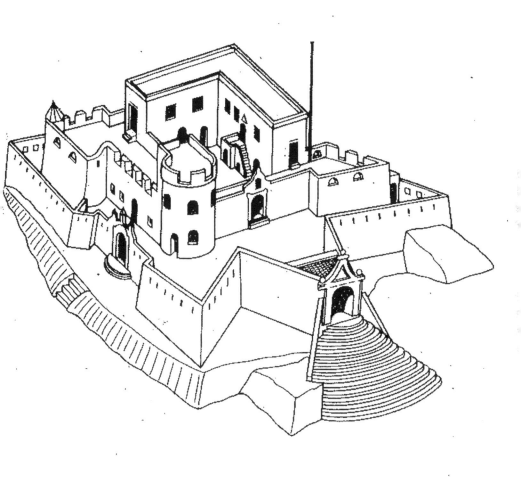

Figure 3.2: Fort São Sebastião - Sketch
Courtesy of Sedco Publishing. Van Dantzig, *Forts and Castles of Ghana*. 19.

Photo 3.12: Fort São Antonio

the drawbridge, the Portuguese built a spur and connected it to the main building. The spur had sufficient space to hold twenty men who could be effective with guns in the event of an attack on the fort. [117] As a result of this the fort's strongest defenses are on the landward side.

The promontory on which the fort stood afforded excellent natural defense on the seaward side. "It runs straight out to sea, ending in a point," and that made it difficult to defend the fort against a fleet of ships attacking from the seaward side.[118] There were two good batteries toward the sea, together with several large and small guns for the defense of the fort.[119] But since this proved inadequate against a well-armed fleet at sea, the Portuguese built seaward walls for protection. They also probably leveled the summit of the promontory, and piled up rocks against the lower part of the seaside slope to create a platform and a stable base to hold the fort. The walls of the fort are thus supported at the base by the rocks mentioned above and the walls are free standing only at the top.[120] Therefore, for most of its height, the walls of the fort formed "a revetment or facing to a platform upon which the fort stands."[121] The structure was faced, and probably indirectly bolstered in its defenses, by several little rocky islands (on one of which a lighthouse now stands) and dangerous reefs which prevented ships from coming very close to the fort. In this way, the fort was protected from a seaward assault by enemies or rival European nations. However, the little islands near the fort would later become its Achilles heel. When the Dutch lost the fort to the English, they installed cannons on these little islands (cognizant of their strategic value), and shelled the fort from those positions and took it back from the English in 1664.[122]

Unsuccessful Dutch attacks of Portuguese Axim in 1596 and 1641 were followed by a very successful one in 1642 after a bombardment of the fort by seven ships. This time the Dutch took possession and completed the forcible expulsion of the Portuguese from the Gold Coast. When an English naval expedition of 1664 took São Antonio, the Dutch located guns on the island in the bay and retook the fort soon afterward. They held it as part of the bargaining chips during the Anglo-Dutch exchange of forts in 1868.

Initially important for holding off competition to Portuguese trading activities east of Elmina, Fort São Antonio in Axim had no major strategic value and became negligible after the Dutch seized it. This is borne out by the fact that the Portuguese had very few guns at the fort. A Dutch list four years after capture put the number of guns at "four brass twelve-pounders, two brass three-pounders, a brass mortar (to fire stone balls of twenty-four pounds) and two iron two-pounders."[123]

Photo 3:14: Islands near the Fort

Photo 3.15: Picture showing location of Fort São Antonio

Photo 3.16: Fort São Antonio – Landward side

Due to the construction of the platform (made by leveling the summit of the promontory and piling rocks against the lower parts of the seaward slope), there is a wall-walk all around the fort. The end of the promontory drops into the sea and while it was not suitable for siting a battery, the platform provides a footing for situating several guns that could pour withering fire out to sea and along the coast.[124] Fort São Antonio's defenses were therefore stronger on the landward side (Photo 3.16). The seaward side was protected by the sea walls created by piling up rocks against the lower part of the seaward slope of the promontory on which the fort stood.

At both ends of the landward side to the front of the fort, there were two bastions that commanded the approaches from both the town and the beaches and were the only means by which the Portuguese ensured the safety of the seaward walls (Photo 3.17). The northeast and south-south east walls connected the battery to the inward corners of the bastions and thus completed the outer ring of defenses of the fort. [125]

The building inside the fort must have housed a fairly large Portuguese garrison but very little evidence remains of this part of the structure (Photo 3.18). The Dutch bombardments, coupled with the excessive rainfall in Axim, may have damaged that part of the structure severely. In 1646, barely four years after the Dutch took the fort from the Portuguese, the Dutch governor at Elmina received information that "a great part of the N. part of the fort has fallen owing to the great rain which falls there daily. The commerce room was made with the same work, and accordingly I ordered that this fallen work should be restored with a high and proper wall ..."[126] The section of the fort that collapsed appeared to have been an office and residential accommodation built of mud and stones laid in mud. This seemed to have been a large building between the main courtyard and the seaward battery and which was documented in 1682. It was restored with stone laid in good mortar.[127]

IMPACT OF THE PORTUGUESE PERIOD

The most lasting impact of the 160-year Portuguese period on the Gold Coast could be found in vocabulary (translated or slightly corrupted) in use on the coast as well as in geographical names of places. Such words include: palaver (palabra), panyar (apanhar), fetish (feitiço), piccaninny (piccin or picania), caboceer (cabeceiro), among others. In terms of place names, the following are the most prominent: Gold Coast (Costa del Oro), Cape Three points (Cabo de Tres Puntas), Cape Coast (Cabo Corso), Elmina (São Jorge del Mina), River Volta (Rio Volta), River Ankobra (Rio Cobre), among several others.[128] The Portuguese also reportedly introduced cattle, prickly pear to fence enclosures, Indian

Photo 3.17: Fort São Antonio – Bastions Commanding Approach from Town and Beaches

corn and sugarcane from the island of São Tomé, and banana and pineapple from the Congo. Finally, the Portuguese maintained missionary priests for the longest time at Elmina to instruct the people in the Christian faith. In the end, however, the level of Christianization remained minimal at best.

Notes

1. See Adam Jones, trans. & ed., *West Africa in the mid-Seventeenth Century: An Anonymous Dutch Manuscript* (Atlanta: African Studies Association Press, 1995).

2. For details of the West African carrying trade and the effects of European presence, see for example, J.D. Fage, "Some Remarks on Beads and Trade in Lower Guinea in the Sixteenth and Seventeenth Centuries," *Journal of African History* 3, 2 (1962): 343-344; Ivor Wilks, "A Medieval Trade-Route from the Niger to the Gulf of Guinea, *Journal of African History* 3, 2 (1962): 339; Harvey M. Feinberg, "Elmina, Ghana: A History of Its Development and Relationship With the Dutch in the Eighteenth Century," Ph.D. Dissertation, Boston University, 1969, 3.

3. Christopher Hibbert, *Africa Explored: Europeans in the Dark Continent, 1769-1889* (London: W.W. Norton & Co., 12-13; Georg Nørregård, *Danish Settlements in West Africa 1658-1850*, trans. Sigurd Mamme (Boston: Boston University Press, 1966), 2.

4. Hibbert, *Africa Explore*, 13.

5. See for example, Peter Frobath, *The River Congo: The Discovery, Exploration and Exploitation of the World's Most Dramatic River* (New York: Harper and Row, 1977); Alta Jablow and Dorothy Hammond, *The Myth of Africa* (New York: Library of the Social Sciences, 1977).

6. Hibbert, *Africa Explored*, 13.

7. For the Arab advance into Egypt and the rest of North Africa, see Robert Brunschvig, "Ibn Adal al-Hakim et la conquéte de l'Afrique du Nord par les arabes," *Al-Andalus* 40 (1975): 129-179; R. Le Tourneau (ed & rev.), *History of North Africa: Tunisia, Algeria and Morocco. From the Arab Conquest to 1830* trans. John Petrie (New York: Praeger, 1970); Jamil M. Abun-Nasr, *A History of the Maghreb* (Cambridge: Cambridge University Press, 1971).

8. For accounts of early and later trade networks see for example, Rhys Carpenter, "A Trans-Saharan Caravan Route in Herodutus," *American Journal of Archaeology* 60, 3 (July 1956), 231-242; Count Byron Khun de Prorok, "Ancient Trade Routes From Carthage Into the Sahara," *Geographical Review* 15, 2 (April 1925): 190-205; Nehemia Levtzion, "Ibn-Hawqal, the Cheque, and Awdaghost," *Journal of African History* 9, 2 (1968): 223-233; E.W. Bovill, *The Golden Trade of the Moors* (Oxford: Oxford University Press, 1958); Robin C.C. Law, "The Garamantes and Trans-Saharan Enterprise in Classical Times, *Journal of African History* 8, 2 (1967): 181-200; Timothy Garrard, "Myth and Metrology: The Early Trans-Saharan Gold Trade," *Journal of African History* 23, IV (1982): 443-461; A. Adu

Photo 3.18: Fort São Antonio – Inside the Fort

Boahen, *Britain, the Sahara and the Western Sudan, 1788-1861* (Oxford: Clarendon Press, 1964).

9. Ibn Batuta, *Travels in Asia and Africa 1325-54*, trans & intro., H.A.R. Gibb (New York: R.M. McBride & Co., 1929); Said Hamdun and Noël King, *Ibn Battuta in Black Africa* (London: Rex Collins, 1975), 22-62. See also Claude Meillassoux, "L'itineraire d'Ibn Battuta entre Walata et Mali," *Journal of African History* 13, 3 (1972): 389-395; Vincent Monteil, "Introduction aux voyages d'ibn Battuta (1325-53)," *Bulletin de l'I.F.A.N*, 30, Series B, 2 (1968): 444-462; John Vogt, *Portuguese Rule on the Gold Coast 1469-1682* (Athens: The University of Georgia Press, 1979), 1-2.

10. Leo Africanus was reportedly captured by Christian corsairs of Jeber and sent to Pope Leo X because he was a widely traveled man. Pope Leo freed him, baptized and christened him Leo, after himself. See Vogt, *Portuguese Rule on the Gold Coast*, 1. See also Ibn Batuta, *Travels in Asia and Africa 1325-54*.

11. For the trans-Saharan trade, see E. W. Bovill, *Golden Trade of the Moors* (Oxford: Oxford University Press, 1958); A. Adu Boahen, *Topics in West African History* (London: Longmans 1966); Boahen, *Britain, the Sahara and the Western Sudan*.

12. See Ivor Wilks, *Forest of Gold: Essays on the Akan and the Kingdom of Asante* (Athens: Ohio University Press, 1993); Wilks, "A Medieval Trade-route from the Niger to the Gulf of Guinea," *The Journal of African History* 3, 2 (1962): 337-341. Enid Schild-krout (ed.), *The Golden Stool: Essays of the Asante Center and Periphery. Anthropological Papers of the American Museum of Natural History* 65, No. 1 (New York: American Museum of Natural History 1987); Claude Meillassoux, *The Development of Indigenous Trade and Markets in West Africa* (London: O.U.P., 1970). See also Edmund Abaka, *Kola is God's Gift: Agricultural Production, Export Initiatives and the Kola Industry of Asante and the Gold Coast, c. 1820-1950* (Oxford: James Currey, 2005); Paul E. Lovejoy, *Caravans of Kola. The Hausa Kola Trade 1700-1900* (London and Zaria: Oxford University Press, 1980).

13. See Nehemia Levtzion, *Ancient Ghana and Mali*. London, 1973; Levtzion, "The Thirteenth and Fourteenth Century Kings of Mali," *Journal of African History* 4, 3 (1961): 341-353; Bovill, *The Golden Trade of the Moors*; Claude Meillassoux, "L'itineraire d'Ibn Battuta entre Walata et Mali," 389-395.

14. Boahen, *Topics in West African History*.

15. Ibid. See Ibn Batuta, *Travels in Asia and Africa 1325-54*; Hamdun and King, *Ibn Battuta in Black Africa*, 22-62; see also Meillassoux, "L'itineraire d'Ibn Battuta entre Walata et Mali," 389-395; Monteil, "Introduction aux voyages d'ibn Battuta (1325-53)," 444-462; Vogt, *Portuguese Rule on the Gold Coast 1469-1682*, 1.

16. Hibbert, *Africa Explored*, 16.

17. A.E. Afigbo, E.A. Ayandele, R.J. Gavin, J.D. Omer-Cooper and R. Palmer, *The Making of Modern Africa. Vol. I. The Nineteenth Century*, 4th ed. (Essex: Longman Group, 1988), 37.

18. For a discussion of the motives of Henry the Navigator in the African enter-prise, see John W. Blake, *West Africa: Quest For God and Gold 1454-1578* (London:

Curzon Press, 1977), 194; John Vogt, "Crusading and Commercial Elements in the Portuguese Capture of Ceuta (1415)," *The Muslim World* 59 (1969): 287-299.

19. Guinea at this time reportedly referred to a vaguely defined expanse of the land lying south of the Sahara with Djenne or Jenne as its chief commercial center. The name Guinea was applied to West Africa after the maritime discovery of the fifteenth century, first in the chronicles of Azurara and later in papal bull Romanus X in 1455, which granted Portuguese rulers control over lands from Cape Bojador to Guinea and beyond. See Blake, *West Africa: Quest for God and Gold*, 195.

20. See W. Walton Claridge, *A History of The Gold Coast and Ashanti from the Earliest Times to the Commencement of the Twentieth Century* (London: Frank Cass, 1964), 18-19, 22-23.

21. Hibbert, *Africa Explored*, 16; Claridge, *A History of The Gold Coast and Ashanti*, 11-13.

22. Vogt, *Portuguese Rule on the Gold Coast*, 1-2; Blake, *West Africa: Quest for God and Gold*, 194

23. Claridge, *A History of the Gold Coast and Ashanti*, 34-35; Vogt, *Portuguese Rule on the Gold Coast*, 2.

24. Hibbert, *Africa Explored*, 16; Christopher DeCourse, *An Archaelogy of Elmina. Africans and Europeans on the Gold Coast, 1400-1900* (Washington, DC: Smithsonian Institution Press, 2001), 21.

25. Albert van Dantzig, *Forts and Castles of Ghana*, (Accra: Sedco Publishing, 1980), i.

26. Some geographers believe that Rio de Ouro is perhaps the River Senegal or even the River Niger since both of them take their sources from what can be considered part of the auriferous region of West Africa – in the Senegambian region.

27. While the impression is often created that African immigrants arrived in Europe after World War II, the reality is otherwise. African arrival in Europe goes back to the time before the Portuguese overseas endeavor in Africa.

28. Claridge, *A History of the Gold Coast and Ashanti*, 38-39. Cognizance is taken of the fact that Portugal, Spain and southern Italy had been part of the Muslim Arab world and were thus used to the presence of enslaved Africans who had arrived in Europe via the trans-Saharan trade across North Africa. The Portuguese continued to participate in the trade in enslaved Africans after the expulsion of Muslim Arabs from the Iberian peninsula, using enslaved Africans and Arabs as builders, water sellers, dock workers and cleaners among others. See P.C. Emmer, *The Dutch Slave Trade, 1500-1850*, trans., Chris Emery (New York: Berghahn Books, 2006).

29. Hibbert, *Africa Explored*, 17; Claridge, *History of Gold Coast and Ashanti*, 41-42; See also Vogt, *Portuguese Rule on the Gold Coast*, 6.

30. Johannus Wartenburg cites a tradition regarding the emergence of *Anomee*. This tradition states that emigrants searching for drinking water accidentally found a stream and their leader exclaimed in the Wassaw dialect, *Be Enya*, meaning

"I have found it." This immigrant group erected a hut by the rivulet and refreshed themselves and called the rivulet *Be enya*. This ostensibly is a reference to the Benya River. See Johannus Wartenberg, *Sao Jorge d'el Mina: Premier West African European Settlement* (Ilfracomb: Arthur H. Stockwell, n.d.), 15.

31. Nørregård, *Danish Settlements in West Africa*, 3.

32. João de Barros, *Asia* [1552], trans. and ed. G.R. Crone, Hakluyt Society 80, 2nd ser., 1937, cited in Freda Wolfson, *Pageant of Ghana* (London: Oxford University Press, 1958), 38. See also Eric Tylleman's account in Nathan, "The Gold Coast at the End of the Seventeenth Century Under the Dutch and the Danes," *Journal of the African Society* 13 (October 1904): 16-17.

33. Rosemary M. Cave, *Gold Coast Forts*. London: Thomas Nelson, [1956]? 3-4. Claridge, *History of the Gold Coast and Ashanti*, 47; Harvey M. Feinberg, *Africans and Europeans in West Africa: Elminans and Dutchmen on the Gold Coast During the Eighteenth Century* (Philadelphia: The American Philosophical Society, 1989), 27-28; Feinberg, "Elmina, Ghana," 15; J. W. Blake, *Europeans in West Africa, 1450-1660*, I. (London, 1942), 73. Historians dispute whether the Caramança of European documents is indeed Kwamena Ansah, the Elmina Chief who acceded to the Portuguese request for land to build a "house." David Henige asserts that Kwamena Ansah does not appear in the king lists of the period.

34. Tony Hyland, *The Castle of Elmina. A Brief History and Guide*. Series No. 3 (Accra: Ghana Museums and Monuments Board, 1972), 3.

35. DeCourse, *An Archaelogy of Elmina*. 21; Feinberg, *Africans and Europeans in West Africa*, 27-28; Feinberg, "Elmina Ghana: A History of Its Development and Relationship With the Dutch," 15; Hyland, *The Castles of Elmina*, 1-2.

36. Wilks, "A Medieval Trade-route from the Niger to the Gulf of Guinea," 337-341; Feinberg, *Africans and Europeans in West Africa*, 10-11; Feinberg, "Elmina, Ghana," 16-17; Schildkrout, *The Golden Stool*; Meillassoux (ed.), *The Development of Indigenous Trade and Markets in West Africa*.

37. See for example, John L. Vogt, "The Early Sao-Tomé-Principé Slave Trade with Mina, 1500-1540," *The International Journal of African Historical Studies* VI, 3 (1973): 464-465.

38. Feinberg, *Africans and Europeans in West Africa*, 47. For the expansion of the plantation complex see Philip D. Curtin, "The Atlantic Slave Trade 1600-1800," in J.F. Ade Ajayi and Michael Crowder, *The History of West Africa. Vol. I.* (New York: Columbia University Press, 1972), 243-250; Curtin, *The Rise and Fall of the Plantation Complex: Essays in Atlantic History* (Cambridge: Cambridge University Press, 1990).

39. Feinberg, *Africans and Europeans in West Africa*, 29.

40. See Kwame Arhin (ed.), *The Papers of George Ekem Ferguson* (Leiden: Afrika-Studiecentrum, 1974), 15 for a description of traditional gold mining on the Gold Coast. George Ekem Fergusson's views as a surveyor is very important. See also *Ghana Notes and Queries*, 1 (1965): 4-5, for information on gold extraction at Bure.

41. J. Sylvanus Wartemberg, *Sao Jorge d'el Mina. PremierWest African European Settlement*, 21.

42. A.W. Lawrence, *Trade Castles and Forts ofWest Africa* (London: Jonathan Cape, 1963), 30.

43. Ibid, 30.

44. Blake, *Europeans in West Africa, 1450-1560*. I, 72; Van Dantzig, *Gold Coast Forts and Castles*, 3; K.Y. Daaku and A. van Dantzig, "An Anotated Dutch Map of 1629," *Ghana Notes and Queries* 9 (Nov. 1966), 14-15.

45. Lawrence, *Trade Castles and Forts*, 32.

46. Ibid., 32.

47. Ibid., 35-36; Hyland, The Castles of Elmina," 2.

48. Lawrence, *Trade Castles of Elmina*, 35-36.

49. Hyland, *The Castles of Elmina*, 3. The castle slaves constituted an important component of the "foot soldiers" whose work made the forts and castles function efficiently. They worked in various capacities as artisans, cooks, servants and even helped to defend the fortified stations during enemy attack, both local and foreign.

50. See Daaku and van Dantzig, "An Annotated Dutch Map of 1629," *Ghana Notes and Queries*," 14. The Portuguese fort at Shama to the east of Elmina became an important service fort supplying timber and firewood.

51. Lawrence, *Trade Castles and Forts*, 34-35; Hyland, *Castles of Elmina*, 2-3.

52. Ibid., 35.

53. Ibid., 91.

54. Paul Redmayne, *The Gold Coast Yesterday and Today* (Cape Coast: Methodist Book Depot, 1941), 50.

55. Colin Flight, "The 'French Battery' at Elmina," *TheWest African Archaeological Newsletter* 10 (1968): 21.

56. Ibid.

57. Ibid, 22.

58. Redmayne, *The Gold Coast Yesterday and Today*. 51; Feinberg, *Africans and Europeans in West Africa*, 27; Blake, *Europeans inWest Africa* I, 73; Claridge, *History of the Gold Coast and Ashanti*, 47.

59. Hyland, *The Castles of Elmina*, 3.

60. Scholars do not agree that Kwamena Ansa and Caramansa are indeed one and the same person and that he was the Elmina chief who dealt with the Portuguese in 1481; Feinberg, *Africans and Europeans inWest Africa*, 28; Feinberg, "Elmina, Ghana: A History of Its Development and Relationship With the Dutch," 15; Blake, *Europeans inWest Africa*, I, 73; Claridge, *History of the Gold Coast and Ashanti*, 47; Hyland, *The Castles of Elmina*, 3.

61. Redmayne, *The Gold CoastYesterday andToday*, 51; Albert van Dantzig, *Forts and Castles of Ghana* (Accra: Sedco Publishing, 1980), 5, 28.

62. Van Dantzig, *Forts and Castles of Ghana*, 3, 9.

63. Redmayne, The Gold Coast Yesterday and Today, 51.

64. Information about local plaster, mortar and wood for construction was provided by local guides such as Mr. Atta Yawson (Fort Amsterdam) and also at Fort St. Anthony at Axim.

65. See for example, Daaku and van Dantzig, "Map of the Regions of Gold Coast in Guinea, Map 743 of the Leupen Collection, the Hague, 25th December 1629," 14.

66. Van Dantzig, Gold Coast Forts and Castles, 6.

67. Ibid.

68. Ibid., 6; Hyland, The Castles of Elmina, 3.

69. Ibid., 6.

70. See Van Dantzig, Forts and Castles of Ghana, 10, fn. 4.

71. Claridge, History of the Gold Coast and Ashanti, 58.

72. Ibid.

73. Ibid.

74. Ibid.; Hyland, Castles of Elmina, 5.

75. Hyland, Castles of Elmina, 5.

76. See for example, H. Morse Stephens, "Introduction," in Waldemar Westergaard, The Danish West Indies Under Company Rule 1671-1754 (New York: Mcmillan, 1917), xix-xx.

77. Lawrence, Trade Castles and Forts, 46; Hyland, Castles of Elmina, 6.

78. David Birmingham, "The Regimento da Mina," Transactions of the Historical Society of Ghana XI; See also Nathan, "The Gold Coast at the End of the Seventeenth Century Under the Danes and Dutch," Journal of African Society, 13, 4 (1904): 15; Hyland, The Castles of Elmina, 6.

79. Birmingham, "The Regimento da Mina," 2.

80. Vogt, "Portuguese Gold Trade: An Account Ledger From Elmina, 1529-1531," Transactions of the Historical Society of Ghana, 14, 1, (June 1973) : 96-97.

81. Birmingham, "The Regimento da Mina," 1; Nathan, "The Gold Coast Under the Danes and Dutch," 15; Hyland, The Castles of Elmina, 6.

82. Birmingham, "The Regimento da Mina," 1-2; Hyland, Castles of Elmina, 7.

83. Birmingham, "Regimento da Mina," 2; Hyland, Castles of Elmina, 7.

84. Birmingham, "Regimento da Mina," 2.

85. Ibid., 2-3; Hyland, Castles of Elmina, 6-7.

86. Vogt, "Portuguese Gold Trade: An Account Ledger From Elmina, 1529-1531," 96; Nathan, "The Gold Coast Under the Danes and Dutch,"15.

87. Feinberg Africans and Europeans in West Africa, 28.

88. Redmayne, The Gold Coast Yesterday and Today, 51; Claridge, History of the Gold Coast and Ashanti, 57-58.

89. Claridge, History of the Gold Coast and Asante, 57-58.

90. Hyland, *Castles of Elmina*, 7.

91. Cave, *Gold Coast Forts*, 4.

92. Nathan, "The Gold Coast Under the Danes and Dutch," 16.

93. Ivor Wilks, "A Medieval Trade-Route from the Niger to the Gulf of Guinea," 337-341; Wilks, *Forests of Gold*, 1-39.

94. David Birmingham, "The Regimento da Mina," 1; Vogt, "Portuguese Gold Trade: An Account Ledger From Elmina," 94.

95. Vogt, "Portuguese Gold Trade: An Account Ledger from Elmina," 94.

96. Birmingham, "The Regimento da Mina," 1.

97. Vogt, "Portuguese Gold Trade: An Account Ledger From Elmina," 94

98. Birmingham, "The Regimento da Mina," 1.

99. Ibid.

100. John Blake, *Europeans in West Africa*, (London: Hakluyt Society, 1942), 240; Vogt, "Portuguese Gold Trade: An Account Ledger From Elmina," 94.

101. A manilla is a bracelet or anklet of metal that served as currency in the Gold Coast until the early twentieth century.

102. Value of reis – 1 reis was roughly £10-£3.

103. Value of milreis is £10-£13.

104. Birmingham, "The Regimento da Mina," 4.

105. Vogt, "Portuguese Gold Trade: An Account Ledger From Elmina," 94

106. Birmingham, "The Regimento da Mina," 4.

107. Ibid.

108. Ibid.

109. Lawrence, *Trade Castles and Forts*, 276.

110. Claridge, *History of the Gold Coast and Ashanti*, 59.

111. Lawrence, *Trade Castles and Forts*, Fn 1, 280.

112. J. Barbot in Lawrence, *Trade Castles and Forts*, 274.

113. Ibid., 174.

114. Lawrence, *Trade Castles and Forts*, 230.

115. Ibid., 229.

116. Ibid., 234.

117. Claridge, *History of the Gold Coast and Ashanti*, 58-59; Lawrence, *Trade Castles and Forts*, 234.

118. Lawrence, *Trade Castles and Forts*, 231.

119. Claridge, *History of the Gold Coast and Ashanti*, 58-59.

120. Lawrence, *Trade Castles and Forts*, 231.

121. Lawrence, *Trade Castles and Forts*, 231.

122. Ibid., 229.

123. Ibid., 230.

124. Ibid., 231.
125. Ibid.
126. Ibid., 235-6.
127. Claridge, *History of the Gold Coast and Ashanti*, 99-100.
128. Claridge, *History of the Gold Coast and Ashanti*. 99-100.

✥ Chapter 4

The Dutch Global Enterprise and the Atlantic Slave Trade: Slave Fort and Castle Construction

The Dutch period on the Gold Coast covered an important conjuncture in Gold Coast history. On the global front, the "golden age" of the Dutch Republic was inextricably linked with the Atlantic slave trade; the great Dutch commercial powerhouses – the Dutch East India Company (1602) and the Dutch West India Company (1621) – all flourished at this time. Side by side with this flourishing commercial explosion, the exploits of sailors who braved the seas to carve out a niche for the nascent state of Holland expanded the reach of this tiny nation to all corners of the globe and set in motion what would become intense competition with England for global supremacy. Second, on the international scene, Dutch commercial supremacy on the Gold Coast became evident just as a corresponding decline of Portuguese hegemony globally, concomitant with a qualitative decline in the gold trade on the Gold Coast, took place. Dutch commercial supremacy on the "Guinea" coast and, to some extent on the global scene, was fueled by the trade in enslaved Africans.

Following the Portuguese example, the Dutch became major carriers of enslaved Africans in the early stages of the development of the Atlantic slave trade. However, English rivalry eventually undermined the Dutch supremacy to the extent that after the abolition of the slave trade in 1807 the Dutch were left with "a few crumbling forts, ill equipped and undermanned (if manned at all), an inadequate staff, demoralized when it had the right to engage in private trade and impoverished when it was without it."[1] However, São Jorge da Mina remained without a doubt a formidable structure right up to the end of the Dutch period in the Gold Coast. By the early nineteenth century, trade, the *raison d'etre* of the Dutch enterprise on the Gold Coast, brought in a deficit balance as the British in part disrupted Dutch commercial activities and cut into profits. The Dutch eventually gave up the headquarters of the Dutch Gold Coast trade, São Jorge da Mina, in 1867, and with that the profitable Dutch-Asante trade.

This chapter examines the rationale for Dutch arrival on the Gold Coast, the Dutch takeover of Portuguese fortifications on the coast and the emergence of São Jorge da Mina as the headquarters of the Dutch commercial enterprise. It discusses Dutch competition with the Portuguese and the English, the resultant slave forts and castle construction, the departure of the Portuguese and the rehabilitation of captured Portuguese forts, the Dutch participation in the Atlantic slave trade and their eventual departure from the Gold Coast.

THE DUTCH REVOLT AGAINST SPAIN

From 1568, the ten provinces of the Netherlands or the Low Countries fought against Philip II (1556-1598) of Spain for independence from the centralization policies of the king and his fierce determination to enforce Catholicism and punish heresy. More important, his arbitrary rule, contrary to his solemn promises not to infringe on the ancient rights, privileges and customs of the seventeen provinces of the Burgundian, and later, the Spanish Netherlands, led to rebellion.[2] The harsh policies of Philip's military commander in the Netherlands, the Duke of Alva (1507-1582), only strengthened the determination of the United Provinces to break away from Spain.[3] In 1581 the northern provinces (which united to become Holland) voted to depose Philip II and several military expeditions sent by the latter to conquer the northern provinces and unite the southern provinces failed.

In 1581, the Portuguese and Spanish crowns were merged and, by implication, the rebellious United Netherlands faced two enemies: Spain and Portugal. As a result, the Dutch were excluded from all Spanish and Portuguese ports and Dutch commercial activities were badly affected. The Dutch took to the sea in search of new ports, sometimes with the help of sea-tested "rogue" or interloper Portuguese and Spanish sea captains, and also intensified their rivalry against the Portuguese and attacked the latter's holdings, including Portuguese fortified stations on the Gold Coast.[4]

Flemish and Dutch navigators, like their Portuguese counterparts, were involved in the early exploration of the West African coast. While the Portuguese crown was encouraging Portuguese mariners in the voyages to the West African coast, it also granted concessions to Flemish captains in the Azores in the early 1460s and four years after the Portuguese arrived on the Gold Coast, Flemish ships were also participating in Gold Coast trade. However, the Portuguese secured a monopoly and thus squelched Dutch-Flemish participation in Gold Coast trade at this early date.[5] The Dutch turned their attention elsewhere and the revolt against Spain kept them very busy for a long time before any maritime ventures to the Gold Coast were undertaken again.

From the 1590s Dutch ships began to embark on voyages of exploration and trade to other lands, following a trail blazed by Prince Henry the Navigator and the Portuguese. A Dutch sailor, Barend Erickszon, opened the channel for Dutch trade on the Gold Coast when his expedition, destined for Brazil, inadvertently sailed to the Gold Coast and later landed on the islands of Principé and São Tomé.[6] Imprisoned by the Portuguese and later released, Erickszon returned to Holland in 1593, fitted out a ship and returned to the Gold Coast to trade. The profitable cargo of gold and other products that Erickszon took to Holland paved the way for the sustained Dutch trading enterprise on the Gold Coast.[7] Thus, by 1598 there were about twenty-five Dutch ships trading on the Gold Coast, largely in gold, but also in other products. In the wake of the protracted war with Spain, no concerted Gold Coast policy was charted by the government of the Netherlands at the time.

The United Provinces succeeded in breaking away from Spain with the signing of the Truce of 1609 (which lasted from 1609 to1621), and four decades later, the Treaty of Westphalia (1648). The Treaty of Westphalia ended the religious wars that had plagued Europe as a result of the Counterreformation and ushered in a period of peace, religious toleration and commercial and political expansion. Spain also granted the Netherlands *de jure* independence by the treaty.[8] It is in this context that the Dutch Republic came into its own (later given the name Holland even though Holland used to be one of the fourteen provinces that made up the United Provinces). In the resultant development and growth of the Dutch Republic – a period described by some historians as the golden age of the Dutch Republic – Dutch mercantile operation touched all corners of the globe. During this period of Dutch global mercantile enterprise, Dutch merchants traded to the Gold Coast, buying pepper, ivory and gold. More important, however, the capture of Dutch Brazil and the introduction of sugar cultivation necessitated availability of a large supply of labor. This forced the Dutch to be more aggressive in acquiring a foothold on the Gold Coast and a large number of enslaved Africans for Dutch Brazil and other Dutch possessions in the New World. The Dutch also supplied other European nations such as Portugal and Spain with the labor needs of their plantations and mines in the New World.[9]

Dutch interest in the Gold Coast occurred in three phases. In phase one, a Dutch captain *en route* to Brazil, as already pointed out, lost his way and ended up on the Gold Coast in 1596. The Portuguese imprisoned this Dutch interloper but the captain, Barend Erickszon, eventually went back to Holland with a sizable amount of gold and other goods.[10] In phase two, a Dutch ship sailed past the Cape of Good Hope *en route* to the Far East and carried spices to Europe in a venture that proved to be very profitable. In phase three, the Dutch chartered the United East India Company (EIC) in 1602, and in 1609, the United Provinces and Spain signed a truce. In 1621, the Dutch set up the West India Company (WIC) as an instrument of colonization and commerce through conquest and gave it control over West African trade.[11] In 1674, the WIC was reorganized and the new company functioned on the Gold Coast until 1791.

THE DUTCH AND THE SLAVE TRADE

The writings of Dutchmen in the service of Portuguese and Spanish kings, such as Pieter de Marees, Jan Huyghen van Linschoten, Pieter van den Broecke and Dierick Ruiters, about their work in the Portuguese colonial empire provided a valuable blueprint for the Dutch as they charted an early global colonial policy.[12] In spite of the initial Dutch reticence in participating in the slave trade, which they considered odious commerce, the demand for labor for sugar cultivation in Dutch Brazil gradually broke down the moral and, to a limited extent, economic resistance to Dutch participation in the trade in enslaved Africans. Consequently, the Dutch West India Company became involved in the slave trade in spite of the protestations of eminent voices including those of Willem Usselincx, a proponent of the founding of the WIC and Hugo Grotius, the renowned Dutch jurist.[13] Proponents of enslavement in Holland, like other apologists for slavery, used Biblical passages, especially Noah's curse of Ham to justify enslaving Africans.[14]

Dutch participation in the slave trade initially took the form of piracy and occasional attacks and occupation of Spanish and Portuguese possessions. For example, 2,356 enslaved Africans were captured by the Dutch and sold for an average price of 250 florins in America between 1623 and 1637.[15] However, the formation of the Dutch West India Company in 1621 changed everything, albeit not for about a decade. War with Spain and Portugal was resumed at this time and a profitable contraband sugar trade with Brazil was affected by the war. In 1628 the Dutch Admiral Piet Heyn captured most of the Spanish treasure fleet sailing with gold, silver coin and tropical produce from Havanna, Cuba, to Spain and used the loot to carry out a large-scale attack on Brazil. In the resultant attack, the Dutch captured part of Brazil and later, New York (New Amsterdam) between 1630 and 1635.[16] The possession of the new colony of Brazil spurred on a system of Dutch exploitation of the African slave trade, since seizure of Portuguese and Spanish ships proved woefully inadequate in supplying labor for the sugar plantations. After the seizure of São Jorge da Mina the Dutch slave trade started in earnest. Between 1636 and 1645 they shipped over 25,000 enslaved Africans to Brazil.[17] In this initial phase, as table 4.1 shows, half of the enslaved Africans in the Dutch slave trade came from West Africa, largely from the Gold Coast.

Table 4.1: Distribution of Enslaved Africans Bought in Guinea According to Region of Embarkation, 1637-1645

Region	Slaves	**Region**	**Slaves**
Gold Coast	238	Bight of Benin	611
Mouree	285	Calabari	2461
El Mina	1,059	Rio del Rey	
Accra	139	Cameroon	432
Total	1,721	Total	3504

Source: Ernst van den Boogart and Peter C. Emmer, "The Dutch Participation in the Atlantic Slave Trade, 1590-1650," in *The Uncommon Market. Essays in the Economic History of the Atlantic Slave Trade*, ed., Henry A. Gemery and Jan S. Hogendorn (New York: Academic Press, 1979), 360. Boogart and Emmer collected the data from OWIC 51-71, especially from communication between Dutch agents on the West African coast to the Council in Brazil and from the Council in Brazil to the *Heren XIX*.

In the period 1637-1645 the Dutch were very active on the Gold Coast. They built Fort Nassau (Moree) and Fort Crevecoeur (Accra), rebuilt a trade lodge at Komenda (1638), dislodged the Portuguese from Elmina (1637) and seized Fort São Antonio (Axim) in 1641. It is very likely that the figures from the "Gold Coast" region in table 4.1 derives from enslaved Africans from the Dutch forts in places such as Shama, Komenda, Anomabu and Butri.

Angola initially supplied the other half of the labor needs of Dutch Brazil, but later on, the Gold Coast supplied twice as many slaves as Angola. Between 1642 and 1645, the Dutch shipped an average of 4,000 enslaved Africans a year to Dutch Brazil[18] (see Table 4.2) The numbers increased significantly after this period.

After Portuguese planters rose in revolt against Dutch colonial authority in 1645, the Dutch began to look for new opportunities on the English Caribbean Islands. From 1650, the initial stream of Irish, English and French Huguenot and other migrants to the Caribbean Islands began to decline, paving the way for Dutch shipment of enslaved Africans to the Caribbean.[19] Demand for labor in the French and English Caribbean colonies for tobacco, cocoa, cotton and indigo had originally been met with indentured servants from Europe (especially in Barbados) but the supply of labor dried up after 1650, largely due to negative feedback that filtered back to Europe. From 1650 onward therefore, enslaved Africans began to arrive in the Caribbean in large numbers.[20]

The Dutch and the English (especially from the time of the Navigation Act in 1651) began to supply large numbers of enslaved Africans to the Caribbean. However, when French minister Colbert banned Dutch traders from the French colonies, the Dutch colony of Curaçao became an important transit point for enslaved Africans. Between 1658 and 1730, 100,000 enslaved Africans were shipped via Curaçao to Spanish America.[21] Thus, at a time when Spanish slave traders were not allowed to operate freely (especially between 1500 and 1640, when the Casa de Contratación in Seville regulated trade with Spanish America) the Dutch filled the vacuum. Spanish slavers, especially after 1662, picked up enslaved Africans from Curaçao for onward shipment to Portobello, Cartagena and Vera Cruz. Many ended up in the silver mines of Peru with the WIC shipping about half of the 3,000-4,000 enslaved Africans and the Royal African Company supplying the other half.[22]

Table 4.2: Dutch Slave Trade – Slave Departures

Years	Total slaves	West Africa (two-thirds of total)	Bight of Benin
1630-1674	70,000	46,200	-
1675-1680	18,302	12,079	-
1630-1680	-	-	39,000
1681-1690	15,437	10,188	10,188
1691-1700	23,155	15,282	15,282
1701-1710	23,822	15,723	12,500
1711-1720	23,624	15592 13,700	
1721-1730	32,639	21,542	8,400
1731-1740	47,794	31,544	8,600
1741-1750	55,243	36,460	-
1751-1760	51,350	33,891	500
1761-1770	62,921	41,528	-
1771-1780	40,300	26,598	600

Source: Patrick Manning, "The Slave Trade in the Bight of Benin, 1640-1890," in The Uncommon Market: Essays in the Economic History of the Atlantic Slave Trade, ed., Henry A. Gemery and Jan S. Hogendorn (New York: Academic Press, 1979), 140. Most of the data are from Postma, "Dimension," 240.

Table 4.3: Value of Slaves

Years	Slave Departures from Africa	% of slaves leaving from West Africa	Slave Departures from West Africa	Average Coastal Price, Pounds	Value of slaves leaving from West Africa, Pounds
1701-1710	457,000	74	339,000	12.6	4,271,400
1711-1720	483,000	81	391,000	16.8	6,568,800
1721-1730	440,000	71	312,000	14.2	4,430,400
1731-1740	580,000	65	377,000	20.2	7,615,400
1741-1760	1,316,000	60	790,000	17.7	13,983,000
1761-1770	753,000	66	497,000	20.0	9,940,000
1771-1776	760,000	60	456,000	21.0	9,576,000
1777-1780	400,000	60	240,000	11.4	2,736,000
1781-1790	1,050,000	48	504,000	29.1	14,666,400
1791-1800	800,000	43	344,000	25.3	8,703,200
Total	**4,249,000**				**79,754,600**

Source: Henry A. Gemery and Jan S. Hogendorn, "The Economic Costs of West African Participation in the Atlantic Slave Trade: A Preliminary Sampling for the Eighteenth Century,"
in *The Uncommon Market: Essays in the Economic History of the Atlantic Slave Trade*, ed. Henry A.
Gemery and Jan S. Hogendorn (New York: Academic Press, 1979), 156.

Table 4.4: Slave Mortality at Various Stages of the Dutch Slave Trade from West Africa

Ship	Year	Cargo	MP		Africa Coast	America
			DEATHS	COAST		
Graf van Laarwijk	1701	488	150	91	-	-
De Son	1703	513	134	-	-	-
Vriendschap	1704	393	72	23	7	-
Quinera	1706	547	?	45	-	-
Justitia	1707	740	152	48	9	1
Catharina Christina	1709	509	?	50	-	-
Amsterdam	1710	520	?	30	-	-
Carolus Secondus	1710	510	32	18	0	-
St. Clara	1710	517	?	17	-	-
Akredam	1713	596	?	51	-	-
Guntersteyn	1715	541	?	29	-	-
Duynvliet	1723	340	27	-	-	49
Akredam	1725	643	32	-	2	3
Amsterdam	1726	466	178	14	-	12

| Ship | Year | Cargo | MP | | Africa Coast | America |
			Deaths	Coast		
Leusden	1727	748	66	25	-	10
Beekesteyn	1733	866	?	57	-	-
Rusthof	1734	716	345	Many	-	43
Beschutter	1735	768	?	13	-	-
Stad en Lande	1735	760	349	Many	-	34
Jonge Daniel	1736	469	58	1	-	5

Source: Johannes Postma, "Mortality in the Dutch Slave Trade, 1675-1795," in *The Uncommon Market. Essays in the Economic History of the Atlantic Slave Trade*, ed. Henry A. Gemery and Jan S. Hogendorn (New York: Academic Press, 1979), 246.

THE DUTCH ON THE GOLD COAST: SUSTAINED PRESENCE

By early seventeenth century, the Dutch were the most enterprising traders on the Gold Coast (Table 4.2 and 4.3). But the Dutch presence grew from the mid to late sixteenth century. The New World demand for slaves at this time fueled and drove Dutch trade. The Dutch capture of Portuguese Brazil and other colonial possessions resulted in a demand for labor to exploit and develop these colonies. This occurred at a time of "New World" discoveries and the need for labor for plantations (sugar, cotton, tobacco etc.) and mines. Therefore, Dutch trade in slaves to the Gold Coast grew in response to this demand. After 1595, the Dutch built two forts, Nassau at Moree and later Batenstein at Butri to the east and west of the Portuguese stronghold of Elmina. In 1637, an expedition from Brazil led by Count Maurice of Nassau captured the Portuguese stronghold of São Jorge da Mina after earlier failures in 1596, 1615 and 1625. These activities constitute the stages in the struggle for hegemony on the West African coast and culminated in the Dutch expulsion of the Portuguese from the Gold Coast. After dislodging the Portuguese from the Gold Coast, the Dutch tried to maintain their own monopoly and insisted that Portuguese merchants pay tax at Elmina for permission to trade on the Gold Coast.[24] 1n 1645 the Dutch had five forts at Moree, Elmina, Shama, Axim and Accra. By 1700 they had eleven forts and by 1725, when the Brandenburgers left the Gold Coast, Dutch holdings tallied up to fifteen forts, and a considerable number of enslaved Africans were shipped from these forts (Table 4.4).

Table 4.5: Expenditure Incurred on Repairs, Maintenance and Consumption in the Different Administrations, and on the Forts on the Coast of Guinea in 1810

The Hospital	426. 7
Lighting – Governor's Residence & guards at forts at Elmina	1,682. 10
Day and Night Shots	2,600
Sunday Custom	732
Maintenance of Elmina Castle and artillery	6,532. 15. 12
Palm Oil	40
Canoe hire: Canoemen	1,657
Rum for Canoemen	480
Making of Flags for the Quarters &c.	102. 10
Pensions for Wounded Natives	462. 10
Rum consumed at Store (Factory: Store)	80
Presents and expenses to the Embassy from the King of Ashantee	625
Expenses of Garden	96
Bedsheets given at confinement of Government Slave Women	8. 12. 8
King's Birthday Custom	1,740
Dinner	320
New Year Custom	1,076. 12. 8
Dinner	320
Yam Custom	49. 2
Government Interpreter or Servant	360
Steward and Umbrella Carrier	480
Office necessaries	488. 56
Military Clothing and Equipment	5,185. 10. 14
Ammunition	1,082
Armory	87. 10

	DOMESTIC EXPENDITURE	MAINTENANCE OF FORT	
Axim	177. 10	22. 8	199. 18
Hollandia	7. 10	-	7. 8
Akwadae (Akwida)	7. 10	-	7. 8
Butri	119. 9	58. 4	177. 13
Sekondi	77. 10	46. 0	123. 10
Shama	71. 2	11. 5	82. 7
Accra	67. 10	50. 17 8 $^{24}/_{35}$	118. 7. 8$^{24}/_{35}$
			f 25,755. 12. 4
	Extraordinary Expenditure		3,026. 13. 8
			f 28,782. 5. 12

Source: *Journal and Correspondence of H.W. Daendels Governor-General of the Netherlands Settlements on the Coast of Guinea* (Legon: Institute of African Studies, University of Ghana, 1964), 74-75.

During the early phase of the Dutch trade to the Gold Coast, the major commodities were textiles, guns, powder, metal ware and alcoholic drinks in exchange for gold, ivory, slaves and, to a lesser extent, pepper and lemon juice.[25] Cognizance is taken of the fact that in as much as treaties between coastal Gold Coast rulers and Europeans purportedly gave the latter monopoly right, the former insisted on what they perceived to be their rights – the right to trade with the people of any nation that was interested in trade on the Gold Coast. This resulted in shifting alliances, dumping of old friends for new ones and local people siding with one European nation against another. This is the context in which the Asebu allied with the Fante and the English against the Dutch and Elmina between 1738 and 1740.[26]

While the Portuguese were the first to build castles, forts and lodges on the Gold Coast (São Jorge da Mina, São Sebastiao, and São Antonio), beginning with Elmina in 1482 in defense of their trading monopoly along the West African coast, French, English and Dutch ships came to trade in what was supposed to be a Portuguese monopoly, backed by papal sanction, in the early sixteenth century.

AT THE HEIGHT OF DUTCH TRADE ON THE GOLD COAST

From 1600 until the Anglo-Dutch exchange of forts in 1867, the Dutch arrived on the Gold Coast in larger numbers and became a very serious rival to the English. De Marees notes that the Dutch wars of independence against Spain resulted in the loss of the port of Lisbon and of profits accruing from Dutch redistribution of European manufactured goods. Consequently, Dutch merchants traded far and wide and to the source of tropical goods. On the Gold Coast, the Dutch exchanged large amounts of Silesian linen[27] (acquired through Baltic trade) and different types of basins – namely Neptunes, barbers' basins, cooking basins, Scottish pans.[28] They also sold large quantities of cauldrons (for carrying water from wells, streams and rivers as well as for storing water), copper stewing pots and iron (for making weapons for agriculture and for war). In addition, the Dutch exported red, blue and green cloth, Spanish serges (used like cloaks), red and yellow copper bangles, pewter bracelets, knives, Venetian beads of all colors, pins (for fish hooks), mirrors and small copper jugs among others, to the Gold Coast.[29] Sometimes, wealthy people in the interior sent their enslaved (domestic slaves) to the coastal towns with gold to purchase these items.

One major trade tactic of the Dutch on the Gold Coast was to undercut competitors. A meeting of the Director-General and Council at Elmina in November 1682 resolved that in order to do damage to the trade of ships of other Nations, which come steadily to do prejudice to the Noble Company, to reduce the price of French Brandy from 16 Angels 1 Ackie to 12 Angels and that of gunpowder from 2 oz to 1 oz 8 Angels.[30]

Similarly, in December of the same year (1602), another resolution reinforced the position above:

D-G and Council resolved, in the service of the Noble Company, the growth of its trade and in order to do damage to the trade of other Nations, to change the price of carbines from 20 Angels to 12 Angels a piece, that of long muskets from 7 to 8 Angels, and that of Brandy from 12 Angels to 10 Angels, 1 Ackie[31]

Furthermore, two years later in December 1684, the Director-General resolved that the Dutch should "buy for a reasonable price from a certain little Portuguese ship called *Nostra Signora de Monserva St. Anthonio*, arriving from Bahia, all the tobacco it has in its hold, on condition that its Captain pay before-hand 3,000 pounds of tobacco as a duty for the licence of free trade ..." and to "buy the remaining tobacco at 8 pounds per Angel, in the hope to sell it at 5 pounds per Angels to the English."[32] After the expulsion of the Portuguese from the Gold Coast in the 1640s, they tried to make a comeback at the end of the century, but with no permanent bases, they paid "recognition-duty" to the Dutch for the right to trade at some of the Dutch forts.

One major concern of the WIC officials at Elmina was the turnaround time for ships on what was considered a disease-ridden coastline at the time. In order to quickly supply return-freight to Dutch ships such as the *Ceurvorst van Brandenburgh* and *Eendragt* the Director-General and Council resolved that

It was considered necessary to set our market-prices in such a way, that the merchants from in-land may be enticed to come to sell their gold to the Noble Company and be diverted from trading with the English at Cabo Cors or on board English and other foreign ships such as the present one from Brandenburg in particular, or the interlopers who continue their prejudicial competition. Resolved to put the bedsheets at the same price as do the English at Cabo Cors and that for which they are sold on board of the ships.[33]

In this way the WIC hoped to steer trade to Dutch forts in particular.

DUTCH PERSONNEL AND GOVERNMENT ON THE GOLD COAST

The Dutch West India Company (1621-1791) officials were concerned first and foremost with the promotion of trade in the interest of its directors. The DWIC was not necessarily a state enterprise and did not always act in the interest of the state except that the state provided its charter.[34] Its trade in the Gold Coast was largely based on gold as a standard of measurement and value. It was "based on the mark (MK), half pound weight of gold" which by 1700 was worth about 300 guilders (£30). In local currency this translated or converted to 4 bendas, or 8 ounces (oz, ø), or 128 Angels (Engels, ..)"[35]

Dutch operations in the Gold Coast were headed by the governor-general who was the commander-in-chief. A Royal Decree dated Brussels 27th July 1815, No. 30, for example stated that the "Governor General shall assume the supreme direction over the Netherlands Establishment on the coast of Guinea, as well as the military, civil and domestic affairs of what ever nature; and shall correspond with the Department of Trade and Colonies alone, on all that concerns the service of these establishments."[36] The governor-general commanded all military units (including naval forces) and was responsible for the defense of the Dutch possessions. He was responsible for admitting Dutchmen into the Dutch establishment and for granting permission to whites or mulattoes who wanted to settle and trade in the Dutch "territory" on the Gold Coast. He was to ensure that the "natives were treated well" and good relations were maintained with all Europeans who settled on the coast to trade. The governor-general was to preside over the Great Council (composed of all the officials up to the rank of First Resident), and meetings with local chiefs at the forts and settle complaints, disputes or breaches of agreement. Furthermore, he was responsible for ensuring the "undisturbed and orderly exercise of public worship," and the supervision, the protection and the instruction of the young, whether local or European.[37]

As the foremost Dutch official and president of the council, he had the power to punish wrongdoers according to law through confinement or some other means but he could not banish or expel Dutch officials from the Guinea coast. For those who deserved the death-penalty, he was to send them back to Holland with all the paperwork for trial.[38]

The governor-general was assisted by a number of officials. The second in rank was the chief merchant (*Oppercomis*), who presided over the council that assisted the governor in his duties. He was later given the title permanent vice president. He succeeded the director-general in case the latter died and was often stationed at Elmina or Fort São Antonio.[39] The other officials in order of rank were the *fiscal* or the chief judicial officer, the bookkeeper-general (in charge of the books and accounts), the commander of the Elmina Castle garrison, chief factors (*commiezen*) – often commanders of out-forts or chief traders in these forts, sub-factors (*onder commiezen*) – usually in charge of receiving most of the gold, assistants (*assistenten*) – lowest in rank of all the administrative personnel, and the chaplain of the Elmina Castle (*predicant*) (table 4.6).[40] This group of officials was assisted by a garrison in the castle and sailors on board ships (cruisers). Eric Tylleman asserts that the military officials included "a chief officer, two constables, two sergeants, three corporals, twelve gentlemen cadets, 150 common soldiers, and one 'profos' (Provost?)."[41] In addition to these, a large number of company slaves and coast men (*makelaers or brokers*) acted as go-betweens and mediated between the (WIC) officials and various African kingdoms. Lastly, there were the "*manceros*" or "young men" who served as the auxiliary military wing of the WIC and who fought periodically in the wars of the Dutch on the Gold Coast.[42]

Table 4.6: Dutch Officials and Their Salaries - Submitted to Department of Trade and Colonies for Approval (1816)

H. W. Daendels	Governor General	f12,000
	Table money	6,000
A. Van Neck Vice President	Comptroller General & Fiscal	5,000
W. Starrenburg	Colonel, Engineer	3,000
F. C. E. Oldenburg	Commandant	2,600
I. G. Coorengel	1st Resident (Shama)	1,800
C 't Hoen	1st Resident (Accra)	1,800
A. H. Abeloos	2nd Resident (Shama)	1,200
R. Roelossen	2nd Resident (Butri)	1,200
P. Loo	2nd Resident (Sekondi)	1,200
J. Oosthout	2nd Resident (Sekondi)	1,200
A. Van Barneveld	2nd Resident	1,200
M. Carillon	Storekeeper	1,200
H. J. J Milet	Acting Secretary	2,400
M. A. Thurkow	Surgeon Major and for	2,500
	administration and medicines	600
M. J. Reinhout	Doctor of Medicine and Botanist	2,500
W. Huydecooper	1st Assistant	900
F. Last	1st Resident	900
C. G. Coorengel	1st Resident	900
C. H. Bartels	1st Resident	900
M. Brouwer	2nd Resident	600
F. Oosthout	2nd Resident	600
T.C. Van der Breggen Paauw	2nd Resident	600
T. Flusz	Factory Master	2,100

C. Schek	Timber-sawing Master	1,200
J. E. Da Costa	Quartermaster in the "Trein"	600
Jacob Van Dijk	Sail Master	120
Dirk Van Dijk	Carpenter	300
Wouter Van Hoften	Smith	300
Lodewijk Kunst	Agriculturist	300
Jacob Homburg	Gardener	300
J. Franzen	Pensioner	120
J. Down	Pensioner	120
J. Klerk	Pensioner	240
		f56,500

Source: *Journal and Correspondence of H. W. Daendels Governor-General of the Netherlands Settlements on the Coast of Guinea* (Legon: Institute of African Studies, University of Ghana, 1964), 73.

In sum, the Dutch officials and the merchants were the best paid of the staff and workers of the Dutch establishment on the Gold Coast in particular and the West African coast in general. They were the administrative personnel of the WIC. The director-general came from their ranks. They constituted 20 percent of Dutch personnel and carried on trade and supervised the company's operations on the West African coast.[43] Artisans constituted the second tier of officials on the Gold Coast. Composed of coopers, carpenters and bricklayers, they constituted about 20 percent of company employees. They were responsible for all repairs of company forts and boats on the Gold Coast.[44] The third tier [of officials] was composed of soldiers who formed the bulk of company employees on the Gold Coast, about 50 percent to 60 percent. Their major function was to protect company property, especially forts and castles, from the depredatory activities of other Europeans as well as from the local people.[45] At the bottom of the totem pole were the coast men and the company slaves who were responsible for cleaning, repair works and all kinds of labor necessary for the efficient running of the castle as a "ship at permanent anchor."

For better protection of the Dutch outposts on the Gold Coast, the Directors of the West India Company "meeting in the Assembly of Ten," directed in 1689, and it was agreed, that no Dutch outpost would be abandoned. Personnel decisions as shown in Table 4.7 and 4.8 were made.

Table 4.7: Personnel Decisions

Axim	30 Europeans (apart from slaves) with a sergeant in charge to keep discipline;
Akwadae	2 Europeans and 8 slaves;
Butri	10 Europeans and 10 slaves
Takoradi	1 European and 1 black man
Sekondi	5 Europeans and 15 slaves, most of them armed

Shama	18 Europeans apart from slaves
Komenda	move personnel
St. Jago & Elmina	maintain sufficient garrison – at least 200 men (St. Iago as Key to the coast)
Moree & Kormantin	25 men each – to be reinforced to 50 in case of an attack.
Accra	50 white men.[46]

Table 4.8: Proposed Reduction in Expenditure for Military Wages That Will Replace the Former Existing Kostgelden (1816)

1 Adjutant	@ £ 20 per month		240
6 Sergeants	@ £ 13 per month	each	936
9 Corporals	@ £ 11 per month	each	1,188
2 Drummers	@ £ 8 per month	each	192
2 Pipers	@ £ 8 per month	each	192
32 Soldiers	@ £ 8 per month	each	3,072
65 Soldier Gov't Slaves	@ £ 7 per month	each	3,780
1 European Pensioned	@ £ 10 per month	each	120
4 Tapoejers pensioned	@ £ 5 per month	each	240
			£ 9,960

THE DUTCH AND GOLD COAST FORTS AND CASTLES

Fort Nassau

In the period before 1600 Dutch ships sent to the Gold Coast by private ship owners and small companies were often chased off the coast by Portuguese carriers determined to keep Gold Coast trade in Portuguese hands. For Dutch merchants to actively participate in Gold Coast trade, which was considered of vital importance to Dutch interests, a more serious attempt was made to break the Portuguese monopoly and secure a foothold on the Gold Coast. This was achieved through the construction of Dutch forts, often in proximity to Portuguese forts. In 1611, an Asebu chief, a Dutch commercial partner, requested the Dutch to construct a permanent stronghold on the Gold Coast in his area (Dutch-Moree contacts dated from 1599). In 1612, "the Admiralty of Amsterdam sent one Calantius with several carpenters and masons on board a ship loaded with a great quantity of bricks to start the construction of the first Dutch fort on the Gold Coast at Mori."[47]

This first Dutch fortification built in 1612 at Moree, named after the Stadtholder, Count Maurice of Nassau, was located fairly close to the Portuguese stronghold of São Jorge da Mina (Figure 4.1). With the construction of Fort Nassau, the Dutch obtained their first foothold on the Gold Coast and used it as a beachhead to construct several forts along the coast. More important, however, was the fact that it gave them a stronghold from which they could challenge Portuguese hegemony along the entire West African coast. Moree was an important trading station for the Dutch. In an assessment of Dutch fortification half a century after the construction of Fort Nassau, Heerman Abramsz noted that

> Moure is one of the best trading places for us as well as for the Acannists and other merchants, because through the land of Sabou, which is situated next to it, they go straight to Atty [Etsii], which belongs to the Acannists, and then further up to Accanien. We must therefore maintain our fort there.[48]

Cognizant that the Portuguese might prevent or interrupt the construction of the fort, the structure was hurriedly built with large quantities of bricks brought directly from Holland in much the same way the Portuguese had constructed Sao Jorge da Mina. One needs not overstate the significance of the Dutch use of bricks in constructing this first Dutch Gold Coast fort. Brick building was the norm in Holland and Dutch masons used the same material for this fort in the Gold Coast. However, the hot tropical climate, coupled with the constant sea breeze and sea salt that sprayed the structure, made the fort wholly unsuitable for the Gold Coast. By using bricks and failing to adapt brick construction to the hot tropical climate and a building near the sea, the Dutch built a high structure "much after Northern European fashion and [it] always remained particularly notorious for its unhealthy atmosphere and foul stagnant air."[49] A large number of Dutch personnel lay buried at Fort Nassau, and consequently, the fort was considered the "Dutch Churchyard."[50]

Fort Nassau served as the headquarters of Dutch commercial operations on the Gold Coast until the conquest of Sao Jorge da Mina in 1637. The fort "had four bastions mounting eighteen cannon and the normal garrison was seventy to eighty men ... it also had four towers."[51] Fort Nassau was expanded into a nearly square building with very high walls and a square tower at each corner. The building mounted eighteen guns on four batteries. The entrance gate into the fort was furnished with a drawbridge and defended by a loop-holed gallery[52] (Photo 4.1 and 4.2).

A very large garrison was maintained in Fort Nassau because it was the Dutch headquarters. The number of Dutch troops was, however, reduced after 1637 when the Dutch headquarters was moved to São Jorge da Mina Castle, Elmina.[53] The Danish official, Eric Tylleman, observed that in the 1690s Fort Nassau was "fortified with 22 cannon, and occupied by one chief factor, one underfactor, two assistants, one barber, one sergeant, one

Figure 4.1: Fort Nassau

Photo 4.1: Fort Nassau
Courtesy: National Archives, Kew, England.

Photo 4.2: Fort Nassau – Guard room
Courtesy: National Archives, Kew, England.

corporal, one constable, four gentleman cadets, one drummer, and 20 common soldiers, besides natives."[54]

The new West India Company took over the new fort in 1621. From this small fort at Moree, the Dutch gradually expanded their area of operation to Anomabu to the west and toward the Portuguese possessions to the east. This extended the Dutch sphere of operation and climaxed the Dutch period on the Gold Coast with the capture of Brazil, and most important, the Portuguese fortress of São Jorge da Mina. In 1596, 1619, and 1625, as already pointed out, the Dutch launched attacks on the Portuguese stronghold of São Jorge da Mina and failed miserably. In 1637, spurred on by the need for large numbers of enslaved Africans for their new sugar colony of Dutch Brazil, the Dutch launched a more effective attack on São Jorge da Mina from St. Iago Hill and bombarded the north side of the castle with heavy guns. The Dutch attack was led by Colonel Coine and consisted of about one thousand European soldiers and many African troops (some from Elmina). The Portuguese garrison in the castle consisted of a little more than thirty European troops but were supported by a large force of the well-trained Elmina men, the *manceros*.[55] The Dutch attack on the Portuguese headquarters, Sao Jorge da Mina, is forever etched (in capital letters) in stone in the plaque below:

Plaque Commemorating the Attack

ILLUSTRISSIMO AC GENEROSISSIMO MAURITIO
NASSQUIAE COMITE BRASILIAM GUBERNANTE
KOINIO TRIBUNO IMPERANTE OCCUPATA FUIT
VI HAEC FORTISSIMA ARX QUA TRIDUO ANNO
MDCXXXVII DIE XX QIR AUGUSTI.

While the most distinguished and noble Count
Maurice of Nassau was Governor of Brazil, this
very strong fortress was taken by force under
the leadership of Colonel Coine after three
days (fighting) on the 29th day of August 1637.

Source: ADM 23/1/341 S.R.J. Kinston, Assistant District Commissioner, Cape Coast to the Honourable, The Commissioner, Central Province, Cape Coast, 18th August, 1942. The translation was agreed to by S.R.J Kingston, Assistant District Commissioner, Cape Coast, Rev. Father Holland and Mr. Watson.

With concentrated canon fire from the landward side the Dutch eventually seized the castle and used it as a stepping stone to capture the two other Portuguese forts, São Sebastïao at Shama and São Antonio at Axim. And not only did the Dutch capture Axim from the Portuguese but they demanded that the people of Axim pay homage to them as conquerors. This attempt at "vassalage by conquest" claimed by the Dutch was met with considerable resistance by the people of Axim.[56] After capturing fort São Antonio at Axim, the Dutch sailed up the Ankobra and established three forts (including Fort Ruychaver), ostensibly as bases for a gold-mining operation. Due to local hostility, the Dutch were eventually driven back to the coast.

Stressing the importance of the slave trade, the Assembly of Ten included in a special memorandum and instructions to Heerman Abramsz, the director of the Second West India Company, that he should direct the factors to apply utmost diligence in acquiring enslaved Africans of good quality. They charged the director-general that "He should also admonish those who are charged with the transport of these slaves, to take proper care of them, whether they are healthy or sick … the surgeons should be well provided with medicines against the runs (dysentry) and other diseases."[57] Responding to the Assembly of Ten in Holland, Abramsz noted that given the importance of the slave trade, proper transportation of enslaved Africans was very necessary but "the sailors drink too much, and the ships are often short of crew. No proper care is taken of the slaves, and they are so badly treated, that those people become so angry (?) (*so na neemen*) that they don't eat and sorrow themselves to death."[58]

São Jorge da Mina (Elmina Castle)

After seizing São Jorge da Mina the Dutch started in earnest to reinforce the defenses of the castle. From 1637 onward, therefore, most of the additions to Elmina Castle were made on the north side, which had been damaged by the 1637 bombardment. The defenses of São Jorge da Mina were anchored by thirty-eight good brass cannon. In addition, there were smaller pieces of cannon and some iron guns on the lower battery, though not necessarily for the defense of the castle but for firing salutes.[59] The main entrance to the castle was heavily defended by a layer of defensive positions. First, there was the drawbridge, which could be pulled in times of war or crisis (Photo 4.3). The Dutch pulled the bridge several times during their war with the people of Elmina between 1638 and 1640 during the tenure of Director-General des Bordes.[60] The drawbridge was guarded or defended by a small redoubt that had eight iron guns trained on the bridge. There is also an iron porticullis that was in turn defended by four small pieces of brass sited within the gates of the castle.[61] All these defensive layers were put in place to ensure that no military force could easily fight its way through the gates and into the castle. The only other door to the castle was high up in the wall facing the river, and was used for carting goods in and out of the castle by means of a crane.[62]

The Dutch divided the moat on the western side of São Jorge da Mina into two (Photo 4.4). While it continued to be part of the defense system of the castle, the Dutch adopted a more utilitarian approach to its use. They used it as a reservoir for fresh water supply for odds and ends and for a fish farm – for fish and turtles. Water supply, especially fresh water, was of utmost concern to all the European officials in the various forts and castles. Each fort or castle administration ensured that an adequate supply of water was always available to the occupants. Thus, in addition to the moat, three large tanks or cisterns were constructed within the walls of São Jorge da Mina to collect rainwater through spokes and thus to ensure adequate water supply for the needs of the castle personnel (over one hundred Europeans, exclusive of officers and about one hundred Africans) as well as for ships that needed to replenish their water supply. The Dutch, fearing that the Portuguese had poisoned the water supply before they surrendered São Jorge da Mina in 1637, built a new water cistern to supply the castle's needs (Photo 4.5).[63]

The water supply system, together with provisions and everything else, was designed to make the castle a "ship at permanent anchor," and able to withstand an attack or a prolonged siege by a hostile European power or by the local people of the Gold Coast.[64]

Due to Dutch modifications to São Jorge da Mina after 1637, the castle compound took the form of a large quadrangle, surrounded by storehouses of stone and bricks. A long hall gave access to a long "gallery" leading to the governor's quarters (Photo 4.6).

The governor's quarters were located high up in the castle, specifically in what was an octagonal tower, and could be accessed only by a large "Staircase of black and white Stone, defended at the Top by two small Brass Guns and four Padereros [small swivel guns] of the same Metal, commanding the Place of Arms, and a Corps-de-Guard."[65] Befitting the status of its occupant, the governor's quarters consisted of several rooms and offices along the ramparts close to the sea with very tall windows to admit fresh air from the sea and protect its occupant from mosquitoes.

Whereas the Portuguese had built a church in the courtyard, the Dutch "constructed" a Chapel on the other side of the building away from the Governor's quarters and the mess hall/meeting rooms and on top of the male dungeon.

Photo 4.3: Drawbridge – Elmina Castle

Photo 4.4: Moat – Elmina Castle

Photo 4.5: Water Cistern, Sao Jorge da Mina

Photo 4.6: Governor's Quarters - Elmina Castle

Photo 4.7: Staircase (With Trapdoor) Leading to Governor's Residence

In reality, the Dutch transformed "The top floor of the western wing of the [castle]" into a Dutch Reformed Church and completely abandoned the large Portuguese church of St. George in the courtyard of the castle. The latter was then horizontally divided in two – the ground floor was used as "house of trade" (*huys van Negotie*) or slave auction hall[66] and the upper floor was turned into a dining room for soldiers. In one sense this was a practical innovation given the fact that there was a big chimney and an open kitchen on the left side of this structure for preparing food for the garrison.[67]

Daily and weekly prayers of the Dutch Reformed Church tradition were held at the new church. On the eastern wall of the church a plate with an inscription of Psalm 132 in Dutch and English: *Zion is des Heeren ruste / Dit is Syn woonplaetse in eeuwigheyt* (Zion is the Lord's resting place / This is His eternal habitation) is still visible (Photo 4.9).[68] In effect, the Dutch Reformed Church in São Jorge da Mina was the Lord's habitation. The only paradox was that the Dutch church sat atop the male dungeon in the São Jorge da Mina castle.

Given the very high mortality rate among Europeans in the Gold Coast at this time, an infirmary or hospital that could house about a hundred men at any particular time was sited along the ramparts on the River Benya side of the castle, next to a large tower overlooking the redoubt but mounting no guns.[69] About 1,879 Europeans working for the Dutch West India Company died between 1719 and 1760.[70]

Right outside the Elmina Castle is another significant Dutch signature addition to the structure that they had captured from the Portuguese. This was a brick compass made by Director General Heerman Abramsz (Photo 4.10). He wrote:

> Outside of the castle, in front of the gate, is a big square, on which it is difficult to walk, because of the unevenness of the rocks. I have leveled it and floored it with big square stones. I also made of yellow bricks a "sun-compass" similar to the one here in the yard of the Admiralty, in the center of which has been put a sun-dial. I also built across the entrance a royal gate of stone, without doors, which is every day guarded by soldiers, and is (also?) done by the natives with a lot of show and dances of their own manner.[71]

OTHER ADDITIONS TO SÃO JORGE DA MINA

After 1637 most of the repairs, renovations and reinforcements to São Jorge da Mina were made on the northern side of the building to repair the damage from the bombardment of 1637 and also to make the structure impregnable. The Dutch greatly improved São Jorge da Mina to secure their position in the new structure. A new bastion was built to replace the

Photo 4.8: Portuguese Church - São Jorge da Mina

Photo 4.9: Dutch Reformed Church with Inscription of Psalm 132

Photo 4.10: Sun-Dial/Sun-Compass in front of São Jorge da Mina

former "French bastion" and this was connected with the main building by a long gallery (turn right after passing over the drawbridge) hallway and heavy curtain walls[72](Photo 4.11). The reinforced castle enclosed a third courtyard, a large riverside yard (about 50 meters square) that was used as a big service yard for repair work. It boasted of carpentry shops, smithies, a bakery, pigsties, and chicken coops to supply eggs for the castle occupants.[73] The service yard was largely for repair work on the castle as well as for work on Dutch boats. The pigsties and chicken coops provided meat to supplement meat supplies from São Tomé and, to a limited extent, from the local people. This service yard was called also a *katteplaets* (cat yard) because, as Dutch soldier Michael Hemmersam put it, it was also used for rearing civet cats whose odorous secretion was used in the perfume industry.[74] The Dutch similarly kept ducks at Fort Amsterdam but in this case, while they supplied eggs for the fort, they acted as a sort of early warning system to the garrison in case of an enemy attack.[75] The ducks flapped their wings and caused a ruckus upon being disturbed and thus alerted the garrison to the presence of an intruder or intruders.[76]

The Dutch extended and improved the fortifications of the São Jorge da Mina castle to the extent that within a few years, the building underwent a dramatic transformation. Willem Bosman notes that Director-General William De La Palm added "four tower-like ornamental structures and some warehouses."[77] One of these towers on the sea-front side of *São Jorge da Mina* is known as Prempeh's rooms. The Prempeh tower has become one of the famous sections of the castle at Elmina. The Asantehene Prempeh I had strengthened the Asante Confederacy through a mixture of diplomacy and war between 1888 and 1896 after the British had defeated the Asante in 1874 and broken up the Asante Empire. Afraid of the restoration of the Asante Empire, the British dispatched an army to Kumasi under Sir Francis Scott and Baden Powell. Asantehene Prempeh counseled against resistance and surrendered to the British but the latter imprisoned him, his mother, who was also the queenmother, his father, his brother and a number of leading men of Asante in the towers of Elmina Castle in 1896. A year later, the British moved them to Sierra Leone and to the Seychelles Island on September 11, 1900.[78]

In addition to these changes, the Dutch also reconstructed the façade of the building in the main courtyard of São Jorge da Mina, and during the time of Director-General Pieter Valckenier, from 1723 to 1727, an arched portico and an iron balustrade were added[79](Photo 4.12)

Photo 4.11: Sao Jorge da Mina

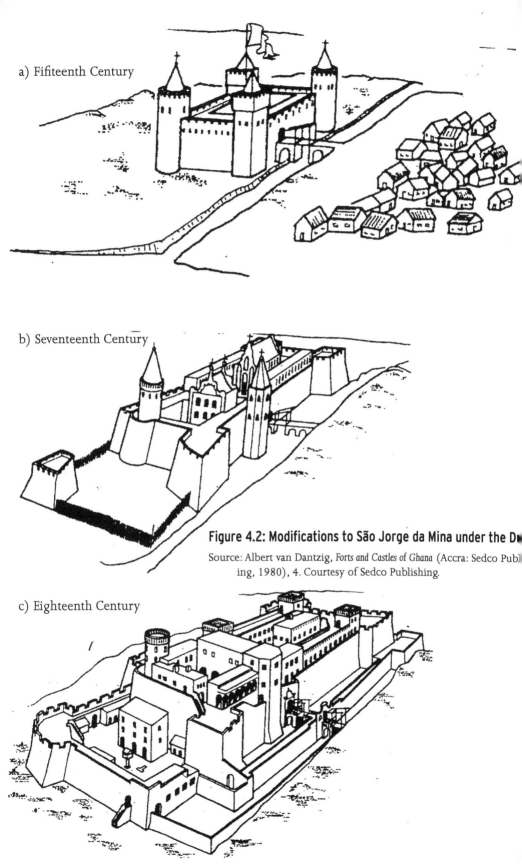

a) Fifteenth Century

b) Seventeenth Century

Figure 4.2: Modifications to São Jorge da Mina under the D[...]

Source: Albert van Dantzig, *Forts and Castles of Ghana* (Accra: Sedco Publ[...]ing, 1980), 4. Courtesy of Sedco Publishing.

c) Eighteenth Century

Photo 4.12: Arched portico, Iron Balustrade and Tomb

Directly below the platform that supported the new arched portico a tombstone chronicles the life of a Dutch official on the Gold Coast. The text on the upper part of the tombstone, insufficient to enable one to ascertain the full scope of his activities, highlights a very brief tour of duty of this Dutch official[80] (Figure 4.3)

Figure 4.3: Text on Tombstone – Courtyard, São Jorge da Mina

Grafsteen ingewerk in 'tkasteel <u>Elmina</u>
Goudkust. W. A.

HIER – RUST
MR. LAMBERT. JACOB VAN TETS
GEBOREN TE SAMARANG. N.O.I. 1717
VAN VEERE MITSGADERS BEWINDHEBBER
DER GEOCTROYEERDE WEST INDISCHE
COMPANIE TER KAMERE ZEELANDT
EN DE LAATS DIRECTEUR GENERAAL
OVER DE NOORD EN ZUYDKUST VAN AFRIKA
ALHIER AANGEKOMEN OP DEN 16de JANUARY
1758 EN OVERLEDEN DEN 12de MAART
DESSELVEN JAAR OUD SYNDE 41 JAREN
GRAF-SCHRIFT
MR. VAN TETS HIER NAAUW OELAND OF DOODT
RUST HY HIER IN VREE THANS LIGHTENSCHOOT
BEZIELD VAN 'T RECHT VAN D' EERLYKHEIT
DEN TOESCHHOUMER EER SYN KOUT GEBEENTE
GEWYD ZY HEM DIT GRAFF GESTEENTE
A.   ANDRIESSEN.
PREDIKANT TE VEERE.

Translation of the Tombstone Inscription at Elmina Castle

Gold Coast

HERE - RESTS
MR. LAMBERT JACOB VAN TETS
BIRTHPLACE - SAMARANG - DUTCH EAST INDIES

IN THE YEAR 1717
FROM <u>VEERE</u>, AND WAS ALSO ADMINISTRATOR
OF THE COMBINED WEST INDIA COMPANY
DISTRICT COUNTY ZEELANDT
AND THE LAST DIRECTOR GENERAL IN THE
NORTH AND SOUTH COAST OF AFRICA
ARRIVED HERE THE 16TH DAY OF JANUARY 1758
AND DIED ON THE 12TH DAY OF MARCH OF THE
SAME YEAR AT THE AGE OF 41 YEARS

EPITAPH

MR. VAN TETS DIED SHORTLY AFTER HIS ARRIVAL HERE
HE RESTS HERE IN PEACE BENEATH THE LAP OF THE EARTH
HIS UNTIMELY DEATH DEPLORED BY MANY WHO INSPIRED
WITH HIS JUSTICE, HONESTY AND FAIRNESS, DEEPLY
MOURNED HIS SACRED MEMORY BY THIS TOMBSTONE
ANDRIESSEN
REV. PREACHER AT <u>VEERE</u>

Source: ADM 23/1/341.

The Dutch also built a stone bridge, with a wooden drawbridge in its center, across the River Benya as part of the early defensive system around São Jorge da Mina. The bridge was specifically designed to control access to the castle. As well, the Dutch cut a wide road from the bridge to connect the new fort with the castle and thus enable them keep an eye on people who moved between the castle and the bridge.[81] Another battery was located on the River Benya side of the castle and mounted with six guns to protect or cover the road to the fort. The guns could also be turned on the castle if and when circumstances warranted it (as in the case of an enemy attack or any attempt to take the Dutch headquarters); a second, albeit smaller battery, was sited on another hill to provide additional fire power to protect the castle in case of need.[82]

Jean Barbot who visited Elmina Castle in 1682 noted that

> This castle has justly become famous for beauty and strength, having no equal on all the coasts of Guinea. Built square with very high walls of dark brown stone so very firm that it may

Photo 4.13: Canals on landside of São Jorge da Mina

Photo 4.14: Police Training at São Jorge da Mina
Source: National Archives, Kew

be said to be cannon-proof. On the land side it has two canals always furnished with rain or fresh water sufficient for the use of the garrison and the ships – canals cut in the rock by the Portuguese (by blowing up the rock little by little with gun-powder). The warehouses either for goods or provisions are very largely and stately always well furnished.[83]

By 1774, Sao Jorge da Mina had been completely transformed by the Dutch from its Portuguese imprint into an impregnable and architectural masterpiece. By that time, the structure had habitable accommodation of about 3,950 meters square within its walls. The enlarged accommodation was home to a garrison of two hundred men and the batteries mounted 48 brass cannon as well as other smaller guns, whilst the main gate was heavily defended.[84] On the land side of the fort canals were cut which augmented water supply from the three large fresh water tanks (Photo 4.13).

Storerooms and offices were also added to São Jorge da Mina together with special quarters for the gunner.[85] The refurbished castle included new buildings in the large riverside yard (50 meters square) which, as the Dutch soldier Michael Hemmersam put it, was designated for rearing civet cats for their odorous secretions.[86]

In 1872, São Jorge da Mina was ceded by the Dutch to Britain as part of the Anglo-Dutch exchange of forts. In the colonial period, it served as the barracks of the Gold Coast Constabulary or Hausa Constabulary, the frontier police force recruited and trained by the British to protect their new colony, and later as Police Recruitment and Training Center . Thereafter, it served as a prison, a hospital and a rest house.

In 1972 the Ghana Museums and Monuments Board took over Elmina and Cape Coast Castles and in the 1980s the two castles were designated World Heritage Sites by UNESCO. In the 1980s São Jorge da Mina's premises were utilized by the Edinaman Secondary School (Senior High School). Students from the University of Cape Coast were assigned to the school in the castle for their teaching practicum. Edinaman Senior High was moved out of São Jorge da Mina to its present site in the late 1990s.

FORT COENRAADSBURG (ELMINA)

Guns	Slaves	Servants

Hardly had the Dutch taken São Jorge da Mina than they set out not only to improve the defenses of the castle, but also, St. Iago Hill which they had utilized as a base for their conquest of the castle. After they strengthened the north-eastern part of São Jorge da Mina, the Dutch built a strong fort on the

Photo 4.15: Fort Coenraadsburg (Elmina)

summit of Iago hill in 1638. This was the only Gold Coast fort built like a military barracks. A stone tablet above the gate near the entrance attributes Fort Coenraadsburg's construction to the Director General of the WIC, J. Valckenburg (1667), and a partly defaced inscription on the outer walls indicate that they were commissioned by Director General Dirck Wilsree in 1671[87] (Photo 4.15)

Named Fort Coenraadsburg and garrisoned by a twenty-five-man guard unit that worked twenty-four-hour rotations, the fort had four batteries and a tower that enabled the Dutch to keep watch on the area around São Jorge da Mina, the town of Elmina itself, and out at sea up to about thirty miles. The Dutch considered Fort Coenraadsburg the key to the security of São Jorge da Mina and took great pains to secure its defenses. They went to great lengths to prevent any one from getting a good look at the defenses of the fort. Consequently, no strangers were ever admitted into the fort under any circumstances.[88]

Fort Coenraadsburg, as it exists today, was the result of a four-fold development process. In the first phase, St. Iago hill was the site of a chapel. In the second phase, this chapel was transformed into an earthwork redoubt or fortified structure sitting atop a hill. Third, the earthwork redoubt was rebuilt into a one-storey, and later, a two-storey rock structure. In the fourth stage of its existence, an extra storey which included three rooms on top of the guardroom, was added by the British in 1872, after they took over the Dutch forts in the Anglo-Dutch forts exchange.[89] The British also reduced the height of the tower and put gabled roofs on the northwest and southeast bastions.[90]

A Portuguese source, Diego de Alvarenga, it is reported, claimed that an Effutu Paramount Chief on the Mina coast, together with some three hundred subjects, were converted to Christianity and baptized by a Portuguese missionary in 1503, and to further the work of proselytization the chief permitted the Portuguese to build a chapel on St. Iago Hill (dedicated to the Portuguese saint, Jago).[91] Thus the Portuguese, by this time ensconced in São Jorge da Mina, held church services at the chapel on top of Iago hill. Later, however, the Portuguese constructed a chapel in the courtyard of São Jorge da Mina.

In 1637, this strategic hill and chapel, which stood about 33 meters above sea level, became the point from which the concentrated firepower of the Dutch breached the northern wall of São Jorge da Mina and forced the Portuguese garrison to surrender. After taking the castle, the Dutch reinforced the structure atop Iago Hill. They built a "redoubt or fortified quadrilateral earthwork with a tower [of baroque military architecture] and a gate and a single-storeyed building within a courtyard all surrounded by an embankment."[92] This earthenwork fortification was replaced with a permanent rock fort in the 1660s and the Dutch called it Fort Coenraadsburg (Photo 4.16).

Photo 4.16: Fort Coenraadsburg (With Dutch Modification)

Fort Coenraadsburg was different from any other fortification - fort or castle - built by Europeans on the Gold Coast. It was built as a purely military fort devoid of the commodious accommodations for merchants, factors or any other European officials.[93] Rather, it was based on the design of baroque military architecture and had "two giant, strong landward bastions on the northeast and northwest sides for defending the castle from land attacks and two smaller seaward bastions on the southwest and southeast sides. The bastions were linked by [continuous] curtain walling" that is 10 meters high.[94] The central courtyard of the fort was surrounded by "two-storeyed apartments on the landward side and a single storey on the seaward side."[95] These apartments housed a Dutch garrison made up of the commandant and sixty-nine officers and soldiers whose main job was the security of São Jorge da Mina over across from the Benya River, a rifle shot away. They served on rotational duty between the fort and the Castle. Coenraadsburg was thus a military barracks par excellence (Photo 4.17). The other rooms in the fort were all for serviceable usage rather than comfort. One served as a kitchen (two huge grinding stones in the yard are leftovers from the kitchen [Photo 4.18]) and other rooms served as armory and prison for disciplining European convicts and misbehaving or offending officials of the Dutch West India Company.[96]

The military complex that was Fort Coenraadsburg - fortifications and residential quarters - was surrounded by an outer wall, about 5-6 meters in height, for further security. This wall has about seventeen arched gun ports cut into it, together with sentry boxes located on top of the bastions.[97] In addition, a "ravelin, or half-moon, outwork, located in front of the fort is linked to the main entrance by a drawbridge overhanging a shallow ditch"[98] (Photo 4.19). The ravelin was like a " 'little island' connected to the main building by a drawbridge" and thus when the drawbridge was pulled up no one could enter or leave the fort, moreso since the entrance gate was about fifteen feet or four and a half meters above ground level.[99]

A final distinguishing feature of the fort is a high watch tower located at the gateway and used as a flagpost to hoist flags when hailing or signaling to ships approaching Elmina, whether they were Dutch ships or ships of other European countries[100] (Photo 4.20)

Fort Coenraadsburg was handed over to the British colonial military authorities on the Gold Coast on January 13, 1944, in fairly good shape.

FORT VREDENBURG - KOMENDA

The Dutch Fort Vredenburg lay a little farther east of the British fort (Fort Komenda) in the same town, Komenda. It is specifically located in

Photo 4.17: Fort Coenraadsburg – Military Barracks for Dutch Soldiers

Photo 4.18: Grinding Stones Used in Fort Coenraadsburg (Elmina)

Photo 4.19: Ravelin - Fort Coenraadsburg (Elmina)

Photo 4.20: Tower - Fort Coenraadsburg (Elmina)

Photo 4.21: Fort Vredenburg

the town of Little Komenda or Dutch Komenda, and within gunshot of the British fort on the other side of the river [in British Komenda] Photo 4.22. Initially, the Dutch built a trade lodge at Komenda in 1638, of wood and thatch, and surrounded it with a fence. It was abandoned and reoccupied several times before a proper fort was built.[101]

The fort was built by Mr. Swerts in 1688 and given the name Vredenburg. It was a square stone building with a small tower and four batteries mounting anywhere from twenty to thirty-two guns (Photo 4.22). Around 1690 it could accommodate, at a maximum, about sixty men but it did not appear to have housed that many Dutchmen at any time.[102] All the same, it was strong enough to defend itself against the rival English fort in Komenda.

Rivalry between the Dutch and English was so bad that in about 1725 the Dutch Commandant at Fort Vredenburg reportedly attacked the factor of the English fort under a tree midway between the two forts. In this encounter, the Dutch commandant lost his life.[103]

DUTCH AND BRITISH FORTS AND ANGLO-DUTCH ACTIVITIES AND RIVALRY ON THE GOLD COAST (1624-1715)

To a large extent, the relationship between the Dutch Republic and England during this period was one of hostility. However the hostility was followed by spells of peace during which the two combatants buried their differences and allied against a common enemy. The Anglo-Dutch wars affected trade on the Gold Coast because the two nations attacked each other's trade post in West Africa. The wars on the Gold Coast were largely precipitated by commercial rivalry. Dutch commercial superiority in the early seventeenth century was increasingly challenged by British sea power. In the global trade the Dutch, throughout the century, were successful rivals to the English in commerce, fisheries, the carrying trade and in colonization. In the seventeenth century the Dutch Republic was eminently superior in overseas commerce to every other state in Europe despite its small population of 2 million and lack of natural resources. As recognizably the most active commercial state in Europe, the Dutch monopolized trade in timber, pitch, maritime stores, spices and carried fish and Scandinavian raw materials to every corner of Europe.

The Dutch lost the Anglo-Dutch War of 1652-54 and were forced to recognize the Navigation Acts which mandated that only English carriers were to carry goods destined for England or the colonies. In spite of this, the Dutch continued to be a major force on the Gold Coast, occupying eight forts at this time as against one by the English.[104]

Photo 4.22: Fort Vredenburg as it Exists Today

FORT LIJDZAAMHEID (PATIENCE) - APAM

Guns   Slaves   Servants

The construction of Fort Lijdzaamheid (Patience) at Apam was begun by the Dutch in 1697 and they continued to use the fort until 1782 when the Dutch garrison surrendered it to the English. The Dutch regained possession of Fort Lijdzaamheid by treaty in 1785 but almost a century later (1881) the fort was attacked and pillaged by the Akyem in their wars against the Asante. The Akyem targeted Fort Lijdzaamheid and other Dutch possessions because the latter were allies and trading partners of the Asante and a major source of guns and gunpowder, which gave the Asante technological superiority in warfare on the Gold Coast.

The English came into possession of Fort Lijdzaamheid during the Anglo-Dutch exchange of forts in 1868. In 1968, the Apam Fort was turned into a police station and, sometime later, a wooden structure was mounted against the west wall of the backyard to serve as a post office like other forts and castles.

Fort Patience is located near a sheltered beach on "the gently rounded summit of a promontory which forms the end of a much larger ridge on the south-west" of the town of Apam.[105] Construction began in 1697 but this little fort was not completed until 1702 due to disagreements with the local people. As a result, the Dutch called the fort *Lijdzaamheid*, meaning Patience, because they suffered annoyances from the obstructionism of the people and from lack of trade "in the roads" next to the town.[106]

In many coastal towns and cities, forts and castles were located at the edge of the town or right on the beach and the *door of no return* opens right onto the seashore. Fort Lijdzaamheid, however, is located on a hill to the south and southeast of the town. A not-too-difficult descent snakes from the fort's door of no return for about a hundred yards to the seashore (Photo 4.23).

Another significant feature of Fort Lijdzaamheid is that the track up to the fort passed right through the town of Apam. Consequently, Dutch control of the fort was at best tenuous because it was easy for the local people to cut off access to the fort and endanger the lives of the Europeans who lived there. As a result, Fort Lijdzaamheid, more than any other fort on the Gold Coast, depended to a large degree on the good will of the people of the town.[107]

The fort started out as a one-storeyed house that later became a small two-storey building between 1701 and 1721 and certainly before 1786 when this oblong structure was strengthened with two semibastions located diametrically opposite each other at two corners.[108] The directors of the

Photo 4.23: Fort Lijdzaamheid (Patience)

Photo 4.24: Door of No Return - Fort Lijdzaamheid

Photo 4.25: Main Gate, Fort Lijdzaamheid

West India Company were not enthused about the construction of the fort due to minimal trade returns along that stretch of the Gold Coast and consented to the construction of Lijdzaamheid on condition that expenses were kept to a minimum, hence the very small size of the fort (Photo 4.23 and Photo 4.25).

The northwest bastion was solid while the southeast bastion, like one of the bastions of Fort Amsterdam, was hollow, and used as a male slave prison by 1786.[109] This appears to be a Dutch architectural design and purposely reserved for use as a male slave prison. At Fort Lijdzaamheid, there was also a small female slave prison opposite this hollow bastion on the other side of the courtyard and very close to the fort's entrance.

The fort was indeed a very small structure. Its central feature is a small central courtyard and spur in front of the two-storey building. Around the central courtyard were ranged the quarters for the European personnel, warehouses or storerooms, a guard room and a tiny slave prison.[110] The outer section of the spur in front of the building was later partitioned and adapted as a guardroom that could be defended from the roof in case of an enemy attack on the main gate of the fort.[111] An outer gateway with a curved gable, possibly built of brick (characteristic of Dutch construction) was part of the original structure, but today, the entrance to the fort is a single brick arch. The gate leading from the original guardroom to the courtyard is now the main gate[112] (Photo 4.25 and Photo 4.27).

Building plans dated 1786 locate storerooms and the powder magazine on the ground floor and the fort commander's quarters upstairs. However, a 1790 plan shows the addition of a storeroom, a male slave prison and soldiers barracks on the ground floor of the fort[113] (Photo 4.25 and Photo 4.26).

Due to the need for more space, the original structure was possibly altered in 1790 to almost double the area enclosed by the fort. A two-storey wing pointing to the south contained the "Orange Hall" for receptions or palavers; no bastions defended these additions.[114] A yard was added at the back of the fort as well as along the west, from the northwest bastion to the corner of the smaller yard. Access to the smaller yard was by way of a descent down the old wall clock. The southeastern portion of the yard accommodated a smithy and kitchens for preparing meals for officers and soldiers.[115] The parapets contain arched gun ports and the sill is about a foot above the platform. The outer wall is ringed with slits for small arms so that the garrison could fire at will when enemies try to break into the fort (Photo 4.26 and Photo 4.29).

Fort Patience was transferred to England in 1868. Since the beginning of the twentieth century, Fort Patience has served as a police station, a post office and at present, as a guest house.

Figure 4.4: Size of Fort Lijdzaamheid

Source: Van Dantzig, *Forts and Castles of Ghana*, 46. Courtesy of Sedco Publishing.

Photo 4.26: Female slave Prison (on the right); Male slave prison (on the left) – Fort Lidjzaamheid

Photo 4.27: Entrance with Curved Gable - Fort Lijdzaamheid

Photo 4.28: Soldiers' Quarters - Fort Lijdzaamheid

Photo 4.29: Slits for Small-arms Fire

During the Dutch period, trade from the fort was largely in enslaved Africans. Two Dutch ships reportedly loaded about nine hundred enslaved Africans at Apam, Beraku and Accra in two months in November 1705 and some slaves were obtained in the Akyem-Akwamu war but trade was generally pitiful due to the Asante-Akyem wars. The Akyem eventually attacked the Asante allies, the Dutch, at the fort and threw the guns over the walls.[116]

FORT AMSTERDAM

Guns   Slaves   Servants

Fort Amsterdam was built by the English in 1638 and seized by the Dutch in 1665 in retaliation for the English seizure of Dutch lodges at Anomabu and Egya. Specifically, Fort Amsterdam is generally believed to be located at Kormantse, generally referred to by Europeans as Cormantine or Kormantine. This town has gained the status of "hallowed place" in Slavery and Atlantic Studies. This is largely due to the accounts of European plantation owners who asserted that Cormantine slaves constituted one of the most rebellious groups of enslaved Africans in the New World, especially in Jamaica, Surinam, Panama, Antigua and other places. At one point, plantation owners cautioned against purchasing enslaved Cormantine people. As well, maroons of Jamaica, and especially Accompong maroons, indicate that their ancestors came from Cormantine or Coromante.[117] The maroons of Jamaica earned their reputation for bravery, hardiness and hard work and resisted British attempts to conquer them and return them to the slave plantations.[118]

But did the ancestors of the Accompong maroons come from Cormantine? Could they have come from Anomabu or even its hinterland about fifteen kilometers or so away? Indeed, both Cormantine and Anomabu were slave ports and the ancestors of the maroons passed through either port after marching from farther inland.

KORMANTE (CORMANTINE): THE LEGEND AND THE LORE

The town of Kormantse was situated on a hill overlooking the sea, a little over a rifle shot away from Fort Amsterdam.[119] The local people provided land for the construction of the fort to the British who built Fort Kormantin in 1638. In response to the presence of the fort, the town of Abandzi developed and at present is next to Fort Amsterdam. Consequently, the fort is currently situated at Abandzi despite the reference to the Kormantin (Kormantine) fort (Photo 4.30).

Photo 4.30: Abandzi – Seen From Fort Amsterdam

The town of Kormantse is today bordered by Saltpond to the east and Abandze to the west. Dutch Admiral de Ruyter captured Fort Kormantin in retaliation for the capture of Dutch forts by Admiral Holmes in 1664. The Dutch rebuilt the fort and named it Fort Amsterdam. It was attacked by the people of Anomabu and almost destroyed in 1811.

FORT AMSTERDAM

Fort Amsterdam was "rectangular in outline with two square bastions and two round bastions at the corners linked by curtain walls."[120] It was fortified with "24 cannon, and occupied by one chief factor, one under factor, two assistants, one barber, one sergeant, one corporal, four gentlemen cadets, one constable, one drummer, and 20 common soldiers, besides natives."[121] Around a central courtyard were arranged (a) a one-storeyed building on the western side, (b) a two-storeyed building along the northern side and (c) a line of two or three-storeyed buildings on the southern side (Photo 4.31).

While the curtain and bastion on the northern side were solidly built, the eastern, western and southern bastions were poorly constructed. Each of them had an earth filling between two walls of stone laid in mortar (Photo 4.32). That this was shoddy construction was borne out by the fact that cracks appeared in these bastions and they disintegrated at the time of the abandonment of the fort.

The southeastern bastion was deliberately designed as a hollow bastion so that it could be used as a slave prison. It had a grated ventilation hole above the entrance to the fort to enable clean air to flow into the fort, but above all, to serve as a means for keeping a close eye on the enslaved people down in the dungeon below. The hollow bastion is believed to be the first of its kind on the Gold Coast[122] (Photo 4.33).

The high point of trade at Fort Amsterdam was between the years 1705 and 1716. But for most of the time of its existence, trade was slow and lethargic, sometimes due to wars and conflicts with the Kormantin people who gave the land to the English and not to the Dutch to build the fort. Thus, the question of suzerainty bedevilled the Dutch period at Fort Amsterdam and the Dutch had to pay money to the people whenever they blocked the trade routes.

Photo 4.31: Fort Amsterdam

Photo 4.32: Walls of Fort Amsterdam

Photo 4.33: Bastion - Fort Amsterdam

FORT SÃO SEBASTIÃO - SHAMA

Guns	Slaves	Servants

When the Dutch captured Fort Sao Sebastiao in 1664 it was in a state of ruin. Between 1664 and 1682 they rebuilt the fort and added substantially to the former Portuguese structure. The Dutch added "an inner rectangular enclosure, pointed bastions located at opposite northwest and southeast corners, smaller round towers located at opposite southwest and northeast corners, an inner courtyard around which were lined two storeys of rooms on the northeast and northwest sides, a single storey of vaulted rooms with battery on the southwest side and a spur"[123] (Photo 4.35) According to Eric Tylleman, it was fortified with twelve small pieces of cannon and, in terms of personnel, had "one factor, two assistants, and twelve common soldiers."[124]

Unlike any other fort in Ghana, Fort São Sebastiao comes closest to Elmina Castle in terms of conceptualization and construction. Several features are of Portuguese origin and mirror the defensive system of São Jorge da Mina. A seventeenth-century turret at the apex of the bastion, together with the "southwest round tower with gun ports, the northeast round tower and the curtain walls which link these towers and enclose the inner courtyard," are remarkable in their original Portuguese design and structure taking much after Elmina Castle.[125] The fortifications are more formidable on the landward side than the seaward side which can be explained by the turbulence of the relations between the Portuguese and the local people and a desire to be ready for any landward attack (Photo 4.36).

Fort São Sebastiao was not a remarkable fort in terms of the slave trade, or general trade for that matter, during the Portuguese period and this did not change much under Dutch control. Rather, it became an important site for water and wood. The Dutch made the fort the source of their wood supply to repair their ships and forts. To compensate for the lack of trade in the area, the Dutch began sugar and cotton plantations in the fertile Pra Valley.[126] Axim was, and still is, the wettest region in Ghana, netting about seventy-four inches of rain a year and near Fort São Antonio, the Dutch planted a garden that produced "apples of China, pomegranates, 'cassu,' 'Anassa,' 'Bankoves,' water-melons, bananas, coconuts, and limes."[127] The Dutch gave out a lot of the fruits to ships that called at the fort.

In 1872 the Dutch fort was ceded to Britain as part of the Anglo-Dutch forts exchange but it was not put to any major use and decay set in. In 1957, however, it was restored to its former Dutch period status and has since

Photo 4.34: Fort Amsterdam – Frontal Section

Photo 4.35: Fort São Sebastiao

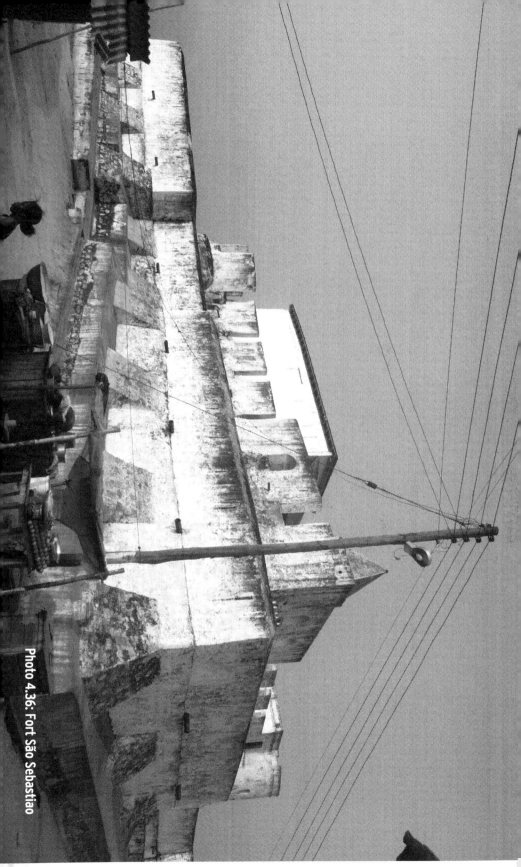

Photo 4.36: Fort São Sebastiao

been put to a number of uses – a meeting place for the Shama Traditional Authority, a post office and offices of the Ghana Commission for Democracy.

FORT SÃO ANTONIO (AXIM)

Guns   Slaves   Servants

The Dutch captured Fort São Antonio in 1642, a little over four years after São Jorge da Mina fell to the Dutch. Soon after they took over the fort, the Dutch made changes to the building. Three-storeyed buildings were erected inside the fort for use as residence, offices and store rooms. The Dutch added a service yard and outworks at this time. They also modified the chief factor's quarters into "a high triangular building of brick with a small plot of ground planted with a few orange trees on its western front."[128]

It was situated at some elevation above the sea and was "fortified with 36 guns. The garrison consists of 28 common soldiers, one chief factor, one under factor, two assistants, one sergeant, two 'Gefriedere" (reservists?), one barber, one constable, and one drummer."[129]

The Dutch do not appear to have changed the structure very much except that they renewed the facing of the seaward walls and the free-standing upper portions of the wall to mitigate decay of the local stone used in its construction.[130] A thin free-standing wall with slits for small arms fire enclosed a service yard that was created out of a shelf on the north slope. A doorway with steps from the main courtyard leads to this service yard, which appears to have been added by the Dutch.[131]

The activities of the Brandenburg Company at nearby Price's Town interposed a rival power between Axim and other Dutch possessions. This, coupled with the emergence of an anti-Dutch faction in the town of Axim, made the Dutch build an outwork "parallel with the existing main fortifications, and far enough away to make space for refugee families and their goods," should the need arise. These local men would help defend this new wall and hence the numerous slits for small arms fire.[132] Behind the outwork, a rock-cut ditch where the drawbridge used to be, probably eight feet deep, according to Barbot, was filled during the Dutch period and the central gateway, which has an ornamental facing of Dutch brick, was probably added when the drawbridge was removed.[133]

Fort São Aontonio was not an extremely important fort in terms of the slave trade. However, it was important in terms of the gold trade. There was no trading post in the gold-rich lands of the Ankobra and Tano River valleys. This implied that Fort São Antonio assumed economic and strategic importance. Located near the mouth of the Ankobra Rriver, gold traders from Waassa, and even, Adanse and Denkyira frequented Fort São Antonio to sell their gold winnings. During the period c. 1650-1720, European competition for bases and trade increased and other forts, such as Fort Ruychaver at Awudua, were built east of Axim.[134] The Dutch constructed a kiln in Axim where they burned oyster shells for the repair of their Gold Coast forts.

After the dissolution of the Brandenburg Company and the death of its principal ally John Conny in the 1720s, inter-European hostile competition in the Axim area abated and Dutch trade increased. With no competition and no interference Dutch trade in gold in the Axim area blossomed. In addition to the gold trade, the tropical rainforests of Axim became an important source of timber for Dutch forts on the Gold Coast. Seeking to augment Dutch trade revenue in the Axim region, the Dutch in the eighteenth century established cotton plantations.[135] The significance of this measure is borne out by the assessment of Heerman Abramsz, the Dutch Director-General in Elmina in 1679, that Axim was important to the WIC because "the surrounding peoples have to come there to put before the factor of the Company all their litigations … and if we lost it, the entire trade of the area would be lost to us."[136] In short, given the abatement of conflicts and the continuous flow of trade, the Dutch riverted back to the role as arbiters in local disputes and conflicts thus enhancing their stature in the eyes of the local people.

In 1872 Fort São Antonio was ceded to the British and from the 1950s, it became an important source of central government and local government offices.

FORT BATENSTEIN AT BUTRI

Guns   Slaves   Servants

The Dutch connection to the village of Butri began in 1598 when the Dutch West India Company established a trade post in this small town lying in a beautiful sheltered bay east of Cape Three Points. In 1650-1652, the Swedish Africa Company, led by Henry Caerlof of Cape Coast Castle fame, established a lodge at Butri. The Dutch took the Swedish threat seriously and in 1653 persuaded the people of Ankassa (probably Wassa) to attack the Swedish lodge. In the resulting conflict the Ankassa people expelled the Swedish Company from Butri, leaving the Dutch in control.[137]

With the expulsion of the Swedes the WIC constructed a fort on a very high hill overlooking the bay at Butri in 1656 and called it Batenstein (Photo

4.37). Bosman argues that the fort deserved a better name, Schadenstein instead of Batenstein (as *Bate* signified profit and *Schade*, loss) because Fort Batenstein was not a profitable fort – trade was pitiful and the WIC lost far more than it invested in it.[138] As a result it was paradoxical that the fort went by the name Batenstein.

Fort Batenstein was a very insignificant, irregularly shaped, oblong building that mounted eight guns on two small batteries; Bosman described it as a "small ill-shaped Fort."[139] According to Bosman, who visited the fort in 1701, "it has a pair of flat-roofed buildings adjoining the bastions. So feeble was the structure, militarily, that it was said that it was shaken itself whenever it had to fire its own guns."[140] In reality the fort's commanding location on top of a steep hill (and its not-so-useful guns) gave it a semblance of impregnability that tended to put off would-be invaders. Close to the end of the eighteenth century, Fort Batenstein was modified by the Dutch. They reshaped the bastions: "the eastern bastions were amalgamated into one strong battery; the northwestern bastion was expanded; and the amorphous apartments rehabilitated into a two-storey building."[141]

The fort's strength lay in the fact that it was considered one of the healthiest stations on the whole Gold Coast. As well, its very strategic position on a very steep hill (possibly the only fort with such a steep incline to the entrance) discouraged would-be attackers because it seemed unassailable (Photo 4.38).

The paradox, however, is that the fort was useless as a militarily fortified position. Batenstein never became an important commercial fort either. Political instability and local wars involving the Ankassa, who blocked the trade routes from time to time, disrupted trade. Similarly, the predations of John Conny also drove away traders. Thus from 1705 to 1716 only about 290 marks of gold and 156 enslaved Africans were purchased. Not surprisingly, Fort Batenstein was abandoned from 1818 to1829. However, Batenstein served as an important "service-fort." The tropical rainforests of the region yielded abundant logs that were used to repair Dutch ships and forts. Thus Dutch ships that needed to be refitted sailed into Butri Bay.[142]

The Dutch also cultivated sugar, coffee and cotton in the Butri district. In 1708 they brought two hundred enslaved Africans from Ouidah to help with sugar cultivation. That experimental farm was aimed at distilling rum, and materials were ordered from Holland and plans made for sugar plantations to feed the factory but the scheme does not seem to have proved successful.[143]

Photo 4.37: Fort Batenstein

FORT ORANJE (SEKONDI)

Guns   *Slaves*   *Servants*

In the seventeenth and eighteenth centuries, not long after the Dutch expelled the Portuguese from Elmina, intense European competition occurred in the region between Elmina to the west and Axim to the east, specifically in the Sekondi-Takoradi area. The Dutch and the English built forts within gunshot of each other. The local Ahanta people became involved in this intense rivalry and supported first one group and them the other. A Dutch lodge built in the 1640s at Sekondi was strengthened, enlarged and fortified as Fort Oranje in 1704[144] (Photo 4.39).

Fort Oranje initially had two bastions in the north and southwest corners of the building but in the course of the eighteenth century, improvements and modifications changed the structure. After the modifications, the fort consisted of a square white building mounting eight or ten guns on the terrace on the roof with cannons and gun ports directed toward the nearby English fort.[145] Oranje at the time was an enclosure with rooms arranged around a central courtyard. A group of two-storey and one-storey buildings served as quarters for the commandant and other officers. Other rooms served as warehouse, kitchen, gun powder magazine, slave prison, and a service yard[146] (Photo 4.40 and 4.41).

Poor trade figures, both in goods and enslaved Africans, were registered by the Dutch at Fort Oranje. The slave prison looks very small. A 1711 audit report from Elmina Castle put the main export figures for the period 1705 to 1716 at three hundred marks of gold and 151 enslaved Africans. These poor trade figures were largely due to local hostilities, especially to Ankassa blockade of the trade routes and the hostility of the Ahanta.[147] As the Dutch had done in other places, they tried to supplement trade with agriculture and established a cotton plantation and an industry in 1703.

In 1872, the Dutch ceded Fort Oranje to the English and from that point on, it was used as a lighthouse (Photo 4.41 and 4.42).

CONCLUSION

The Dutch impact on the Gold Coast after almost two and a half centuries of interaction can be seen in very remarkable ways. The Dutch language did not proliferate on the Gold Coast to any appreciable extent, but the Dutch presence in the Gold Coast, and especially Elmina, is epitomized in the Dutch cemetery in Elmina and Dutch-Ghanaian families in several coastal cities. While there is virtually no remnant of an older Dutch cem-

Photo 4.38: Fort Batenstein - Hilly ascent to Fort

Photo 4.39: Fort Oranje

Photo 4.40: Fort Oranje

Photo 4.42: Fort Oranje – Now Used as a Lighthouse by the Ghana Ports and Harbors Authority

etery near the castle, a second cemetery further away boasts an impressive
list of Dutch merchants and missionaries who spent their last days in the
"Dutch city" of Mina. A few of the houses built by Dutch merchants for
their African families still exist in Elmina. Given the importance of Dutch-
Ghana relations today, the government of Ghana, with the help of some
international organizations, has rehabilitated such houses as heritage sites. A
number of descendants of Dutch-Ghanaian families can be found in various
coastal cities and these families still carry their Dutch names. Schnapps, a
very popular drink in Ghana even today, was one of the staple items of Dutch
trade in the Gold Coast. The drink, imported as well as produced locally, is
an integral part of customary marriage celebrations, funeral celebrations
and is very prominent in rites that accompany local festivals.

Finally, the appendix below provides a list of the types of commodities
that the Dutch carried to São Jorge da Mina for trade on the Gold Coast and
beyond to other parts of West Africa. As already pointed out in this chapter,
one of the most important items of trade was cloth and the list below (Table
4.9) provides examples of the types of cloth that the Dutch exchanged on
the Gold Coast. The list includes Silesian linen, unbleached linen, Cape Verde
cloth, neptunes and perpetuanas. Brass pans, basins, pans, iron bars, knives
and hooks were also itemized as important in the Gold Coast trade (Table 4.9)

Table 4.9
Proposed Merchandise

**Proposal for a Gold Coast Cargo, drawn up by General Jacob Ruÿchaver
and Counselors at the Castle St. George d'elMina [São Jorge da Mina] in
Guinea, 8 April 1653**

//F.29R//	UNIT COST	COST (FL)
50,000 ells Silesian linen, akraas or none (*slesiger lÿwaay akraas of geen*)	15 [1/2-stuivers] per ell	18,750,-
1,000 ells unbleached linen (*rouw hessens*)	9 fl.apiece	9,000,-
6,000 p. bed-sheets (*slaaplakens goet*)	34 st.	10,200,-
3,000p. say cloths (*zaÿe cleeden*)	30st.	4,500,-
800 p. blue says (*zaeÿ*), including 100 p. bluish black (*geblaut swart*)	34fl.	27,200,-
100 p. Turkey rugs (*turcx tapÿten*)	15 fl. Apiece	1,500,-
400 p. Turkey carpets (*ditto carpetten*)	10 fl. Apiece	4,000,-
400 p. friezed blankets, including 100 p. white (*gefriseerde dekens 100 p. witte daeronder*)	4 fl. 10 st.	1,800,-

//f.29r//	UNIT COST	COST (fl)
200 p. perpetuanas 150 p. azure, 50 p. Verdon green (perpetuanen[..] hemels blauw [..] verdon groen)	25 fl. Apiece	5,000,-
200 p. Cyprus cloths with red and white Flowers (ciperse cleede root en wit geblomt)	6 fl. Apiece	1,200,-
600 p. etticons	6 fl. apiece	3,600,-
1,000 p. Cape Verde cloths as per sample (cabo Verdse cleede alst monster)	5 fl. apiece	5,000,-
20,000 lb large neptunes (groote nepten) }		
10,000 lb small ditto }		
10,000 lb brown pots (diggelen) }	60 fl. per cwt.	27,000,-
5,000 lb pans (taatsen) }		
8,000 lb hammered basins (gedreve akers)	70 fl. per cwt.	5,600,-
10,000 lb brass bracelets (gele ringen)	50 fl. per cwt.	5,000,-
6,000 lb assorted pewter basins, good or none (gesorteerde tinne commen goet of geen)	54 fl. per cwt.	3,240,-
8,000 p. iron bars at 32 p. in the thousand (staven iser a 32 p. int duÿsent)	45 st. apiece	18,000,-
6,000 doz. burnt-handle knives (gebrande messen)	15 st. apiece	4,500,-
1,000 lb zalte, each box 6 oz. (zalte ider bos 6 oncen)	27 st. per lb	1,350,-
500 bunches of large hooks (bos groote hoecken)	2 fl. per bos	1,000,-
1,000 bunches of small hooks (bos cleyne hoecken)	2 fl. per bos	2,000,-
1,200 p. small sheepskins, not to be forgotten (schape velletjes niet te vergeten)	2 fl. per doz.	200,-
4,000 lb mutton tallow (schapesmeer)	4 st. per lb	800,-
150 p. earthenware basins with lids (aerde kommen met litten) holding 4 stoop	1 fl. apiece	150,-
150 p. ditto without lids	15 st.	112,10
400 p. small ditto with lids	10 st. apiece	200,-
1,000 p. ditto without lids	5 st.	250,-
20 p. half-cases of French brandy (halve leggers france brandewÿn)	135 fl.	2,700,-
3-4 stoopen of spirits (starck water)		-
Total		**163,852,10**

Proposal of merchandise drawn up by the General and Counselors in Guinea, 27 December 1653, sent with the Roode Leeuw [from Sao Jorge da Mina]

	UNIT COST	COST (fl)
100,000 ells Silesian linen (slesiger lÿwaat)	14 [1/2 —stuivers] per ell	35,000,-
600 p. half-bleached (halfgebleeckt)	10 fl. apiece	6,000,-

4,000 p. bed-sheets (slaaplakens)	34 st.	6,800,-
600 p. says (zaeÿ), including 50 p. black and 50 red	34 gl. [= fl.]	20,400,-
20 p. serge of Chalon, assorted colours	50 gl. [=fl.]	1,000,-
400 p. Turkey carpets (turcxse carpetten)	10 fl.	4,000,-
400 p. white and green blankets (deeckens)	4 fl. 10 st	1,800,-
30 p. rapÿnen, green and white	13 fl.	390,-
200 p. tick (tÿckten)	4 fl.	800,-
20,000 lb large neptunes (nepten) }		
10,000 lb small ditto }		
10,000 brown pots (diggelen) }	60 fl. per cwt.	
5,000 earthenware pans (taatsen) }		27,000,-

//F.29v//

8,000 lb hammered basins (*gedreve akers*)	70 fl. per cwt.	5,600,-
600 lb ditto dishes (*schotels*)	70 fl. per cwt.	420,-
10,000 lb brass bracelets (*gele armringen*)	50 fl. per cwt.	5,000,-
4,000 lb brown band-kettles (*ketels met banden*)	36 fl. per cwt.	1,400,-
4,000 lb copper rods (*copre staafjes*)	60 fl. per cwt.	2,400,-
6,000 lb assorted basins, light and good or none (*commen, licht en goet off geen*)	59 fl. per cwt.	3,240,-
2,000 lb lead (*loot*)	7 fl. per cwt.	140,-
5,000 p. iron bars (*staven iser*)	45 st. apiece	11,250,-
6,000 doz. boatswains' knives	29 st.	7200,-
100 doz. sheepskins (*schape vellen*)	2 fl. per doz.	200,-
2,000 lb tallow (*smeer*)	4 st. per lb	400,-
1,600 oz. fine beads of colour Nr. 1 (*fÿn corael pmo. couleur*)	23 st. per oz.	

Venetian goods (*goedt veneets*):

4,000 lb lemon-coloured past}		
3,000 lb white q. }		
1,000 lb red q. }	16 st. per lb	9600,-
2,000 lb torquyn q. }		
2,000 lb blue lavender q. }		
1,200 lb straw-yellow lemon (*stroogeel lemoen*)	16 st. per lb	960,-
2,000 lb black rosados with white stripes	12 st.	1200,-
1,200 lb striped crystal (*christalÿn*)	16 st.	960,-
500 lb violet q.	16 st.	400,-
1,000 lb roo madrigette with white and blue stripes	10 st.	500,-

1,000 lb blue-violet madrigette with white stripes	10 st.	500,-
20 p. half-cases French brandy (halve leggers france brandewyn)		2700,-
6 p. half [-case] Spanish wine (halve spaense wyn)		800,-
Total		**159,940,-**

Source: Adam Jones (ed.), *West Africa in the Mid-Seventeenth Century. An Anonymous Dutch Manuscript* (Atlanta, GA: The African Studies Association Press, 1995), 175-177, 178-180.

Table 4.10
Slave Origins Based on WIC Departures from the Gold Coast, 1700-1736

PERIOD	NO. OF SLAVES	NO. OF SHIPS
1700	100	1
1701		
1702		
1703		
1704	279	1
1705	896	2
1706	1,277	3
1707	424	1
1708		
1709		
1710		
1711		
1712		
1713		
1714	166	1
1715	410	2
1716	146	1
1717	175	1
1718	719	1
1719		
1720		
1721	1,483	3
1722	562	1
1723	865	2
1724	423	1
1725	2,028	4
1726	991	2

Period	No. of Slaves	No. of Ships
1727	1,224	2
1728	1,028	2
1729	525	1
1730	323	1
1731	1,558	3
1732	1,140	2
1733	1,514	2
1734	1,549	4
17351	1,194	3
Total	**20,891**	**47**
1675-99	136	5
1700-1709	2,866	287
1710-19	1,616	162
1720-29	9,129	913
1730-35	7,278	1,213
1736-	5,618	

TABLE 4.11 SAMPLE ORIGIN OF SLAVES, 1741-1788
Year of Slave Purchase

Place of origin	1741	1746	1753	1753	1754	1755	1755	1756	1756	1757
Assine to Axim	-	13	8	-	-	1	2	-	1	6
Axim	3	4	-	2	-	12	1	-	4	2
Poquesoe	-	-	-	-	-	-	-	-	-	-
Akwida	-	-	-	-	-	-	2	-	3	4
Butri	-	-	-	-	-	-	-	-	-	-
Takoradi	-	-	-	-	-	-	-	-	-	-
Secondi	-	-	1	-	-	-	9	-	7	1
Shama	2	-	-	-	-	-	-	-	-	-
Komenda	32	-	-	-	-	-	-	-	-	-
Elimina	-	20	3	84	13	-	52	1	-	55
Cape Coast	-	-	-	-	-	-	-	-	-	-
Mori	-	-	-	-	-	-	-	-	-	-
Annamabu	61	3	10	9	37	-	-	90	62	-
Kormantin	-	-	-	-	-	-	-	-	-	-
Apam	-	-	52	124	-	-	-	44	54	-
Berku	-	-	-	-	-	-	-	-	-	-
Accra	-	-	12	-	-	-	-	-	-	-
Keta	-	-	1	-	-	-	-	-	-	-
Eppee	-	-	-	-	-	-	-	-	-	-
Popo	-	-	34	-	-	-	-	-	-	-
Not identified	-	62	28	-	40	-	-	32	-	-
Gold & Slave Coasts Combined	**102**	**89**	**141**	**219**	**90**	**12**	**64**	**167**	**130**	**62**

PLACE OF ORIGIN	1758	1761	1762	1763	1763	1764	1765	1765	1765	1767
Axim	2	-	11	-	-	3	-	-	6	18
Poquesoe	-	-	-	-	-	-	-	-	-	-
Akwida	-	-	-	-	-	2	-	-	-	-
Butri	4	-	-	-	-	-	-	-	2	-
Takoradi	-	-	-	-	-	6	-	-	-	-
Secondi	-	-	-	-	-	-	-	1	1	-
Shama	-	-	-	-	-	-	-	-	-	-
Komenda	-	-	-	-	-	-	-	-	-	-
Elimina	9	97	80	-	24	48	-	16	16	32
Cape Coast	-	-	-	-	5	-	-	-	-	-
Mori	-	-	-	-	6	-	-	-	-	-
Annamabu	-	73	-	-	13	-	-	-	-	40
Kormantin	-	-	-	-	15	-	-	-	25	-
Apam	-	-	-	-	-	-	-	-	4	-
Berku	-	-	-	-	-	-	-	-	5	-
Accra	-	-	-	-	-	-	71	-	8	-
Keta	-	-	-	-	-	-	-	-	-	-
Eppee	-	-	-	-	-	-	-	-	-	-
Popo	-	-	-	-	-	-	-	-	-	-
Not identified	-	-	-	-	-	-	-	-	13	-
Gold & Slave Coasts Combined	**15**	**170**	**91**	**-**	**-**	**59**	**71**	**17**	**80**	**90**

PLACE OF ORIGIN	1767	1768	1769	1769	1769	1770	1771	1771	1771	1772
Axim	35	-	-	7	-	5	3	9	34	-
Poquesoe	-	-	-	-	-	-	-	-	-	-
Akwida	-	-	-	-	-	5	-	3	-	-
Butri	-	-	-	6	-	14	7	4	18	-
Takoradi	-	-	-	7	-	6	12	-	-	29
Secondi	10	-	-	7	-	3	-	-	-	-
Shama	-	-	-	-	-	17	-	-	-	-
Komenda	-	-	-	-	-	-	-	-	-	-
Elimina	-	61	-	55	-	23	28	-	-	118
Cape Coast	-	-	-	-	-	-	-	-	-	-
Mori	-	7	-	-	-	-	-	-	-	-
Annamabu	-	-	-	-	-	-	-	-	-	-
Kormantin	-	-	-	-	-	-	-	-	-	-
Apam	-	1	-	-	-	-	-	64	-	-
Berku	-	-	-	-	-	-	-	-	-	-
Accra	-	-	-	-	-	-	-	-	-	10
Keta	-	-	4	-	-	-	-	-	-	-
Eppee	-	-	-	-	-	-	-	-	-	-
Popo	-	-	-	-	-	-	-	-	-	-
Not identified	-	-	63	-	-	-	-	-	-	-
Gold & Slave Coasts Combined	**45**	**69**	**67**	**82**	**-**	**73**	**50**	**80**	**52**	**157**

PLACE OF ORIGIN	1772	1773	1773	1774	1774	1775	1775	1775	1776
Axim	-	2	-	-	-	114	-	-	6
Poquesoe	-	-	-	-	-	-	-	-	10
Akwida	-	-	-	-	-	-	-	-	8
Butri	-	-	-	-	-	-	-	-	-
Takoradi	-	-	-	-	-	-	-	-	-
Secondi	-	-	-	-	-	-	-	-	-
Shama	-	-	-	-	-	-	-	5	-
Komenda	-	-	-	-	-	-	-	2	-
Elimina	-	-	-	1	169	-	10	51	6
Cape Coast	-	-	-	-	-	-	-	-	-
Mori	-	12	27	-	-	-	80	-	-
Annamabu	-	-	-	4	-	-	-	-	-
Kormantin	-	-	-	40	-	-	-	-	-
Apam	-	-	-	54	-	-	-	-	-
Berku	-	12	27	47	-	-	-	-	-
Accra	-	-	-	-	-	-	-	-	-
Keta	-	-	-	4	-	-	-	-	-
Eppee	-	-	-	5	-	-	-	-	-
Popo	-	-	-	118	-	-	-	-	-
Not identified	106	-	-	-	-	-	-	-	-
Gold & Slave Coasts Combined	**106**	**26**	**54**	**273**	**169**	**114**	**90**	**58**	**30**

PLACE OF ORIGIN	1777	1777	1778	1778	1778	1779	1779	1780	1787	1788
Axim	11	-	-	16	-	-	-	-	-	4
Poquesoe	-	-	-	-	-	-	-	-	-	-
Akwida	-	8	-	-	-	-	-	-	-	-
Butri	-	2	-	-	3	-	14	-	-	-
Takoradi	-	-	-	-	-	12	-	-	-	-
Secondi	-	-	-	-	-	-	-	-	-	-
Shama	-	-	-	-	-	-	-	-	-	-
Komenda	-	-	-	-	-	-	-	-	-	-
Elimina	112	42	154	-	11	63	-	103	-	47
Cape Coast	-	-	-	-	-	-	-	-	-	-
Mori	-	-	-	17	-	-	-	-	-	-
Annamabu	-	-	-	-	-	-	-	-	-	-
Kormantin	-	-	-	17	-	-	-	-	-	-
Apam	-	-	-	-	-	-	-	-	-	-
Berku	-	-	-	-	-	-	-	-	-	-
Accra	-	-	-	-	-	-	-	-	-	-
Keta	-	-	-	-	-	-	-	-	-	-
Eppee	-	-	-	-	-	-	-	-	-	-
Popo	-	-	-	-	-	-	-	-	47	-
Not identified	-	-	-	-	-	-	-	-	-	-
Gold & Slave Coasts Combined	**123**	**52**	**154**	**16**	**48**	**75**	**14**	**103**	**47**	**51**

PLACE OF ORIGIN	1792	TOTAL
Axim	-	314
Poquesoe	-	10
Akwida	-	35
Butri	-	74
Takoradi	-	72
Secondi	-	40
Shama	6	30
Komenda	-	34
Elimina	78	1,682
Cape Coast	-	5
Mori	-	149
Annamabu	-	402
Kormantin	-	97
Apam	-	397
Berku	-	91
Accra	-	101
Keta	-	9
Eppee	-	5
Popo	-	152
Not identified	-	395
Gold & Slave Coasts Combined	**84**	**4,094**

Notes

1. Douglas Coombs, The Gold Coast, Britain and the Netherlands 1850-1874 (London: Oxford University Press, 1963), 1-2.

2. Amry Vandenbosch, Dutch Foreign Policy Since 1815. A Study in Small Power Politics (The Hague: Martinus Nijhoff, 1959), 44; C.R. Boxer, Four Centuries of Portuguese Expansion, 1415-1825: A Succinct Survey (Johannesburg, 1961), 48.

3   See Geoffrey Parker, The Dutch Revolt rev ed. (Ithaca, NY: Cornell University Press, 1988); Cecil John Cadoux, Philip of Spain and the Netherlands: An Essay on Moral Judgment in History (Hamden, CT: Archon Books, 1969); Maarten Park, The Dutch Republic in the Seventeenth Century: The Golden Age, trans. Diana Webb (Cambridge: Cambridge University Press, 2005); Jonathan Israel, The Dutch Republic: Its Rise, Greatness and Fall, 1477-1806 (Oxford: Clarendon Press, 1998).

4. It is in this context that the Dutch attacked São Jorge da Mina in 1596, 1603, 1606, 1616 and 1625, and though these attacks failed, the Dutch eventually prevailed in 1637 and also took São Antonio, Axim, in 1642. The capture of the Portuguese headquarters and other forts forced the Portuguese out of the Guinea coast altogether. See George Masselman, The Cradle of Colonialism (New Haven, CT: Yale University Press, 1963), 47. Masselman puts emphasis on Dutch need for salt. Also, Pieter de Marees, Description and Historical Account of the Gold Coast Kingdom of Guinea (1602), trans. and ed. Albert van Dantzig and Adam Jones, (Oxford: Oxford University Press [for the British Academy], 1987), xv.

5   De Marees, Description and Historical Account of the Gold Coast Kingdom of Guinea (1602), xiii.

6. Michael R. Doortmont, "An Overview of Dutch Relations with the Gold Coast in Light of David van Nyendael's Mission to Ashanti in 1701-02," in ed. I. van Kessel Merchants, Missionaries & Migrants: 300 Years of Dutch-Ghanaian Relations, (Legon, Accra: Sub-Saharan Publishers, 2002), 21; De Marees, Description and Historical Account of the Gold Kingdom of Guinea (1602), viv.

7. De Marees, Description and Historical Account of the Gold Kingdom of Guinea, xiv; Harvey Michael Feinberg, "Elmina, Ghana: A History of Its Development and Relationship with the Dutch in the Eighteenth Century," Ph.D. Dissertation, Boston University, 1969, p. 28, footnote 1.

8. Feinberg, "Elmina, Ghana," 28-29.

9   See C.R. Boxer, The Dutch in Brazil, 1624-1654 (Oxford: Clarendon Press, 1957), 7-8.

10. De Marees, Description and Historical Account of the Gold Kingdom of Guinea. xiv; K. Ratelband, (ed.) Vijf Dagregisters van het Kasteel Sao Jorge da Mina (The Hague, 1953), in Feiberg, "Elmina Ghana," 28.

11. Boxer, The Dutch in Brazil. 7-8; H. M. Feinberg, "New Data on Europeans Mortality in West Africa: The Dutch on the Gold Coast, 1719-1760," in ed. Anthony Disney An Expanding World. The European Impact on World History 1450-1800. Vol. 4. His-

toriography of Europeans in Africa and Asia, 1450-1800. (Aldershot: Variorum, 1995), 361.

12. Peter C. Emmer, *The Dutch Slave Trade 1500-1850,* trans. Chris Emery. New York: Berghahn Books, 2006, 11.

13. Ibid., 14. See also Ernst van den Boogart and Peter C. Emmer, "The Dutch Participation in the Atlantic Slave Trade, 1590-1650," in, *The Uncommon market. Essays in the Economic History of the Atlantic Slave Trade,* ed., Henry A. Gemery and Jan S. Hogendorn (New York: Academic Press, 1979), 355-356.

14. This reference is to the Biblical story of Noah and his sons Ham, Shem and Japheth. Ham who saw his father's nakedness told his brothers who covered up their father. Noah cursed Ham when he later found out what had happened. However, how this specific curse of Ham transferred to mean that Africans were cursed to be enslaved has not been proved anywhere.

15 Van den Boogart and Emmer, "The Dutch Participation in the Atlantic Slave Trade, 1590-1650," 355; C.C. Goslinga, *The Dutch in the Caribbean and on the Wild Coast, 1580-1680* (Gainesville: University of Florida Press, 1971), 344-345.

16 Boxer, *The Dutch in Brazil,* 7-8. See also Ludewig Ferdinand Rømer, *A Reliable Account of the Coast of Guinea (1760)* trans. and ed. Selena Axelrod Winsnes (Oxford: Oxford University Press [for the British Academy], 2000), xii.

17. Emmer, *Dutch Slave Trade,* 17-18.

18 Emmer, *Dutch Slave Trade,* 19; Boogart and Emmer, "The Dutch Participation in the Atlantic Slave Trade, 1590-1650," 359-360.

19. Emmer, *Dutch Slave Trade,* 23.

20. Ibid., 24-25.

21 Ibid., 28; Boogart and Emmer, "The Dutch Participation in the Atlantic Slave Trade, 1590-1650," 373-374.

22. Ibid., 28-29; Boogart and Emmer, "The Dutch Participation in the Atlantic Slave Trade," 373-374.

23. In Table 4.4 MP refers to the Middle Passage. The data are culled from Postma Data Collection.

24. Rømer, *A Reliable Account of the Coast of Guinea (1760),* xiii.

25. Ineke van Kessel, Introduction to *Merchants Missionaries & Migrants. 300 Years of Dutch-Ghanaian Relations* (Legon, Accra: Sub-Saharan Publishers, 2002), 13; Emmanuel Akyeampong, *Drink, Power and Culture Change: A Social History of Alcohol in Ghana, c. 1800 to Present Times,* (Portsmouth, 1966).

26. Kessel, Introduction to *Merchants, Missionaries & Migrants,* 12.

27. Silesian linen was used in making clothes.

28. De Marees, *Description and Historical Account of the Gold Kingdom of Guinea (1602),* 52-53. The basins were used on the Gold Coast to store oil, carry or convey materials, for bathing, to keep ornaments and trinkets, to hold meat and food and for other uses.

29. De Marees, *Description and Historical Account of the Gold Kingdom of Guinea* (1602), 52-53.

30. Document 34, WIC 124: Resolutions of the Director-General and Council at Elmina, 8th November 1682, in *The Dutch and the Guinea Coast 1674-1742: A collection of Documents From the General State Archive at the Hague*, comp. and trans, A. Van Dantzig (Accra: Ghana Academy of Arts and Sciences, 1978), 36.

31. Document 36. WIC 124: 3rd December 1682. In *The Dutch and the Guinea Coast 1674-1742. A collection of Documents From the General State Archive at the Hague*. Comp. and trans., A. Van Dantzig. 37. Angel - ; Ackie - …

32. Document 55, 10th December 1684, in *The Dutch and the Guinea Coast 1674-1742*, 45.

33. Document 36, WIC 124, 3rd December 1682, in *The Dutch and the Guinea Coast 1674-1742*, 40.

34. Van Dantzig, *The Dutch on the Guinea Coast, 1672-1742*, 4.

35 Ibid.

36. Royal Decree, dated Brussels 27th July 1915, No. 31 (King William I of Netherlands) in *Journal and Correspondence of H.W. Daendels, Part I, November 1815 to January 1817*, 3.

37. Ibid. See also M. Nathan, "The Gold Coast at the End of the Seventeenth Century Under the Danes and the Dutch," *Journal of African Society* 13, 4 (1904): 15.

38 Royal Decree, dated Brussels 27th July 1915, No. 31, 10-11.

39. Feinberg, "Elmina, Ghana," 34; Nathan, The Gold Coast at the End of the Seventeenth Century Under the Danes and the Dutch," 15.

40. Van Dantzig, *The Dutch and the Guinea Coast 1672-1742*, 4; Feinberg, "Elmina, Ghana," 34; Nathan, The Gold Coast Under the Danes and the Dutch," 15.

41. Nathan, "The Gold Coast Under the Danes and the Dutch," 15.

42. Van Dantzig, *The Dutch and the Guinea Coast 1672-1742*, 4; Nathan, "The Gold Coast Under the Danes and the Dutch," 15.

43. Feinberg, "Elmina, Ghana," 33-34; Feinberg, "New Data on European Mortality in West Africa," 362.

44. Feinberg, "New Data on European Mortality in West Africa," 362.

45. Ibid.

46. Document 64, 17 January 1689, in *The Dutch and the Guinea Coast 1674-1742*, 48-49.

47. Albert van Dantzig, *Forts and Castles of Ghana*, 13.

48. Doc. 3 ARA: Rademacher Arch, No. 587: Heerman Abramsz to Assembly of Ten, 23rd November 1679 (written after his return), in van Dantzig, *The Dutch and the Guinea Coast 1674-1742*, 14-15. The term Accanists often refers to the people of Assin.

49. Van Dantzig, *Forts and Castles of the Gold Coast.*, 13.

50. Nathan, "The Gold Coast Under the Danes and the Dutch," Fn. 3, 20.

51. Rosemary Cave, *Gold Coast Forts* (London: Thomas Nelson & Sons, 1900), 9.

52. W. Walton Claridge, *A History of the Gold Coast and Ashanti* (London: Frank Cass, 1964), 169.

53. Claridge, *A History of the Gold Coast and Ashanti,* 170

54. Nathan, The Gold Coast Under the Danes and the Dutch," 20.

55. Cave, *Gold Coast Forts,* 12.

56. Van Dantzig, *Forts and Castles of the Gold Coast.* 9. Feinberg, "Elmina, Ghana."

57. Doc. 2, WIC 831, Special Memorandum & Instruction for Heerman Abramsz, Director-General of the Coast of Africa in Guinea, April 1675. Art. 18 & 19, in *The Dutch and the Guinea Coast 1674-1742,* 12-13.

58. Document 3, ARA: Rademacher Arch. No. 587: Heerman Abramsz to Assembly of Ten. 23rd November 1679 (written after his return) in *The Dutch and the Guinea Coast 1674-1742,* 19.

59. Claridge, *A History of Gold Coast and Ashanti.* 165.

60. Van Dantzig (trans) *The Dutch and the Guinea Coast 1674-1742.* .

61. Claridge, *A History of the Gold Coast and Ashanti.* 166.

62. Ibid., 165-166.

63. Ibid., 165-166. Information provided by tour guide at Sao Jorge da Mina during Study Abroad tour of the Castle with students from the University of Miami in June 2005.

64. See the Dutch-Elmina War 1738-1740 .

65. Claridge, *A History of the Gold Coast and Ashanti.* 166.

66. Van Dantzig, *Forts and Castles of Ghana,* 15.

67. Ibid.

68. Ibid.

69. Claridge, *A History of the Gold Coast and Ashanti,* 166.

70 For a good account of European mortality on the Gold Coast see Feinberg, "New Data on European Mortality in West Africa," 363-364.

71. Document 3, ARA, Rademacher Arch. No. 587, in *The Dutch and the Guinea Coast 1674-1742,* 20.

72. ADM 23/1/337. Monuments and Relics Commission. Ancient Forts and Castles in the Central Province.

73. Claridge, *A History of the Gold Coast and Ashanti,* 101; van Dantzig, *Forts and Castles of Ghana.* 15.

74. Van Dantzig, *Forts and Castles of Ghana,* Footnote 3, 20; Kwesi J. Anquandah, *Castles and Forts of Ghana* (Paris: Atalante [for Ghana Museum and Monuments Board] 1999), 61.

75. Information provided by Mr. Ata Yawson, caretaker, Fort Amsterdam in June 2005.

76   Ibid.

77. van Dantzig, Forts and Castles of Ghana, 15-16.

78. For details see " 'Prempeh I in Exile," and "A Nation in Exile: The Asante on the Seychelles Islands, 1900-24,' " in ed. Toyin Falola, Africa in the Twentieth Century: The Adu Boahen Reader (Trenton, NJ: Africa World Press, 2004), 355-370, 371-391.

79. Van Dantzig, Forts and Castles of Ghana. 15

80. Van Dantzig, Forts and Castles of Ghana. 15.

81. ADM 23/1/337, Monuments and Relics Commission, Ancient Castles and Forts in the Central Province.

82. Claridge, A History of the Gold Coast and Ashanti, 101.

83   Anquandah, Castles and Forts of Ghana, 59; Jean Barbot, A Description of the Coasts of North and South Guinea (London, 1942), 59-60.

84. Cave, Gold Coast Forts, 15.

85. Cave, Gold Coast Forts, 15-16.

86. Anquandah, Castles and Forts of Ghana. 61.

87. Ibid., 63; van Dantzig, Forts and Castles of Ghana, 16.

88. Anquandah, Castles and Forts of Ghana. 62; Nathan, "The Gold Coast Under the Danes and the Dutch," 16.

89. van Dantzig, Forts and Castles. 17; James R. Anquandah, "Archaeological Investigation at Fort St. Jago, Elmina, Ghana," Archaeology in Ghana, 38; R.M. Wiltgen, Gold Coast Mission History 1471-1800 (Accra, 1956).

90. van Dantzig, Forts and Castles of Ghana 17

91. Anquandah, Castles and Forts of Ghana. 62.

92. Anquandah, Castles and Forts of Ghana. 62; Anquandah, "Archaeological Investigation at Fort St. Jago," 38.

93. van Dantzig, Forts and Castles of Ghana, 17; A.W. Lawrence, Trade Castles and Forts of West Africa, (London: Jonathan Cape, 1963), 80; Anquandah, "Archaeological Investigation at Fort St. Jago," 38.

94. Anquandah, Castles and Forts of Ghana. 61; Anquandah, "Archaeological Investigation at Fort St. Jago," 38.

95. Anquandah, "Archaeological Investigation at Fort St. Jago," 38.

96. Ibid.

97. Ibid.

98. Anquandah, Castles and Forts of Ghana, 63.

99. Van Dantzig, Forts and Castles, 17; Anquandah, "Archaeological Investigations at Fort St. Jago," 38-39.

100. Van Dantzig, Forts and Castles of Ghana, 16-17; Anquandah, "Archaeological Investigations at Fort St. Jago," 38.

101. Doc. 3 ARA: Rademacher Arch. No. 587, in *The Dutch on the Guinea Coast 1674-1742*, 13, 20.

102 Willem Bosman. *A New and Accurate Description of the Coast of Guinea*, (London, 1967), 26-27.

103. Claridge, *A History of Ashanti and the Gold Coast.*

104 Cave, *Gold Coast Forts*, 15.

105. Lawrence, *Trade Castles and Forts.*

106. Van Dantzig, *Forts and Castles of Ghana.*

107. Lawrence, *Trade Forts and Castles,*

108. Ibid.

109. Anquandah, *Castles and Forts of Ghana*, 35-36.

110. Ibid., 36; Van Dantzig, *Forts and Castles of Ghana*, 45-46.

111. Bosman. *A New and Accurate Description of the Coast of Guinea*, (London, 1967).

112. Anquandah, *Castles and Forts of Ghana*, 36; Van Dantzig, *Forts and Castles of Ghana*, 46.

113. Anquandah, *Castles and Forts of Ghana*, 36; Van Dantzig, *Forts and Castles of Ghana*, 46.

114. Van Dantzig, *Forts and Castles of Ghana*, 46; Anquandah, *Castles and Forts of Ghana*, 36.

115. Anquandah , *Castles and Forts of Ghana*, 36.

116. Ibid, 34.

117. I interviewed a number of Accompong maroons in 1998 when I went on a field trip to Accompong and all recounted the fact that they were of Cormantine ancestry.

118. For the maroons of Jamaica see Bev Carey, *The Maroon Story: the Authentic and Original History of the maroons in the History of Jamaica, 1490-1880* (Gordon Town, Jamaica: Agouti Press, 1997).

119. I am grateful to Phillip Atta Yawson, caretaker of Fort Amsterdam, for this piece of information .

120. Anquandah, *Castles and Forts of Ghana*, 38.

121. M. Nathan, "The Gold Coast Under the Danes and the Dutch," 21.

122. Anquandah, *Castles and Forts of Ghana*, 38. Philip Ata Yawson, caretaker of Fort Amsterdam, also repeated that information.

123. Anquadah, *Castles and Forts of Ghana*, 64-65.

124. Nathan, "The Gold Coast Under the Danes and the Dutch," 15.

125. Anquandah, *Castles and Forts of Ghana*, 67.

126. Ibid.

127. Nathan, "The Gold Coast Under the Danes and Dutch," 13.

128. Claridge, *A History of the Gold Coast and Ashanti.* 162

129. Nathan, "The Gold Coast Under the Danes and the Dutch," 13.

130. Lawrence, *Trade Castles and Forts*, 233.

131. Ibid.

132. Ibid., 233-234. Lawrence writes that the information comes from Jean Barbot.

133. Ibid., 234.

134. See Merrick Posnansky and Albert van Dantzig, "Fort Ruychaver Rediscovered," *Sankofa* 2 (1976), 7-9.

135. Anquandah, *Castles and Forts of Ghana*. 94.

136. Doc. 3 ARA: Rademacher Arch. No 587, in *The Dutch and the Guinea Coast 1672-1742*, 13-14.

137 Anquandah, *Castles and Forts of Ghana*, 74; Van Dantzig, *Forts and Castles of Ghana*, 25.

138. Willem Bosman, *A New and Accurate Description of the Coast of Guine*, 15.

139. Ibid. Cave, *Gold Coast Forts*, 8.

140. Anquandah, *Castles and Forts of Ghana*, 74.

141. Ibid., 74-75.

142. Ibid., 74.

143. Claridge, *A History of the Gold Coast and Ashanti*, 163; Van Dantzig, *The Dutch and the Guinea Coast 1674-1742*.

144. Anquandah, *Castles and Forts of Ghana*, 70.

145. Ibid., 72.

146. Ibid.

147. Ibid.

✥ Chapter 5

English Hegemony: the Slave Forts, Castles and Dungeons and the Atlantic Slave Trade

In an introduction to Paul Redmayne's book, *The Gold Coast Yesterday and Today*, Sir Arnold Hodson, K.C.M.G., governor of the Gold Coast wrote

> England's first contact with the Gold Coast was in the days of the great Queen Elizabeth, and what a lot of water has run under the bridge since then and what startling amazing changes have taken place! It is best, I think, to draw a veil over the old days of the iniquitous slave trade with its attendant horrors and miseries, and to confine ourselves to the present and future. The Gold Coast of today is a peaceful and contented country, probably one of the most peaceful and progressive countries in the distracted world we live in at the present time.[1]

Rather than draw the veil over the work of the English in Ghana, however, this chapter highlights the period of English hegemony over the Gold Coast and their eventual domination of the Atlantic slave trade from the West African subregion to the Caribbean and the Americas. Headquartered in Cape Coast, and later, in Accra, the English eventually bought out the Danes, and later the Dutch, from the West African trade. Not only did the English monopolize the slave trade and the so-called legitimate trade that followed, but they also established colonial domination over large parts of West Africa. They pontificated on the idea that the Gold Coast was a model colony of the British empire until political disturbances provided a jolt of reality and a recognition that all people yearn to be free from foreign domination.[2]

The English period on the Gold Coast had a lasting impact on what became the colony of the Gold Coast and, later, Ghana. This chapter looks at the early English presence on the coast, the period of English struggle for hegemony with the Dutch, the construction of fortified bases in the Gold Coast for English personnel and the eventual takeover of Danish and Dutch slave forts and castles. At the peak of the slave trade from 1700 to 1808, when more enslaved Africans were transported to the New World than at any other time, the English were the largest carriers, shipping more than a quarter of all enslaved Africans. The role of Cape Coast Castle in particular, and other British forts on the Gold Coast such as Anomabu, cannot be overemphasized.

THE ENGLISH ON THE GOLD COAST

English contact with the Gold Coast began in the days of Portuguese hegemony in that area when interlopers appeared in West Africa to trade. The Dutch, followed by the English, broke the Portuguese trade monopoly in the Gold Coast (granted by a papal bull). The earliest English voyages were the work of interlopers or semipiratical adventurers and aroused the bitterest enmity of the Portuguese. The first English voyage to West Africa was made in 1553 by Captain Thomas Windham, accompanied by a Portuguese pilot, Antonio Anes Pinteado, who traded both east and west of São Jorge da Mina. Though Windham and Pinteado died, the remnant of their 140-man crew brought back a large quantity of gold and sparked interest in the Guinea coast.[3] Subsequently, Captain John Lok in 1554 sailed for the Gold Coast with three ships - the *Trinitie, John Evangelist* (both 140 tons) and the *Bartholomew* (90 tons) - passing Axim and Shama and trading near Cape Coast, Saltpond and Beraku and returned home with a sizable quantity of gold and other trade items.[4] Lok returned to England with 400 pounds weight of gold, 36 *butts* of pepper grains (a *butt* is about 120 gallons), 250 elephant teeth (ivory) and the head of an elephant.[5] Lok was followed by Captain William Towerson who in 1555 undertook three voyages to West Africa. The quantity of goods that Lok and Towerson sent to England, coupled with their accounts of trade on the Gold Coast, inspired a serious effort at trade on the Gold Coast.[6] Towerson was told by the King of Eguafo to send men and materials to build a fort, and in 1561 a syndicate, the Company of Merchant Adventurers for Guinea, was established to look into the possibility of constructing this fort.

Almost a century earlier, the Portuguese had taken a party of ten Africans to Portugal in 1441 and by 1470 the Spaniards had begun to take slaves to Spain, the Canary Islands and the West Indies. After John Lok's journey in 1554, other English ships began to visit the Gold Coast. English participation in the slave trade on the West African coast did not begin until sometime after these early English voyages. In 1562 Captain John Hawkins carried three hundred enslaved Africans in three ships from the Guinea coast and sold them in the West Indies. Even though an Act legalizing the purchase of Africans was passed in 1562 or 1563, it was not until after 1660, when the English were more successful with their North American colonies, that the English slave trade began in real earnest.[7] For the exploits of John Hawkins, Queen Elizabeth gave him "a coat of arms on which a negro bound in chains was a prominent feature."[8]

At this early stage, the Portuguese fiercely guarded their trade monopoly on the Gold Coast, operating out of their fortified positions at Elmina, Axim, Shama and Accra. African traders who did business with European rivals of the Portuguese were severely punished by the latter to deter them from such activities. As a result, the English were forced in the early decades of the seventeenth century to focus on the coasts of Senegal, the Gambia and other parts of the Gold Coast for trade until they could secure a foothold or forti-fied stronghold from which they could challenge Portuguese hegemony.

The English came to the realization that without a permanent base or foothold on the Gold Coast, a place to store goods from England as well as goods purchased from African merchants and, more important, to hold enslaved Africans, they could not effectively operate the slave trade on the Gold Coast.[9] In 1618 James I granted a royal charter to the Company of Merchants who were trading to Africa. That is the context in which the first English stronghold on the Gold Coast was begun at Kormantse (or Korman-tine, as the Europeans called it), not far from the Dutch headquarters of Mouri.[10] The first English trade post was constructed at Kormantine in 1618 and later developed into a large stone fort with four bastions in 1631. In 1662 the Company of Royal Adventurers of England Trading to Africa was given the sole right to trade in Africa from Gibraltar to the Cape of Good Hope by Charles II. In return for this concession, the Company was to ship three thousand enslaved Africans a year to the Americas and to establish fortified bases in the region.[11] War broke out in 1664 when English Captain Robert Holmes commanded a fleet of two men-of-war, six frigates and a number of smaller craft to capture all Dutch forts on the Gold Coast except Elmina and Axim.[12] However, the Anglo-Dutch war was fatal to the survival of this new company's enterprise on the Gold Coast as Admiral de Ruyter took all British forts except Cape Coast Castle.[13]

In 1672 the new monopolistic Royal African Company of England took the place of the Company of Royal Adventurers. Appointing agents on the Gold Coast to supervise the slave forts and trading activities, the company proceeded to build or rebuild English forts at Dixcove, Sekondi, Komenda, Anomabu, Winneba and Accra. More important, it strengthened

Cape Coast Castle to the point of making it almost impossible to capture.[14] The formation of the African Company of Merchants Incorporated in 1750 and dissolved in 1821 "was an attempt to provide an adequate government for the slave trade posts which were the British West African settlements of the mid-eighteenth century."[15] Company rule in the slave forts and castles represents a case study of local government and was a precursor to colonial administration that operated out of the forts and castles on the Gold Coast as elsewhere in Africa. Of course, it was also an attempt to run government on the cheap, a phenomenon that characterized British colonial administration on the Gold Coast. The use of the African Company of Merchants obviated the need for government by officers commissioned by the Crown just as the use of African rulers in the celebrated indirect rule system saved the British colonial administration the salaries of Crown agents. Not surprisingly, both the British and French used chiefs or "warrant chiefs" as important cogs in the administrative machinery of the colonies.[16] Cognizance is taken of the fact that the use of chiefly authority was also considered an important element in controlling large areas and people since chiefs exercised some element of control over their people. In effect, the Cape Coast Castle and other British forts served another important function that is hardly mentioned in the annals of the history of the slave trade. They served as the platform or space for experimentation with a model for the administration of the British Empire in the eighteenth century.

In 1821, company rule was abolished and the British government took over responsibility for the Gold Coast and Sir Charles MacCarthy was posted as governor of Sierra Leone with responsibility over the Gold Coast. However, MacCarthy's disastrous 1824 campaign against the Asante resulted in the British government's "neglect" of the Gold Coast and the reintroduction of company rule. It also resulted in the arrival of one the best representatives of both government and company administration the British ever saw on the Gold Coast – Captain George Maclean.

It is not surprising that company rule which was "established to assist the development of the slave trade," survived after the abolition of the trade.[17] Castle administration provided another important development in the evolution of British colonial administration. Joint stock companies of the seventeenth century tended to be monopolistic because of the fact that the company was answerable to the Crown but the Company of Merchants Trading to Africa could not afford to be monopolistic. However, it needed government support against unfriendly rivals and local people and, therefore, could not afford to go against the interests of the crown.[18]

As a base for slave operations in Africa, the forts and castles anchored British trade and British prosperity deriving from the Caribbean. If the Caribbean was the goose that laid the golden egg, Africa was the lifeline needed to keep the goose alive. This was evidenced in a treatise on the trade of Great Britain to Africa (1772), which eloquently spelled out British views on trade in Africa:

> How vast is the importance of our trade to Africa, which is the first principle and foundation of all the rest; the main spring of the machine, which sets every wheel in motion: a trade which arises almost entirely of ourselves, our exports being chiefly our manufactures, or such as are purchased with them, and the returns gold, ivory, wax, dyeing woods and negroes the first four articles of home consumption, or manufactured for exporting the last affording a most prodigious employment to our people, both by sea and land without whom our plantations could not be improved or carried on, nor should we have any shipping passing between the colonies, and the mother country; whereas by their labours our sugars, tobacco, and numberless other arti-cles are raised, which employ an incredible number of ships, and these ships in their turn must employ a much greater number of handicraft trades at home; and the merchandises they bring home and carry out, pay such considerable sums to government, that of them consist the most flourishing branches of revenue; so that both for exports and imports, the improvement of our national revenue, the encouragement of industry at home, the supply of our colonies abroad, and the increase of our naviga-tion, the African trade is so very beneficial to Great Britain, so essentially necessary to the very being of her colonies, that without it neither could we flourish nor they long subsist.[19]

If England was a nation of shopkeepers, the slave forts and castles of the Gold Coast constituted the fulcrum around which British trade on the West African coast revolved, enabling the country to produce and sell in Africa, using to some degree the forts and castles (Tables 5.1 and 5.2). The point being made here is that European trade in West Africa and the Atlantic slave trade were both organized with the Gold Coast forts and castles as the linchpin of both commercial enterprises. Granted that some ships loaded enslaved Afri-cans away from the slave forts and castles, especially the work of interlopers and freebooters, and others did so at the time of the abolition and suppression of the trade, Cape Coast, Anomabu, Elmina, Sekondi, Axim and other forts and castles became, in aggregate terms, very essential to the Euro-African trade.

A number of pamphlets written before and during the Seven Years War fought between England and France linked the African trade to the West Indian trade. Once again, in such a scheme of things, the slave forts and castles loomed large. A 1745 tract notes that

> The trade to Africa involves in it no less than the consideration of our whole West Indies in general; a Trade of such essential and allowed Concernment to the Wealth and Naval Power of Great Britain that it would be as impertinent to take up your Time in expatiating on that subject as in declaiming on the common Benefits of Air and Sunshine in general.[20]

It is important to reiterate that the forts and castles were of tremendous importance to the English plantation trade in America and the Caribbean. They not only supplied labor for plantation agriculture but they also served as conduits for the sale of British manufactured goods. And certainly, in the period of mercantilism, and long before the period of free traders, the African trade was of tremendous importance to the "well-being" of Europe. A writer asserted in 1788, after the loss of the American colonies that

> The African Trade connected as it is with the West Indian commerce, and that to the remaining continental colonies, and Newfoundland Fishery, is of the utmost consequence to the employment of many thousands of our Fellow-subjects, to the Naval Power of Britain, and to the Royal Revenues; all of which are conjoined by sympathetic ties. [21]

This explains why the English government stepped in from time to time to exert control over the Gold Coast settlements and periodically the Crown took over control of the slave forts and castles whenever the companies were on the brink of bankruptcy.

Table 5.1: Volume of British Slave Trade 1690-1807 (Gold Coast)

1690 - 1700	18,300	18.4%
1701 - 1710	37,300	31.2%
1711 - 1720	44,000	31.2%
1721 - 1730	54,200	38.3%
1731 - 1740	56,100	27.1%
1741 - 1750	59,400	23.3%
1751 - 1760	36,500	15.8%
1761 - 1770	43,600	16.6%
1771 - 1780	31,400	16.0%
1781 - 1790	43,900	13.5%
1791 - 1800	27,000	8.3%
1801 — 1807	22,000	8.3%
Total	473,800	18.4%

Source: K.G. Davies, *The Royal African Company* (London: Longmans, 1957), Table 36 143.

Table 5.2: English Slave Trade 1680-1800 Expressed in Percentages of Varying Sample (Gold Coast)

1680 - 1685	20.9%
1688	18.4%
1713	31.2%
1724	38.3%
1752	32.0%
1771	16.0%
1771	13.0%
1788	13.5%
1798	6.2%
1799	9.7%

Sources: Davies, *Royal African Company*, 225, 233, 363; Philip D. Curtin, *The Atlantic Slave Trade: A Census* (Madison: University of Wisconsin Press, 1969), 129.

CAPE COAST CASTLE: DEVELOPMENT AND GROWTH

Table 5.3 shows the significance of castle slaves in the operations of the forts and castles on the Gold Coast. These enslaved Africans were artisans and servants who were largely responsible for cooking, cleaning, washing, repairing and in some cases helping to defend the fort or castle from external attack.

Table 5.3: Cape Coast Castle: Enslaved Africans and Ordnance

CASTLE SLAVES

Carpenters	10	Blacksmith	7	Armourers	3
Brick makers	3	Bricklayers	9	Gunner	1
Goldsmiths	3	Slave Cooks	2	Chief Cooks	3
Doctor's Servants	2	Coopers	3	Chapel Servants	7
Gold Takers	2	Men	137	Canoe men	20
Women	79	Children	76	Grand Total	367

ORDNANCE

On the Platform	29 guns, iron
On the S.E. Baston	6 guns, iron
On the S.W. Round Bastion	6 guns, iron
On the N.W. Bastion	5 guns, iron
On the N.E. Bastion	6 guns, iron
On Greenhill Point	8 guns, iron
On the Parade	1 gun, brass

In the Spur	4 guns, iron, unserviceable
On the lieutenant's Room	1 gun, brass
At Fort Royal	8 guns, iron, dismounted and nailed up
At Phipp's Tower	1 gun, iron
	75 Total

Source: J. J. Crooks, *Records Relating to the Gold Coast Settlements from 1750-1874*, new ed. (London: Frank Cass, 1973).

Cape Coast Castle, like its counterpart in Elmina, is a major historical landmark in West Africa and captures vividly the scope of the slave trade in Western Africa. As one of the largest European structures outside of Europe at the peak of the slave trade, Cape Coast Castle was, and still is, very impressive by all standards (Photo 5.1 and 5.2). It is strategically located on a sheltered beach where waves break against the rocks to the east of the Castle making it difficult to attack. Cabo Corso, Portuguese for Cape Short, was one of the better landing places along the Gold Coast, hence the choice of the location for the castle.

Cape Coast Castle began its life as Fort Carolusburg, a fort built by Heindrick Caerlof in 1652 for the Swedish African Company. This Polish architect also built other Swedish lodges such as the one at Butri, east of Cape Three Points. The fort at Cabo Corso was named Carolusburg after Charles X of Sweden (1655-1660). In 1657, Carolusburg, which was then the headquarters of the Swedish African Company, was captured by the Danish Guinea Company. Two years later, the Danish commander of Fort Carolusburg, Samuel Schmidt, sold the fort, through treachery, to the Dutch.[22] It reportedly changed hands a number of times, including seizure by the local people of Cabo Corso, before 1664, when a joint English-Danish alliance (the Danes were in nearby Fort Fredericksborg) captured Carolusburg from the Dutch. It remained in English possession and Admiral de Ruyter considered its defenses sufficiently improved to be impossible to capture in 1667 without the help of local allies during the Anglo-Dutch war.[23]

Around 1665 the English rebuilt Cape Coast Castle, even though they kept about 75 per cent of the original Swedish structure, and made it the headquarters of the Royal African Company. The English expanded and strengthened the castle at this time because from the Restoration period (1660), English trade on the Guinea coast was revived and the Company of Royal Adventurers of England Trading to Africa was chartered for that purpose. But more important, the 1660s was a period of intense rivalry between the Dutch and the British. In 1664 England seized New Amsterdam (renamed New York) and along the West African coast, Captain Holmes,

Photo 5.1: Cape Coast Castle

Photo 5.2 Cape Coast Castle

Photo 5.3 Cape Coast Castle

along with two men-of-war, six frigates and six smaller ships, took the Dutch forts on the Island of Gorée (Senegal) and on the Gold Coast, at Cabo Corso (Carolusburg), Takoradi, Shama, Mouri, together with small lodges at Anomabu and Egya.[24] After a bombardment by land and sea for about eight days, Governor Tobia Pensado (a Frenchman) surrendered Fort Carolusburg to Captain Holmes.[25] However, the Dutch Admiral de Ruyter replicated the feat of the English Admiral Holmes and took Gorée, and later Kormantin. He blew up the English fort at Takoradi after capturing it but could not take the reinforced Carolusburg. A garrison of fifty men left with stores for six months, together with materials and laborers and helped by the Danes in neighboring Fort Fredericksborg, had rebuilt Fort Carolusburg to make it more difficult to capture. The English subsequently turned it into Cape Coast Castle and the headquarters of the English enterprise on the Gold Coast. However, the Anglo-Dutch competition, the disruption of trade and the resources expended in the war bankrupted the Company of Royal Adventurers.

In 1672, this company, which had been chartered in 1663 by Charles II with the exclusive right to trade to Africa, was abolished and the Royal African Company was established.[26] Based in Cape Coast Castle, the company sent considerable quantities of gold to London but the slave trade overshadowed the gold trade and a much expanded Cape Coast Castle became the focal point for one of the largest removals of enslaved Africans from West Africa. From 1672 onward, the Royal African Company transported about seventy thousand enslaved Africans a year from Cape Coast Castle to the New World. The company built forts at Dixcove (Metal Cross), Sekondi (Orange), Komenda, Anomabu, Tantumquerry (Otuam), Winneba and Accra (James Fort) - all on the Gold Coast and at Whydah on the Slave Coast.[27]

In 1682 Jean Barbot asserted that the castle was situated, "on a round head jutting out into the sea towards the south south-east, and its being compassed on that side and the south-west by several rocks and the sea itself, render it inaccessible on that side."[28] Brodie Cruickshank noted that it [Cape Coast Castle] is protected from the raging surf "by an immense rock, against which the heavy rollers beat with an incessant roar, casting their angry spray over the adjoining bastions."[29] Bosman also noted that Cape Coast Castle was "next to that of St. George d'Elmina the Largest and most Beautiful on the whole Coast; within it is well furnished with fine and well-built Dwelling-places."[30] It was strengthened with four large batteries. One observer noted that "On the battlements are ten guns and twenty-five on the flankers, from minions to nine-pounders and on a rock called Tabora, twenty paces from the Castle, are four, or six twelve pounders, in a round tower, [the base of the present Dalzel Tower] which serves to keep the blacks of the town the better in awe."[31] In addition to the four large batteries is a large platform on the southeast wall of the castle, on which are mounted thirteen pieces of heavy cannon, all about eight-pounders. These are directed toward the sea (pointing on the "road" or the "water passage") to hinder any enemy ships anchoring there.[32] Furthermore, various types of small arms scour all the landing places, and together with these, Cape Coast Castle also enjoyed some natural protection from a great rock lying just before the castle and thus acted as a shield that could absorb shots from the sea.[33] Cruickshank describes the castle thus,

> Many additions have been made to the original structure ... At present it is a large, irregular building, ill-suited for the purpose of defense, but containing within its precincts good and com-modious apartments for the governor and officers, as well as a variety of barrack rooms and warehouses of a very indifferent description. It is calculated to mount from 50 to 60 pieces of ordnance, and there is about that amount of nearly unserviceable cannon at the present battlements.[34]

Between 1766 and 1773, the Committee of Merchants made further modifications to the castle to give it its present look. The expansion and changes made to the castle at this time made it one of the most, if not the most, strongly fortified stronghold on this side of the Atlantic. Not only did the Committee of Merchants gradually rebuild Cape Coast Castle but they also strengthened many of their subordinate forts and replaced walls of unsound structure to make the British settlements on the Gold Coast more durable and able to withstand competition with other European rivals. It was at this time (early 1770s) that the low platform that could mount several cannons was added to the Cape Coast Castle defenses, an addition that made the castle's position unassailable.

As well, the changes to the castle included the addition of a very large underground dungeon, ventilated with grates and a few small holes along the sides of the structure. The underground dungeon was a "spacious arched vault, subdivided into several rooms and entered through an iron gate, in which the slaves were kept while awaiting the arrival of a slave ship. It could hold about one thousand."[35] The underground dungeon of Cape Coast Castle represents one of the most significant slave prisons in the entire history of the Atlantic slave trade (Photo 5.4). Not only could these dungeons hold up to a thousand slaves at any particular time but these "underground bunkers" of the castle are admittedly one of the most remarkable designs for prevent-ing slave rebellions. Literally locked up in the bowels of the castle, there was no way the slaves could mount an effective insurrection. Additionally,

MALE SLAVE DUNGEON
(CIRCA 1792)

Photo 5.4: Underground Dungeon – Cape Coast Castle

Photo 5.5: People Buried at the Courtyard

Photo 5.6: Courtyard – Cape Coast Castle

Photo 5.7: The Platform on the Eastern Side of the Castle

peep holes were cut through the thick walls into the courtyard of the castle grounds so that the activities of the enslaved Africans who were locked up in the bowels of the earth could still be monitored from above ground in the courtyard. This is important in underscoring the fact that slave revolts did not occur only during the Middle Passage. The fear of slave revolts was at the heart of the architectural changes made to the Cape Coast Castle at a time when the British were the largest carriers of enslaved Africans to the Caribbean and the Americas. The same consideration was instrumental in the design and construction of Fort William at Anomabu.

Cape Coast Castle has a very large square or courtyard. It is bounded on one side (the eastern side) where it is open to the sea, by a large platform mounting thirteen guns while on three other sides it was enclosed by buildings containing quarters for the officers and garrison and warehouses for goods (Photo 5.6 and 5.7). The courtyard was also a large grave yard.

The courtyard, which was large enough to parade four to five hundred men was raised about twenty feet above the rock on which the castle stood. The castle was garrisoned by about two hundred red coats, half of whom were Africans, under the command of a captain.[36] Bosman, however, did not see the garrison as any serious force designed to both protect the castle and ward off attackers, local or foreign. Rather, he saw the garrison as a weak force that was addicted to drinking, and that, "the Soldiers are such miserable Wretches that they raise your Pity rather than Fear."[37] In spite of Bosman's characterization of the garrison, a fairly high level of alertness was maintained at the castle. At eight o'clock every night the castle gates were shut and a strong guard mounted, together with sentinels at post on the seaward side of the castle (Photo 5.8). The officer in charge of the guard was provided with a pass-word by the chief agent (the governor) and had to challenge anyone who wanted to be granted access to the castle at night.[38]

Like Elmina Castle, Cape Coast Castle had a large underground cistern beneath the courtyard for the storage of fresh water (Photo 5.9). All the same, whenever the supply was low for whatever reason, company ships were supplied from a pond known as Domine's Hole. This, in all likelihood, is a reference to the lagoon west of Cape Coast, which Barbot described as "lying at some distance towards the sea, between Cabo Corso and Mina ... at a place called Domine."[39] This lagoon is now located at Bakano, a suburb of Cape Coast.

There was also a special dungeon in the courtyard (near the main gate), in which European criminals or insubordinate soldiers were confined before being sent to England to stand trial. Since such personnel were to be shipped off to England to stand trial, they were given the necessities of life before the time of reckoning. However, next to the same dungeon was

Photo 5.8: Sentinel Post – Cape Coast Castle

Photo 5.9: Underground Cistern – Cape Coast Castle

Photo 5.10: Condemned Cell - Cape Coast Castle

a "special" one for recalcitrant enslaved Africans. This "special" dungeon replicated the condemned cells at São Jorge da Mina with its trademark skull and crossbones (Photo 5.10). Enslaved Africans who were kept in this dungeon hardly lived to tell their story. The vital signs of life were gradually squeezed out of them through lack of sustenance, breathable air and appropriate room temperature, all of which were near impossible in this musty, hot and stuffy room.

Finally, on the south side of the parade ground was a "large well-built Chapel, the back part of which joins to the Castle wall, having a great body of the rock Tabora on the outside of it."[40] This chapel became a very significant feature of the castle.

All ships, whether English or foreign, that anchored off the castle or passed within gunshot range of the castle were required to announce their presence by saluting the castle with a prescribed number of shots and by lowering their topsails. Any ship that did not follow these procedures of salutation was considered an enemy vessel and fired upon. The importance of this system of saluting the castle and identifying oneself is vividly portrayed by Barbot, who noted that the French warship *Le Jolly* saluted the castle with seven guns and was answered with five, and when it tried to anchor near the castle the latter fired three guns at the ship.[41] This shows that firing the right number of guns in salute was one way of determining who was an enemy and who was not. In Barbot's words when the captain of the French ship sent a party to investigate why the castle had fired on them, the governor told him in plain words that his orders were to strictly observe regulations concerning security of the Castle.[42]

Early in the 1750s Cape Coast Castle became the springboard for the introduction of Western education to the Gold Coast. The Society for the Propagation of the Gospel sent Phillip Quacoe to England to train as a minister. After his ordination as an Anglican priest, Quacoe became chaplain and schoolmaster of the chapel and Cape Coast castle school.

In the 1870s, Cape Coast Castle first became the headquarters of the West Indian Regiment and, later, the Hausa Constabulary, all of which were mobilized against Asante stranglehold on the Coastal states in 1874.

PERSONNEL

The first staff of Cape Coast Castle after it was rebuilt in 1662 consisted of a "Chief Agent assisted by two other merchants, a warehouse keeper, a gold-taker, two assistants, three assistant factors" and the garrison was composed of fifty soldiers and thirty enslaved Africans. Not surprisingly, the castle could not withstand Dutch firepower during the Anglo-Dutch War.

Photo 5.11: Chapel – Cape Coast Castle

Tylleman reports that Cape Coast Castle was staffed in the 1680s and 1690s by a director or governor who was in control of all the commerce of the area, and was assisted by two merchants or underfactors, a bookkeeper and four assistants and two barbers. In addition, there was a garrison composed of two sergeants, three constables, three corporals, six gentlemen cadets, two drummers, eighty common soldiers and two "Provosts." There were also mulattoes, enslaved Africans and servants.[43]

After the 1660s, Cape Coast Castle became a virtually self-sufficient community, with an administrative body headed by the governor, clerical and mercantile staff responsible for bookkeeping, record keeping and communication with other British establishments as well as with company headquarters in England. There were also workmen, largely castle slaves skilled in all essential handicrafts and in the daily minutiae of cleaning, cooking and other daily comforts of life.[44]

On April 3, 1751, the Committee of the Company of Merchants met in London and decided on the personnel and emoluments for Cape Coast Castle as shown in Table 5.4.

Table 5.4: Personnel and Salaries, Cape Coast Castle, 1751

NAME	POSITION	SALARY PER ANNUM
Thomas Melville, Esq.	President of the Council Chief Agent, Treasurer & Warehouse Keeper	£ 400
William Husbands	Chief Agent	£ 200
Thomas Boteler	Chief Agent & Accountant	£ 200
Ebenezer Young	Assistant to Mr. Melville & Successor to all his Titles, etc., In Case of his Death and Member Of the Council Upon his Arrival	£ 100
Matthew Mackaile	Physician and Surgeon	£ 100
William Tymewell	Factor	£ 80
Joseph Harmer	Factor	£ 80
John Emerton	Factor	£ 80
John Russell	Factor	£ 80
James Wickliffe	Factor	£ 80
Charles Bonville	Writer	£ 60
Andrew Farquhar	Writer	£ 60
Joseph Sayer	Writer	£ 60
John Andrews	Writer	£ 60

NAME	POSITION	SALARY PER ANNUM
James Perrott	Surgeon Mate	£ 60
Richard Westgate	Surgeon's Mate	£ 60
John Slater	Engineer and Surveyor	-
10 Tradesmen	as shall be hereafter agreed	-
30 Soldiers		£ 27

Source: J.J. Crooks, *Records Relating to the Gold Coast Settlements from 1750 to 1874*, new ed. (London: Frank Cass, 1973), 14.

The Company of Merchants meeting on April 8, 1789, made a more extensive provision that included local personnel in the employ of the Company at Cape Coast Castle. The appropriation for personnel is shown in Table 5.5.

Table 5.5: Personnel - Cape Coast Castle, 1789

1 Governor, per annum	£ 400
For the Public Table	400
1 Accountant and Register	200
1 Deputy Accountant	130
1 Secretary	150
1 Deputy Secretary	130
1 Surgeon	100
1 Assistant Surgeon	80
1 Deputy Warehousekeeper	100
Ditto as Gunner	36
1 Chaplain	80
Ditto as Writer	60
1 Officer of the Guard	80
Ditto as Inspector of the Hospital	50
1 Surveyor	100
1 Deputy Surveyor	80
4 Factors @ £ 80	320
4 Writers @ £ 60	240
1 Serjeant	50
2 Corporals @ £ 36	72
30 Soldiers @ £ 27	810
2 Drummers @ £ 27	54

2 Fifers @ £ 13 : 10	27
1 Drum Major	36
1 Gardener	50
1 Butler	<u>50</u>

40 Non-Commissioned Servants

20 Commissioned Servants

60 In Garrison	
	———
	£ 3,885

African Servants

1 Cabbocer	100
1 Linguist	100
1 Captain General of the Town	60
2 Black Writers @ £ 40	80
	———
	£ 4,225

Table 5.6: Royal African Company (English) Personnel in the Gold Coast Forts and Castles 1673-1713

	1673 DEC.	1674 SEPT.	1683 APR.	1684 JULY	1685 APR.	1686 JAN.	1687 JULY	1688 MAY	1689 JAN.	1690 NOV.
Cape Coast	39	53	64	80	55	73	105	115	102	84
In sloops attending	-	-	26	23	22	61	19	21	28	23
Accra	2	4	8	10	10	11	12	12	19	16
Alampo	-	-	-	-	-	-	-	-	-	-
Anashan	-	-	-	-	2	-	1	2	2	-
Anomabu	-	-	9	10	8	9	13	13	11	7
Dixcove	-	-	-	-	-	-	-	-	-	-
Egya (Agya)	-	3	2	2	2	3	2	3	3	-
Fredericksborg (Fort Royal)	-	-	-	-	7	4	15	11	18	12
Komenda	2	4	1	1	1	2	2	-	-	-
Lagoo	-	-	-	-	-	-	-	-	-	-
Qn. Anne's Pt	-	-	-	-	-	-	-	-	-	-
Sekondi	-	-	2	2	3	6	9	13	7	6
Shido	-	-	-	-	-	-	-	-	-	-

Tantumkweri	-	-	-	-	-	-	-	-	-	-
Takoradi	2	-	-	-	-	-	-	-	-	-
Winneba	2	4	-	-	-	-	-	-	-	-

	1691	1693	1694	1695	1696	1697	1701	1702	1703	1704
	June	Mar.	Apr.	Jan.	Aug.	Apr.	-	Sept.	Mar.	Jan.
Cape Coast	97	114	75	80	66	67	?	55	71	86
In sloops attending	-	-	13	-	-	-	13	7	-	-
Accra	16	12	16	18	17	16	17	12	17	16
Alampo	-	-	-	-	-	-	2	6	3	4
Anashan	-	2	2	1	1	1	-	-	-	2
Anomabu	9	8	10	11	12	10	16	14	13	8
Dixcove	1	7	13	9	12	13	12	10	8	9
Egya (Agya)	-	2	2	2	2	-	1	2	3	2
Frederiksborg (Fort Royal)	8	9	9	4	4	4	-	-	-	-
Komenda	-	-	-	8	17	17	18	16	18	11
Lagoo	-	-	-	-	-	-	-	-	-	-
Qn. Anne's Pt.	-	-	-	-	-	-	-	-	-	-
Sekondi	7	5	-	-	-	-	-	-	-	-
Shido	-	-	-	-	-	-	-	-	-	-
Tantumkweri	-	2	-	-	-	-	3	2	2	2
Takoradi	-	-	-	-	-	-	-	-	-	-
Winneba	-	-	2	9	11	11	16	14	15	10

	1705	1706	1707	1708	1710	1711	1712	1713
	Jan.	Mar.	Sept.	Oct.	Feb.	Apr.	Aug.	June
Cape Coast	81	53	90	62	59	55	91	73
In sloops attending	-	-	-	-	-	-	-	-
Accra	21	11	17	19	13	14	18	20
Alampo	-	3	-	-	-	-	-	-
Anashan	-	-	-	-	-	-	-	-
Anomabu	11	6	7	7	7	7	9	9
Dixcove	9	6	7	9	8	12	13	13
Egya (Agya)	2	2	2	1	1	-	-	-
Frederiksborg Fort Royal	4	3	4	4	5	5	5	5
Komenda	9	12	8	8	9	10	8	11
Lagoo	2	-	-	-	-	-	-	-
Qn. Anne's Pt.	5	3	3	4	5	3	5	5
Sekondi	6	10	10	6	7	13	14	11
Shido	-	4	3	2	1	-	-	2

Tantumkweri	1	-	-	2	2	2	2	5
Takoradi	-	-	-	-	-	-	-	-
Winneba	9	9	11	11	8	14	15	12

Source: Davies, *The Royal African Company*, 247-248.

The size of the British personnel at the various fortified stations, as can be seen from table 5.6, depended on the size of the station as well as its strategic and economic importance. Some of these fortified stations were abandoned and reoccupied during the period under consideration, December 1673 to June 1713. For example the English Fort at Komenda was occupied by British personnel in December 1673 but was abandoned in 1687 due to the Komenda wars or Dutch-Komenda wars. The Fort was later resettled and in January 1695, there were eight officials in residence and was occupied right through 1713.[45] Similarly, the little factory at Anashan (modern Biriwa) was occupied and abandoned several times in the forty-year period under consideration.

The author of the document *A Treatise upon the Trade* gave a terrible indictment of the administration of Cape Coast Castle when he noted that

> The Committee-men (of the African Committee) ... are self-chosen, and consequently independent of the real African merchants, unattentive of the publick good, and industrious only to raise fortunes for themselves, by means of that publick money annually allowed them for the general advantage of the whole trade. They make their own dependents the governors of the forts, and carry on their trade by their means, either evading or boldly acting in defiance of the law of their country; and having the advantage of house and warehouse room, their servants abroad and freight of their goods out of the publick defence, can afford to overbid the private traders. ...
>
> The governors of the forts though to appearance forbidden to ship off slaves for their own use in pain of dismission, yet knowing they can depend on the committee-men for their protection, as they are secretly interested in their trade, do it clandestinely, and when they leave the Coast, always take care to have a noble cargo of the very best negroes to carry with them. The poor soldiers are obliged to do all their work and labour for them, though miserably supplied, at the dearest rates with the common necessaries of life."[46]

It is important to point out that merchant oversight of Cape Coast Castle and other British forts on the Gold Coast came under periodic review in England such as the Select Committee of 1865.

Since Ghana's independence in 1957, Cape Coast Castle has served as a police training depot, a historical museum, regional headquarters of the Ghana Museums and Monuments Board and a UNESCO World Heritage site.

ANOMABU FORT

Sandwiched between the English base at Cape Coast and the Dutch base at Fort Amsterdam, Anomabu was strategically located and from the middle of the seventeenth century, European companies vied with each other to establish a foothold at Anomabu. In 1640 the Dutch built the earliest trading post, an earthwork lodge that became a victim of European rivalry on the Gold Coast. The little trade lodge changed hands four times – the Swedes, the Danes and the Dutch (1665) all took turns with ownership of the lodge until it finally reverted back to the English.

When Admiral de Ruyter wreaked havoc on English forts as part of the Anglo-Dutch wars, the English fort at Anomabu became the site for one of the bloodiest battles of the war, culminating in Admiral de Ruyter's capture of the fort from the English.[47] It was fortified with "12 cannon, besides some small ones of no value, and occupied by one chief factor, one under-factor, one assistant, one constable, one corporal and 8 common soldiers."[48]

Anomabu Fort, in its present form, was built by the English in 1673-1674 (Photo 5.12). Redmayne described it as "a rectangular shell of windowless walls, with projecting towers at the corners, so that every wall was covered by the guns of the battlements. Within the court there is ample trading and barrack accommodation; but this building – unlike many in Dutch and Portuguese West Africa – is bare and ill-proportioned."[49] This definitely indicates that the fort was built more for utilitarian purposes than as a luxurious residence for officials and merchants. It was a slave prison par excellence.

In 1698 the English Royal African Company adopted other measures to exploit the presence of a large number of merchants trading around Anomabu. They granted licenses to ships belonging to foreign nations or individuals to trade in the region between Cape Coast and Otuam or Tantumquery on condition that they paid a 10 per cent "affiliation fee.[50] While this was an attempt to regulate illegal trade by these freebooters and interlopers who were eating into the profits of the Company, a large number of these interlopers flooded the Gold Coast. Anomabu became a popular haunt for these traders who were despatching vast numbers of enslaved Africans to the New World until their licensing was stopped in 1712.

K.J. Anquandah notes that the Dutch director-general at Elmina, Engel-graaf Robbertsz, quoting an English captain on Anomabu Slave Trade figures, stated in 1717 that "From January 1702 to August 1708 [the 10 percenters] they took to Barbados, Jamaica a total of not less than 30,141 slaves and in this figure are not included transactions made for other ships sailing to such Islands as Nevis, Montserrat, St. Christopher, for the South Sea Company, with New Netherlands and others which would increase the above number considerably, and of which Annemaboe alone could provide about one third." [51]

Fort William (Photo 5.13), built between 1753 and 1770 as an entirely new fort close to the partially demolished Fort Charles (Photo 5.14), and named after King Willian IV, was changed in appearance in the early nineteenth century when a new storey was added.

It was built largely of local and imported bricks and lime on an eroded shelf of hard rock close to a sandy beach indentation with a sheltered anchorage. [52] The rock base extends from far out to sea right onto the beach where the fort stands. It is believed that the rocky outcrop is the abode of a deity, *Obonoma*, from whom the town derives its name, Anomabu. The rocky outcrop not only undergirds the fort but also appears in the male slave dungeon where a shrine dedicated to the deity can be seen today [53] (Photo 5.15)

Structurally, Fort William is a square building with larger, solid brick bastions in the northeast and southeast and smaller bastions in the southwest and northwest corners, and a three-storey main building complex constructed of stone. [54] Like other forts and castles, imported bricks were specifically used to design the vaults.

Unlike other Gold Coast slave forts and castles, Fort William's original design and structure are unique in the sense that it was conceived and planned specifically as a large slave prison (the northwest bastion) to hold significant numbers of enslaved Africans awaiting transport to the New World. [55] This slave prison has tall vaults, rock floors, and very high dark walls as compared to other similar structures on the Gold Coast (Photo 5.17). Fort William is a deceptively small fort in the sense that it could accommodate more enslaved Africans than many other such forts, and compares favorably with Cape Coast Castle in the number of enslaved Africans it could hold at any particular time. Not surprisingly, a large number of enslaved Africans were shipped by the British and other European slave traders from Anomabu. Another significant feature of the slave prison in Fort William is that unlike any other fort or castle, there are numerous iron stakes driven into the floors to hold enslaved Africans in chains (Photo 5.18).

Photo 5.12: Fort William - Anomabu

Photo 5.13: Fort William

Photo 5.14: Fort Charles

Photo 5.15: Shrine in Fort William dedicated to Obonoma

Photo 5.16: Fort William

Photo 5.17: Fort William - High Walls and Tall Vaults

Photo 5.18: Iron Stakes in Floors of Slave Prison (Fort William)

The fort is a solid architectural piece and heavily armed with the "best stock of cannons" of the eighteenth and nineteenth century forts that various Europeans nations built on the Gold Coast.[56] It was built at the height of the slave trade and the Royal African Company was bent on a large slave prison that could be a clearinghouse of its slave purchases along the coast from Accra to Cape Coast. Fort William served Anomabu and Ghana well into recent times as a rest house, a post office and a prison.[57] At present a non-governmental organization plans to use the rooms on the second floor as classrooms for a university college. In the meantime, one of the rooms is used as public library (Photo 5.19).

In 1807 Anomabu fort witnessed the might of the resurgent Asante power on the Gold Coast. In that year, the fort almost capitulated to the Asante who had conquered most of the states of the then Gold Coast, between the interior and the seacoast. The Asantehene Mensah Bonsu reportedly earned his name Bonsu (whale) by dipping his foot in the sea at Anomabu, a remarkable feat for the leader of an inland nation such as Asante.

According to Claridge,

> Anamabu was very large and populous, but the people bore a very bad character and were particularly turbulent. The English Factors dare not in the least contradict them but are rather obliged to bear with them ... The great wealth of the Fantineans makes them so proud and haughty that a European trading there must stand bare to them. They often extorted money from the Factor by shutting the garrison up in the Fort, closing all the paths so that no traders could come down, and compelling him in a very short time to purchase peace and a renewal of trade at their own price.[58]

But this was certainly not the case when the Asante invaded the coastal states of the Gold Coast in the early nineteenth century. It was the guns of the fort that prevented a catastrophic defeat of the Fanti states.

At the April 8, 1789, meeting, the Committee of Merchants appropriated £ 818 for the following personnel at Fort William: 1 chief factor, 1 factor, 1 sergeant, 1 gunner and 8 soldiers.[59]

In 1941, Anomabu fort served as a government rest house. "Its white-washed walls gleam on the shore – but the walls of the courtyard are cracking and the maintenance grant insufficient for their repair."[60] In the 1940s, Fort William served as a local telephone office.

Photo 5.19: Fort William - Community Library

FORT METAL CROSS (DIXCOVE)

Fort Metal Cross was one of the smallest as well as one of the most elegantly built of the British possessions on the Gold Coast. Built at Mfuma (better known as Dixcove, a corruption of Dick's Cove) by the English in 1691, "Its triangular courtyard, with the apex cut off and replaced by an inner rectangular court, is one of its main features. Its style of architecture is reminiscent of the earlier Portuguese work."[61] It was not, in the end, a terribly profitable fort for trade in enslaved Africans.

The English and Brandenburgers struggled for control of Ahantaland around Mfuma in the late 1680s. The English were particularly interested in building a fort at Dixcove to disrupt the activities of English interloper captains who traded at the Brandenburger Fort *Gross Friedrichsburg* at Pokesu. A secure foothold in the neighborhood of the Brandenburg fort would enable them to vigorously chase away the interlopers who were cutting into English trade. The English fort at Dixcove was built in 1691 after several disputes with the Brandenburgers who were also interested in Dixcove, not far from Pokesu. It was fairly well defended (Table 5.7)

Table 5.7: Ordnance at Fort Metal Cross

S. platform	9 guns, iron
N.E. Bastion	5 guns, iron
S.W. Bastion	5 guns, iron
S.E. Bastion	2 guns, iron
S.W. Platform	1 gun, iron
N.W. Bastion	3 guns, iron

The Brandenburgers had earlier (before the 1800s) planted the flag of the Elector of Brandenburg at Dixcove but found the area unprofitable and quietly gave it up to the English. It was in these circumstances that the English won over the chief of Upper/Greater Dixcove who gave land to the former to build a fort on a promontory near Mfuma village.[62] The Royal African Company commenced construction of the fort in the large, sheltered bay, whose calm waters and sandy beach made it ideal to launch canoes and small boats from the shoreline to the ships that anchored offshore on the high seas (Photo 5.21).

The town of Dixcove or Mfuma was located in

Photo 5.20: Caretaker – Anomabu Fort (right)

a deep Valley encircled with a high rising ground overtopped with high, close, and ever verdant trees of an African Forest, and the village encircled and ever shaded with tall Majestic Cocoa nut trees.[63]

The British Fort Metal Cross was located, according to the Slave ship Captain Brooks, near the entrance into Dix's Cove,

on a rising eminence about 80 feet above the level of the sea …its rising declivity enables it to have an entire view and command of the native town below and the surrounding Country. Its situation would enable it to sustain a considerable siege in case of difficulties with the different native tribes, and afford releaf and permanent protection to the town under its Charge[64] (Photo 5.21)

The Royal African Company commenced fort construction in 1691 but could complete construction only seven years later in 1698 because of the hostility of the local people. This hostility, manifested in occasional attacks by the Ahanta people, was not unconnected with the Dutch presence at the nearby fort Batenstein at Butre.

The original fort, as described by Jean Barbot, was a "square structure with a pointed bastion at each corner except for the southwest corner which had a round tower. The bastions and tower were linked by curtain walls. The inner structure comprised apartments, storage rooms and kitchen arranged around a small courtyard."[65] (Photo 5.22). This original structure underwent several alterations in the eighteenth century, most especially, a spur ending with a bastion which consisted of garrison apartments, storage rooms and a workshop.[66] In the eighteenth century, the Dutch and the English extended their spurs and outworks to enable them to hold more enslaved Africans, and following this practice, one of the hollow bastions in the main section of Fort Metal Cross was used as a slave prison. The fort was built of stone and lime with two round flankers and four batteries mounting twenty guns and, by 1750, it was equipped to mount 25 canons. It had a spur on the western side and a moderately high square tower. It was defended by a garrison of about thirty men, half of whom were European and the other half African.[67]

Captain Edward Harrington described Fort Metal Cross as a

quadrangular Building with an open Brick paved square in the center. Along the sides of the square are erected Rooms, and apartment occupied as soldiers quarters, armory, ammunition, and provision stores. In the Center and underneath of the open square is a tank or a large Cistern which is filled with water by the conductors from the flat roofs and Battery terrace above during the rainy

Photo 5.21: The Sheltered Bay of Mfuma

season, and which is sufficient to supply the fort during the rest of the year. On the eastern angle of the Fort above the basement stores are Built the apartments for the commanding officers, consisting of a large Hall three other rooms (say Bed rooms) and a Kitchen. The top of this building as well as the stores are composed of flat cemented roofs, which with the Batteries afford pleasant and cool promenade of an evening all around this buildings and the top of the terrace. On top of the outside wall of the Fort is the battery consisting of about 30 guns. Long 18 & 24 Pounders or they carry 24 & 18 Pound shot to a long distance[68] (Photo 5.22)

Fort Metal Cross was a small fort and at the time of Captain Harrington's visit, Mr. Frank Swanzy was the official in change of the fort. Mr. Swanzy performed the functions of

> Governor, Commander, Judge, magistrate, Doctor, School Inspector, and Clergyman. Reading services and Himms after the custom of the Church of England in his Hall to a considerable number of Blacks, Molattoes, and quadroons on Sundays, and in the same Hall holding a court of Justice during a part of week days, when the cases are brought from his own clan or those over whom he holds an immediate Influence and Jurisdiction but also by parties a Month's Journey from the interior.[69]

Dixcove's chief claim to fame, as stated by Claridge and others, lay in its notoriety in trading in counterfeit gold (diluted) with European traders. It was noted that

> Dixcove Fort had only recently been finished [1692], and in this year the people laid siege to it, and very nearly succeeded in taking it. As it was, they compelled the Factor to submit to their terms, by which he acknowledged that he had no power or authority over them, and agreed to join them in cheating all ships that called there by passing imitation gold to them. This compact was so well kept that the place soon became known as the "false mint of Guinea" and in 1701 two small ships, the cargo on one of which alone was valued at £1,700 sold their whole stock there and received nothing but this false gold in exchange. The manufacture of this imitation gold was a regular industry at Dixcove, and it was sold by the makers at the rate of a crown in good gold for false gold at the apparent value of twenty pounds.[70]

Fort Metal Cross, like Batenstein, was not of tremendous commercial importance. While gold was mined and traded in the region in the sev-

Photo 5.22: Fort Metal Cross

enteenth and eighteenth centuries, substantial quantities of false gold was also peddled to the unsuspecting stranger. Not surprisingly, whatever little economic activity at the fort declined after the abolition of the slave trade. The British traded textiles, metal bars, rum and gunpowder for limited quantities of gold, ivory and palm oil at Mfuma or Dixcove in exchange but generally, Fort Metal Cross was not a very viable commercial fort. Slave supply was pitiful. However, the fort served other interests of its British occupants. The forests of Mfuma and its surrounding areas, located in the tropical rain forest region of the Gold Coast, produced substantial quantities of timber for building operations (both forts and ships). As well, the area was important for quality lime, limestone and clay for locally-made bricks. These resources of Mfuna proved vital to the English commercial enterprise in the region. Thus, while Dixcove lacked gold or large numbers of enslaved Africans, Fort Metal Cross became an indispensable service fort for the repair of English ships and English forts on the Gold Coast.[71]

In 1867 the English transferred the Dixcove fort to the Dutch in an exchange of forts and territory on the Gold Coast. The Dutch renamed the fort, Metalen Kruis (Brass Cross), after one of the gunboats sent from Holland to enforce the exchange and suppress revolts by locals who rose up in revolt against the swap of territory by different European powers in this 1867 Anglo-Dutch exchange of forts.[72] The exchange of territory, which eventually transferred various peoples from one overlord to another and from one trading partner also to another, was initiated without the knowledge and the consent of the local peoples involved. Consequently, there was a lot of commotion in Mfuma and the surrounding areas during this transfer to the Dutch, for the people were averse to Dutch rule. The troubles between the people and the new Dutch "masters" continued until the fort and all other Dutch possessions on the Gold Coast were eventually bought by the English in 1872 and thus ended the Dutch period on the Gold Coast.[73]

In 1872, the British purchased Dutch possessions on the Gold Coast and the fort reverted back to England. Subsequently, the name Metalen Kruis was changed to the anglicised Metal Cross. During the colonial period, the English used Fort Metal Cross as District Officers' residence and offices, State Council offices, police and post offices. This continued in the period after Ghana's independence.

PERSONNEL

In a meeting on April 8, 1789, the Committee of Merchants earmarked £ 385 for the following personnel at Fort Metal Cross: 1 chief factor, 1 writer, 1 Sergeant, 1 gunner, 5 soldiers and 1 Black writer.[74] In addition to the above personnel, the company had sixty two enslaved Africans as fort workers. Out of these, four were sawyers, four carpenters, four smiths, two masons and forty-three all-purpose workers, and five sick enslaved Africans at the time the data were recorded.[75]

FORT ORANGE - SEKONDI

Fort Orange at Sekondi is a small fort and insignificant architecturally. It was built by the Dutch in 1640 and called Fort Oranje. In 1694 it was captured and pillaged by the Ahanta. It then came into English possession until 1872. In the 1940s it was used as a prison.

Fort Orange was much like Fort Metal Cross at Dixcove but with larger and stronger guns. It was a "square white house in a yard, mounting eight or ten guns on a terrace on the roof."[76] In all respects, it was very much like an earlier English fort that was neglected for such a long time that the guns became "literally honey-combed with rust and the carriages rotten and useless" and thus was easily captured by the people of Ahanta and pillaged in 1694.[77]

Fort Orange at Sekondi had the following ordnance: the north bastion had six iron guns, the west bastion had four iron guns, the south one had six iron guns, the east bastion nine and the north-east curtain five.

The Committee of Merchants made allocation for the following fort personnel at Sekondi in its April 8, 1789, meeting: one chief factor, one surgeon, one sergeant, one gunner and five soldiers. The total emoluments for these personnel amounted to £ 387.[78] In addition to the paid personnel, the fort was also staffed by ten enslaved Africans - five women, two women and three children.

CONCLUSION

It was not for nothing that the English outlasted all European nations on the Gold Coast. First, they purchased all the Danish settlements and brought the Danish period on the Gold Coast to an end. Later, the English exchanged forts and settlements with the Dutch in 1867. The Sweet River between Elmina and Cape Coast demarcated the new boundary between English and Dutch settlements. In 1872 the English purchased all Dutch settlements on the Gold Coast and lowered the curtain on the Dutch period on the Gold Coast. Cape Coast Castle continued to be the headquarters of English commercial and, later, political operations on the Gold Coast. In 1874, the English defeated the Asante in the Sagrenti war and in 1900-1901 finally brought Asante under British rule after the Yaa Asantewaa War. Tables 5.8, 5.9, 5.10

and 5.11 in the Appendix to this chapter, refer to the Sekondi Fort Day Book, English exports from the Gold Coast, numbers of enslaved Africans and ordnance and travel times. Table 5.8 shows the stores and the number of castle slaves in the English fort at Sekondi for the two month period of January and February 1766, together with the movement of personnel on company business to other English forts and castles on the Gold Coast/Ghana. Finally, Table 5.9 itemizes some of the major items of English trade in the slave forts cand castles and, Table 5.10 shows the ordnance at various English forts.

Table 5.8: Succondee (Sekondi) Fort Day Book for the Months of January and February 1766

January 1st
Inventory of Slaves, Stores, Ordnance & Ordnance Stores Belonging to the Company of Merchants Trading to Africa Remaining Here This Day

NAMES	OCCUPATION	CONDITION	YEARS (AGE)	PAY PER MO.	PAY DUE 2 MO. £	s	d
Men							
Cruzoe (Cudjoe)	Bricklayer	Sickly	13	20/-	2	-	-
Twitee	Laborer	Superanuated	63	10/-	1	-	-
Adougia	Canoemen	Superanuated	58	10/-	1	-	-
Quashie Cumah	Laborer	Healthy	36	15/-	1	10	-
Succondee (Sekondi)	Laborer	Healthy	39	15/-	1	10	-
Adoom	Laborer	Healthy	45	15/-	1	10	-
John	Laborer	Healthy	-	20/-	2	-	-
Women							
Ambah	Laborer	Superanuated	58	10/-	1	-	-
Abruah	Laborer	Healthy	68	5/-	-	10	-
Adjuah & child	Laborer	Healthy	21	12/6	1	5	-
Jackoo & child	Washerwoman	Healthy	28	12/6	1	5	-
Marimba	Laborer	Healthy	31	10/6	1	-	-
Adjua Coomah	Laborer	Healthy	18	7/6	-	15	-
	Amount of their pay for these 2 months				16	5	-

INVENTORY OF STORES		ORDNANCE
1 Pile 4 MK Weights;	Incompleat	3 9 Pounders good
2 Sifters (?);	1 Message Stick	2 6 Pounders good
1 Dorman Lanthern;	1 mortar and pestle	12 4 Pounders 9 good & 3 bad
1 Gun & Bayonet;	1 Scabbard	7 1 Pounders 1 bad
1 Gold Chizzle;	4 Rings	5 3 Pounders 2 good & 3 bad
1 Half hour glass;	1 Hammer	The carriages of most of the
2 Masons Towels;	1 Garden Watering Pot	above guns are bad

3 Spades	820 shot of sorts
2 Pick axes	A quantity of cast iron for
	Patridge Shot
	1 powder horn
	1 Castle flag

January 1st
Balance of Supplies Remaining Here this Day

500 Billets wood 10/100	£	2	10	0

Memorandum Feb. 28th

Sent John Coe (?) slave @ 20/- per Month to Winneba Fort to commence there March 1st

January 26th

John Shupten arrived from Cape Coast to commence this day

February 28th

Received from Cape Coast Castle these 2 months the following Supplies for the support of this fort

1 Fustian Coat		2	10	0
2 lbs Pepper	2/6	-	5	0
20 Yards Osnabrigs	1/1	1	1	8
2 Bottles Fine Oil	2/-	-	1	0
	£	4	8	0

Castle Stores

200 6 penny sail (?)	12/100	£ -	1	2			
200 8 penny sail	10/100	-	1	8			
200 10 penny sail		-	2	0			
22 Yards Canvas	1/6	1	13	0			
10 lbs Yellow Paint	1/1	-	10	0			
2 Large Extra padlock	5/-	-	10	0	2	17	10

Furnished by David Mill in these 2 Months the Following Supplies for the Support of the Fort

		£	s	D
70 Fathoms Tobaco	2/6	8	15	0
1 Guinea Staff		-	7	6
28½ Gallons Rum	6/-	8	11	0
9 Kegs Tallow	10/-	4	10	-
8 Long Ells	60/-	24	0	0
7 Brass Pans	3/4	1	3	4
6 Halfsays	35/-	10	10	0
7 Cotton Romauls	5/-	3	0	0
		67	16	10

Castle Charges in These Two Months

January 26	Subsistence to a Messenger from Commenda [Komenda] With a letter from this place	£	s	d
	½ Fathom Tobacco 2/6	-	1	3
January 28	Subsistence to 5 Company Slaves Canoemen with Letter from Appollonia Settlement			
	1 Fathom Tobacco 2/6	-	2	6
February 2	Paid a Dutch Carpenter for making a frame to a filtering Stone and Other jobs			
	1 Guinea Staff	-	7	6
February 4	Subsistence to a Messenger from Commendah [Komenda] with a Letter for Dixcove			
	½ Fathom Tobacco 2/6	-	1	3
February 4	Subsistence to a Messenger from Dixcove With the Accounts of that Fort			
	½ Fathom Tobacco 2/6	-	1	3
February 4	Subsistence to a Messenger carrying this Fort's [Dixcove] accounts to Commendah [Komenda]			
	½ Fathom Tobacco 2/6	-	1	3
February 8	Subsistence to a Messenger from Commendah [Komenda] with a letter for Appollonia Settlement			
	½ Fathom Tobacco 2/6	-	1	3
February 8	Paid 3 free Canoemen carrying the above Letter on board Capt. Gullan's boat/she Being off Chamah [Shama]			
	1 ½ Fathoms Tobacco 2/6	-	3	9
February 14	Paid free people for assisting the Company Slaves in cutting palisades to stop up the breaches in the bastions			
	2 Gallons Rum 6/-	-	12	0

February 18	Subsistence to a Messenger from				
	Commendah [Komenda] with a letter for this place				
	¼ Gallon Rum	6/-	-	1	6
February 28	Expended in the Hall Case in these 2 mos.				
	16 Gallons Rum	6/-	4	16	-
February 28	Expended in Lights for the Forts				
	1 Keg Tallow		-	10	-
February 28	Delivered on Garrison Pay in these 2 months as per Garrison Ledger				
	1 Fustian Coat		2	10	-
	2 lbs Pepper	2/6	-	5	-
	20 Yards Osnabrigs	1/1	1	1	8
	2 Bottles Fine	2/-	-	4	-
	8 Long Ells	60/-	24	-	-
	4 Kegs Tallow	10/-	2	-	-
	7 Brass Pans	3/4	1	3	4
	¼ Gallon Rum	6/-	-	1	6
	6 Halfsays	35/-	10	10	-
	6 Cotton Romauls	20/-	6	-	-
	6 Gallons Brandy	5/-	1	10	-
	£		49	5	6
February 28	Balance of Supplies remaining here this day				
	500 Billets Wood	10/100	2	10	0

Castle Stores

200 6 penny nails @ 7^d/100		-	1	2
200 8 penny nails @ 10^d/100		-	1	8
200 10 penny nails @ 1/100		-	2	0
22 Yards canvas	1/6	1	13	0
10 lbs Yellow paint	1/-	-	10	0
2 Large Padlocks	5/-	-	10	0
		2	17	10
		£52.3.4		

Delivered on Black Men's Pay in the 2 Months
as per Garrison Ledger

10 Gallons Rum	10/-	5	0	0
1 Cotton Romaul		1	10	0
6 Gallons Brandy	10/-	3	0	0
4 Kegs Tallow	15/-	3	0	0
		12.10.0		

Paid the Company's Slaves their Pay for these 2 Months

65 Fathoms Tobacco	5/-	16.5.0

Total Amount of Castle Charges Carried Over   £ 87.17.10

Amount Thereof Brought Over   £87   17   10

Defrayment Thereof viz:

		£	s	d
5 Fathoms Tobacco	2/6	-	12	6
1 Guinea Stuff		-	7	6
8 ½ Gallons Rum	6/-	5	11	0
5 Kegs Tallow	10/-	2	10	0
1 Fustian Coat		2	10	0
2 lbs Pepper	2/6	-	5	0
20 Yards Osnabrigs	1/1	1	1	8
2 Bottles Fine Oil	2/-	-	4	0
8 Long Ells	60/-	24	0	0
7 Brass Pans	3/4	1	3	4
6 Halfsays	35/-	10	10	0
6 Cotton Romaul	20/-	6	0	0
6 Gallons Brandy	5/-	1	10	0
10 Gallons Rum	10/-	5	0	0
1 Cotton Romaul		1	10	0
6 Gallons Brandy	10/-	3	0	0
4 Kegs Tallow	15/-	3	0	0
65 Fathoms Tobacco	5/-	16	5	0
		85	**0**	**0**

Castle Stores

		£	s	d
200 6 penny nails	7/100	-	1	2
200 8 penny nails	10/100	-	1	8
200 10 penny nails	1/100	2	0	0
22 Yards Canvas	1/6	1	13	0
10 lbs Yellow Paint	1/-	-	10	0
2 Large Extra Padlocks	5/-	-	10	0
		2	17	10
		87	17	10

Source: Succondee [Sekondi] Fort in Charge of David Mill. Accounts for the months of January and February 1766.

Table 5.9: Items of Trade on the Gold Coast (British Exports) 1673-1702

1. Metal and Metalware
    a. Iron bars
    b. Copper bars
    c. Brassware
    d. Pewterware

2. British Wollens
    f. Perpetuanas
    g. Says
    h. Welsh plains

3. East India textiles
    a. Allejaes
    b. Baftes
    c. Brawles
    d. Guinea Stuffs
    e. Long cloths
    f. Longees
    g. Nicconees
    h. Pautkes
    i. Tapseels

4. Miscellaneous textiles
    a. Annabasses
    b. Carpets
    c. Sletias
    d. Sheets
    e. Boysados

5. Gunpowder, firearms and knives

6. Miscellaneous
    a. Cowries
    b. Beads
    c. Coral

Source: Culled from T 70/910-920 in Davies, 351-357.

Table 5.10: Castle Slaves and Ordnance

Komenda

Slaves: - Bomb boy 1, sawyers 10, women 6, children 5

	Ordnance
S.W. Bastion	9 guns, iron
S.E. Bastion	8 guns, iron
-	6 guns iron

Tantumquerry

Slaves: - Men 6, women 4.

	Ordnance
S.E. Bastion	4 guns, iron
S.W. Bastion	3 guns, iron
N.E. Bastion	4 guns, iron
N.W. Bastion	4 guns, iron
In the Tower	3 guns, iron
	unserviceable

N.B. – All hardly fit for use

Winneba

Slaves: - Men 8 women 5.

	Ordnance
S.E. Bastion	4 guns, iron
S.W. Bastion	3 guns, iron
N.E. Bastion	3 guns, iron
N.W. Bastion	3 guns, iron
Platform	2 guns, iron
Over the gate	2 guns, iron

Accra

Slaves: - Men 7, women 15, children 4, canoe men 6

	Ordnance
N.W. Bastion	6 guns, iron
N.E. Bastion	5 guns, iron
S.W. Bastion	4 guns, iron
S.E. Bastion	4 guns, iron
Platform	14 guns, iron

Whydah

Slaves: - Men 33, women 46, children 27, canoe men 12

	Ordnance
S.W. Bastion	9 guns, iron
S.E. Bastion	8 guns, iron
N.E. Bastion	6 guns, iron
N.W. Bastion	11 guns, iron
Parade	1 gun, iron

Source: Crooks, *Records Relating to the Gold Coast Settlements.*

Table 5.11: Time of Traveling from Apollonia to Cape Coast Castle by Hammock, at 3 1/4 mph

	Hrs.	Mins.	Hrs.	Mins.
From Apollonia to Axim	8	0	-	-
Axim to Dixcove	7	35	-	-
Dixcove to Butri	1	15	-	-
Boutrie to Takoradi	4	30	-	-
Taccorary to Sekondi	1	10	-	-
Secondee to Shama	2	30	-	-
Shama to Komenda	3	0	-	-
Commendah to Elmina	2	25	-	-
Elimina to Cape Coast Castle	2	0	-	-
From Apollonia to Cape Coast Castle	32	25	-	-

From Accra to Cape Coast Castle at the same rate of travelling:-

	Hrs.	Mins.
Accra to Lacoom River	2	0
Fettah	5	20
Beraku	6	30
Winneba	9	10
Winneba to Manguadie	1	20
Asam	2	15
Mumford	3	7
Lagos	4	12
Tantum	4	40
Tantum to Anaguah	3	0
Anomabu	6	0
Cape Coast Castle	9	15
Distance from Accra to Cape Coast Castle	23	5
Apollonia to Cape Coast Castle	32	25
Apollonia to Accra	55	30

Source:

Notes

1. Arnold Hodson, "Introduction" in Paul Redmayne, The Gold Coast Yesterday and Today (Cape Coast: Methodist Book Depot, 1941), 8-9.

2. For a broad survey on the literature for struggle in the model colony see for example, A. Adu Boahen, African Perpectives on Colonialism (Baltimore, MD: Johns Hopkins University Press, 1987), especially 80-84; Toyin Falola (ed.), Africa in the Twentieth Century: The Adu Boahen Reader (Trention, NJ: Africa World Press, 2004). Chapter 8 – Asante, Fante and the British, 1800-1888, 201-204; and "Struggle for Ghana's Independence, 415-431.

3. Rosemary Cave, Gold Coast Forts (London: Thomas Nelson & Sons, 1900), 16.

4. Ibid.

5. Ibid., 5-6.

6 W. Walton Claridge, History of the Gold Coast and Ashanti (London: Frank Cass, 1964), 60-72.

7. Cave, Gold Coast Forts, 7.

8. Redmayne, Gold Coast Yesterday and Today, 16.

9. Cave, Gold Coast Forts, 10.

10. Vice-Admiral Sir John Dalrymple Hay, Ashanti and the Gold Coast: What We Know of It (London: Edward Stanford, 6, 7, & 8, Charing Cross, 1874), 33; J.J. Crooks, Records Relating to the Gold Coast Settlements from 1750-1874, new. ed. (Dublin: Browne and Nolan, 1923), 2.

11. Redmayne, The Gold Coast Yesterday and Today, 19; Crooks, Records Relating to the Gold Coast Settlements, 2.

12. Redmayne, The Gold Coast Yesterday and Today, 20.

13. Hay, Ashanti and the Gold Coast. 33; Brodie Cruickshank, Eighteen Years on the Gold Coast of Africa: Including an Account of the Native Tribes, and Their Intercourse with Europeans (London: Frank Cass, 1966), 20-21; Crooks, Records Relating to the Gold Coast Settlements, 2.

14. Hay, Ashanti and the Gold Coast. 34; Crooks, Records Relating to the Gold Coast Settlements, 3.

15. Eveline C. Martin, The British West African Settlements 1750-1821. A Study in Local Administration (London: Longmans, Green, 1927), ix.

16. Michael Crowder, "Indirect Rule: French and British Style." In Perspectives on the African Past, ed. Martin A. Klein and G. Wesley Johnson (Boston: Little, Brown, 1972), 358-370 ; Adu Boahen, African Perspectives on Colonialism (Baltimore: Johns Hopkins University Press, 1987); Adu Boahen, UNESCO General African History. Vol. VII. (Paris: UNESCO, 1987).

17. Martin, The British West African Settlements, ix.

18. Ibid., x.

19. "A Treatise upon the Trade of Great Britain to Africa. London, 1772," 4-5, in Eveline Martin, The British West African Settlements, 1-2.

20   The African Trade the Great Pillar and Support of the British Plantation Trade in America. London, 1745, 2, in Martin, *British West African Settlements*, 2.

21.   Martin, *The British West African Settlements*, 2.

22.   Kwesi J. Anquandah, *Castles & Forts of Ghana*. 24; Redmayne, *The Gold Coast Yesterday and Today*, 48. See also the account of Eric Tylleman, in M. Nathan, "The Gold Coast at the End of the Seventeenth Century Under the Danes and the Dutch," *Journal of African Society* 13, 4 (1904) 4, 17.

23.   Redmayne, *The Gold Coast Yesterday and Today*, 48.

24.   Claridge, *A History of Ashanti and the Gold Coast*; Albert van Dantzig, *Forts and Castles of Ghana* (Accra: Sedco Publishing, 1980), Nathan, "The Gold Coast Under the Danes and the Dutch," 17.

25.   Nathan, The Gold Coast Under the Danes and the Dutch," 17.

26.   See Crooks, *Records Relating to the Gold Coast Settlements*, 2-3.

27.   Ibid., 3.

28.   Jean Barbot, *A Description of the Coasts of North and South Guinea* (London, 1732).

29.   Cruichshank, *Eighteen Years on the Gold Coast*, 23.

30   Willem Bosman, *A New and Accurate Description of the Coast of Guinea*, London, 1705), 48.

31.   Claridge, *A History of the Gold Coast and Ashanti*, fn3, 167; Barbot, 169.

32.   Bosman, *A New and Accurate Description of the Coast of Guinea*, 49; Claridge, *A History of the Gold Coast and Ashanti*, 167.

33.   Bosman, *A New and Accurate Description of the Coast of Guinea*, 49.

34.   Cruickshank, *Eighteen Years on the Gold Coast*.

35.   Claridge, *A History of the Gold Coast and Ashanti*, 167; Redmayne, *The Gold Coast Yesterday and Today*, 49.

36.   Claridge, *A History of the Gold Coast and Ashanti*, 167-168. See fn 1 p. 168: "The African members of the garrisons are usually referred to as 'Gromettoes,' a corruption of the Portuguese 'grumete,' meaning a ship's boy. The majority, if not all, of them were the domestic slaves of the Company, and were possibly Kruboys."

37.   Bosman, *A New and Accurate Description of Guinea*.

38.   Claridge, *A History of Ashanti and the Gold Coast*, 168.

39.   Ibid., 69; Barbot, *A Description of the Coasts*, 171.

40.   "The rock upon which the Castle stands is the reputed residence of the marine deity *Tabi*, whose wife, *Tabi Yir* (*Tabora*), is said to inhabit a group of rocks a little further westward." See Claridge, *A History of the Gold Coast and Ashanti*, fn. 1, p. 167;' Barbot, *A Description of the Coasts*, 69.

41.   Barbot, 271.

42.   Barbot, Photo 5.11.

43.   Nathan, "The Gold Coast Under the Danes and the Dutch," 16.

44.   Ibid.

45. For details of the English-Komenda wars that resulted in the abandonment of the English Fort at Komenda see T. 70/11/17. Also Bosman, *A New and Accurate Description*.

46. Martin, *The British West African Settlements*.

47. Redmayne, *The Gold Coast Yesterday and Today*. 54.

48. Nathan, The Gold Coast Under the Danes and the Dutch," 20.

49 Redmayne, *The Gold Coast Yesterday and Today*. 54.

50. Ibid.

51. Ibid.

52 Ibid., 45.

53. Interview with the caretaker of Anomabu Fort in June 2006.

54. Anquandah, *Castles and Forts of Ghana*, 45,

55. Ibid.

56. Ibid.

57. Interview with caretaker of Fort William in June 2006. See also Anquandah, *Castles and Forts of Ghana*, 45.

58. Claridge, *A History of the Gold Coast and Ashanti*.

59. Crooks, *Records Relating to the Gold Coast Settlements, 79*.

60. Redmayne, *The Gold Coast Yesterday and Today*. 54.

61. Redmayne, *The Gold Coast Yesterday and Today*. 58.

62. Interview with Caretaker at the Fort in June 2006. See also, Anquandah, *Castles and Forts of Ghana*, 78.

63. George E. Brooks Jr., "The Letter Book of Captain Edward Harrington," *Transactions of the Historical Society of Ghana* 6 (1962): 72. Entry dated June 15th (1840).

64. Ibid., 73.

65. Barbot, *A Description of the Coasts*, utilized in Anquandah, *Castles and Forts of Ghana*, 78.

66. Anquandah, *Castles and Forts of Ghana*, 78.

67. Claridge, *A History of the Gold Coast and Ashanti*. 163

68. Brooks, "The Letter Book of Captain Edward Harrington," 74.

69. Ibid.

70. Redmayne, *The Gold Coast Yesterday and Today*. 58; Bosman, *A New and Accurate Description of the Coast of Guinea*, 15.

71. Anquandah, *Castles and Forts of Ghana*, 82.

72. Ibid.

73. Redmayne, *The Gold Coast Yesterday and Today*. 58.

74. J.J. Crooks, *Records Relating to the Gold Coast Settlements*, 79.

75. Ibid.

76. Claridge, A History of the Gold Coast and Ashanti. 163.

77. Ibid.

78. Crooks, Records Relating to the Gold Coast Settlements, 79.

✦ Chapter 6

The Danes on the Eastern Seaboard of the Gold Coast: "The Baltic-African Complex" and the Atlantic Slave Trade

The story of the Atlantic slave trade (and for that matter the Black Atlantic) is the story of hundreds of thousands if not millions of Africans chained in the slave forts, castles and dungeons, awaiting shipment to the New World as well as those who could not make it to the slave forts and castles but succumbed to brutality, hunger, disease or death. It is also the story of the canoemen of the Gold Coast, the Kru laborers from the Liberian coast and castle slaves who toiled to keep the "ships at permanent anchor" afloat. The latter group has become one of the invisible groups of the Atlantic slave trade. Finally, the story of the slave trade is also about another cohort of people - European slavers, ship captains, merchants and officials - who did or did not survive on the Gold Coast but lost the fight against "climate fever." Above all, it is the story of the Africans who landed in the New World and the experiences they went through. All of these experiences constitute component parts of an Afro-European frontier experience that would be incomplete without the story of the Danish-Norwegian participation in the European slave trade on the Gold Coast. This Danish participation centered on the eastern seaboard of the Gold Coast from Accra to Keta, away from the western seaboard that was dominated, first by the Portuguese, and then by the Dutch and the English.

Lack of a substantial economic or industrial base in the seventeenth century militated against active participation in the Guinea trade or the trade in enslaved Africans by Baltic countries. Additionally, economic losses due to enemy depredation, coupled with losses from shipwreck, made it almost impossible and economically not feasible for many Baltic nations to participate in the Guinea trade.[1] It is, therefore, remarkable that Denmark was the only Baltic power to participate in the slave trade to West Africa but, more important, that it held onto its West African settlements for almost two centuries. The Dutch were not only preeminent in Europe (arts, culture, education, literature, manufacturing, commerce, industry) but Dutch influence also extended to Scandinavian activities on the Guinea coast and was the main stimulus for what Georg Nørregård calls the seventeenth-century Baltic-African complex. The Danish were no less influenced, and inspired, by the Dutch success on the Gold Coast to participate in the African trade.[2]

Like the British, the Dutch, the French and the Brandenburgers, the Danish-Norwegians participated in seventeenth century Gold Coast trade at a time of heightened competition in Europe, the Caribbean and on the West African coast. The earliest Danish trading vessels arrived on the West African coast in the mid-seventeenth century, returning with gold, ivory, rich wood, tropical fruit and glowing tales that stirred the imagination of Danish investors and adventurers.[3] From the middle of the seventeenth century until the middle of the nineteenth century, Danish-Norwegians purchased enslaved Africans for the Atlantic economies of Latin America and the Caribbean, and especially so after the Danes purchased the Caribbean Islands of St. Thomas (1671), St. John (1712) and St. Croix (1733).[4] It is in this context that the Danes constructed slave forts and a castle on the Gold Coast. The Danes built three forts (Friedensborg, Kønigstein and Prinzenstein), one castle (Christiansborg), and six lodges at Labadi, Teshi, Tema, Kpong, and Aflao along a fifty-mile stretch from Accra to Keta. Apart from Christiansborg Castle, most of their forts have not survived the test of time. As Thorkild Hansen noted, "'Forts are after all no mushrooms that mature one day and disappear the next!' That was, however, exactly what Kiøge's forts were. They appeared all over, a lot of shoddy work, and because trade was in decline, they were not maintained, so today there is not much left of Kiøge's ambitious constructions."[5] The Danish enterprise on the Gold Coast went through hard times in the late seventeenth century, especially due to hostile Dutch action which reached a climax in the Dutch attack on and, subsequent plunder and burning of, Fort Fredericksborg.[6] As well, disease took a terrible toll on Dutch personnel.

While Portugal, France and Britain despatched a combined total of about 5,419,200 enslaved Africans between 1701 and 1810, Denmark and Norway, according to Per Hernaes, sent only 97,850 enslaved Africans to the New World at the same time.[7] Others estimate that the Danes shipped over 50,000 enslaved Africans between 1733 and 1802 while 53,000 more were sent to the Danish West Indies. At the same time, 70,000 enslaved Africans were sent on from the Danish West Indies.[8] Paiewonsky notes that

Danish historians agree that Danish ships "carried but a fraction of the total number of slaves transported. In retrospect, it was not worth the stigma nor the trouble. As it was, the Danish colonies had been able to buy their slaves cheaper from the Dutch, the British or the interlopers."[9] This means that the Danish contribution was modest, but not insignificant.

Apart from the trade in enslaved Africans the Danes set up plantations in the area where their forts and castle were concentrated – from the coast eastwards from Accra to Keta as well as in the Akwapim mountains and along the banks of the River Volta.[10] The sphere of Danish influence was defined in a royal instrument issued by the king of Denmark to the governor of the Gold Coast in 1820 thus: "the whole stretch of coast from Osu by Christiansborg Fort to Keta by Prinsensten Fort, together with the inhabitants with the sole exception of the two negro towns of Great Prampram and Little Prampram which for the time being are under a foreign power."[11]

The Danes were on the Gold Coast from 1658, when they took over Swedish forts, until they sold the Danish holdings to the English in 1850. Altogether, they stayed on the Gold Coast for 192 years and managed to survive a long period of Dutch and English rivalry on the Gold Coast – certainly no small feat for a small country with no major industrial base. Denmark's entry into the African trade was part of a Danish "big century" in which Denmark fought to regain provinces lost to Sweden about a century after the rupture of the Union of Kalmar.[12] In 1625 Denmark chartered its first trading company but Danish participation in the Thirty Years War, especially the losses incurred by Christian IV, delayed Danish participation in the African trade. However, by 1660, Frederick II, supported by the mercantile elite, some of whom were interested in the African trade, began to promote overseas trade.[13] Quoting from Danish archive sources, Paiewonsky notes that "Suddenly it seemed a good idea to send Danish ships with Danish merchandise to Guinea and from there with slaves to the West Indies and from there on home to Denmark with West Indian goods."[14] Furthermore, he points out how Danish historians explain Danish participation (the Danish Crown and the Danish West India Company) in terms of a "widely held concept of many monarchs and capitalists of the seventeenth and eighteenth centuries," that "trading in slaves meant huge profits. It was believed to be the best way to bail out bankrupt colonial companies that were operating constantly in the red and showing no dividends or returns to stockholders."[15]

During the governorship of Johan Lorentz (1694-1702) of the Caribbean island of St. Thomas, the Danish West India and Guinea Company mapped out a plan for the slave trade, and did brisk business until losses at sea by 1733 crippled the company and opened the door for private participation.[16] In 1699, the Danish ship *Christianus Quintus*, sailed from Christiansborg Castle to St. Thomas with 549 enslaved Africans (295 men and 254 women), 61 elephant tusks weighing 2,371 pounds, and gold dust to the value of 2,488 rix dollars.[17] Almost a year later, the *Fredericus Quartus* sailed from Christiansborg to St. Thomas with 542 enslaved Africans and 7,185 pounds of ivory; and in 1705, the *Cron-Printzen* left Christiansborg with 820 enslaved Africans (460 men and 360 women) bound for St. Thomas.[18] However, the trip was characterized by misfortune from start to finish. After a brief hiatus, in 1709 (October 2) the two company ships, the *Fredericus Quartus* (with 435 enslaved Africans and about 4,000 pounds of gold), and the *Christianus Quintus*, with about 334 enslaved Africans and another 4,000 pounds of gold set sail from Christiansborg Castle but neither ship arrived at the Caribbean destination. Both ships were lost at sea.[19]

Table 6.1: Slave Cargoes on Danish Ships From Guinea to the West Indies 1767-76

Year	No/Name of Ship	Slave Departures	Slave Arrivals	Death Rate %
1767	1. Christiansborg	245	224	8.6
	2. Eleonora	171	159	7.0
1768	3. Fredensborg	260	240	7.7
	4. Ada	201	184	8.5
1769	5. Christiansborg	323	288	10.8
	6. Eleonora	203	176	13.3
	7. Montaguerre*	244	-	-
	8. Ada	164	162	1.2
1771	9. Le Miere*	262	-	-
	10. Le Bon Fils	235	-	-
	11. Christiansborg	267	246	7.9
	12. Ada	166	146	12.0
	13. Montaguerre*	369	-	-
1773	14. Brison*	196	-	-
	15. Langlois*	255	-	-
	16. Berthaud*	207	-	-
1774	17. Eleonora	218	207	5.0
	18. Fortuna	111	-	-
	19. Ada	221	135	38.9
	20. Christiansborg	336	254	24.4
1776	21. Ada	145	142	2.1
	Total	**4,799**		

Source: Per O. Hernæs, *Slaves, Danes, and African Coast Society: The Danish Slave Trade from West Africa and the Afro-Danish Relations on the Eighteenth-Century Gold Coast*. Trondheim Studies in History, No. 6. (Trondheim, Norway: Department of History, University of Trondheim, 1995), 261.

Hernæs notes that the French-named ships on the list (Table 6.1), apparently chartered by a French firm, arrived at Christiansborg to carry enslaved Africans to the Danish West Indies due to an agreement the Danish Company, the Bargum Trading Society, signed with the French firm, David & Dubuque. Accordingly, these French ships have been classified as "Danish" in contradistinction to French ships that carried enslaved Africans from Christiansborg.

Danish participation in Gold Coast trade began with the work of Henry Caerlof, the renegade Dutch official who seized Swedish trading lodges and constructed other lodges at Cape Coast and Butri. In 1657 the Danish Guinea Company, then headed by Caerlof, captured Fort Carolusburg, headquarters of the Swedish African Company. Two years later, the Danes sold Fort Carolusburg and other Danish possessions in Accra to the Dutch.[20] The Gã Paramount Chief Okaikoi, who was not a Dutch ally, subsequently revoked Dutch ownership of Osu lodge. K. Anquandah notes that in 1661 the Danish official Jost Cramer acquired land from Chief Okaikoi for 3,200 florins and built a stone fort in place of an earlier earthen lodge. He named the stone fort Christiansborg (Christian's fortress) in honor of the former king of Denmark, Christian IV (d. 1648).[21]

From 1679 through the next decade, the Danish fortress had a checkered history. First, Peter Bolt, reportedly a Greek commandant at Christiansborg, instigated the murder of his boss, the Danish Johan Ulrich (of Gluckstad). Subsequently, he sold the fort to Julian de Campo Baretto, a former Portuguese governor of São Tomé for 7 marks of gold or 224 pounds.[22] The Portuguese, booted out of Elmina Castle by the Dutch and driven from their stronghold along the western stretch of the Gold Coast, improved the bastions of the fort, garrisoned it and renamed it St Francis Xavier.[23] The Portuguese sent a garrison from São Tome that occupied the fort for three years. The Portuguese also added a Roman Catholic chapel to the structure (much like the setup at Elmina) but despite the improvements they could not achieve any traction in trade due to their unpopularity among the Gã. Poor management of the Osu fort coupled with paucity of trade goods and ill-treatment of the garrison by their commander led to a revolt by the Portuguese garrison. Added to this was the fact that the Portuguese commercial enterprise on the Gold Coast was on its last legs at the time (1670s) and thus they were unable to withstand English and Dutch trade competition.[24] Facing stiff competition from the local people on the one hand and European competition (Dutch and English) on the other and running progressively into debt, the Portuguese resold the Osu fort to the Danes in 1683. Two years later, the Osu fort became the headquarters of the Danish commercial operations on the Gold Coast.[25]

The first major Danish foothold on the Gold Coast was Fort Fredericksborg in Cape Coast, and later the Osu fort in Accra was added to Danish possessions in 1683, as already pointed out. These served Danish commercial interests at the time. Fredericksborg continued to be the headquarters of the Danish enterprise on the Gold Coast until the English purchased it in 1685. From this point on, the Danes concentrated their energies in the eastern part of the coast of Ghana and made Christiansborg Castle, enlarged and transformed from a fort into a castle, their headquarters. The Danes continued to trade on the Gold Coast for the next one hundred years or so, largely in the vicinity of Accra before embarking on a major expansion eastward all the way from Accra to Keta.

In the eighteenth century, Denmark-Norway concentrated their activities east of Accra, between Accra and Whydah, leaving the region from Accra to Assinie to the Dutch and the English. Earlier, they had abandoned the Danish lodge at Cape Coast in 1675 before giving up Fort Fredericksborg. In 1781 the Danish government chartered the Baltic Guinea Company to trade to Guinea and the West Indies and the move put Danish activities on the Coast on a more business-like footing.

FORT FREDERICKSBORG

The Danish base in the Gold Coast was initially a new fort called Fredericksborg, located on a very high hill later known as Danish Mount. This high hill, three hundred steps in height and located at Amanful, lay about twelve hundred yards east of the Cape Coast Castle and overlooked the latter. The land was obtained from Fetu leaders at a cost of 50 benda gold.[26] The fort was built in 1659 by the Danish Governor Jost Kramer. Given its strategic location, the Danes could fire into Cape Coast Castle and launch an assault to possibly seize it but this depended on whether Fredericksborg was well supplied with cannon. Fortunately for the English in Cape Coast Castle, Fredericksborg was in a state of perpetual disrepair and the defenses of the fort were so weak that the Danes made no attempt to drive the English from Cape Coast Castle.[27]

Fort Fredericksborg was described as a triangular enclosure with a wall of stone and clay and as such not a very strong fort. It had small bastions, a round flanker facing the sea and two batteries toward Cape Coast and Mouree. It was fortified at one time with twenty-two cannons and was occupied by a governor, one chief factor, one under factor, one preacher, one lieutenant, one barber, two assistants, one sergeant, one constable, two corporals, six gentleman cadets, one drummer and 28 common soldiers with one under officer and one constable.[28] There were living quarters of thatched huts within the enclosure. Cognizant of the strategic position of Fort Fredericksborg in relation to Cape Coast Castle, the commander at Cape Coast Castle bought Fort Fredericksborg from the Danes in 1685. He renamed the structure Fort Royal.[29]

Fort Fredericksborg was triangular in shape but the "new" fort built by the English after 1685 was square and could be reached only by a narrow winding path up the hill. This made it easier to defend with a single, powerful and well-placed cannon. The rebuilt fort mounted eighteen or twenty guns, eleven of which were on the platform. The English fort was garrisoned by six whites and twelve blacks.[30] When the work of reconstruction was completed the English stopped the practice of firing salutes from Cape Coast Castle. Instead, all salutes from ships in the Cape Coast 'road' were acknowledged from this fort. This new practice minimized the noise made by constantly firing cannon to salute ships passing by the Castle.

CHRISTIANSBORG CASTLE

Christiansborg lies on 5 degrees 44 minutes north latitude, in the middle of Accra province. It was built on a cliff at the edge of the sea. The sea was consistently rough and therefore it was difficult for boats to land. It was the largest Danish possession on the Gold Coast and was for the longest time the headquarters of the Danish settlements in West Africa. Its history is as tumultuous as it is interesting. It began life as a Portuguese fortified lodge. The Portuguese had used it only as a secondary fort where they had some white servants to maintain the Accra [Akra] trade. It was at that time a small but very durably built fort.[31] Originally founded by the Portuguese, the fort was taken by the Swedes in 1645 and then by the Danes (under Henry Caerlof) who rebuilt it in 1659 on the orders of the Danish Governor of Fredericksborg, Henning Albrecht.[32] In 1662 it was taken over by the Portuguese, when they were trying to recover lost ground on the Gold Coast. Danish governor John Ulrichs was murdered in a conspiracy led by the Greek officer Peter Bolt, who later sold the fort to the Portuguese ex-governor of São Tomé, Julian de Campo Baretto for £224 or 36 pounds of gold.[33] The Portuguese garrisoned the fort and "raised the curtains and batteries another 3 feet; built a small chapel inside the Castle where mass was said by a Black priest who had been ordained in São Tomé."[34] The Danes took back the fort in 1682, and in 1691 Nicolaus Janssen, the new Danish governor, further improved the structure and provided all the essentials. Christiansborg was at this time, according to Eric Tylleman, "armed with 28 cannon and occupied by a Vice-Governor, one Factor, one preacher, one barber, three assistants, one Sergeant, one Corporal, one Constable, three gentlemen cadets, one drummer, and 26 common soldiers."[35]

From its initial design, Christiansborg Castle underwent several architectural changes when different European countries took control. One significant indication of these changes could be found in the huge disparity in size between the southwestern and southeastern bastions, both of which overlook the sea. The southwestern bastion, dated 1780, according to a plaque on the wall, was more durable than the southeastern bastion, which is too small to be compatible with a castle of this size. The latter could have been part of the original Portuguese structure, a Portuguese bastion of 1550.[36]

Another sign of change in structure is manifested in a low tower near the north-eastern corner of the castle at the foot of the stair leading to the Assistant District Commissioner's office. Here "there is a rubble wall with an obtuse angle," which defies explanation.[37] In all likelihood, this was part of the Danish changes designed to strengthen the earlier Portuguese fort. Similarly, a "very pointed demi-bastion at the north-western angle, which now contains the electric light engine room" also appears to have been part of the Danish structure of 1659, and so was a "new bastion built at the north-eastern angle of the old enceinte, butting against the small early bastion."[38] According to Mr. Seale, governor architect, "A curtain connecting the flanks of these two bastions would have run east and west 20 feet south of the present wall containing the main entrance into the Castle, and this seems to be represented by a piece of thick wall jutting out westward from under the chapel building."[39]

An inscription of 1734, and the cistern head of 1753, both point to the fact that the final shape of the courtyard and the construction of the cistern occurred in the mid-eighteenth century, just before the final burst of Danish construction of forts on the eastern seaboard of the Gold Coast.[40] This was during the reign of Christian VI (1730-1746). Further changes were made in the last decades of the eighteenth century, namely, the great new southwestern bastion of Christiansborg (1780). The present main entrance to Christiansborg was constructed by 1790.[41] This was when Major Conrad Hansen Hemsen was Governor and Christian VII (1766-1808) was king. According to Isert, two 24-pound, 18-pound and 6-pound guns were then mounted on the ramparts. About half a dozen of these bronze guns were still in position when the castle was handed over to the English. King Christian VII's cipher was still visible.[42]

In addition to these, the wall containing the main entrance

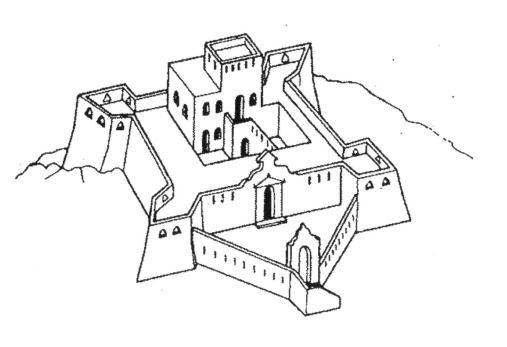

Figure 6.1: Christiansborg Castle – Seventeenth Century

Source: Albert van Dantzig, *Forts and Castles of Ghana* (Sedco Publishing 1980), 30.
Courtesy of Sedco Publishing.

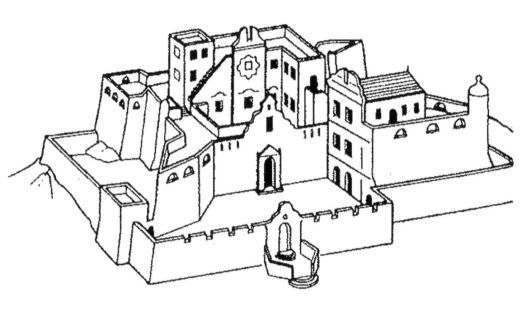

Figure 6.2: Christiansborg Castle – Eighteenth Century

Source: Albert van Dantzig, *Forts and Castles of Ghana* (Sedco Publishing 1980), 30.
Courtesy of Sedco Publishing.

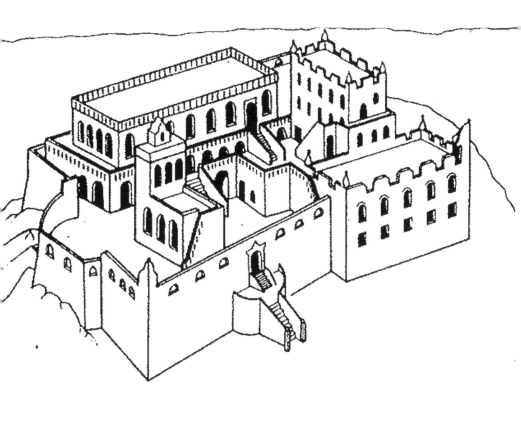

Figure 6.3: Christiansborg Castle - Nineteenth Century

Albert van Dantzig, *Forts and Castles of Ghana* (Sedco Publishing 1980), 30.

seems to have been part of part of an outer curtain wall, which
enclosed the earlier castle on all sides except towards the sea,
where it was unnecessary. The wall enclosing the western court
seems to be part of it, and it may have broken out into a re-entrant
or bastion at the northwestern angle under the present offices,
but recent work has made it difficult to decide this point.[43]

In addition to this, "the wall enclosing the barbican or garden on the eastern
side of the castle must be later still, since it is apparently not shown in the
engraving of 1806."[44] Late in the eighteenth century, the internal buildings
were refurbished and embellished. O'Neil notes that "Apart from the Chapel
Tower, which must surely have housed bells, the chief remaining part of this
is the main stair in the courtyard, which has an arcaded parapet, like similar
arcades in contemporary work at Elmina and Cape Coast Castle"[45] (Figures
6.1, 6.2, and 6.3).

In 1692 Nicolaus Janssen became governor of Christiansborg Castle and
further improved the building. In that same year the Akwamu general/chief
Asameni captured the castle from the Danes at a time when the Akwamu
were in control of the Accra region. Asameni made the Danish governor
believe that he would bring in a large number of Akwamu merchants to buy
firearms. Under the pretext of testing the guns, the eighty-odd Akwamu
trading contingent loaded their guns with powder and shot and turned
them on the thirty-member Danish garrison at Christiansborg Castle and
overpowered them.[46] For one year, Asameni occupied Christiansborg,
having reportedly stripped it of about seven thousand pounds of loot.[47]
Asameni dressed up in the Danish governor's uniform and fired continuous
salutes in his own honor.[48] In 1693 the Danes, having sent a considerable
gift to the king of Akwamu through the intercession of the Dutch, bought
the castle back from Asameni.[49]

Paul Erdman Isert, with interest in natural science as his chief motive,
went on a sixteen week trip via the ship *Prinz Friedrichs Hofnung* (*Prince Frederick's Hope*) from Denmark to the Gold Coast in October 1783. By the time
of Isert's arrival, Christiansborg had been considerably enlarged and had a
fairly large administrative setup and personnel in place.[50] The various guns
were also used to salute ships of other nations, and especially, when necessary, the Dutch Fort Crèvecoeur and the English Fort James, all of which
were nearby in Accra. Isert also noted that "At its highest point the Castle has
four storeys which might be very disadvantageous in the event of a siege by
Europeans"[51] (Photo 6.1)

Christiansborg Castle looked very beautiful and imposing on the outside
in 1783. However, it was lacking in comfort in the interior. This was because

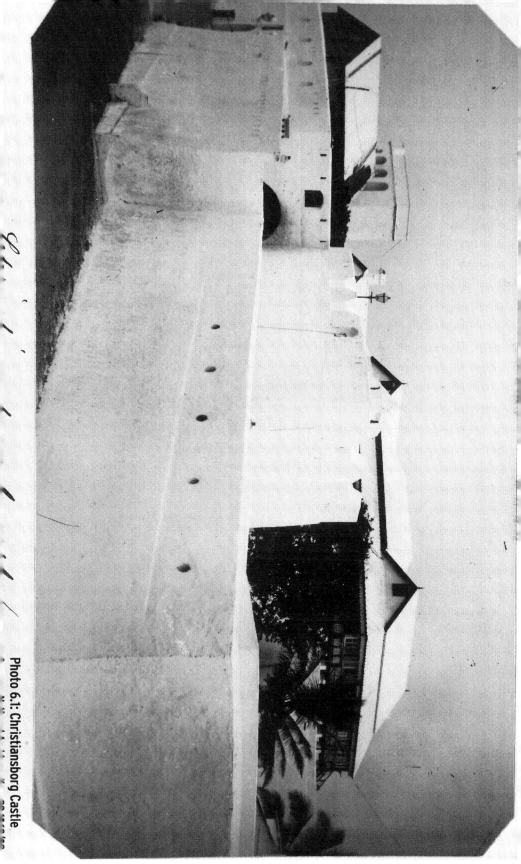

Photo 6.1: Christiansborg Castle

not only are the rooms extremely cramped, even those for the officers, but they are so low that a grown man can barely stand upright in some of them. Moreover, the walls in the old part of the fort are up to four feet thick and the windows so small that it is barely possible for a man to put his head out.[52]

The cramped quarters made it impossible to catch the draft from the sea in the hot tropical climate of the Gold Coast and, therefore, was a recipe for disaster in the event of the outbreak of a contagious disease like smallpox.[53]

Henry Meredith notes that all the Danish governors made additions to Christiansborg Castle until, by the time of Danish Governor Christian Schionning, Christiansborg was a "large and irregular pile of buildings."[54] Meredith adds that a school was held in the chapel under the chaplain. The chapel was built in the north-eastern part of the castle in the 1790s. It was shortly afterwards converted into a store.[55]

Jens Adolph Kiøge, the man who singe-handedly prosecuted the Danish expansion eastward from Accra to Keta, was first appointed underassistant at Christiansborg Castle in 1776. He had earlier been posted as factor of Ada trading lodge in 1770, and established a trading station at Little Popo (Anecho) in 1772, after the Ada-Anlo war. Kiøge became acting governor of Christiansborg Castle at the death of Governor Hensen in 1780. Kiøge laid the foundation for the first string of Danish forts on the Gold Coast – Kongensten at Ada in 1783, ostensibly to protect the Danish ally Ada against the Anlo. It was for this new fort that Kiøge supported his ally Ada and the nations west of the Volta against the Anlo in the Sagbadre War, named after a Danish trader who was reportedly robbed by the Anlo in 1783.[56]

Christiansborg continued to be the headquarters of the Danish African settlements until the Danes transferred the castle to the British in 1849 with Danish Governor Carstensen handing over the keys to British Governor Sir W. Winniet. Winniet reported to Earl Grey, that "the Castle was a fortification of considerable extent and strength, mounting on its battlements forty guns and with good officers' quarters"[57] (Photo 2.4 – Christiansborg castle).

In 1862 Christiansborg Castle was destroyed by an earthquake. When the seat of government of the Gold Coast was transferred from Cape Coast to Accra in 1873, Christiansborg Castle became the residence of the British governors: Ussher died at Christiansborg Castle in 1883; Governor Young died there in 1884.[58] Between 1884 and 1902, when a building between Christiansborg and Accra became Government House, Christiansborg was first used as a constabulary mess and later as a lunatic asylum. In 1902, however, it was converted into the residence of the British governor and is at present in use as the seat of the government of Ghana.

Photo 6.2: Christiansborg Castle
Source: National Archives, Kew CO 1069/30
Gold Coast General Views 1887

Photo 6.4: Fort Augustaborg
Courtesy of National Archives, Kew, England

FORT AUGUSTABORG

The Danish Fort Augustaborg, which has almost disappeared now, was located in the western part of Teshie, about 50 meters from the sea (Photo 6.4). Even though the four bastions were pulled down a long time ago, remnants of the foundations hardly remain visible. The intervening walls stood partly in full height, erected as dry walls in sandstone. Most of the structure has succumbed to the elements and only two window arches and a vaulted portal from the gallery near the fort's courtyard are nearly intact and speak to the fort's presence.[59] In addition, six cannons lie on the ground in the area adjacent to the structure. Two of those cannons were from the original location of the fort but they have been dragged into an open space and utilized by the people in ritual ceremonies. They are at present serving much the same functions like the cannons in the sacrificial grove near Fort Friedensburg at Ningo.[60]

FORT FRIEDENSBURG

The Danish fort at Ningo was called Fort Friedensburg. It was built between 1735 and 1741, two miles beyond Prampram-Ningo. It was "a regular long rectangle with four bastions and a spacious courtyard."[61] Surrounded by an outwork or wall, Fort Freidensburg was spacious enough to provide shelter to the local people in case of an attack.

Under the leadership of the chief merchant and commander, Mr. Kipnasse, a very serious effort was made to improve the defenses of the Fort, especially the outwork. In addition to this, the fort was provided with a solidly built storehouse and living quarters for craftsmen and soldiers. In spite of all of these, however, the fort was generally weak, which derived from its unusable northern bastion. While attempts were made to repair the walls of this bastion, it was obvious that a single shot from the four cannons that the bastion carried was sure to exacerbate the cracks in the wall. From an architectural standpoint, the wall was likely to crack again in spite of whatever efforts were put into its repair. The only solution, which was problematic at best, was to rebuild the bastion or the fort.[62]

Photo 6.5: Fort Friedensburg at Old Ningo
Courtesy of Sub-Saharan Publishers

FORT KONGENSTEEN (KÖNIGSTEIN)

The cornerstone for fort Kongensteen was laid on October 15, 1783, by Jens Adolph Kiøge. The fort lies about one mile inland from the sea and a good musket shot from the bank of the Volta River, across from the island of Ada. It was "a regular rectangle measuring 136 alen long and 130 alen wide, with four bastions which are intended to carry six cannons each."[63] It was erected on "quite flat and clayey ground, where for a full ten miles around surely no stone larger than a bean could be found, even if one were willing to pay a million for it."[64] Kongensteen means "Kingstone" and the governor explained to Isert that "the name is even more fitting because all the stones which were used for the building came either from Christiansborg or all the way from Europe at the King's expense."[65]

The fort was built in stages. In the first phase of construction, only the two bastions toward the river were built. Accommodations (shelters or cabins) were built between the new fort and the Volta River for the white and mulatto soldiers serving the new Danish settlement. Close to the river, breastworks were erected, equipped with cannons to repel enemies on the other bank of the river who might try to interfere with the construction of the new fort. A "tall flagstaff from which the royal flag waves has been erected in the middle of the row of cannons."[66]

The major rationale for the construction of Fort Kongensteen was that whenever the Danes sent their company slaves with supplies, either over land or by the lagoon, destined for the Danish station at Keta about twelve miles away on the east side of the river, the company's slaves, wares and boats were often seized.[67] The people of Ada were cognizant of the strategic importance of the fort and the prospect of using it as a safe refuge in case of war against their enemies, and supported the Danes in this endeavor in any way they could.[68]

ADMINISTRATION OF THE DANISH FORTS

The head of all Danish possessions on the Gold Coast was the governor. He was paid an annual salary of about 1,000 thalers and an allowance of 500 thalers. He was assisted by a council that consisted of the commanders of the other forts. This council acted as a consultative body on all important matters.[69] The second in command to the governor was the chief trader or commander of Fort Friedensburg. He was paid an annual salary of 500 thalers while the commanders of the other forts received 400 thalers.[70] The commanders of the other forts – Königstein and Prinzenstein – were called traders and their seniority was based on length of service on the Gold Coast.

Photo 6.6: Remnant of Fort Kongensteen
Courtesy of Sub-Saharan Publishers

The lodges or smaller trade establishments, especially the prominent ones, were commanded by Factors and the less important ones by assistants, junior officers and, in a few cases, a soldier. The Factors, that is, the commanders of the prominent lodges and the two chief assistants, were responsible for the bookkeeping and secretarial work of the Danish establishments and received a remuneration of 400 thalers. The other chief assistants at the forts and lodges were paid 300 thalers, while underassistants received 250 thalers. A reserve assistant took home 120-140 thalers a year[71]

The spiritual oversight of the Danish officials was in the hands of a clergyman who was paid 400 thalers per annum while a catechist received 250 thalers.[72] Medical service was provided by a chief surgeon who was stationed at Christiansborg; his deputy was stationed at Friedensburg. The former was paid 400 thalers and the latter 300. The chief surgeon at Christiansborg was also assisted in his work by a mulatto whose major responsibilities included performing minor surgical tasks as well as bandaging wounds. The chief surgeon's assistant was paid 144 thalers annually.[73] The surgeons received additional incentives for their work. For every enslaved African who shipped out of the Danish establishments on the Gold Coast the chief surgeon and the surgeons were paid a bonus. In good times, the bonus could be equal to or even more than their salaries.[74]

As a ship at permanent anchor, the fort or castle was usually well protected, especially if it was a fairly important fort or lodge. The military contingent at Christiansborg Castle was made up of "a sergeant, two corporals, a drummer, two pipers, twenty musketeers, one chief gunner, one assistant gunner, two constables, and two assistant constables"[75] who were black. The other forts were guarded by a sergeant, a corporal, a drummer, a piper, ten musketeers, two constables, who were gunners and a few company slaves.[76]

A gunner in the Danish service was paid 20 thalers, a sergeant 16, and a corporal 14. Apart from the three levels or differences in salary ranges, European soldiers were paid more than "colored" soldiers. For example, a European soldier was paid 10 thalers and a mulatto soldier 8. Obviously black soldiers received the lowest wages.[77]

For the maintenance and upkeep of the Danish forts and lodges, a number of artisans were employed, headed by a baas who was paid 20 thalers. The masons, smiths, joiners and coopers were paid according to the level of their skill, but on average they received 14 thalers a month.[78] In all about thirty-eight Europeans worked in the Danish settlements at the time Isert was on the Gold Coast.

The Danes maintained a contingent of 200-250 "castle slaves" or company slaves who were in service in Christiansborg Castle and the various forts and lodges. The males were paid 1 thaler a month; females received

half a thaler and girls were paid one-quarter of a thaler every month.[79] According to Isert, "these wretched souls are most poorly paid for their work, and if they were not able to supplement their pay by one means or the other, they could not possibly manage."[80]

The Danish Crown paid the company 25,000 thalers for their operations and this was often supplemented through the company's trading activities. The company had a monopoly over all trade from the Gold Coast and paid the officers considerable commissions as an incentive to promote trade.[81]

Mortality for Danish officials on the Gold Coast was very high. Isert attributes the high mortality to a variety of factors. He notes that the salubrious climate was not the only problem that Europeans faced. The first and foremost problem was the limited public diversions, as a result of which "the refuge of such gentlemen is usually Bacchus, gaming and Venus, in all of which a number of former citizens have so excelled that they have had to pay prematurely with their lives of debauchery."[82] But added to this is the very rich meals they enjoyed soon after their arrival from Europe to their new locale – "the extraordinary amount of meat which it is customary to serve at the tables of the rich here is veritable poison to the Europeans, if they do not take it in moderation."[83]

Due to the high mortality rate, even people from the lowest ranks such as soldiers, artisans or even cabin boys could gain promotion to the rank of governor. But with no opportunity for training, such individuals tended to be problematic governors – confrontational and combative, inefficient, arrogant and cruel.[84] The result of this was that the Danish Company was sometimes served by governors who were liabilities rather than assets to the company.

The wares the Danes generally exchanged for male and female enslaved Africans are shown in Table 6.2.

Table 6.2: Wares Exchanged for Enslaved Africans

Males

5 muskets at 6 rthlr.	= 30 rthlr.
80 pounds of gunpowder	= 40 rthlr.
2 rods of iron at 3 rthlr.	= 6 rthlr.
1 anker of brandy	= 16 rthlr.
4 dozen small knives	= 4 rthlr.
2 tin basins	= 2 rthlr.
1 piece of flowered cotton of 24 ells	= 10 rthlr.
1 piece of *chellos* (East Indian ware)	= 10 rthlr.
1 piece of *bajuttenpauts* (East Indian ware)	= 10 rthlr.
½ piece of striped taffeta (East Indian ware)	= 10 rthlr.

1 piece of East Indian kerchiefs in 10 units	= 12 rthlr.
1 brass basin	= 4 rthlr.
3 rods of copper at 1 rthlr.	= 3 rthlr.
2 rods of lead at 1 rthlr.	= 1 rthlr.
to the guard	= 1 rthlr.
Total	**=160 rthlr.**

Females

5 muskets at 6 rthlr.	= 30 rthlr.
60 pounds of gunpowder	= 30 rthlr.
1 crate containing 9 bottles brandy	= 12 rthlr.
4 dozen small knives	= 4 rthlr.
Various kinds of glass beads	= 12 rthlr.
2 brass kettles	= 8 rthlr.
1 piece *Neganepaut* (East Indian ware)	= 10 rthlr.
1 piece *Nicones* (East Indian ware)	= 10 rthlr.
1 piece half *Say*	= 10 rthlr.
Boss [cowries]	= 1 rthlr.
For the guard	= 1 rthlr.
Total	**=128** rthlr.

a. *Chellos* were chequered East Indian cotton. See Isert, 83, fn. 12, Sixth Letter. Fort Kønig-stein at Ada on Rio Volta in Guinea, September 24, 1784.

b. *Bajuttenpauts* was a coarse white cotton cloth. See Ibid.

c. *Neganepaut* were cotton cloth of primary colors originally produced and obtained from the East Indies, but later, obtainable from Europe, specifically from Rouen.

d. *Nicones* refers to the blue and white striped East Indian cotton cloth. See Ibid.

e. *Says* were fine-textured cloth initially manufactured from silk but later made entirely of wool. See Ibid.

Source: Paul Erdman Isert, *Journey to Guinea and the Caribbean Islands in Columbia*, 82-83, Sixth Letter, Fort Kønigstein at Ada on Rio Volta in Guinea, September 24, 1784.

Isert notes that these commodities were not almost always the preference of slave merchants. Muskets, gunpowder and knives were highly prized and Asante merchants exclusively preferred guns, powder and fine fabric or silk cloth,[85] the latter of which could possibly be put to service in weaving kente cloth.

Tables 6.3 and 6.4, in the Appendix to this chapter, refer to supplies for Christiansborg Castle and Danish slave ships.[86]

Table 6.3: Supplies on the Danish-Norwegian Ship Fredensborg Bound for Christiansborg Castle

White rice	3,400 kg	Ginger
Red rice	1,000 kg	saffron 3 lodd (46.5 g)
Horse beans	9,320 litres	Prussian beer
Peas	10,200 l	Raisings
Ship's bread	5,800 kg	Pepper
Soft bread	450 kg	Cinnamon
Butter	2,055 kg	Cloves
Brandy	64,265 lbs	Coffee beans
(for use on board)	3,872 lbs	Brown sugar
Beer for officers	9,530 lbs	Congo tea
Barley groats	200 barrels	Nutmeg
Pork	4 barrels	Rock candy
Ham	60 whole	Green tea
Beef	44 barrels	Cardamon
Lamb		Granulated sugar
Dutch cheese		Bohea (black) tea
Stock fish		10 ducks
Klip-fish		10 chickens
Pickled herring		2 geese
Salt cod		400 eggs
Oats		Vegetable seeds – 2 kg
Fish oil		160 large water casks
Rye meal		8 barrels of gunpowder
Red wine		Muskets, 40 cases
Old wine		Gun-flint, 32,000
New wine		Iron bars
Rhine wine		Cartridge paper
Wheat flour		Shoes
French brandy		Textiles
Pearl barley		West Indian coral necklaces
Tapioca		
Dried cherries		
English mustard		
Wine vinegar		
Prunes		
Currants		

f. Horse beans was normally used as animal fodder but became an important part of the diet of the enslaved.

g. Most of the brandy was offloaded at Christiansborg castle.

h. The egg supply was supplemented by eggs of chickens or ducks on board the ship.

i. The vegetable seeds were planted during the voyage.

j. Of the barrels of gunpowder carried on board 8.695 kg was for Christiansborg Castle and 420 kg of gunpowder for the ship.

k. Most of the muskets, gun-flint, iron bars, cartridge paper, shoes, textiles and West Indian coral was to be exchanged for enslaved Africans, gold and ivory.

Source: Leif Svalesen, The Slave Ship Fredensborg, trans. Pat Shaw and Selena Winsnes (Accra: Sub-Saharan Publishers, 2000), 37-38.

Table 6.4: Danish Slavers That Came to Saint-Domingue, 1781-1791

A. SHIPS COMING DIRECTLY FROM THE GOLD COAST

DATE OF ARRIVAL	NAME OF SHIP	CAPTAIN	NUMBER OF ENSLAVED AFRICANS	
October 1781	Accra	S. A. Møller	?	(172)
November 1781	Christiansborg (Hiorth)	Jørgen Andreas	200	(199)
April 1782	Kammerherre Schack	Jens Møller	400	(400)
June 1782	Upernavik	Niels Iversen Schmidt (Smith)	207	(203)
November 1782	Gregers Juel	Henrik Lind	?	(186)
July 1784	Christiansborg	Severin Kock (Kocq)	380	(347)

B. SHIPS COMING FROM ST. THOMAS WITH ENSLAVED AFRICANS, PARTICULARLY FROM THE GOLD COAST

DATE OF ARRIVAL	NAME OF SHIP	CAPTAIN	NUMBER OF ENSLAVED AFRICANS
April 1782	La Patience	Joseph Wesey	?
May 1782	La Fancy	Daniel Couling	200
October 1782	Elsinor	Collins	100
November 1782	L'Aventure	Joseph Lightbourn	?
November 1782	Le Phénix	?	?
January 1783	L'Expedition	?	200
January 1783	One Schooner	?	80
January 1783	La Betsy	Maurice Stack	?
January 1783	Le Phénix	Pyring Yates	?

Source: Svend E. Green-Pedersen, "The Danish Negro Slave Trade, Some New Archival Findings in Particular With Reference to the Danish West Indies," in De La Traite à L'Esclavage. Actes du Colloque International Sue la Traites Des Noirs, édités par Serge Daget, Tome I: Vᵉ-XVIIIᵉ Siècles, Nantes, 1985, 450.

Notes

1. Georg Nørregård, Danish Settlements in West Africa 1658-1850, trans., Sigurd Mammen (Boston: Boston University Press, 1966), xx. See also, James Duffy, Shipwreck and Europe (Cambridge 1995) for the economic cost of shipwrecks to European nations.

2. Nørregård, Danish Settlements in West Africa 1658-1850, xviii.

3. Isidor Paiewonsky, Eyewitness Accounts of Slavery in the Danish West Indies (New York: Fordham University Press, 1989), 1.

4. Ibid., 6-7, 12; Thorkild Hansen, Coast of Slaves, trans, Kari Dako (Accra: Sub-Saharan Publishers, 2005), 12.

5. Hansen, Coast of Slaves.

6. Paiewonsky, Eyewitness Accounts of Slavery, 2.

7. Per Hernæs, Slaves, Danes, and African Coast Society. The Danish Slave Trade from West Africa and the Afro-Danish Relations on the Eighteenth-Century Gold Coast. Trondheim Studies in History, No. 6. Trondheim: Department of History, University of Trondheim, 1995.

8. See Svend Erik Green-Pedersen, "The Danish Negro Slave Trade, 1733-1807," 214, 219.

9. Paiewonsky, Eyewitness Accounts of Slavery, 5-6.

10. See for example, Yaw Bredwa-Mensah, "Slavery and Plantation Life at the Danish Plantation Site at Bibease, Gold Coast (Ghana), EAZ, Ethnogr. Archäol. Z. 38 (1996).

11. Reindorf, 1980, 6; Bredwa-Mensah, "Slavery and Plantation Life at the Danish Plantation Site," 447.

12 Nørregård, Dutch Settlements in West Africa 1658- 1850, xiii. By the Union of Kulmar (1397), Queen Margaret united Denmark, Norway and Sweden.

13. Nørregård, Dutch Settlements in West Africa 1658- 1850, xvi.

14. Paiewonsky, Eyewitness Accounts of Slavery, 6.

15. Ibid.

16. Ibid., 6-7.

17. Ibid., 7.

18. Hansen, Coast of Slaves, 50; Paiewonsky, Eyewitness Accounts of Slavery, 7.

19. Paiewonsky, Eyewitness Accounts of Slavery, 10.

20. James Anquandah, Castles and Forts of Ghana (Paris: Atalante [for Ghana Museums and Monuments Board], 1999), 24. See also M. Nathan, "The Gold Coast at the End of the Seventeenth Century Under the Danes and Dutch," Journal of African Society 13, 4 (1904): 2, 4, for the account of Eric Tylleman. Tylleman's version of the beginnings of Cape Coast Castle differs from that of Jean Barbot, A Description of the Coasts of North and South Guinea (London, 1732).

21. Anquandah, Castles and Forts of Ghana, 24.

22. Nathan, "The Gold Coast under the Danes and Dutch," 6. See also Anquandah, *Castles and Forts of Ghana,* 24.

23. B. H. St. J. O'Neil, *Report on Forts and Castles of Ghana* (Ghana Museums and Monuments Board). (Accra-Tema: State Publishing Corporation, October 1961), 16; W. Walton Claridge, *A History of the Gold Coast and Ashanti* (London: Frank Cass, 1964), 120-121.

24. Rosemary Cave, *Gold Coast Forts* (London: Thomas Nelson and Sons, 1900), 21-22; Anquandah, *Castles and Forts of Ghana,* 24, 27.

25. Anquandah, *Castles and Forts of Ghana,* 27.

26. Paiewonsky, *Eyewitness Accounts of Slavery,* 1-2.

27. Cave, *Gold Coast Forts,* 21.

28. Nathan, "The Gold Coast Under the Danes and the Dutch," 18.

29. Cave, *Gold Coast Forts,* 21. See also Claridge, *A History of the Gold Coast and Ashanti,* 169.

30. Claridge, *A History of the Gold Coast and Ashanti,* 169.

31. Paul Erdman Isert, *Letters on West Africa and the Slave Trade. Paul Erdmann Isert's Journey to Guinea and the Caribbean Islands in Columbia* (1788), trans & ed. from German by Selena Axelrod Winsnes, (Oxford: Oxford University Press, 1992), 1783, 28-29. First Letter.

32. Nathan, "The Gold Coast Under the Danes and the Dutch," 23.

33. Ibid., 24; St. J. O'Neil, *Report on Forts and Castles of Ghana* [for Ghana Museum and Monuments Board], October 1951, 16.

34. O'Neil, *Report on Forts and Castles of Ghana,* 16; Claridge, *A History of Ashanti and the Gold Coast,* 120-121.

35. Nathan, "The Gold Coast Under the Danes and the Dutch," 23.

36. O'Neil, *Report on Forts and Castles,* 17.

37 Ibid.

38 Ibid.

39. Information provided by Mr. Seale, governor architect and cited in O'Neil, *Report on Forts and Castles,* p. 17, fn. 1.

40. O'Neil, *Report on Forts and Castles,* 17.

41. Ibid.; Nathan, "The Gold Coast Under the Danes and the Dutch," 7.

42. Isert, *Journey to Guinea and the Caribbean Islands of Columbia.*

43. O'Neil, *Report on Forts and Castles,* 17.

44. Ibid., 17-18.

45. Ibid., 18.

46. Nathan, "The Gold Coast Under the Danes and the Dutch," 24-25.

47. Redmayne, *The Gold Coast Yesterday and Today* (Cape Coast: Methodist Book Depot, 1941), 59; Nathan, "The Gold Coast Under the Danes and the Dutch, 6.

48. Redmayne, *The Gold Coast Yesterday and Today*, 59; Nathan, "The Gold Coast Under the Danes and the Dutch," 7.

49. Nathan, "The Gold Coast Under the Danes and the Dutch," 24-25.

50. Isert, *Journey to Guinea and the Caribbean Islands in Columbia*, 29.

51. Ibid.

52. Ibid.

53. Ibid.; Nathan, "The Gold Coast Under the Danes and the Dutch," 7.

54. Nathan, "The Gold Coast Under the Danes and the Dutch," 7.

55. Ibid.

56. Isert, *Journey to Guinea and the Caribbean Islands in Columbia*, 30, fn. 1, Second letter, In camp at Ada on the Rio Volta, 29 December, 1783.

57. Nathan, "The Gold Coast Under the Danes and the Dutch," 8.

58. Ibid.

59. Hansen, *Coast of Slaves*, 113.

60. Ibid.

61. Isert, *Journey to Guinea and the Caribbean Islands*, 34.

62. Ibid., Second Letter

63. Ibid., 38. Second Letter.

64 Ibid., 37. Second Letter.

65. Ibid. See fn. 19. Second Letter

66. Ibid., 37-38. Second Letter.

67 Ibid. 42. Second Letter

68 Ibid., 43.

69. Isert, *Journey to Guinea and the Caribbean islands in Columbia*, 151. Ninth Letter. Main Fort Christiansborg in Guinea, 20 April, 1786.

70. Ibid., 151.

71. Ibid.

72. Ibid., 152.

73. Ibid.

74. Ibid., 152.

75. Ibid., 152

76. Ibid.

77. Ibid.

78. Ibid.

79. Ibid.

80. Ibid., 152.

81. Ibid,. 152-153.

82. Ibid., 156, Ninth Letter.

83. Ibid. 153, Ninth Letter.

84. Ibid., 158, Ninth Letter.
85. Isert, Letters on West Africa and the Slave Trade, 83. Sixth Letter.
86. Includes food and drink for crew of 40 and most of the food for slaves during the Middle Passage.

✤ Chapter 7

Brandenburg-Prussia: Latecomers to the Atlantic Slave Trade on the Gold Coast

While the slave trading activities of the Portuguese, the English and the Dutch are very well known, one hardly hears about the Brandenburger-Prussian participation in the construction of slave forts, castles and dungeons on the Gold Coast or their participation in the Atlantic slave trade. In fact the flag of the Elector of Brandenburg can still be found at Fort Groot Friedrichsburg at Pokesu or Princestown, even though Brandenburg-Prussian's participation in the Atlantic slave trade pales in comparison with that of any of its illustrious competitors. This chapter examines the role of Brandenburg-Prussia in the construction of European fortified stations on the Gold Coast and their participation in the Atlantic slave trade.

The earliest recorded Brandenburg-Prussian commercial activity in West Africa dates from the 1600s when ships from Hamburg and Lübeck visited the islands of São Tomé and Principé. While it is likely that the merchants of Brandenburg-Prussia were invited by the Portuguese who controlled these islands at this time, there is no information about the Brandenburg-Prussian participation in the coastwise carrying trade involving the shipping of slaves from São Tomé to the Gold Coast, especially to Elmina.[1] The second recorded evidence of Brandenburg-Prussia participation in African commerce dates to 1651 when an expedition sent by the Duke of Courland established a trading post on James Island on the Gambia River. The purpose of the post was to establish a base for participation in the lucrative Atlantic slave trade to the Americas. However, as Adam Jones notes, there is little evidence of any serious participation in the trade in enslaved Africans to the Americas at this time.[2]

From this point forward, a smattering of fragmentary evidence paints the following picture about Brandenburg-Prussia and the carrying trade in enslaved Africans:

> First, six enslaved Africans were purchased in November 1651, for 30 iron bars on the Gambia River; second, a 1652 ship's cargo included beans and other items that were supposedly to be exchanged for enslaved Africans; and third, in 1658, when the Dutch took James Island, the Courland governor reportedly escaped to Jamaica with an unspecified quantity of goods and enslaved Africans.[3]

Adam Jones asserts that, while Courland obtained the island of Tobago as a colony in 1654, ostensibly to receive enslaved Africans from its Gambian trading post, there is very little evidence of any substantial slave trading activity, not even in the 1670s, when Courland reestablished its link to Africa. In short, the very few extant documents available (because many of the documents were lost) indicate that this early Courland enterprise was indeed only in name, even though it is also possible that the near nonparticipation was a by-product of the fact that Courland had neither the human nor material resources to compete with its more powerful and illustrious competitors, especially the English and the Dutch.[4]

Overall, though, while there is very little information about Brandenburg-Prussian participation in the slave trade, there is some evidence to the effect that they managed to send a few hundred enslaved Africans to the New World. The *Patriarch Jacob*, Jones notes, left Glückstadt, one of the three ports on the Elbe, in 1668 and early 1669, and "transported a hundred enslaved Africans from the West African mainland to São Tomé."[5]

Brandenburg-Prussian participation in the trade in enslaved Africans owed much impetus from the Baltic-Africa complex. Holland, until the third Anglo-Dutch war (ended 1674), was the preeminent industrial and commercial power in Europe. The Dutch were similarly prominent in West Africa, and especially on the Gold Coast where they competed with the English for control over the coast. Dutch influence on the Guinea coast, like its preeminent position in seventeenth-century Europe, played no small role in the Brandenburg participation in the African trade. Brandenburg and Courland's interest in the Africa trade, like those of their Swedish and Danish counterparts, were also influenced by Dutch success. Elector William of Brandenburg, who had spent part of his youth in the Netherlands, and who had also married into the Dutch royal house of Orange,[6] was inspired by Dutch success in the Baltic and on the Guinea coast to plunge Brandenburg into the Guinea trade and, for that matter, the trade in enslaved Africans.

The appearance of Brandenburger-Prussians on the Gold Coast took the initial form of an "interloper company" designed to break the Dutch West India Company's monopoly on the Gold Coast. In 1674-1678, when Brandenburg was not at war with Sweden, one Benjamin Raule, "a member of a great Huguenot corsair family from Dunkirk," offered his corsairs to the great Elector to attack Dutch shipping carrying military stores to Sweden.[7] For his services and friendship, Raule was appointed minister of marine in 1679. In 1680, Joris Bartelson, the captain of a Zeeland privateer, was permitted to sell enslaved Africans in Cadiz, Lisbon or the Canary Islands, and to bring six young enslaved Africans aged 14 to 16 to the Bradenburg Elector's court.[8]

In 1682, Raule, with the help of a number of financiers and ship owners in Amsterdam, organized a chartered company, the Brandenburg Africa Company, to break what was believed to be the Dutch West India Company stranglehold on the Gold Coast and West Africa.[9] To better compete with its more established competitors, the Company received subsidies and diplomatic protection from the Great Elector. Cognizant of the profits from the slave trade accruing to other European countries, the Brandenburgers (Prussians) appeared on the Gold Coast to participate in the trade. The Elector of Brandenburg, on the advice of his Zeeland-born Director-General of the Brandenburg Navy, Raule, dispatched two frigates (a thirty-two gun boat manned by sixty men and an eighteen-gun boat and fifty men) commanded by Captains Mathieu de Vos and Philip Pieter Bloncq to West Africa, specifically to the Gold Coast in 1682 on a private trading enterprise.[10] Armed with instructions to start a settlement, de Vos, Bloncq and the men landed off Cape Three Points in May 1682, at Pokeso (Princestown).[11] A plaque on the wall of Fort Gross Friedrichsburg notes that one "Major Otto Frederick von der Groeben hoisted the red-white flag with the red eagle on the rock Manfro on the peninsula near Poqueso, perhaps an African village on the site of the present Prince's Town on January 1, 1683,"[12]

In 1685, Raule wrote to the Great Elector that

> Everyone knows that the slave trade is a source of wealth which the Spaniards draw from their Indies, and that he who knows how to supply the slaves will share this wealth with them. Who can guess how many millions the Dutch West India Company has gained by this delivery of slaves.[13]

It is worthy of note that Dutch success in the trade in enslaved Africans had become the yardstick for Brandenburg participation in the trade and Raule wanted Brandenburg-Prussia "to take its rightful place in the West African sun" and reap some of the profits accruing from the trade in enslaved Africans. It is also worthy of note that Bloncq and his team were also to trade in malaguetta pepper, ivory, gold and enslaved Africans. Some six hundred enslaved Africans were to be purchased at Allada or Ardra; one hundred of the enslaved Africans were to be shipped separately; sixty were to be sold at São Tomé; and forty aged 8-11 and 25 to 30 were to be brought to Europe, probably to the Brandenburg court.[14] Another ship would carry a large kettle, fifty pounds of tobacco, a drum and two hundred shackles from Brandenburg to West Africa, and would carry five hundred enslaved Africans for the outbound journey to the Van Pere property on the Berbice River in Guiana.[15] Bloncq was permitted to trade on his own account on condition that he sent five to six enslaved Africans between the ages and 8 and 16 to Europe, but the trip, unfortunately, fell below expectations.[16]

Bloncq, who had already made several voyages to the Gold Coast, secured the permission of the Pokesu chief to build a fort on Manfro (or Montfort) Hill as a warehouse for trade goods. To protect this initial settlement, the Brandenburgers dragged some cannons from the shore and up the hill to the settlement. The cannons were mounted and surrounded by earthworks to convert the settlement into a fortified defensible structure. Next, they built a large palisade fence around the structure and, having secured the perimeter, built rooms within the compound for storing ammunition and provisions and as accommodations for the Brandenburg garrison.[17]

After building a settlement and planting the Brandenburg flag on the Gold Coast (Photo 7.1), the company began to trade in the western part of the Gold Coast in an area believed to be rich in gold. Bloncq returned to Hamburg, and thence to Berlin, with ambassadors of the Pokesu chief. The African guests were received by the Elector and treated to the pomp and pageantry of his court. Bloncq and the Pokesu ambassadors returned to the Gold Coast a year later.[18] The result of this visit was that the Pokesu chief formed an alliance with the first Brandenburg Governor, Major Otto Frederick von der Groeben. Subsequently, the chief ceded a promontory near Pokesu to the Brandenburgers to build a fort in return for a promise to protect the people against the Dutch and not to sell anyone in the area into slavery.[19]

FORT GROSS FRIEDRICHSBURG

The principal fort of the Brandenburgers, Gross Friedrichsburg, was the headquarters of the Brandenburg Company on the Gold Coast, at Mamfro. Originally, the Brandenburgers erected temporary defenses in May 1682 and completed the fort the following year. It was "fortified with 30 guns, and manned with 60 common soldiers and a Director-Governor, one Chief Factor, one underfactor, three assistants, one lieutenant, one ensign, two

Photo 7.3: Fort Gross Friedrichsburg

sergeants, two corporals, one chief and one under barber, one constable, some gentlemen cadets, and one drummer."[20] Two and a half decades later the Brandenburgers abandoned the fort, and it could have been given to, or was appropriated by, John Conny.[21] After an unsuccessful attack in 1720, the Dutch captured the fort in 1725 and renamed it Fort Hollandia.

The Brandenburg Africa Company constructed the heavily-fortified fort, Gross Friedrichsburg to countermand Dutch influence in the region. The fort is an interesting structure. "From the middle of its western curtain there projects a tower of elongated D-Plan with battered walls, apparently solid from the ground up to the wall-walk level."[22] This round tower, probably built at an earlier date, and "designed to take cannon in the formative period of defense with artillery," could have preceded the Brandenburger structure, probably dating back to an earlier Portuguese lodge or fort at the same site.[23] The existing masonry "which follows the same D-form," "contains a room, roofed, and has round-headed windows, like the windows of the storerooms."[24]

By 1684, Fort Gross Friedrichsburg was protected by thirty-two heavy cannons, "4 bastions, with unusually thick parapets and linked by wide curtain walls made of solid masonry," and was an enclosure with some two-storey buildings that could house about ninety-one Europeans.[25] The structure is square in form, "enclosed by a thick curtain of rubble masonry, well mortared but not plastered externally. From each corner there projected a large bastion with an acute salient angle."[26] Due to lack of maintenance over the years, the northwestern and northeastern bastions are in ruins and overgrown with weeds and the southwestern bastion has lost much of its parapet, and remnants of the south-eastern bastion show that each face (60 ft. long) had three gunports and each flank (24 ft. long), had two."[27]

With its monumental gateway and a big bell tower, Fort Gross Friedrichsburg, like other late seventeenth-century Brandenburg structures, was designed to impress all who saw it.[28]

Bosman described Gross Friedrichsburg as "handsome and reasonably large, strengthened with four large batteries furnished with forty six Pieces of Ordnance, but too light and small."[29] It had a very beautiful gate which was proportionally much too large for the structure and did not make too much sense from a security standpoint. However, the greatest weakness of Fort Friedrichsburg was that "the Breast-works are built no higher than a man's knee, and the men thereby are continually exposed defenseless to the shot from without."[30] On the east side of the fort is a beautiful out-work, but paradoxically, this out-work "deprives the fortress of a great part of its strength," and therefore made it easier to breach and difficult to defend on that side of the fort; the local people could easily fire on any one who appeared on the battery to man the guns.[31]

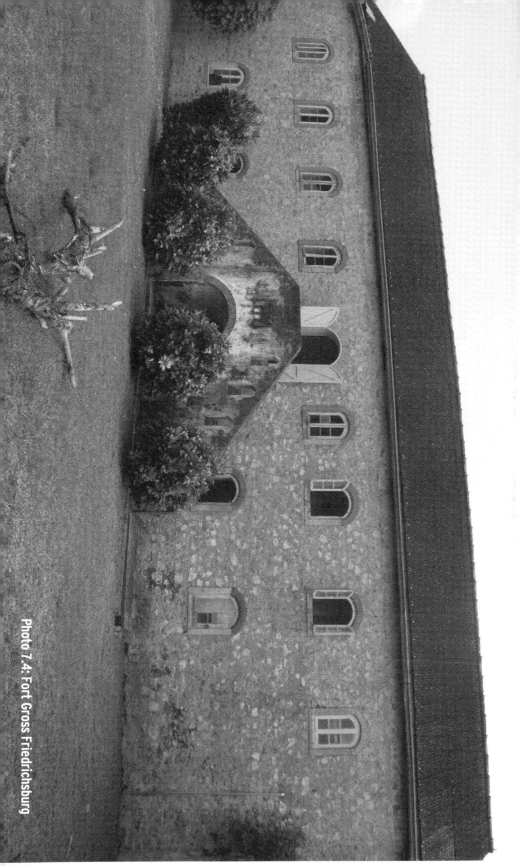

Photo 7.4 Fort Gross Friedrichsburg

The rest of Fort Gross Friedrichsburg is composed of accommodations for the Bradenburg merchants, officials and the few troops who defended the fort. These quarters, in 1700, stood "two storeys high, without roofs and floors on the north, east and south sides of the courtyard. The southern storehouse is especially impressive even in ruins, with its row of eight windows and a door in each long wall at first floor level."[32] An external staircase was added to the western side of the eastern storehouse to facilitate entrance to the first floor and all the buildings had "roundheated windows turned in brick and rebated for external shutters."[33]

Overall, only a handful of enslaved Africans were received in the late seventeenth century. In 1685 Brandenburg negotiated a treaty with Denmark to enable the Brandenburg Africa Company to sell enslaved Africans in St. Thomas, together with establishing plantations, but the venture bore very little fruit.[34] Gross Freidrichsburg supplied very few enslaved Africans. In 1686, the director-general of the fort received two enslaved boys (said to be worth 35 – 35 rix-dollars) as a present from a trader, but overall, the trade was fitful and pitiful for the Brandenburgers as well as their Dutch neighbors to the west at Axim, Butre and Sekondi, and even for the English at Dixcove or Mfuma. The focus of slave trading activity at this time was further east from Shama, towards the slave coast (of modern day Togo, Benin and Nigeria).[35]

The best documentation of Brandenburg slave trading on the Gold Coast involved the *Frederick Wilhelm*, which left Emden in July 1892 bound for Alampi or the area between Accra and the River Volta, and also to Whydah. About a dozen enslaved Africans were obtained in Accra but it was in only in Whydah that the *Frederick Wilhelm* purchased 700 enslaved Africans, about 659 of whom eventually reached St. Thomas, having survived two slave uprisings.[36] The plaque on one of the walls of Gross Friederichsburg notes that after selling the enslaved Africans on the island of St. Thomas, the *Frederick Wilhelm* left the island on August 29, 1892, "with a cargo of cocoa for Cadiz/Spain. The Captain Le Sage changed it for Spanish vine, then for cheap European industrial products. For them he changed again for slaves, when he returned [sic] to Africa in the begin [beginning] of November 1693."[37]

Unlike its European competitors, Brandenburg-Prussia did not have the economic and military power for colonial ambitions and the trade in enslaved Africans on the Gold Coast and West Africa so far from the Baltic. Consequently in 1711, the Brandenburg Africa Company went bankrupt and King Frederick William I, the "Soldier King" (1717/1721) sold Gross Friedrichsburg to the Dutch West India Company but without notifying the chief of Poqueso or the African agent of the Brandenburg Africa Company. Subsequently, John Conny, the African agent, defended Fort Gross Friedrichsburg and fought against

Photo 7.5: Fort Gross Friederichsburg – Slave Dungeons

Photo 7.6: Fort Gross Friedrichsburg – Plate with Photo of the Great Elector

Photo 7.7: Fort Gross Friedrichsburg

Photo 7.8: Fort Dorothea - Remnants

Photo 7.9: Fort Dorothea

against the new Dutch owners between 1720 and 1724. This would be later enshrined in history in the legend of the "Black Prussian."[38]

FORT DOROTHEA AT AKWADAE (AKWIDA)

The Brandenburg Africa Company built another fort (Dorothea) in the vicinity of Fort Gross Friedrichsburg, ostensibly to defend their principal fort. As well, they built a small fortified structure (Fort Louise) at Takarama near Cape Three Points. Fort Dorothea near Akwadae (generally called Akwida by Europeans) was a small triangular structure located east of Cape Three Points and visible from Fort Fredericksburg. It was "situated on a promontory at the end of a peninsula between the mouth of the Suni River and the sea."[39] The Dutch seized it soon after its construction but returned it to the Brandenburg Africa Company in light of an alliance against Louis XIV.

Fort Dorothea was little more than a lodge when it was first built, but after it was captured by the Dutch in 1690 the latter considerably improved the structure. In 1698 the Dutch West India Company ordered its officials to hand over the fort back to the Brandenburger-Prussians.[40] Fort Dorothea was again strengthened and improved, and later expanded into "a square building with two bastions pointing landwards."[41]

In general appearance, Fort Dorothea was a "House covered with a flat Roof, on which are two small Batteries and half Curtaines, upon which they have planted several light Pieces of Cannon; it is indeed furnished with a sufficient number of Rooms and Conveniences, tho' but slightly built and somewhat crowded."[42]

PERSONNEL OF THE BRANDENBURG GOVERNMENT SETTLEMENTS IN THE GOLD COAST

For most of its existence on the Gold Coast, the Brandenburg Africa Company personnel in their two forts and one lodge, most especially commanders and servants, were largely Dutch. These were renegades who had left the employment of the Dutch West India Company. Some were dismissed for various infractions and others deserted their positions out of disagreement with their superiors and official WIC policies. But almost all the common soldiers were Brandenburgers.[43] The head of the Brandenburg enterprise in the Gold Coast was the commander-in-chief of Fort Friedrichsburg at Pokesu who had the title of director-general under his Electoral Highness of Brandenburg and his African company.[44] For the fourteen-or-so years that Bosman spent on the Gold Coast from about 1688 to1702, seven directors

Photo 7.10: Fort Dorothea

served at Fort Friedrichsburg. His descriptions of the activities of these men point to the qualities of the men involved in running the Brandenburg forts and highlight the difficulties of getting well qualified men to travel to the Gold Coast at the time, the promises of making fortunes notwithstanding.

The first Brandenburg director, John Nyman of Embden, is described as an experienced, conscientious and honorable man who discharged his duties to the best of his abilities. His successors, a father-son team of John and Jacob Ten-Hooft, are described as reputable officials who kept their subordinates in line. The younger Ten-Hooft is singled out as having gained the affection of the local people by his good nature and civility. Consequently, he left "Brandenburghian Affairs in a much better Condition than any before him … and they never had a better Governor."[45] Surprisingly, however, Jacob ten-Hooft was removed from office and replaced with Gysbrecht van Hoogveldt, a defector from Dutch service at Axim, who was discharged on the grounds of incompetence and cruelty, especially for ill-treating subordinates. His work for the Brandenburgers ultimately led to the ruin of the company and so he was booted out of office through the joint instrumentality of both the Brandenburg officials and the local people. Van Hoogveldt was replaced by John van Laar, an Anabaptist with a much better talent at drinking brandy than with business activities.[46] He was replaced after death by John Visser, who is described as a man lacking in common sense. Soon after assuming office as commander at Pokesu, Visser's factor at Akwadae was killed but Visser was too weak to intervene, let alone punish those who had killed the Brandenburg official. Interestingly, Visser himself was later seized by the local people; his limbs were broken and he was drowned in the sea, all with the complicity of other officials at Fort Friedrichsburg.[47] Adrian Grobble, reportedly chosen by the local people because of his complicity in the death of Visser, replaced him as commandant of Fort Friedrichsburg.

It stands to reason that the Brandenburg officials were not necessarily an impressive cast of the type that was often necessarily needed in the task of negotiating trade and exerting company control on the Gold Coast.

Compared to the Portuguese, the Dutch and the English, the Brandenburger participation in the slave trade on the Gold Coast appears modest to negligible. Their presence on the Gold Coast, however, points to the pull of the Atlantic slave trade to various European nations. It speaks to the period of European rivalry and its ramifications for other parts of the world. In all the Brandenburgers built three main fortified strongholds on the Gold Coast – Friedrichsburg, Dorothea and Louise. The Brandenburg period on the Gold Coast was very brief – from 1682 to 1708 – and the overall impact of their presence on the Gold Coast was negligible.

Notes

1. See Adam Jones, "Brandenburg-Prussia and the Atlantic Slave Trade," in *De La Traite á L'eEsclavage. Actes du Coloque International sue la Traite des Noirs*, édités par Serge Daget, Tomes I: Ve - XVIIIe Siècles (Nantes, 1985), 283.

2 Ibid.

3. Ibid.

4. Ibid., 283-284.

5. Ibid., 284.

6. Georg Nørregård,. *Danish Settlements in West Africa 1658- 1850*, trans. Sigurd Mammen (Boston: Boston University Press, 1966), xviii.

7. Albert Van Dantzig, *Forts and Castles of Ghana* Accra: Sedco Publishing, 1980. 37.

8. Jones, "Brandenburg-Prussia and the Atlantic Slave Trade," 285.

9. Van Dantzig, *Forts and Castles of Ghana*, 37.

10. Jones, "Brandenburg-Prussia and the Atlantic Slave Trade," 284.

11. W. Walton Claridge, *A History of the Gold Coast and Ashanti* (London: Frank Cass, 1964), 123.

12. Information from plaque on one of the walls of Fort Gross Friedrichsburg titled "A Short Summary of the History of the Castle."

13. ZSTA Meresburg, R.65. 11 ff.., 387-90, Raule 26.10.1687 to Elector, in June in Jones, "Brandenburg-Prussia and the Atlantic Slave Trade," 285.

14. Ibid.

15. Ibid., 285-6.

16. Ibid.

17. Claridge, *A History of the Gold Coast and Ashanti*, 123.

18. Ibid.

19. Van Dantzig, *Forts and Castles of Ghana*, 37.

20. M. Nathan, "The Gold Coast Under the Danes and the Dutch," *Journal of African Society* 13, 4 (1904): 12-13.

21. B.H. St. J. O'Neil, *Report on Forts and Castles of Ghana* (Accra-Tema: State Publishing Corporation, October 1951 [for Ghana Museums and Monuments Board], 48.

22. Ibid.

23. Ibid.

24 Ibid.

25. Van Dantzig, *Forts and Castles of Ghana*, 38. Claridge, *A History of the Gold Coast and Ashanti*, puts the number of guns at 46.

26. O'Neil, *Report on Forts and Castles of Ghana*, 48.

27. Ibid., 49.

28. Van Dantzig, *Forts and Castles of Ghana*, 38; O'Neil, *Reports on Forts and Castles*, 49.

29. Willem Bosman, *A New and Accurate Description of the Coast of Guinea*, 7.

30. Ibid.

31. Ibid.

32. O'Neil, *Report on Forts and Castles of Ghana*, 50.

33. Ibid.

34. Jones, "Brandenburg-Prussia and the Atlantic Slave Trade," 286.

35. Ibid., 287.

36. Ibid., 288-289

37. Information from plaque on the wall of Fort Gross Friedrichsburg titled "A Short Summary of the History of the Castle."

38. Information is culled from the plaque on one of the walls of the fort.

39. Van Dantzig, *Forts and Castles of Ghana*, 38.

40. Claridge, *A History of the Gold Coast and Ashanti*, 123.

41. Van Dantzig, *Forts and Castles of Ghana*, 39.

42 Bosman, *A New and Accurate Description of the Coast of Guinea*, 10.

43. Ibid., 8.

44. Ibid.

45. Ibid.

46. Ibid., 9.

47. Ibid., 9.

✦ Chapter 8

Conclusion: From "Gates of No Return" to "Gates of Return": PANAFEST and Emancipation Commemoration in Ghana

The slave forts, castles and dungeons of Ghana constitute an important prism for a discussion of the Euro-African frontier. Over the long *durée* this experience encompasses commodity trade, the odious commerce in enslaved Africans and the colonial encounters of the nineteenth and twentieth centuries. Of the three distinct historical conjunctures, the period covering the Atlantic slave trade is the one that has been given prominence, and rightly so. At the same time, the other dimensions of the Euro-African encounter are important to fully comprehend different facets of the history of Ghana in particular and West Africa in general. For many people, but moreso for diaspora Africans, the forts, castles and dungeons symbolize the epitome of the degradation, humiliation and powerlessness that characterized the world of slavery for about four hundred years. The virulent racism, oppression and the badge of inferiority that became the hallmark of slavery, despite the many accomplishments of Africans in the diaspora (scientific, economic, the arts, education), one can argue, was a by-product of the forts, castles and dungeons experience. At the same time, however, these edifices were also the structural elements that linked the African diaspora to Africa, that "supposedly mysterious," distant, ancient continent with its glorious past (exemplified by Egypt, Nubia, Kush, Meroe, Ethiopia, Ghana, Mali, Songhai), and which in the twenty- first century, beckons to its sons and daughters to return home in the same way the emigrationists of the eighteenth and nineteenth centuries strove to go back to Africa. This is all in spite of the perceptions of Africa as mired in intractable civil wars and poverty.[1]

The slave forts, castles and dungeons have, over time, become increasingly important in the search for many diaspora Africans for closure to a virulent past that has been difficult and problematic to deal with, to say the least. At the same time, the forts and castles have also come to signify the strength, the resilience and the indomitable human spirit in the face of indescribable odds. Grim, foreboding, yet impressive against the skyline, the forts and castles also represent a coming to terms of an aspect of African diaspora historical experience that has been difficult to digest, much less deal with: how could slavery happen? How was it possible for large numbers of Africans to be enslaved and sold like chattel? These are two of the questions that are often asked by some diaspora Africans who frame their return to Africa in the context of the horrors of the Atlantic slave trade. In the early decades of the twentieth century and through the civil rights era of the 1960s, Africans disapora expatriates "framed their 'return' to Africa as a locus of racial and national freedom"[2] as well as repatriation; but since the late 1990s the return has been framed as a search for roots or genealogical projects, tourism and emancipation commemorative activities. The central argument of this concluding chapter is that the slave forts, castles and dungeons of the Gold Coast, once the site of rupture and "social death," have increasingly become "sites of return" and reunification - all the problems of reunification of long-lost families notwithstanding. Thus, the story of the slave forts, castles and dungeons of Ghana has gone full circle to link up some Africans on the continent and diaspora Africans.

The slave forts and castles along the coast of Ghana have, since the early twenty-first century, become a focal point of Africa-African diaspora relations, through the biennial Emancipation commemoration ceremonies and the Pan African Historical Theatre Festival (PANAFEST). During these commemorative and celebratory events, many diaspora Africans, especially African Americans, respond to the Ghana government's invitation to "come back home" to the land of their forbears, often for a few short weeks but, in some instances, months, and even years.[3] The slave forts, castles and dungeons of Ghana and the infamous *Maison des Esclaves* of Senegal have become sites of "pilgrimage" and sites of "return." In this way, diaspora Africans have reframed Atlantic narratives and transnational discourses in the African diaspora. As a result, many heritage and tourism activities have been planned around the biennial PANAFEST and Emancipation activities when many Africans and people of African descent in the diaspora return to the continent to connect or reconnect, as the case may be, with the land of their ancestors. Abraham Padi of Silicon Tours, Accra, captured the mood of many in 1998 when he noted that "We must forever break the myth of 'No Return.' And we must pay tribute to our ancestors' resilience. They finally attained their freedom. Today the chains are no more. Now we must restore the broken walls, heal the deep cuts, knit together the torn threads."[4]

Former U.S. Presidents George W. Bush and Bill Clinton visited Gorée Island and the *Maison des Esclaves* as part of their respective visits to Africa, while President Barack Obama visited Cape Coast Castle. The symbolism of the visits to the slave house on Gorée Island and the slave forts, castles and dungeons, I argue, highlights the crucible in which the Africa-African Diaspora and, for that matter, the larger Atlantic encounter with Africa, is being played out in our time and continues to be viewed and negotiated. As well, their visits show the extent to which the memory of slavery has been integrated into the American and African American national consciousness in the post-Du Bois period. Above all, this book also emphasizes the extent to which the "structural amnesia of slavery in the American landscape" has been brought back front and center in African American popular discourse, especially over the past decade. This is even more poignant after the election of the first African American president of the United States in 2008.[5]

This book demonstrates the role of the forts and castles in the "recreation" and revalorization of Africa and African diaspora exchanges – whether it is to Gorée Island (Senegal) or to the slave castles of Elmina and Cape Coast (Ghana). Though built on African soil, the architects of the forts and castles on the Gold Coast came from Europe: Portuguese, Dutch, French, British, Brandenburger-Prussians, Danes and Swedes. They utilized resources from Europe but the bulk of the manpower and resources for the construction of the slave forts and castles came from the various locales where the structures were built.

The warehouses of the forts and castles teemed with gold and ivory and export products to Europe in the fifteenth century, later to be replaced with enslaved Africans destined for the New World. But these "ships at permanent anchor," as one scholar calls the forts and castles, later became European enclaves on the Gold Coast where the foundations for trade in raw materials, Western education, Christianity, and a colonial civil service were laid.[6] In the recent past, however, these buildings and sites have become places for "recreating" historical memory and reestablishing Africa-African diaspora linkages that date back to the Friendship Societies of eighteenth century African American communities in Philadelphia, Baltimore and other places, including the 1817 back-to-Africa project of Paul Cuffee. These were the emigrationists who preferred the difficulties of "home" in Africa to the alienation of the New World in America. At the same time it is important to point out that there were others who were adamantly opposed to any move to Africa.

Today, through the PANAFEST and Emancipation ceremonies in Ghana, Africa-African diaspora relations are being realigned, not necessarily on a government-to- government basis, but through the drive of people of African descent in the diaspora, especially African Americans, who go on a "pilgrimage" to their roots. In these encounters, the slave forts and castles have served as an important frontier for the acceptance, contestation and negotiation of Africa-African diaspora relations. Thus the forts, castles and dungeons constitute another prism to examine an emerging element in this relationship: a grassroots approach to diplomatic relations. This time, the site of historical memory is the space in which the relations are crafted. As previously mentioned, all American presidents of the recent past have included a visit to the *Maison des Esclaves* (House of Slaves) on Gorée Island or Cape Coast Castle in their itineraries when they have visited Africa.

Apart from the African American presence in the United States, there is also the contribution of the returnees (people of African descent from the United States, Canada's Nova Scotia maroons and people from the Caribbean) to Liberia and Sierra Leone's development. Therefore, in capping their African trips with the visit to the House of Slaves, American presidents who have visited Africa have affirmed the significance of the forts, castles, and dungeons and other sites of historical memory in American History.

HOW DID WE GET TO THIS POINT?

During the period of the slave trade, over 12 million Africans, according to the estimates of scholars, were forcibly uprooted from their homes and transported to the New World.[7] Demographic studies show that throughout a greater part of the slave trade, the enslaved who were born in Africa formed a majority of the slave population in the Atlantic basin, especially in the Caribbean and South America. This trend established some continuity between the experiences of succeeding generations of Africans in the Americas. Though taken from different places, the enslaved Africans drew on familiar ethnic-African ways of being and doing in order to survive as a people.

The survivors of chattel slavery and their descendants filtered through their shared experiences functional borrowings from both their white masters and, in some cases, Indian nations,[8] to create distinctive local and regional "African"cultures, broad patterns notwithstanding. Thus, contrary to Stanley Elkins' concentration camp analogy, enslaved peoples who undertook the dreaded Middle Passage did not forget important aspects of their culture.[9] Faced with the dreaded plantation system, the enslaved redefined and held on to their religious, cultural and ethnic identities as a means of survival. Survival under slavery required adjustment and change and these

342

were in large part sought in connections with the past: language, religion and cultural practices. The mechanisms of self-identity were nurtured and came to influence the host societies, and were in turn influenced by them in very profound ways.[10] The vivacity and resiliency of those "identities" forged by the enslaved Africans have left lasting imprints on New World societies. "The world the slaves made" has had a tremendous impact on several facets of life in the Atlantic basin.[11]

The number of Africans involved in the Atlantic world afforded opportunities, albeit directly or indirectly, of influencing, of being exposed to and contributing to the cultures of the New World. In the end, peoples of African descent have made tremendous contributions to the economies and cultures of the Atlantic basin: music, festivals (carnival), religion, art, food items and cuisine, science, literature and many other aspects of life.[12] All these contributions came into full flower in the postslavery period.

Relations between Africans and their kinsmen and -women on this side of the Atlantic have been complex and multidimensional. Deep historical and cultural roots have linked the two groups together. Yet there is, on the one hand, a largely negative view of Africa in the minds of many people of African descent in the diaspora, which makes it difficult for some to identify with the continent. On the other hand, many Africans see diaspora Africans through the lens of the media stereotype - for example as wealthy Americans or Europeans rather than people of African descent. Consequently, the relationship between the two groups is plagued by distrust, negative media portrayals and stereotypes, perceived superiority complexes, economic and ideological differences.[13]

Early Africans in America certainly designated themselves African as exemplified in their poems, songs, names, schools and churches[14] to keep the link with their ancestral homeland and thus define their identity. However, the constant barrage of stereotypes and negative images about Africa discredited their mother continent, especially at a time when the educational system did not teach the history of African Americans as integral to the founding of America, much less the history of Africa. At the same time, virulent racism and discrimination, lack of voting rights, lack of access to equal education in the land of the free made the African American a product of two worlds – the essence of the "double consciousness" that W.E. B. Du Bois articulates. He eloquently wrote that the history of the American Negro,

> Is the history of this strife – this longing to attain self-conscious manhood, to merge his double self into a better and truer self. ...
> He would not Africanize America, for America has too much to teach the world and Africa. He would not bleach his Negro soul

in a flood of white Americanism for he knows that Negro blood
has a message for the world.[15]

In spite of this sense of double consciousness African Americans maintained
the African or black nomenclature for their churches thus pointing to a
psychological, if not a physical, return. But the physical return had already
begun in the eighteenth century and reached a crescendo in the last decade
of this new twenty-first century.

THE RETURN TO AFRICA: HISTORICAL CONTEXT

Physical return to Africa was sought by some members of the free
African societies that emerged in the late eighteenth century in New York,
Philadelphia, Rhode Island and other places. The Methodist preacher, Prince
Hall, and a party of African Americans sought the help of the Massachu-
setts legislature to return to "their country" in 1787 and set the stage for
the "back-to-Africa" schemes that reached an apogee in the Garvey movement.[16] Similarly, Paul Cuffee, an African-American sailor, shipbuilder and
owner, captain and entrepreneur, after a trip to Sierra Leone in 1811, took
a party of thirty-eight African-American emigrants to Africa in 1815 at his
own expense. Cuffee attempted to develop regular commercial relations
between the United States and West Africa almost a century before Marcus
Garvey.[17] However, these emigrationists differ from the twenty-first century
diasporans who are searching for their roots or going back to Africa to live.
The response of these early "returnees" was a response to racial prejudice
and discrimination in the land of freedom. As well, some of them saw themselves as returning to bring civilization to the motherland, having internal-
ized the European civilizing argument in the United States. In essence, their
American "upbringing" made them see the need to go back to Africa on a
"black civilizing mission."

The American Colonization Society (ACS), formed in 1817, actualized
the aspirations of some African American leaders who supported repatriation
and settlement of free blacks in Africa. African American participation in the
American Revolutionary War did not yield the anticipated results of emancipation and justice. Two main schools of thought, migration and integration, competed as solutions to the conditions of blacks in America. Prominent
leaders like James Forten and Paul Cuffee supported migration to Africa.[18]

In 1820 the ACS acquired a parcel of land from a local chief on Sherbro
Island near Sierra Leone and, in 1821, sent the first batch of eighty-six freed
enslaved Africans on the ship *Elizabeth* to the nascent West African nation.
Sherbro Island and its swampy surroundings exacted a high mortality rate

from the settlers. To save the colonization project from collapse, the ACS sent Eli Ayres to look for a healthier site for the settlers. With the help of Naval Lt. R.F. Stockton and the armed Schooner *Alligator*, Ayres navigated the Sierra Leone-Liberia coast in November 1821. The two men selected territory around Cape Mesurado as the site for the new settlement. Through persuasion and threat of force, they obtained land from the Bassa people. Ayres and the remnant of the colonists at Sherbro moved to Cape Mesurado. However, fever and conflicts with the local people made life difficult for the settlers. The new settlement fought for its very survival.[19]

In August 1822 a ship carrying immigrants from Baltimore (including recaptured Africans) arrived at Cape Mesurado under the leadership of the Methodist missionary and ACS representative, Jehuda Ashmun. Disease, especially malaria, and conflicts with the local people militated against a peaceful development of the settlement. On November 11 and November 30, 1822, for example, the colonists fought against the local people. Thankfully, a peace treaty later ushered in an era of peace and stability. Ashmum continued to work in the colony for five years until his departure for the United States on March 25, 1828.[20] Due to virulent racism in America and a continuation of plantation slavery, some African American leaders championed a return to Africa as a solution to the problems African Americans faced in the United States.

The London Committee for the Black Poor (established in 1786), in collaboration with the British government, sent about 141 immigrants (including some emancipated blacks) to Sierra Leone on May 14, 1787, and settled them at a place near the western tip on the Sierra Leone Peninsula, called Granville Town (named after the British abolitionist, Granville Sharp), later to be called Freetown.[21] About 1,196 Nova Scotia maroons,[22] sent to Canada from Jamaica originally, together with African-descended peoples from Britain, left Nova Scotia for Sierra Leone in January 1792 while a second contingent left Nova Scotia in March 1792. This group was augmented with Africans taken from slave ships by the British naval squadron stationed on the coast of West Africa and were sent to Sierra Leone. This group included, among several others, Yorubas, Ekitis, Igbos, Calabaris, Popos, Congolese, Asantes and other liberated Africans from other parts of Western Africa and who were all settled in Sierra Leone.[23] The towns the Nova Scotians planned with the other migratory groups were given such names as Westmooreland, Bathurst, Liverpool, Putney and so on.[24] These groups represent some of the early waves of return from the diaspora back to Africa. Other groups included the return of African-descended peoples from Brazil back to West Africa, especially to Nigeria and Ghana. Other diaspora Africans from the Caribbean were formally recruited to work as civil servants in the fledgling colony of Liberia. From the late nineteenth century to the early twentieth century, African American missionaries went to Southern Africa in another wave.

The slave forts, castles and dungeons of Ghana, especially in our time, have become the conduit for many Africans in the diaspora to connect with Africa. A 1998 *USA Today* front-page photograph of former U.S. President Bill Clinton, silhouetted in the infamous "Door of No Return" epitomizes Africa-African diaspora relations and the yearning to reconnect with Africa. Clinton visited Africa in 1998 to promote the Africa Growth and Opportunity Act (AGOA) and to strengthen fragile democracies on the continent.[25] For the longest time the shadow of the United States has been cast over West Africa because of the historical reality of a relationship that is at once ambivalent and at the same time celebratory, including the role of the United States in the founding of Liberia.

Speaking at a school in Uganda prior to his visit to Gorée Island, Clinton noted that "European Americans received the fruits of the slave trade … and we were wrong in that."[26] In the ensuing furor over whether the U.S. president had apologized for slavery or not, Clinton and his aides walked back the statement and insisted that the president had not apologized for slavery. On Gorée Island, Clinton asserted that "We cannot push time backward through the door of no return. We have lived our history, America's struggle to overcome slavery and its legacy forms one of the most difficult chapters of that history."[27] Tillet argues that by using the phrase "We have lived that history," Clinton was situating "slavery and its legacy in a bygone past."[28] If that is the case, this book asserts that the PANAFEST and Emancipation commemorations of Ghana, focused as they are on the slave forts, castles and dungeons, have situated "slavery, its legacy, and African diaspora history back in popular discourse," Atlantic histories and the genealogical projects of our time. But even before this time, they were inspired, first by Alex Haley's Roots, and later by technological advances in decoding the human genome. These have sparked renewed interest in Ghana and the slave forts, castles and dungeons that dot its coastline.

When U.S. President George Bush visited Africa in 2003 his first stop was Senegal and, once again, the *Maison Des Esclaves* became the backdrop against which President Bush reiterated the relationship between the United States and Africa. In that speech, President Bush spoke about the forced migration of Africans and celebrated African ties to the United States. He declared that

> In America, enslaved Africans learned the story of the exodus from
> Egypt and set their own hearts on a promised land of freedom.

Enslaved Africans discovered a suffering Savior and found he was more like themselves than their masters. Enslaved Africans heard the ringing promises of the Declaration of Independence and asked the self-evident question, then why not me?[29]

President Bush continued:

Among those Americans was Phyllis Wheatley, who was dragged from her home here in West Africa in 1761, at the age of seven. In my country, she became a poet, and the first noted black author in our nation's history. Phyllis Wheatley said, 'In every human breast, God has implanted a principle which we call love of freedom. It is impatient of oppression and pants for deliverance.'[30]

These words, uttered against the backdrop of the infamous *Maison des Esclaves* on Gorée Island makes the sites of historical memory and the forts, castles and dungeons of West Africa and especially Gold Coast/Ghana an important point of departure as well as point of convergence for Africa-African diaspora relations.

It is worthy of note, and has already been pointed out, that Africa-African diaspora relations have a long historical trajectory dating long before the end of slavery. The exploits of Paul Cuffee, Martin Delaney, the American Colonization Society and Britain in founding new settlements in Sierra Leone and Liberia all speak to this relationship.[31] Delaney reportedly was the first to use the phrase "Africa for Africans" and Delaney and Edward Wilmot Blyden, Molefe Kete Asante argues, established the intellectual basis for an African-centered regeneration of Africana history.[32] Delaney undertook a voyage of exploration throughout Yorubaland (Niger Valley) as a place where African Americans could migrate. However, the British forced the Alake of Abeokuta to repudiate the treaty he had signed with Delaney and Campbell. Moreover, the outbreak of the Civil War in the United States diverted Delaney's attention from Africa.[33] Additionally, the work of the emigrationists of the African American community, whose work was climaxed in Marcus Garvey's back-to-Africa movement, all underlie this relationship.

THE "RETURN" OF OUR TIME

A wave of African Americans started to "go back home" to West Africa from the time of Ghana's independence in 1957. This return was partly a response to the call by Dr. Kwame Nkrumah for African Americans to "take their talents to Ghana."[34] This generation, dubbed "Revolutionist Returnees" by Maya Angelou, included Marxists and Garveyites by orientation and comprised of doctors, journalists, entrepreneurs and other professionals who "brought to Africa varying talents, energies, vigor, youth and terrible yearnings to be accepted."[35] Ghana's independence celebrations in Accra were attended by the crème de la crème of African American society.[36] Thereafter, an exodus of African American political activists began a new pilgrimage to the continent, especially to Ghana. In Angelou's words, "We had come home, and if home was not what we had expected, never mind, our need for belonging allowed us to ignore the obvious and create real places or even illusory places, befitting our imagination."[37] Thus, many African Americans, descendants of those enslaved and taken from Africa, returned, "weighted with a heavy hope to a continent which they could not remember, to a home which had shamefully little memory of them."[38] As one African American intoned in the presence of Angelou and her companions in Ghana, "I belong here. My ancestors were taken from this land."[39] To many African Americans, coming to Ghana was coming home and as Maya Angelou tells it:

> Some travelers had arrived at Ghana's Accra airport, expecting customs agents to embrace them, porters to shout 'welcome,' and taxi drivers to ferry them, horns blaring, to the city square where smiling officials would cover them in ribbons and clasp them to their breasts with tearful sincerity. Our arrival had little impact on anyone but us.[40]

African and African diaspora relations have become more defined and celebrated since the 1990s, partly through Ghana's Emancipation commemorative events of our time. These events have become a cultural paradigm that use the biennial meeting centered around the slave forts, castles and dungeons, and through PANAFEST as a vehicle for reuniting the African family. The events bring together Africans and the diaspora from all corners of the world and have become the basis of cooperation and interaction. It is thus a rare opportunity, and has the potential, to realize the dreams of Marcus Garvey, W.E.B. Du Bois and Kwame Nkrumah, who made Pan-Africanism the cornerstone of their political activism.[41] These events have the potential to become an "African Marshall Plan" to unite the economic potential of Africans in the diaspora with that of their brothers and sisters on the continent.[42]

A long interregnum occurred between 1966 when the first military coup d'etat in Ghana toppled Dr. Kwame Nkrumah and the Convention People's Party and the PANAFEST activities that seek a reunification of African peoples. However, Alex Haley's search for his roots, and the Roots movie he produced, brought West Africa into the African American political and social discourse once again. Haley's work inspired "a lot of African Americans in their desire to replicate his journeys" to West Africa in search of their ancestors.[43] In the absence of national symbols that capture the slavery experience in the United States, African Americans and other diaspora Africans have made trips to the slave forts, castles and dungeons of Ghana with a view to understanding and situating the formation of African diasporic identities in the larger context of the Atlantic slave trade.[44]

PANAFEST AND THE AFRICAN DIASPORA

PANAFEST was inspired by a paper written by Mrs Efua Sutherland, a distinguished Ghanaian dramatist and pan-Africanist, in 1980. The aim was the portrayal of contemporary and historical issues between Africans in the diaspora and on the continent through drama.[45] In 1991, the idea gained favorable review in some corridors of power in Ghana, culminating in the Pan-African Historical Theatre Festival. In October 1991, PANAFEST was officially launched, and in December of that year the national phase of the festival took place at Cape Coast as the end product of a series of activities that included, among others, a national play-writing competition, seminars and workshops across the country on Pan-Africanism.[46] The success of the inaugural PANAFEST in 1991 led to a national PANAFEST celebration in 1992. This event focused on Cape Coast and Elmina where the United Nations World Heritage Sites of Cape Coast and São Jorge da Mina Castles and dungeons are located.

PANAFEST is a cultural event dedicated to the enhancement of the ideals of Pan-Africanism and the development of the African continent. It is organized biennially for Africans and peoples of African descent as well as persons committed to the well-being of Africans on the continent and in the diaspora. The essential thrust of PANAFEST is development. In this way, PANAFEST hopes to put the topstone on the long task of unification and "nation building" started by the Garvey-Dubois-Nkrumah triad.[47]

The Pan-Africanism of the 1900s to the 1950s focused on the struggle for equal and civil rights and was a struggle for dignity and against racism. In the 1940s, 1950s, and 1960s, decolonization became an important element of the pan-African struggle. The Pan-Africanism of the 1990s, promoted through PANAFEST, was done through the prism of the Atlantic slave trade.[48] The focal point of the festival is rooted in the slave forts, castles and dungeons through which enslaved Africans were sent into the New World. Today, the same slave forts, castles, and dungeons have become the vehicle for re-uniting Africans and diaspora Africans.

Launching PANAFEST 94 at the Africa Centre in London, Kojo Yankah, the Deputy Minister of Information, emphasized the fact that "Pan-Africanism is as relevant today as it was when it was conceived years ago."[49] Mr. Yankah continued that "PANAFEST is not merely a carnival over the tragedies, pain and anguish that continue to afflict parts of the continent but a 'rare opportunity for people of African descent to collectively actualize their experience in history, science, technology, in music and dance, as well as in the human and spiritual development of the African.'"[50]

PANAFEST aims to establish the truth about the history of Africa and the experience of its people using the vehicle of African arts and culture. Furthermore, it would provide a forum to promote unity between Africans on the continent and in the diaspora and affirm the common heritage of African peoples the world over. Finally, it would define Africa's contribution to world civilization.

PANAFEST draws participants from different parts of Ghana, some African countries, Europe, the Caribbean and the United States and Canada. In 1998 Jerry John Rawlings, then president of Ghana, added the celebration of Emancipation Day to the Pan-African Historical Theatre festival after a visit to Jamaica. Since then, participants are urged every year to foster African cultural identity and integration and to break cultural and economic barriers. On July 28 2003, Mr. Jake Obetsebi-Lamptey, Minister of Tourism and Modernization of the Capital City (Accra, Ghana), gave the opening address at the Emancipation commemoration activities and stressed that the festival must move away from putting too much emphasis on music and clothes to issues which will move the continent forward. Stressing the fact that the diaspora has more to give by way of skills, and that the African continent certainly has urgent need for such skills, Obetsibi-Lamptey hoped that the festival would achieve its goal of reversing the harm done to the physical and psychological well-being of the people of African descent and pull the African race together to develop Africa. On his part, the chairman of Ghana's National Commission on Culture, Prof. George Hagan, expressed optimism that the festival would be used to build bridges between all peoples of African descent to help fight poverty, ignorance and disease.

THE FORTS, CASTLES AND DUNGEONS AS WORLD HERITAGE SITES

The forts, castles and dungeons along the Coast of Ghana were designated World Heritage Properties in 1979. These structures carry different meanings for different people. To Europeans they may represent, to a large extent, European adventurism and military architecture in far-flung "colonies," as well as precolonial African encounters (including trade, the slave trade), and colonialism. To diaspora Africans, the forts, castles and dungeons, encapsulate the very epitome of degradation, slavery and humiliation. To Ghanaians, there is the added dimension of the role of the slave forts and castles in the colonial enterprise, and serving as the headquarters of the British colonial administration down to independence in 1957, and still playing a functional role as seat of government, despite the construction of a presidential palace complex. The government of Ghana made no serious attempt at rehabilitating the forts, castles and dungeons in the 1980s, even when some of them were designated World Heritage sites, and the Ghana Museums and Monuments Board (GMMB), the custodians of the monuments, did not have the resources to renovate the twenty-seven fortified properties including those with the World Heritage site designation.

In 1988, however, the Government of Ghana successfully launched a major regional integrated development program to refurbish the World Heritage sites in partnership with the United Nations Development Programme (UNDP) and the United States Agency for International Development (USAID).[51] This led to the Central Region Integrated Development Program (CERIDEP) launched in 1989, and which made the preservation and revitalization of three major national monuments – Cape Coast Castle, São Jorga da Mina Castle, Elmina and Fort St. Jago, Elmina – the centerpiece of its historic preservation program.[52] It was funded by the UNDP with additional funding from USAID in 1991.

A newly designed museum in Cape Coast Castle was opened to the public during PANAFEST in December 1994. The museum represents an exhibition on the historic role of the forts and castles titled "Crossroads of People, Crossroads of Trade," which articulates an "inclusivist" view of the role of the slave forts, castles, and dungeons in Gold Coast/Ghana history and sets out to interpret to visitors the architectural history of these structures and dungeons, and the history of the communities that had grown up around them.

The forts, castles and dungeons of Ghana have become important vehicles in preserving intangible values in memory, monuments and sites, especially as major focal points for the continuing encounter between Africans, Africans in the diaspora and Europeans, together with the ramifications of that encounter. Consequently, the forts, castles and dungeons, have become gateways, not of despair, but rather of hope, for the millions of Africans who crossed the Atlantic to various parts of the world as slaves. The slave dungeons of the forts and castles, especially Cape Coast Castle and Elmina Castle, and the "Gates of No Return," have become major points of call for Africans in the diaspora who visit Ghana every summer. In the dank, fetid confines of the dungeons, many diaspora Africans have been moved to tears after coming face to face with the horrors of the encounters in the forts and castles.[53]

It was not surprising that when PANAFEST was conceptualized, the forts, castles and dungeons, were situated front and center in the program. Cape Coast Castle, with its spectacular "Great Court," which opens out to the sea, which in turn laps the walls of the castle, was utilized during the third PAN-AFEST (1994). The harrowing atmosphere of the slave dungeons – fetid, damp, eerie and "haunted" were featured in large part in the film Sankofa,[54] which made such profound impact in North America and Europe in 1994. A Jamaican modern dance company performed in Cape Coast Castle during PANAFEST 1994, and two actors from the National Black Actors Touring Collective of New York put up a splendid performance of a new play about Zora Neale Thurston, the celebrated Florida-born, African American literary giant in Cape Coast Castle. All of these testify to the outsize role of the slave forts and castles in African diaspora literary and emotional imagination.

The importance of the slave forts and castles in the conscious imagination of various segments of the African diaspora is also significant in the periodic disputes and debates concerning activities in the hallowed confines of the Cape Coast or Elmina Castles. During PANAFEST 1993, the members of a Jamaican dance ensemble refused to perform in Cape Coast Castle because it is hallowed ground and any performance would desecrate the memories of their ancestors who passed through it enroute to the New World.[55] Similarly, some diaspora Africans periodically boycotted lunch served at a restaurant near the courtyard, contending that the place was so sacred and hallowed that it was disrespectful to serve meals on, or near, the premises.[56]

Some diaspora Africans see the slave forts and castles as the epitome of the evils of the slave trade, the inhuman trade that dehumanized enslaved Africans, and have argued that to rehabilitate the structures, whether it is in the context of conservation, maintenance, restoration or any other name amounted to nothing but whitewashing the history of the slave forts and castles.[57]

In sum, the forts and castles that dot the coastline of the Gold Coast were built by Europeans from Portugal, Holland, England, Brandenburg-Prussia, Denmark and Sweden and they have left imprints in the sands of time – imprints that have affected every facet of African and African diaspora history. These forts and castles became centers of global commercial activity – they teemed with gold, ivory and enslaved Africans who were sent to Europe, the Americas, the Caribbean and Asia from the fifteenth century until the nineteenth century. The period of the slave trade was indeed an era of globalization and the slave forts, castles and dungeons constituted a linch-pin in that global network that linked three different continents. The Portuguese, then the Dutch, English, Danes, Swedes and Brandenburgers, moved goods and enslaved Africans from one corner of the world to the other with Africa as the link between the various continents. In this way, the slave forts and castles of the Gold Coast became the fulcrum that anchored a global commercial system that facilitated the enterprise and ingenuity of Europeans. Tables 8.1 and 8.2 list all the Dutch and Danish governors who stayed and worked in these Houses of Slaves between 1638 and 1850.

Table 8.1: List of European Governors Who Used the Slave Forts and Castles of the Gold Coast/Ghana During the Trans-Atlantic Slave trade and the Colonial Period

Dutch Governors

NAME	RANK	LENGTH OF TIME IN OFFICE	PERIOD IN OFFICE
N. Van Iperen	Dir. Gen.	9 Mons. 17 days	Oct. 1, 1638 -18 Jul. 1639
A. J. Montford	Dir. Gen.	1 Yr. 5 Mo. 19 days	
R. Ruyghaver	Dir. Gen.	4 Yr. 11 Mo. 12 days	
J. Van der Well	Dir. Gen	4 Yr. 3 Mo. 22 days	
H. Doedens	Dir. Gen	2 Mo. 2 days	
A. Cocq	Gov.	9 Mo. 4 days	
J. Ruyghaver	Dir. Gen.	4 Yr. 10 Mo. 9 days	
J. Valkenburg	Dir. Gen.	3 Yr. 3 Mo. 20 days	
C. Van Houssen	Dir. Gen.	2 Yr. 11 Mo. 11 days	
D. Wilré	Dir. Gen.	8 Mo. 16 days	
J. Valkenburg	Dir. Gen	4 Yr. 5 Mo. 11 days	
H. Van Ongerdonk	Gov.	1 Yr. 6 Mo. 10 days	
D. Wilré	Dir. Gen	6 Yr. 4 Mo. 0 days	
J. Root	Dir. Gen.	1 Yr. 3 Mo. 1 day	
A. Meermans	Dir. Gen.	3 Yr. 6 Mo. 13 days	
D. Verhoutert	Dir. Gen.	3 Yr. 4 Mo. 6 days	
T. Ernsthuis	Dir. Gen.	1 yr. 11 Mo. 14 days	
N. Sweerts	Dir. Gen.	5 Yr. 6 mo. 14 days	
J. Smits	Dir. Gen	4 Yr. 1 Mo. 24 days	
J. Staphorst	Dir. Gen.	2 Yr. 2 Mo. 15 days	
J. Van Sevenhuysen	Dir. Gen.	5 Yr. 11 Mo. 24 days	
W. de Palma	Dir. Gen.	3 Yr. 5 Mo. 3 days	
P. Nuyts	Dir. Gen.	2 Yr. 11 Mo. 5 days	
H. Van Weesel	Gov.	10 mo. 4 days	
A. Schoonheidt	Dir. Gen.	1 Yr. 8 mo. 2 days	
H. Haring	Dir. Gen.	5 Yr. 1 mo. 26 days	
A. E. Roberts	Dir. Gen.	1 Yr. 9 mo. 29 days	
W. Bullier	Dir. Gen.	4 Yr. 6 mo. 5 days	

A. Houtman	Dir. Gen.	- 8 mo. 2 days	
M. de Kraane	Gov.	- 6 mo. 14 days	May 28, 1723- Dec. 14, 1723
P. Valkenier	Dir. Gen.	3 Yr. 2 mo. 24 days	Dec. 14, 1723- Mar. 10, 1727
R. Norri	Dir. Gen.	2 Yr. 11 mo. 25 days	Mar. 11, 1727- Mar. 5, 1730
Jan Pranger	Dir. Gen.	4 Yr. – mo. 6 days	Mar. 6, 1730- Mar. 12, 1734
Ant. Van Overbeck*	Dir. Gen.	1 Yr. 11 mo. 20 days	Mar. 13, 1734- Feb. 21, 1736
M. Francis Des Bordes*	Dir. Gen.	3 Yr. 5 mo. 3 days	Oct. 15, 1736- Mar. 16, 1740
Francis Barbrins*	Gov.	- 11 mo. 20 days	Mar. 17, 1740- Mar. 7, 1741
J. Baron de Peterson	Dir. Gen	6 Yr. 1 mo. 8 days	Mar. 8, 1741- Apr. 10, 1747
Jan Van Voorst	Dir. Gen.	7 Yr. 3 mo. 3 days	Apr. 11, 1747- Jul. 14, 1754
N.M.V. Nood-de-Gieterre*	Dir. Gen.	1 Yr. 3 mo. 10 days	Jul. 14, 1754- Oct. 14, 1755
Roelof Ulsten*	Gov.	2 Yr. 2 mo. 22 days	Oct. 25, 1755- Jan. 16, 1758
Mr. L. J. Van Tets*	Dir. Gen.	1 Yr. 1 mo. 28 days	Jan. 16, 1758- Mar. 12, 1759
Mr. J.P.T. Huydecooper	Dir. Gen.	- 6 mo. 17 days	Mar. 13, 1759- Oct. 1, 1760
David Pieter Erasmi*	Dir. Gen.	2 yr. 9 mo. 8 days	Oct. 2, 1760-Jul. 10, 1763
Henrick Walmbeck*	Gov.	1 Yr. 1 mo. 20 days	Jul. 11, 1763- Aug. 31, 1764
M. J. P. T. Huydecooper*	Gov.	2 Yr. 9 mo. 6 days	Sept. 11, 1764- Jun. 7, 1767
	Gov. Gen.	2 Yr. 0 mo. 1 day	Jun. 8, 1767- Jun. 9, 1769
Pieter Woortman*	Dir. Gen.	10 Yr. 10 mo. 1 day	June 10, 1769- Apr. 11, 1780
Jacobus Van der Puye*	Gov.	- 7 mo. 20 days	May, 10, 1780- Dec. 30, 1780
Pieter Volkmar*	Dir. Gen.	3 Yr. 2 mo. 10 days	Dec. 30, 1780- Mar. 12, 1784
G. Servis Gallé	Gov. Gen.	- Yr. 10 mo. 29 days	Mar. 15, 1784- Feb. 14, 1785

Adolph Thierens*	Dir. Gen	1 Yr. 3 mo. 12 days	Feb. 14, 1785- May 26, 1786
G. Servis Gallé	Gov. Gen.	1 Yr. 2 mo. 22 days	Jun. 2, 1786- Aug. 24, 1787
Mr. L. Van Bergen Vander Gryp	Pres.	2 Yr. 6 mo. 8 days	Sept. 8, 1787- Mar. 1790
Jacobus De Veer	Dir. Gen.	4 Yr. 1 mo. 19 days	Mar. 19, 1790- Mar. 23, 1794
Mr. L. Van Bergen Vander Gryp*	Pres.	0 Yr. 8 mo. 10 days	May 26, 1794- Jan. 10, 1795
Otto Arnoldus Duim*	Gov.	1 Yr. 4 mo. 24 days	Jan. 10, 1795- Jun. 3, 1796
G.H. Van Hamel*	Gov.	1 Yr. 8 mo. 17 days	Aug. 10, 1796- May 1, 1798
Cornelius L. Bartels*	Gov. Gen	5 Yr. 11 mo. 10 days	May 8, 1798- Apr. 28, 1804
J. de Roever	Pres.	1 Yr. 1 mo. 17 days	Apr. 29, 1804- Jun. 15, 1805
Pieter Linthorst*	Gov. Gen.	2 Yr. 1 mo. 5 days	Jun. 16, 1805- Jul. 21, 1807
J. P. Hoogenboom	Pres.	1 Yr. 0 mo. 15 days	Jul. 22, 1807- Aug 11, 1808
J. F. Koning	Pres.	1 Yr. 6 mo. 13 days	
A De Veer	Comm. Gen.	6 Yr. 0 mo. 6 days	
H. W. Daendels	Gov. Gen.	2 Yr. 1 mo. 21 days	
F. Ch. E. Oldenburg	Pres.	1 Yr. 8 mo. 19 days	
J. Oosthout	Pres. Com.	1 Yr. 6 mo. 17 days	
F. F. L. U. Last	Com. a.i.	1 Yr. 5 mo. 15 days	
L. J. Timmink	Com. a.i.	0 yr. 3 mo. 25 days	
W. Poolman	Lt. Col. C	1 Yr. 0 mo. 8 days	
J. H. A. Mourve	Com. a.i.	0 Yr. 7 mo. 11 days	
J. D. C. Pagenstecher	Com. a.i.	0 Yr. 0 mo. 8 days	
F. F. L. U. Last	Com. a.i.	1 Yr. 10 mo. 10 days	
J. C. Vander Breggen Paauw	Com. a.i.	1 Yr. 10 mo. 23 days	
F. F. L. U. Last	Lt. Col. C.	4 Yr. 6 mo. 13 days	
J. T. K. Cremer	Com. a.i.	0 Yr. 1 mo. 0 days	
E. D. L. Van Ingen	Com. a.i.	0 Yr. 8 mo. 16 days	
M. Swarte	Com. a.i.	0 Yr. 1 mo. 14 days	
C. E. Lans	Lt. Col. C.	3 Yr. 6 mo. 21 days	
H. J. Tonneboeyer	Com. a.i.	0 Yr. 10 mo. 26 days	Oct. 28, 1837
A. Van der Eb	Com. a.i.	0 Yr. 9 mo. 7 days	
H. Bosch	Lt. Col. Gov.	1 Yr. 7 mo. 2 days	
A. Van der Eb	Lt. Col. Gov.		

Danish Governors

Erik Tyllemann	1698	died
Erik Oehlsen	1698	died
Johan Tranne	1703	Aug. 31, died
Hartvig Meyer	1704	Apr. 23, died
Peter Swerdrup	1705	June 6, died
Peter Peterson	1706	May 6, died
Erik Lygaard	1711	August 17, died
Frantz Roye	1717	November 26, died
Knud Röst	1720	August 30, died
Peter Ostrup	1722	January 24, died
David Hernn	1723	January 22, died
Niels F. Ostrup	1723	October 30, died
Chr. Syndermann	1724	April 30, died
Hendrik von Suhm	1727	March 1, returned to Europe
Fred Pahl	1727	September 18, died
And. Willumsen	1728	December 24, died
Andr. Waeroe	1735	August 12, returned to Europe
Severin Schilerup	1736	June 14, died
Enewold Borris	1740	June 20, died
Peter Forgensen	1743	May 26, died
Chr. Dorph	1744	February 3, died
Jörgen Bilsen	1745	March 13, died
Thomas Brock	1745	March 23, died
F. Wilder	1745	April 23, died
A.F. Hackenborg	1746	June 21, returned to Europe
Foost Platfusz	1751	February 21, returned to Europe
Magnus Litzow	1751	March 8, died
Magnus Hacksen	1752	July 21, died
Carl Engmann	1757	March 10, returned to Europe
Christian Fessen	1762	February 14, returned to Europe
Carl Resch	1766	October 20, returned to Europe
Chr. Tychsen	1768	January 11, died
Frantz Khyberg	1769	July 2, returned to Europe
Gerhardt F. Wrisberg	1770	June 1, returned to Europe
Joachim Otto	1770	June 13, died
Johan D. Frölich	1772	June 15, died
Niels A. Aarestrup	1777	June 24, returned to Europe
Conrad Hemsen	1780	December 7, died
Jens Kjoge	1788	March 31, returned to Europe
Johan Kipnasse	1789	October 23, returned to Europe
Andreas Biörn	1793	January 25, returned to Europe

And. Hammer	1793	June 30, returned to Europe
Bendt Olrich	1793	August 3, died
Fr. Chr. V. Hagen Baron	1795	August 17, died
Johan P. D. Wrisberg	1799	December 31, returned to Europe
Johan D. Anholm	1802	October 1, returned to Europe
Johan P.D. Wrisberg	1807	April 15, returned to Europe
Chr. Schionning	1817	March 1, died
Johan E. Richter	1817	October 5, died
J. Reiersen	1819	May 15, died
Chr. Svanekjaer	1821	January 1, superceded
Peter S. Steffens	1821	September 10, died
Mathias Thonning	1823	December 23, returned to Europe
Johan Ch. von Richelieu	1825	March 16, returned to Europe
Niels Broch	1827	September 30, superceded
Jens P. Findt	1828	August 1, returned to Europe
Heinrich G. Lind	1831	January 20, returned to Europe
Ludvig v. Hein	1831	October 21, died
Helmuth v. Ahrenstorff	1831	December 4, died
Niels Bröch	1833	March 1, superceded
Henrich G. Lind	1833	July 21, died
Niels Bröch	1834	December 2, superceded
Frederick S. Mörck	1839	March 18, died
Hans A. Giede	1839	August 18, died
Lucas Dall	1842	May 24, returned to Europe
Bernhardt C. Wilkens	1842	August 26, died
Ed. J. A. Carstensen	1850	in April returned to Europe
R. E. Schmid	1850	in April returned to Europe

Table 8.2: English Governors in the Slave Forts and Castles of Ghana, 1751-1817

Governors of the Possessions on the Gold Coast of the Trading Corporation Formed under the Acts of Parliament 23 George II., C. 31 and 25 George II., C. 40, the Company of Merchants Trading to Africa

NAME	DATE	
Thomas Melville	1751	died on the Gold Coast
William Tymewell	1756	died on the Gold Coast
Charles Bell	1756	
Nassau Senior	1757	
Charles Bell	1761	
William Mutter	1763	
John Heppersley	1766	died on the Gold Coast
Gilbert Petrie	1766	
John Grossle	1769	
David Mill	1770	
Richard Miles	1777	
John Roberts	1780	
J. B. Weuves	1781	
Richard Miles	1782	
James Morgue	1784	
Thomas Price	1787	
Thomas Morris	1787	
William Fielde	1789	
John Gordon	1791	
Archibald Dalzell	1792	
Jacob Mould	1798	
John Gordon	1799	
Archibald Dalzell	1800	
Jacob Mould	1802	
Colonel G. Torrane	1805	
E. W. White	1807	
Joseph Dawson	1816	
John Hope Smith	1817	

Governors of the Settlements on the Gold Coast after the Acquirement by the Crown in 1821 of the Possessions of "The Company of Merchants Trading to Africa."

Sir Charles McCarthy	1822	
Major Chisholm	1822	

Sir Charled McCarthy	1822	Killed on the coast
Major Chisholm	1824	
Major Purdon	1824	
Major General Charles Turner	1824	
Sie Neil Campbell	1826	
Captain Ricketts	1826	
Lt. Col. Lumley	1827	
Captain Hingston	1828	
Major Ricketts	1828	

Governors of the British Possessions on the Gold Coast Transferred by the Crown to the Committee of Merchants in 1828

John Jackson	1828
Captain George Maclean	1830
William Topp	1836
Captain George Maclean	1838

Governors of the Settlements on the Gold Coast on their Resumption by the Crown in 1843

Commander Hill, R.N.	1843
James Lilley	1845
William Winniett	1846
J.C. Fitzpatrick	1849
William Winniett	1850
James Bannerman, Lt. Gov.	1850

Source: List of European Governors on the Gold Coast – Carl C. Reindorf, *History of the Gold Coast and Asante*, 3rd ed. (Accra: Ghana Universities Press, 2007), 344-347; John Vogt, *Portuguese Rule on the gold Coast 1469-1682* (Athens: The University of Georgia Press, 1979), 214-215; J.J. Crooks, *Records Relating to the Gold Coast Settlements from 1750-1874*, new ed. (Dublin: Browne and Nolan, 1923).

Notes

1. Afropessimists would argue that Africa is a lost cause, given all the instability and political violence in various parts of the continent. For a discussion of perceptions of Africa see for example, "Coverage of Africa in American Popular Magazines," *Issue. A Journal of Opinion* XXII I (1994): 24-29.

2. Salamishah Tillet, "In the Shadow of the Castle: (Trans)Nationalism, African American Tourism, and Gorée Island," *Research in African Lieratures* 40, 4 (Winter, 2009) , 124.

3. Messages from various Ghanaian officials during Emancipation and PANAF-EST underscore the importance of return for African Americans and Africans in the diaspora.

4. *Panafest Brochure*, "The World & I: Return, Return, Ghana Celebrates Pan-African Heritage," 1998.

5. Tillet, "In the Shadow of the Castle," 123.

6. The most comprehensive coverage of the forts and castles to date can be found in Albert van Dantzig, *Forts and Castles of Ghana* (Accra: Sedco Publishing Ltd., 1980); Kwesi J. Anquandah, *Castles and Forts of Ghana* (Paris: Atalante [for Ghana Museums and Monuments Board], 1999) ; A. W. Lawrence, *Trade Castles and Forts of West Africa* (London: Jonathan Cape, 1963).

7. See for example, Philip D. Curtin, *The Atlantic Slave Trade: A Census* (Madison: University of Wisconsin Press, 1969); J.E. Inikori, "Measuring the Atlantic Slave Trade: An Assessment of Curtin and Anstey," *Journal of African History* 17, 2 (1976): 197-223; J.E. Inikori, Measuring the Atlantic Slave Trade: A Rejoinder, *Journal of African History* XVII, IV (1976), 607-627; Paul E. Lovejoy, "The Volume of the Atlantic Slave Trade: A Synthesis," *Journal of African History* 23 (1982): 473-501; David Eltis, "The Volume, Age/Sex Ratios, and the African Impact of the Slave Trade: Some Refinement of Paul Lovejoy's Review of the Literature," *Journal of African History* 31, 3 (1990): 485-492; and David Eltis and David Richardson, eds., *Extending the Frontiers: Essays on the New Transatlantic Slave Trade Database* (New Haven, CT: Yale University Press, 2008).

8. The history of the Black Seminoles, for example, speaks to this relationship between Africans and Indians in the United States. Runaway slaves lived near and among Seminoles in Florida. Some intermarried with Indians and subsequently Black Seminoles such as John Horse rose to be leaders of the Seminole nation.

9. Stanley Elkins, *Slavery: A Problem in American Institutional and Intellectual Life* (Chicago: University of Chicago Press, 1969). See also John Blassingame, *The Slave Community: Plantation Life in the Antebellum South* (New York: Oxford University Press, 1979); John Blassingame, *Slave Testimonies: Two Centuries of Letters, Speeches, Interviews, and Autobiographies* (Baton Rouge: Louisiana State University Press, 1977); Herbert Gutman, *The Black Family in Slavery and in Freedom, 1750-1925* (New York: Pantheon Books, 1976).

10. Sterling Stuckey, *Slave Culture: Nationalist Theory and the Foundations of Black America* (New York: Oxford University Press, 1987).

11. See, for example, Eugene D. Genovese, *Roll Jordan Roll: The World the Slaves Made* (New York: Vintage Books, 1976).

12. See, for example, Pedro de la Hoz, *Africa in the Cuban Rrevolution: Our Search for Full Justice*, Cuidad de La Habana, Cuba: Editorial José Marti, 2005; Lorenzo D. Turner, *Africanisms in the Gullah Dialect* (Chicago: University of Chicago Press, 1949); Jose Honorio Rodrigues, *Brazil and Africa* (Berkeley: University of California Press, 1968); Leonard E. Barett, Soul-Force: African Heritage in Afro-

American Religion (New York: Doubleday, 1974); Roger Bastide, The African Religions of Brazil: Toward a Socioilogy of the Interpretation of Civilization, trans., Helen Sebba (Baltimore: Johns Hopkins University Press, 1978).

13. See, for example, F. Ugboaja Ohaegbulam, "Continental Africans in America: The Progression of a Relationship," in Africana Studies. A Survey of Africa and the African Diaspora. 2ⁿᵈ ed., ed. Mario Azevedo (Durham, NC: Carolina Academic Press, 1998), 219-220.

14. The African Methodist Episcopal Church and others with a similar nomenclature sprang up in the later eighteenth century.

15. W.E.B. Du Bois, The Souls of Black Folk. Ed., with an introduction by David W. Blight and Robert Gooding-Williams (Boston: Bedford/St. Martins, 1997).

16. See for comparative purposes, Eli Seifman, "The United Colonization Societies of New York and Pennsylvania and the Establishment of the African Colony of Bassa Cove," Pennsylvania History 35 (1968): 33-44.

17. See Lamont D. Thomas, Paul Cuffe: Black Enterpreneur and Pan-Africanist. Urbana and Chicago: University of Illinois Press, 1988; Rosalind Cobbs Wiggins, Captain Paul Cuffe's Logs and Letters, 1808-1817. Washington D.C., 1996; G.E. Saigbe Boley, Liberia: The Rise and Fall of the First Republic. London: Macmillan, 1983.

18. See also ACS, Information About Going to Liberia: Things Which Every Emigrant Ought to Know. Washington: American Colonization Society, 1848.; Paul Cuffee, Memoir of Captain Paul Cuffee, A Man of Color: To Which is Subjoined the Epistle of the Society of Sierra Leone in Africa & etc. York: W. Alexander, 1812 [1817].

19. Eric Burin, Slavery and the Peculiar Institution: A History of the American Colonization Society. Gainesville: University of Florida Press, 2005. See also, Allan E. Yasema, American Colonization Society: an Avenue to Freedom? University Press of America, 2006; Albert P. Blaustein and Robert L. Zangrando (eds.), Civil Rights and the Black American. A Documentary History. Washington Square Press, 1968.

20. See The African Intelligencer 1, 1 (July 1820): 1-31; The African Repository and Colonial Journal 1, 4 (June 1825), 129.

21. Elliott Skinner, "The Dialectic Between Diasporas and Homelands," in The Global Dimensions of the African Diaspora, 2ⁿᵈ ed., ed. Joseph Harris (Washington D.C.: Howard University Press, 1982), 342-343.

22. The maroons, reputedly descendants of the "Coromantees" of Ghana, were deemed intractable and ungovernable by the British in Jamaica. The maroons fled into the cockpit country and other inhospitable parts of Jamaic and waged a successful campaign against interdiction by the British colonial authorities in Jamaica. They founded settlements such as Accompong, Nanny Town and Trelawney. They fought against the British in countless wars and some were finally shopped off to Nova Scotia where the disagreeable climate eventually resulted in the British government agreeing to transfer them to the more congenial climate, but not before they had created more problems for the British in Nova Scotia. See Akintola J.G. Wyse, "The Sierra Leone Krios: A Reappraisal

From the Perspective of the African Diaspora," in *Global Dimensions of the African Diaspora*, 344-345

23. Ibid., 339-340

24 Ibid., 17.

25 The African Growth and Opportunity Act, signed into law on May 18, 2000, by President Bill Clinton, offered incentives for African countries to continue their efforts to open their economies and build free markets. The Act authorizes the president to designate countries as eligible to receive the benefits of AGOA if: they are determined to be making progress toward the establishment of market-based economies, the implementation of the rule of law and popular participation in the political process or multi-party democracy. Other criteria include, among others, protection of human rights, intellectual property rights and the provision of educational facilities and healthcare to the people.

26. Cited in Douglass, "Confronting" A21; Tillet, "In the Shadow of the Castle,"123.

27. Seeing Slavery's Door" A 04; Tillet, "In the Shadow of the Castle," 123.

28. Tillet, "In the Shadow of the Castle," 123.

29. "Remarks by the President on Goree Island, Senegal. 11:47 A.M. (Local). http://www.whitehouse.gov/news/releases/2003/07/print/20030708-1. html 5/9/2006. From this perspective, is it surprising that Frederick Douglass asked: What to me is your 4th of July celebrations?

30. Ibid.

31. See Toagbe Ogunleye, "Dr. Martin Robinson Delaney, 19th Century African Womanist Reflections on His Avant-Garde Politics Concerning Gender, Colorism, and Nation Building," *Journal of Black Studies*, 28, 5 .. 629; Frank A. Rollin, *The Life and Public Service of Martin Delaney* (New York: Kraus Reprint Co., 1969). William Whipper wrote the book under the pseudonym Frank A. Rollin.

32. Asante, 1990.

33. See Howard Brotz (ed.), *Negro Social and Political Thought 1850-1920. Representative Texts* (New York: Basic Books, 1966), 101-111; Martin Delaney, *The Condition, Elevation, Emigration and Destiny of Colored People of the United States Politically Considered.* 1852/1968.

34. A play on the Lebron James announcement to take his talents to South Beach, Florida.

35. Maya Angelou, *All God's Children Need Traveling Shoes* (New York: Vintage Books, 1991), 18-19.

36. Kevin Gaines, *American Africans in Ghana. Black Expatriates and the Civil Rights Era* (Chapel Hill: The University of North Carolina Press, 2006).

37. Angelou, All God's Children, 19.

38. Ibid., 20.

39. Ibid., 40.

40. Ibid., 21

41. Kwame Nkrumah's ideas are clearly articulated in his book *Africa Must Unite* (London: Panaf Books, 1963). For Pan-Africanism see, for example, Colin Legum, Pan-Africanism. A Short Political Guide. rev. ed. (New York: Praeger, 1965).

42. See for example, J.B. Taylor, *Biography of the Elder Lott Cary, Late Missionary to Africa* (Baltimore: Armstrong & Berry, 1837).

43. Tillet, "In the Shadow of the Castle,"124.

44. Tillet, "In the Shadow of the Castle," 125.

45. PANAFEST '94, *Horizon*, 14 December 1994.

46. PANAFEST Brochure.

47. W. E. B. Du Bois (U.S.), Marcus Mosiah Garvey (Jamaica) and Kwame Nkrumah (Ghana) are considered by some to be the Fathers of the Pan-African movement. And to this group must be added George Padmore.

48. See Holsey, Routes of Remem brance, 162-163.

49. PANAFEST '94, *Horizon*, 14 December, 1994; "Seeds of Hope in Panafest," *The Weekly Advertiser*, 1, 10 (1994), 7.

50. "Seeds of Hope in Panafest," *The Weekly Advertiser*, 1, 10 (1994), 7.

51 Turner, "Tourism"

52. Ibid.

53 The accounts of Imakhus Robinson, Sadiya Hartman and others vividly encapsulate this point.

54. *Sankofa* is an Akan term that means to go back to the roots. The essence is essentially knowing the past in order to move forward.

55. See Holsey, *Routes of Remembrance*.

56. Ibid.

57. Imakhus Robinson " Is the Balck Man's History Being Whitewashed?"

✤ Appendix A

Gold Coast/Ghana Slave Forts and Castles: A Historical Timeline

1430s-1440s Period of intense Portuguese exploratory activity down the Western African coast.

1471 Portuguese arrive off the Gold Coast at Edina (Elmina or la Mina, the Mine).

1482 Portuguese begin construction of São Jorge da Mina (Elmina Castle), the first castle or fort on the Gold Coast, and name it after their patron saint, St. George. First structure on such a scale outside of Europe at the time.

1515-1526 Portuguese continue construction of forts on the eastern littoral of the Gold Coast to protect their trade monopoly and to keep rival European nations out of the region.

1515 Portuguese build Fort São Antonio at Axim, further east of Elmina to protect the "roads" and Portuguese monopoly over Gold Coast trade.

1553 Portuguese build Fort São Sebastião at Shama, east of Elmina. São Sebastião becomes an important service station for the supply of timber. It is bombarded by the Dutch, rebuilt in 1640 and used until 1872. In the post independence period the fort has been used as a post office, a traditional authority court (for chiefs) and offices of the District Electoral Commission. A caretaker lives in the fort and takes care of the structure, besides conducting tours for visitors.

1596	Dutch attempt to capture Elmina castle but fail – the first of three attempts.
1612	Dutch build Fort Nassau at Moree, named after Count Nassau. From 1612-1637 Fort Nassau is the Dutch headquarters on the Gold Coast. Taken over by the British in 1868 after the Anglo-Dutch forts exchange. A visit to the site shows very few traces at this time.
1623	Portuguese build fort at Rivers Ankobra and Duma confluence to guard Akwaso or Dwete-bo gold mine. Later abandoned after disaster at the mine. Locals believe that evil spirits resided in the mine, hence the disaster that occurred, and did not want anything to do with the mine and the fort.
1630	Dutch build fort at Anomabu. Occupied the fort from 1630 to1664. English build Fort Charles at Anomabu. English abandon fort in 1730s to concentrate on Cape Coast Castle but rebuild it in 1756 near the old Fort. Fort Charles expanded in the nineteenth century and renamed Fort William. Used as a prison for a long time before the prisoners were moved elsewhere. Currently in a restoration phase. A non-governmental organization plans to use the rooms on the second floor as classrooms for tertiary education in Ghana.
1631	The English build Fort Kormantin at Kormantine/Cormantine [Abandzi]. Used as headquarters of English operations on the Gold Coast (1631- 1665). English operations headquarters later moved to Cape Coast Castle after capture of Fort Carolusburg from the Dutch. Carolusburg is partly rebuilt to enhance security and discourage possible attack. Fort Kormantin is captured by the Dutch and renamed Fort Amsterdam. Reverts to English control in 1868. It is presently partially ruined – part of the southern wall has collapsed. Though there are efforts at conservation, there should be a very serious effort to rebuild the ruined sections of the fort.
1637	Dutch conquer and take over São Jorge da Mina from the Portuguese after earlier failures to seize the castle. The takeover begins the process of eventual Portuguese departure from the Gold Coast as the Dutch proceed to attack all Portuguese forts on the western seaboard of the Gold Coast.

1637	English build fort at Biriwa or Anashan. There are presently no traces of ruins of this fort.
1637/8	Reports indicate that Dutch and English lodges are built at Egyaa near Biriwa (also called Anashan) in the seventeenth and eighteenth centuries. No traces of ruins of these lodges are found at the site.
1640	The Dutch dislodge the Portuguese from Shama and Fort Sebastião.
1649	Dutch build Fort Crèvecoeur at Accra on the site of an earlier lodge. Fort largely destroyed by earthquake in 1863. Handed over to English as part of the Anglo-Dutch exchange of forts on the Gold Coast. English rename it Ussher Fort (after English Governor Ussher). Presently in use as one of the major prisons in Accra, located on what is now High Street.
1650	Henry Caerlof, renegade fiscal of the Dutch West India Company, builds a thatched-roofed trade lodge at Butri, on a steep hill overlooking the bay.
1654	Dutch build Fort Ruychaver at Old Awudua located on the right bank of Ankobra River. Blown up in 1659.
1656	Dutch build Fort Batenstein at Butri in place of the lodge built by Caerlof; transferred to the British in 1872. Abandoned in the late nineteenth century. Partially restored in the 1980s but is currently in ruin. Overgrown with weeds.
1656	Dutch build Fort Witsen at Takoradi. Blown up in 1665 by the Dutch work of Admiral Ruyter in the Takoradi region. Later rebuilt but ruins are no longer visible. Other lodges by Dutch, Swedes, Brandenburgers, English and French. But no traces can be found at the present time.
1657	Swedes build Fort Carolusburg. Later changes hands – Dey of Fetu (1661-1664) and the Dutch (1664-1665). English take over and rebuild Carolusburg into what is now Cape Coast Castle, at Carbo Corso, now Cape Coast.
1661	Danes build Fort Frederiksborg on Mount Amanful – a hill about a rifle shot from, and overlooking, Cape Coast Castle. Danes sell fort to English who are concerned about its strategic location in relation to Cape Coast Castle in 1685. English rebuild fort and rename it Fort Royal.

1661	Danes begin construction of Christiansborg Castle at Osu, Accra. Between 1681 and 1686 Portugal controls what became Christiansborg Castle and rename it Fort St. Francisco Xavier. Difficulties with the Gã lead to Portuguese giving up the fort. In 1693 Akwamu general, Asameni, seizes Christiansborg Castle from the Danes and lives in it for a year. The English use Christiansborg Castle as the seat of colonial administration from 1876 until 1957. Seat of government of Ghana from 1957 to 2011. A presidential palace would be ready for the transfer of the offices of the government of Ghana, probably in late 2011, from Christiansborg Castle.
1662	Company of Royal Adventurers Trading to Africa founded as a chartered company in England.
1665	The English capture Cape Coast Castle from the Dutch. Began as Swedish Fort Carolusburg and changed hands a few times among Swedes, Dey of Fetu and, later, Dutch. English acquire and rebuild fort into Cape Coast Castle. Royal African Company makes Cape Coast Castle headquarters of its operations on the Gold Coast. Cape Coast Castle used as British headquarters and seat of the colonial government of the Gold Coast until 1876 when the capital of the Gold Coast is moved from Cape Coast to Accra.
1665	Fort Coenraadsburg is built on top of the strategically located St. Iago Hill, replacing an earlier fortification built in 1637. Smaller fortifications of the nineteenth century built. They include Veersche Schans near Bantama; Beeckesteyn near the Benya Lagoon, Coebergh, later known as Schomerus (named after Dutch official) near St Joseph School and Cattoenbergh, later known as Java on Java-hill (Dutch- Indonesia connection), and Nachgtlas, named after Dutch governor Natchglas, near the eastern entrance to Elmina. Unfortunately the ruins of these smaller fortifications have all disappeared over time.
1672	Monopolistic Royal African Company takes over from the Company of Royal Adventurers Trading to Africa.
1673	English extend an earlier Dutch lodge into a fort at Winneba (given no definitive name). English bombard fort in 1812 when the people of Winneba kill the British governor of the fort, Henry Meredith. Very few traces exist now. The only visible remnants of the forts are in the form of building materials (bricks/stones) used in the construction of the Methodist Church building on that site.

1673	English build James Fort at Accra. Since independence in 1957 fort used as one of the prisons in Accra.
1681	Arrival of Brandenburgers (Prussians) on the Gold Coast.
1682	English build a fort at Sekondi. Very few traces exist.
1682	Dutch build Fort Vreedenburgh at Dutch Komenda or Kankan on the site where a lodge initially stood. The fort is badly ruined. People who have built houses in the vicinity of the fort have appropriated some of the construction materials from the fort (stones and bricks) for use in their own buildings.
	Dutch, and later, English lodges at Mount Congh or Queen Anne's Point (known to the local people as Ekon), near Moree. No trace of ruins at this time.
1683	Brandenburgers (Prussians) build Fort Gross Friedrichsburg at Princes Town (Pokesu). From 1717 to 1725 John Conny controls the fort. From 1725 to 1872 the Dutch take over the fort. Rename it Hollandia. 1980s – used as a residence for nurses of German hospital in the area. There is a caretaker at the fort.
1685	Brandenburg lodge Luisa at Takrama. Dutch take over lodge in 1717 but soon abandon it. Impossible to locate at the present time since there are no traces.
1687	Brandenburgers (Prussians) build Fort Dorothea at Akwida (Akwadae to the local people); Dutch take over fort in 1717. Abandoned in late eighteenth century. The ruins of the fort are now overgrown with trees and climbers. Most of the walls have tumbled down and the structure may not survive for long if no effort is made to restore and preserve it.
1687	English build fort at Komenda. Dutch take over fort from 1868 to 1872. Fort now in ruins. Some of the walls have collapsed but outlines of parts of the ruined section can still be traced on the ground.
1687	French lodge built at Komenda; later destroyed.
1690	Dutch build Fort Oranje (Orange) at the site of an earlier lodge in 1642. From the late 1970s to date, Fort Oranje has been used as a lighthouse by the Ghana Railways and Ports (now Harbors) Authority. An attendant lives in the fort.

1693	English build Fort Metal Cross at Dixcove. Dutch take over fort from 1868 to 1872 and call it Fort Metalen Kruis. 1980s used as a Rest house. Fort presently maintained by a "white man," I was told by the caretaker. He keeps the fort whitewashed and is building a rest house for European tourists in the bay next to the fort. After the construction of the rest house, Fort Metal Cross would be the focal point of a tourism complex in the Dixcove area.
1693	The Akwamu general, Asameni, seizes Christiansborg Castle from the Danes and lives in the castle as governor, for a year. He fires the guns of the castle to salute ships passing by the castle.
1694	Danes negotiate the return of their castle and eventually buy it back.
1698	Dutch begin construction of Fort Leydsaemheyt (Patience) at Apam. Takes a long time to complete this small fort (completed in 1704) hence the name Patience because the Dutch had to exercise patience to see to its completion. Remains in Dutch hands until 1868 when it reverts to English control. At present in use as a guest house.
1701	Dutch lodge at Tema and Kpone. Tema lodge expanded into a fort in 1714. No visible trace of either exists today.
1702	English fort at Tantumquery (now Otuam). Extended in 1702. Very few traces of ruins
1702	Period of intense Dutch activities on the Gold Coast. Dutch build Fort de Goede Hoop (Good Hope) at Senya Beraku. Later expanded. In 1868 it reverts to English control. Dutch build lodge at Nyinyanu in early eighteenth century. No trace exists today. Dutch and Danish lodges at Labadi in early eighteenth century. Search yielded no results.
1721	Phipps Tower built as an Out-fort in Cape Coast. Fort Victoria built in the nineteenth century as an out-fort. The two forts are very well-preserved, one a rifle shot away from Cape Coast Castle, and used to signal the approach of enemy ships on the sea. A sentinel at post in the Cape Coast Castle picks up the signal and relays it to the garrison.
1721	Finding trade on the Gold Coast not as profitable as they thought it would be Brandenburgers (Prussians) leave the Gold Coast.

1734	Dutch Fort Singelenburgh built at Keta. Blown up in 1737. Dutch and Danish lodges built afterward. Later rebuilt as Fort Prindsensten by the Danes. Used as a prison after independence. The Keta sea erosion has continued to buffet the Danish fort to the point where it would disappear soon unless the sea erosion is checked.
1745	English build Fort Vernon at Prampram. Few traces remain today. Bricks and rocks from the fort can be found in the walls of the rest house that is built on the site.
1750	Company of Merchants in England invested with control over the British slave forts and castles on the Gold Coast. Company appoint agents to supervise the slave forts and castles.
1751	Rev. Thomas Thompson of the Society of the Propagation of the Gospel arrives on the Gold Coast and begins the first major Protestant missionary effort on the Gold Coast.
1752	Rev. Thomas Thompson returns to England due to ill health. He takes three boys from the Gold Coast to England to be educated. Two of the boys die but Philip Quacoe survives to become the first African to be ordained as an Anglican priest.
1754	French build fort at Anomabu. Lasts for four years. No trace of ruins.
1756	Rev. Philip Quacoe returns to the Gold Coast. Appointed as missionary, schoolmaster and catechist at the Cape Coast Castle. He lays the foundation for western education on the Gold Coast through what became known as the castle school system.
1756	English build Fort Apollonia at Benyin. Becomes Dutch Fort William from 1868 to 1872. Rest house in the 1980s. Still in very good shape.
1783-1788	Period of intense fort construction by the Danes – a period described as the golden age of the Danes on the Gold Coast and represents increased Danish slave trading activity and profit. All this occurs during the time of Governor Jens Adolf Kiøge who lays the foundation for four Danish forts on the Gold Coast – all east of Accra.
1783	Jens Adolf Kiøge lays the foundation stone for Fort Kongensteen at Ada. Names fort Kongesteen in honor of the burnt bricks that King Christian VII paid to be shipped to the Gold Coast for the fort. Fort reverts to English control in 1850. Few visible traces exist today.

1784	Jens Adolf Kiøge lays the foundation for Fort Prindsensteen at Keta. Names fort Prindsensteen because Kiøge considered the Ada and Keta forts on opposite sides of the Volta as twins. 1850 – Prindsensteen taken over by the English. Used as a prison in the 1980s but at present on the verge of destruction due to the disastrous erosion problem on the Keta shoreline.
1787	Danes build Fort Augustaborg at Teshie, named after the sixteen-year-old half sister of Crown Prince Frederick of Denmark. Very little of the fort exists today.
1787-1807	French build a fort at Amoku near Saltpond. Very few traces exist now.
1788	Jens Adolf Kiøge lays the foundation stone for Fort Fredensborg at Kpone or Old Ningo (between Kongesteen and Augustaborg). He names it Isegram (a corruption of Isegrim, the wolf in German animal fables).
1802	Denmark abolishes the slave trade. First European nation to do so.
1807	England abolishes the slave trade – legal abolition – and tries to get other European nations to sign treaties to do the same.
1807	First major Asante invasion of the coast. Asante besiege Fort William at Anomabu and almost overwhelm the garrison in the fort.
1812	Henry Meredith, governor of the English fort at Winneba, is murdered by the townspeople.
1816	Philip Quacoe dies and is buried in the courtyard of Cape Coast Castle; English warship bombards Winneba from the sea in response to the murder of Governor Meredith.
1821	Royal African Company abolished. British government takes control of Gold Coast settlements. 1824, Sir Charles McCarthy becomes governor of Sierra Leone with responsibility for the Gold Coast.
1828	British government relinquishes control over the Gold Coast forts and castles as difficult and expensive to manage. British merchants on the Gold Coast take over the management of the forts and castles.
1828-1848	Committee of Merchants in charge of the Gold Coast appoint Capt. George Maclean as governor from 1830.
1841	Madden Committee sitting in England investigates the administration of the Gold Coast forts and settlements.

1844	British government resumes control of the Gold Coast forts, castles and settlements. Commander Hill signs the Bond of 1844 with the Fante chiefs. Bond designed to bring about peace so that trade, especially to the interior of the Gold Coast, could continue.
1850	Only Danes, Dutch, and British occupy forts and castles on the Gold Coast at this time.
1850	Denmark sells its Gold Coast possessions at Osu, Teshie, Ada and Keta. The British government buys all Danish forts and castles on the Gold Coast. The Danes leave the Gold Coast, bringing the Danish period to an end.
1850	Danes sell Christiansborg Castle to the English who would go on to make Christiansborg Castle the seat of the colonial administration on the Gold Coast after 1874.
1868	The Dutch and English exchange forts and castles on the Gold Coast with the Sweet River on the border between Cape Coast and Elmina as the boundary between English and Dutch-controlled forts and castles.
1872	English take over all Dutch forts and castles on the Gold Coast, bringing the Dutch chapter in Gold Coast/Ghana's history to a close.
1874	English defeat Asante in the "Sagrenti War," named after the British commander of British forces on the Gold Coast, Maj. Gen. Garnett Wollselley. War marks the beginning of the end of Asante hegemony over the Gold Coast and the beginning of the English process of consolidating Asante, the Northern Territories, and the coastal states into the Gold Coast Colony.
1876	The English transfer the seat of the colonial government from Cape Coast Castle to Christiansborg Castle at Osu, Accra.
1957	Ghana becomes independent nation, the first in Africa south of the Sahara. Dr. Kwame Nkrumah becomes the first prime minister of Ghana.
1960	Ghana becomes Republic with Dr. Kwame Nkrumah as President.
1994	Ghana begins commemoration of "Emancipation from Slavery" after the President of Ghana, Flt. Lt. Jerry John Rawlings (rtd.), visit Jamaica during Emancipation commemoration activities in that Caribbean nation.

1999   Former slave forts, castles, and dungeons become sites of memory and sites of return as African-descended peoples come to Ghana by the thousands during the Pan-African Historical Theatre Festival (PANAFEST) and Emancipation commemorative events. The two biennial events seek to re-unite African and African-descended peoples and are often organized around the themes of resurgence of African civilization and re-unification of African peoples.

2005   Seat of Government of Ghana continues to be in Christiansborg Castle. Construction efforts underway to complete a presidential palace and to move seat of government out of Christiansborg Castle.

Sources: J. J. Crooks, *Records Relating to the Gold Coast Settlements from 1750-1874*, new edn. (London: Frank Cass, 1973); Freda Wolfson, Pageant of Ghana (London: Oxford University Press, 1958); A. W. Lawrence, *Trade Castles and Forts of West Africa* (London: Jonathan Cape, 1963); Albert van Dantzig, *Forts and Castles of Ghana* (Accra: Sedco Publishing Ltd., 1980); Kwesi J. Anquandah, *Castles and Forts of Ghana* (Paris: Atalante [for Ghana Museums and Monuments Board] 1999); Thorkild Hansen, *Coast of Slaves*, trans. Kari Dako (Accra: Sub-Saharan Publishers, 2005); Brodie Cruickshank, *Eighteen Years on the Gold Coast of Africa, Vol,* I. 2nd. ed. (London: Frank Cass, 1966); W. Walton Claridge, *A History of the Gold Coast and Ashanti from the Earliest Times to the Commencement of the Twentieth Century* (London: Frank Cass, 1964); Willem Bosman, *A New and Accurate Description of the Coast of Guinea*, 4th ed. (New York: Barnes and Noble, 1967).

✢ Appendix B

European Powers and Their Principal Forts and Castles on the Gold Coast (from the southwestern seaboard [near Côte d'Ivoire] to the southeastern seaboard)

FORT/CASTLE	LOCATION	EUROPEAN NATION
Benyin Fort	Appollonia	English, later Dutch
Ankobra Fort	Ankobra	Dutch
Ruychaver	Old Awudua (Ankobra)	Dutch
São Antonio	Axim	Portuguese, and later, Dutch
Groot Friedrichsburg	Princes Town (Pokesu)	Prussian (Brandenburger) Headquarters; later Dutch
Dorothea	Akwida (Akwadae)	Brandenburg-Prussian; later, Dutch
Metalen Kruis/Metal Cross	Dixcove	Dutch, and later, English
Bantenstein	Butre	Dutch
Witsen	Takoradi	Dutch
Oranje/Orange	Sekondi	Dutch, and later, English
São Sebastiao	Shama	Portuguese, and later, Dutch
Vreedenburgh	Dutch Komenda	Dutch
Komenda Fort	Komenda	English, and later, Dutch
São Jorge da Mina	Elmina	Portuguese Headquarters, and later, Dutch headquarters
Coenraadsburg	Elmina	Dutch
Carolusburg/ Cape Coast Castle	Cape Coast	Swedish, later English
Phipps Tower	Cape Coast	English

Frederiksborg (Later Fort Royal)	Cape Coast	Danish, English
Victoria	Cape Coast/ Amanful	English
Nassau	Moree	Dutch
Charles	Anomabu	English
William	Anomabu	English
Kormantine/Amsterdam	Abandzi	English, and later, Dutch
French Fort	Amoku	French
English Fort	Tantumquery/ Otuam	English
Leydsaemheyt (Patience)	Apam	Dutch
English fort	Winneba	English
Goede Hoop	Senya Beraku	Dutch
James Fort	Accra	English
Crèvecoeur/Ussher Fort	Accra	Dutch, English
Christiansborg Castle	Osu	Danes; English
Augustaborg	Teshie	Danes
Dutch Fort	Tema	Dutch
Vernon	Prampram	English
Fredensborg	Old Ningo	Danes
Kongensteen	Ada	Danes
Singelenburgh	Keta	Danes
Prindsensteen	Keta	Danes

FORTS AND CASTLES (DISTRIBUTION BY NATION)

PORTUGUESE

São Jorge da Mina	Elmina
São Sebastiaõ	Shama
São Antonio	Axim
Fort Xavier	Accra

DUTCH

Fort Nassau	Moree
Fort Amsterdam	Kormantine/Abandzi
São Jorge da Mina	Elmina
Fort Conraadsburg	Elmina
Fort Crevecouer	Accra
São Sebastiaõ	Shama
São Antonio	Axim
Fort Hollandia	Princesstown
Fort Goede Hope	Senya Beraku

Fort Bantensteyn	Butri
Fort Vreedenburg	Komenda
Fort Oranje	Sekondi
Fort Leydsaemheyt	Apam
Fort Metalen Kruis	Dixcove
Fort Ruychaver	Old Awudua, Ankobra
Fort Xavier	Accra

DUTCH LODGES

de Veer	Elmina
Natglas	Elmina
Java	Elmina
Schomarus	Elmina

ENGLISH

Fort Kormantine	Abandzi
Cape Coast Castle	Cape Coast
James Fort	Accra
Fort Appollonia	Benyin
English Fort	Sekondi
Fort Vernon	Komenda
Winneba Fort	Winneba
Fort Victoria	Cape Coast
Fort Royal	Cape Coast
Tamtumquery Fort	Otuam
Fort Vernon	Prampram
Fort Metal Cross	Dixcove
Fort William	Anomabu

ENGLISH LODGES

Queen Anne's Point	Ekon
Anashan	Biriwa
Egyaa	Egyaa

BRANDENBURGERS-PRUSSIANS

Fort Groot Friedrichsburg	Princes Town (Pokesu)
Fort Dorothea	Akwadae

DENMARK

Fort Frederiksborg	Cape Coast
Christiansborg Castle	Accra
Fort Augustaborg	Teshie
Fort Fredensborg	Old Ningo
Fort Knogensteen	Ada
Fort Singelenburgh	Keta
Fort Prindsensteen	Keta

SWEDEN

| Fort Carolusburg | Cape Coast (later developed into Cape Coast Castle by the British) |
| Fort Witsen | Takoradi |

✢ Appendix C

Final Phase of European Competition on the Gold Coast Seen Through the Prism of the Slave Forts and Castles (1850-1872)

1850 – Government of Denmark transfers all Danish forts on the Gold Coast to England for £ 10,000.

1867 – England transfers all its forts and rights to territory east of the Sweet River to Holland; Holland transfers in exchange to England all Dutch possessions and rights to territory west of the Sweet River, which marks the boundary between Elmina and Cape Coast

1872 – Holland transfers to England all its forts and rights to territory on the Gold Coast, including possessions and rights to territory that had earlier been transferred by England to Holland in 1867.

Fort Prindsensteen	Keta	formerly Danish
Fort Kongensteen	Ada	formerly Danish
Fort Augustaborg	Teshie	formerly Danish
Christiansborg Castle	Osu	formerly Danish
Fort Fredensborg	Ningo/Nungua	formerly Danish
Fort Crévecoeur	Accra	Dutch till 1867
Fort Amsterdam	Abandzi	Dutch till 1867
Fort Patience	Apam	Dutch till 1867
Fort Nassau	Moree	Dutch till 1867
São Jorge da Mina	Elmina	Dutch till 1867
Fort Vernon	Komenda	British till 1667; Dutch till 1872

Fort São Sebastiao	Shama	Dutch till 1872
Fort Oranje	Sekondi	Dutch till 1872
Fort Batenstein	Butri	Dutch till 1872
Fort Metalen Kruis	Dixcove	British till 1867; Dutch till 1872
Fort Dorothea	Akwadae	Dutch till 1872
Fort São Antonio	Axim	Dutch till 1872
Fort Apollonia	Apollonia	British till 1867; Dutch till 1872

Source: Vice-Admiral Sir John Dalrymple Hay, *Ashanti and the Gold Coast: And What We Know of It* (London: Edward Stanford, 6, 7, & 8, Charing Cross, 1874), 9-10.

✣ Appendix D

Site Plans of Some of the Slave Forts, Castles and Dungeons

DIRECTIONAL MAP
CAPE COAST CASTLE

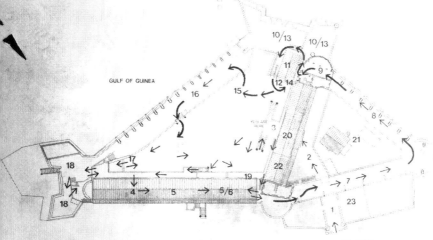

GULF OF GUINEA

∾ L E G E N D ℘

n Entrance Yard
ess Yard
eption ou Are Here)
ntation Room
eum Gallery (First Floor)
ver Hall (Second Floor)
t east Battery (With Cannons)
thwest Battery (With Cannons)

9 alzel Tower (Governor's Residence)
1 . South Bastion (First Floor
1l. Broadcasting / Church
12. Entrance to Male Slave Dungeon
13. Male Slave Dungeon (Ground Floor)
4. agazine (Storage of Cun Powde)
15. Graves (Courtyard)
b. Southeast Battery (With Cannon)

17. Exit for Slaves
1⒏. Female Slave Dungeon
19. Ce l
2 . Mac ean Hal
21. Barracks
22. Museum Shop
23. Washroom •
24. Building History Museum

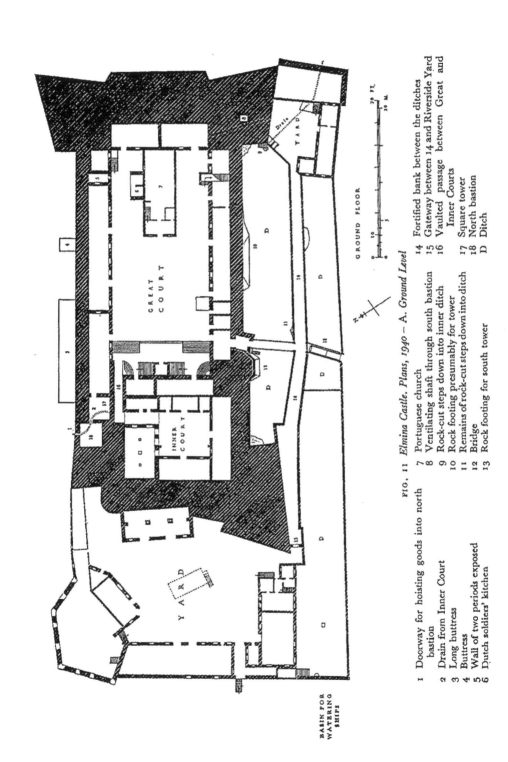

FIG. 11 *Elmina Castle. Plans, 1940 — A. Ground Level*

GROUND FLOOR

GREAT COURT

INNER COURT

YARD

BASIN FOR WATERING SHIPS

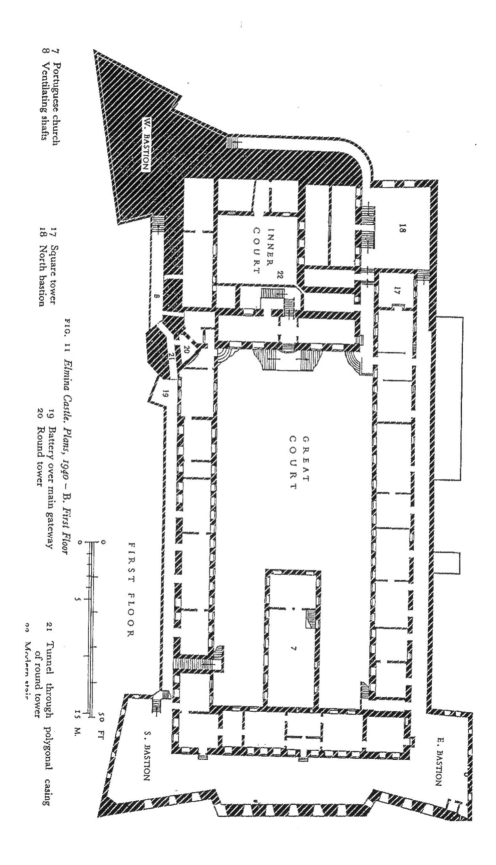

7 Portuguese church
8 Ventilating shafts

17 Square tower
18 North bastion

FIG. 11 *Elmina Castle, Plans, 1940 — B. First Floor*

19 Battery over main gateway
20 Round tower

21 Tunnel through polygonal casing
       of round tower
22 Modern stair

W. BASTION

INNER COURT

GREAT COURT

FIRST FLOOR

18

17

8

20
21

19

7

S. BASTION

E. BASTION

0   5   50 FT

15 M.

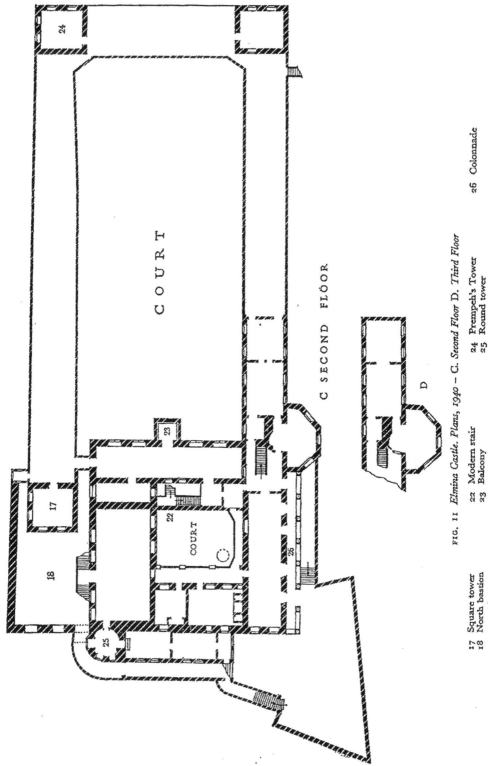

COURT

24

17

18

25

COURT

22

23

26

25

C SECOND FLOOR

D

FIG. 11 *Elmina Castle. Plans, 1940* – C. *Second Floor* D. *Third Floor*

17 Square tower
18 North bastion

22 Modern stair
23 Balcony

24 Prempeh's Tower
25 Round tower

26 Colonnade

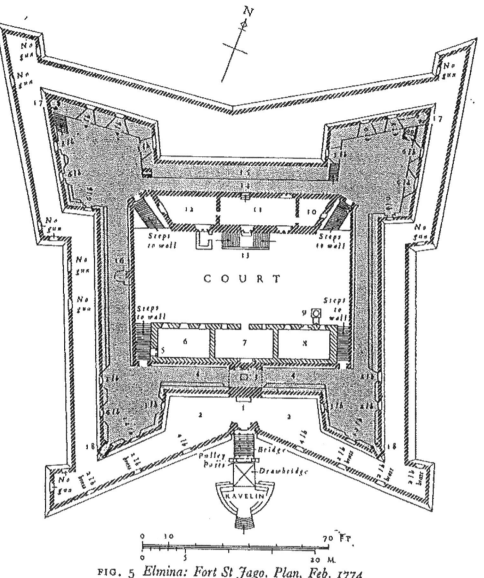

FIG. 5 *Elmina: Fort St Jago. Plan, Feb. 1774*

1   Inner gate
2   Outwork
3   Base of tower
4   Inner wall-walk
5   Door to powder magazine under bastion
6   Armourer's bedroom
7   Guardroom
8   Sergeant's bedroom
9   Cistern
10 Commander's room
11 Commander's hall, over barracks
12 Commander's bedroom, over powder store
13 Stair, over porch to storeroom
14 Inner wall-walk
15 Raised walk
16 Bread oven
17 Shelter
18 Shelter

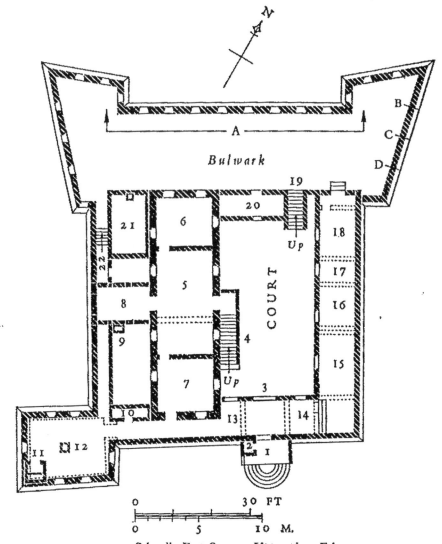

FIG. 40   *Sekondi: Fort Orange. Upper plan, Feb. 1791*

1	Gate of guard ; bell-house above
2	Shelter
3	Inner gate of guardroom
4	Stair to hall
5	Hall over storeroom
6	Bedroom over Assistant's lodging
7	Another room over a storeroom
8	Balcony to bridge a gap
9	Cistern
10	Small larder
11	Latrine
12	Under this bastion is a storeroom (entered under the curtain at 13)
14	Powder magazine, and another behind it

15	Soldiers' lodging
16	Sergeant's lodging
17	Armourer's lodging
18	Slave-prison and small prison behind
19	Stair to battery
20	Doctor's dwelling over Corporal's lodging
21	Kitchen
22	Stair to kitchen from curtain
A	Battery towards the English fort
B	18-lb. cannon
C	18-lb. cannon
D	8-lb. cannon

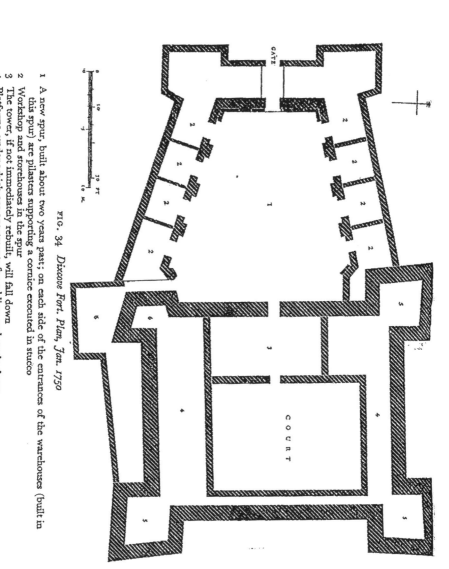

FIG. 34 *Dixcove Fort, Plan, Jan. 1750*

1 A new spur, built about two years past; on each side of the entrances of the warehouses (built in this spur) are pilasters supporting a cornice executed in stucco
2 Workshop and storehouses in the spur
3 The tower, if not immediately rebuilt, will fall down
4 Platforms, under which are apartments for soldiers and castle slaves
5 Three bastions very much out of repair
6 Bastions almost demolished; the end of the spur next the bastion not finished

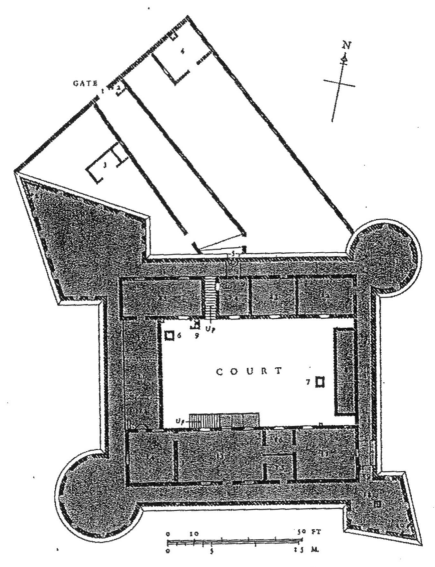

FIG. 19 *Cormantin: Fort Amsterdam. Upper plan, 1790–1*

1	Outer gate, near which is:	15	Larder } over vaulted
2	A shelter	16	Larder } storerooms
3	Soldiers' kitchen	17	A large room }
4	Commander's kitchen	18	Under the bastion is the slave-prison
5	Gate of the guard	19	Flagstaff
6	Small cistern	20	Shelter
7	Large cistern	21	Shelter
8	Granary raised on arch	22	Room over storeroom
9	Latrine in front of soldiers' dwelling	23	Room over storeroom
10	Corporal's and armourer's dwelling	24	Room over the guardroom
11	Sergeant's dwelling	25	Orange Hall, over which is the soldiers'
12	Powder magazine		dwelling
13	Great Hall } over vaulted storerooms		
14	Bedroom }		

Above room 14 is the quadrangular tower of the same size.

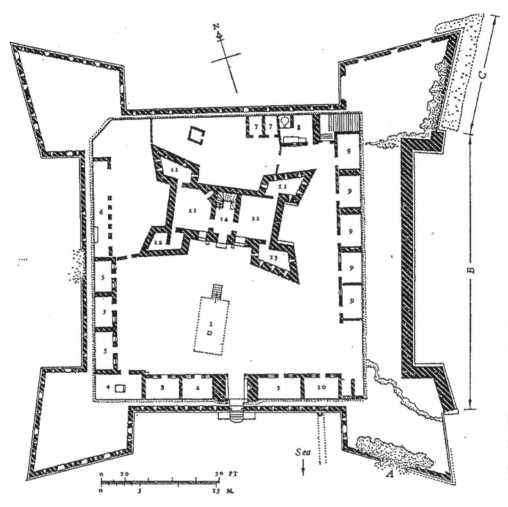

FIG. 31 *Commenda: English Fort. Ground plan, April 1756*

1 Cistern	8 Kitchen (thatched)	13 Slave Hole
2 Sergeant's barrack	9 Barracks (thatched)	14 Base of tower
3 Gunner's barrack	10 Carpenter's shop	
4 Smithy	(thatched)	A Fallen
5 Storerooms (thatched)	Inner Fort:	B This part already built
6 Stock shed (thatched)	11 Store	C Ground prepared for
7 Shed for logs, etc	12 Magazine	rebuilding

✛ References

ARCHIVAL MATERIAL

Public Record Office

CO 1069/30   Gold Coast General Views 1887

CO 1069/31

CO 96/1   Correspondence Between the Government of Cape Coast and Elmina 1753-1756

F.O. 925/747

T 70 1926

T 70 379

Public Records and Archives Administration of Ghana

ADM 23/1/337. Ancient Castles and Forts in the Central Province. Upkeep of

ADM 23/1/341. Maintenance of Ancient Castles

ADM 23/1/340   Ancient Forts and Castles

ADM 23/1/715   Elmina Castle

Printed Sources

Allison, Robert J. *The Interesting Narrative of the Life of Olaudah Equiano Written by Himself*. Bedford Series in History and Culture. 2nd. ed., 2007.

Astley, Thomas (ed.). *A New General Collection of Voyages and Travels*. London, 1968.

Barbot, Jean. *A Description of the Coasts of North and South Guinea*. London, 1732.

Blake John W. *Europeans in West Africa 1450-1560*. 2 vols., London, 1942.

Blassingame, John. *Slave Testimonies: Two Centuries of Letters, Speeches, Interviews, and Autobiographies*. Baton Rouge: Louisiana State University Press, 1977.

Bosman, Willem. *A New and Accurate Description of the Coast of Guinea. Divided into The Gold, The Slave, and the Ivory Coast*. New edn. With an Introduction by John Ralph Phillips. New York: Barnes & Noble, 1967.

Bowdich, T. Edward. *Mission from Cape Coast Castle to Ashantee*. London 1819., reprinted London, 1966.

Boyle, F. *Through Fanteeland to Coomassie*. London, 1874.

Burton, Richard F. *To the Gold Coast for Gold*. 2 vols. London, 1883.

Cardinall, A.W. *The Natives of the Northern Territories of the Gold Coast*. London, 1927.

Cruickshank, Brodie. *Eighteen Years on the Gold Coast*. London: Frank Cass, 1966.

Crummell, Alexander. *The Relations and Duties on the Free Colored Men in Americas to Africa*. Hartford, CT., 1861.

Cuguano, Ottobah. *Thoughts and Sentiments on the Evil and Wicked Traffic of Slavery and Commerce of the Human Species*. London, 1787.

Curtin, Philip D (ed.), *Africa Remembered: Narratives by West Africans from the Era of the Slave Trade*. Prospect Heights, Illinois: Waveland Press, 1967.

Crooks, J.J. *Records Relating to the Gold Coast Settlements From 1750-1874*. Dublin: Browne and Nolan, Ltd., 1923.

Cuffe, Paul. *Memoir of Captain Pal Cuffee, A Man of Color: To Which is Subjoined the Epistle of the Society of Sierra Leone in Africa & etc.* York: W. Alexander, 1812 [1817].

Daendels, H. W. *Journal and Correspondence of H.W. Daendels. Governor-General of the Netherlands Settlements on the Coast of Guinea. Part 1. November 1815 to January 1817*. Legon: Institute of African Studies, University of Ghana, 1964

Dantzig, Albert van. *The Dutch and the Guinea Coast 1674-1742. A Collection of Documents from the State Archive at the Hague*. Accra: Ghana Academy of Arts and Sciences, 1978.

Dantzig, Albert van and Adam Jones (trans). Pieter de Marees, *Description and Historical Account of the Gold Kingdom of Guinea (1602)*. Oxford: Oxford University Press, 1987.

Delaney, Martin R. *The Condition, Elevation and Destiny of the Colored People of the United States*, and Official Report of the Niger Valley Exploring Party. New York: Arno Press, 1968.

Delaney, Martin R. *Official Report of the Niger Valley Exploring Party*. New York, 1861.

Donnan, Elizabeth. *Documents Illustrative of the History of the Slave Trade to America*. 4 vols., Washington, 1930-1935.

Dupuis, Joseph. *Journal of a Residence in Ashantee*, London, 1824, reprinted London, 1966.

Isert, Paul Erdman. *Letters on West Africa and the Slave Trade. Paul Erdmann Isert's Journey to Guinea and the Caribbean Islands in Columbia* (1788). Oxford: Oxford University Press, 1992.

Makepeace, Margaret (ed.), *Trade on the Guinea Coast 1657-1666. The Correspondence of the English East India Company*. Madison: African Studies Program, University of Wisconsin-Madison. African Primary Texts, 4.

Marees, Pieter de. Description and Historical Account of the Gold Coast Kingdom of Guinea (1602), trans. and ed. Albert van Dantzig and Adam Jones (Oxford: Oxford University Press [for the British Academy] 1987.

Law, Robin and Paul E. Lovejoy (eds.), *The Biography of Mahommah Gardo Baquaqua. His Passage From Slavery to Freedom in Africa and America*. Princeton: Markus Weiner, 2003.

Nichols, Charles H. *Many Thousands Gone: The Ex-Slaves Account of Their Bondage and Freedom*, Leyden, 1963.

Nørregård, Georg. *Danish Settlements in West Africa 1658-1850*. Trans., Sigurd Mammen, Boston: Boston University Press, 1996.

O'Neil, B. H. St. J. *Report on Forts and Castles of Ghana* (Ghana Museums and Monuments Board). Accra-Tema: State Publishing Corporation, October 1961.

Rømer, Ludewig Ferdinand. *A Reliable Account of the Coast of Guinea* (1760). Selena Axelrod Winsnes (trans. and ed.). Oxford: Oxford University Press.

Smith, Venture. *A Narrative of the Life and Adventures of Venture, A Native of Africa, but Resident above Sixty Years in the United States of America, related by Himself*, New London, 1835.

Smith, William. *A New Voyage to Guinea*. London: Frank Cass & Co. Ltd., 1967, 138.

Secondary Sources

Abaka, Edmund. "Traders, Slaves and Soldiers": The Hausa Diaspora in Ghana (Gold Coast and Asante) in the Nineteenth and Early Twentieth Centuries," in Toyin Falola and Aribidesi Usman (eds.), *Movements, Borders, and Identities in Africa*. Rochester, NY: Rochester University Press, 2009, 185-199.

Angelou, Maya. *All God's Children Need Traveling Shoes*, N.Y.: Vintage Books, 1991.

Anquandah, Kwesi J. *Castles and Forts of Ghana*. Paris: Atalante, [for Ghana Monuments Board] 1979.

Anstey, Roger. *The Atlantic Slave Trade and British Abolition, 1760-1810*, London, 1975.

Asiamah, A.E.A. *The Mass Factor in Rural Politics: The Case of the Asafo Revolution in Kwahu Political History*. Accra: Ghana Universities Press, 2000.

Austin, Allan D. *African Muslims in America: Transatlantic Stories and Spiritual Struggles*. New York: Routledge, 1997.

Barnet, Miguel "La Regla de Ocha: The Religious System of Santeria," in Margarite Fernandez Olmos and Elizabeth Paravisini-Gilbert (eds.), *Sacred Possessions: Vodou, Santeria, Obeah, and the Caribbean*. New Brunswick , NJ.: Rutgers University Press, 1977.

Bech, Niels and Hyland, A.D.C.. *Elmina. A Conservation Study*. Kumasi: University of Science and Technology. Occasional Report # 17, 1978.

Bennett, Lerone. *Before the Mayflower: A History of Black America*, Chicago: Johnson Publishing Company, 1969.

Blake, John W. *West Africa: Quest for God and Gold 1454-1578*, London, 1977.

Blakely, Allison. *Russia and the Negro: Blacks in Russian History and Thought*. Washington D.C.: Howard University Press, 1986.

Blassingame, John. *The Slave Community: Plantation Life in the Antebellum South*. New York: Oxford University Press, 1977.

Blassingame, John. *The Black Family in Slavery and Freedom, 1750-1925*. New York: Vintage Books, 1976.

Boahen, A. Adu. *Topics in West African History*. London: Longmans, 1986.

Boahen, Albert Adu. *African Perspectives on Colonialism*. Baltimore: Johns Hopkins University Press, 1987.

Boxer, C.R. *The Dutch Seaborne Empire 1600-1800*. London, 1965.

Boxer, C. R. *Four Centuries of Portuguese Expansion, 1415-1825: A Succinct Survey*. Johannesburg, 1961.

Boxer, C.R. *The Dutch in Brazil, 1624-1654*. Oxford, 1957.

Boogart, Ernst van den and Pieter Emmer, "The Dutch Participation in the Atlantic Slave Trade, 1596-1650," in H. Gemery and Jan Hogendorn, *The Uncommon Market: Essays in the Economic History of the Atlantic Slave Trade*. New York: Academic Press, 1979, 353-375.

Boxer, C. R. *The Dutch Seaborne Empire 1600-1800*. London, 1965.

Breitman, George (ed.), *Malcolm X Speaks*. New York: Pathfinder Press, 1989.

Cadoux, Cecil John. *Philip of Spain and the Netherlands: an Essay on Moral Judgment in History*. Hamden, Conn.: Archon Books, 1969.

Cave, Rosemary. *Gold Coast Forts*. London: Thomas Nelson & Sons, 1900.

Clair, William St. *The Grand Slave Emporium. Cape Coast Castle and the British Slave Trade.* Exmouth market, London: Profile Books, 2006.

Claridge, W. Walton. *A History of the Gold Coast and Ashanti From the Earliest Times to the Commencement of the Twentieth Century.* 2 Vols. London: Frank Cass, 1964.

Coombs, Douglas. *The Gold Coast, Britain and the Netherlands 1850-1874.* London: Oxford University Press, 1963

Curtin, Philip D. "The Atlantic Slave Trade 1600-1800," in J.F. A. Ajayi and M. Crowder (eds.), *History of West Africa*, 2 vols., London, 1971, vol 1, 240-268.

Curtin, Philip D. *The Atlantic Slave Trade; A Census.* Madison: University of Wisconsin Press, 1969.

Curtin, Philip D. *The Rise and Fall of the Plantation Complex: Essays in Atlantic History*, 1st Edition, Cambridge University Press

Daaku, K.Y. *Trade and Politics on the Gold Coast 1600-1720.* Oxford: Oxford University Press, 1970.

Dalzel, Archibald. *The History of Dahomy*, London, 1793, reprinted London, 1967.

Da Mota, A. Teixeira and Hair, P.E.H. *East of Mina. Afro-European Relations on the Gold Coast in the 1550 and 1560s. An Essay With Supporting Documents.* Madison, Wisconsin: The Board of Regents of the University of Wisconsin, 1988.

Dantzig, Albert van. *Forts and Castles of Ghana.* Accra: Sedco Publishing, 1980.

Davies, K.G. *The Royal African Company*, London, 1957.

Dickson, Kwamina B. *A Historical Geography of Ghana.* Oxford: oxford University Press, 1971.

Doortmont, Michael R. "An Overview of Dutch Relations with the Gold Coast in Light of David van Nyendael's Mission to Ashanti in 1701-02," in I. van Kessel (ed.), *Merchants, Missionaries & Migrants. 300 Years of Dutch-Ghanaian Relations.* Legon, Accra: Sub-Saharan Publishers, 2002.

Doortmont, Michael R., and Natalie Everts, "Vrouwen, familie en eigendom op de Goudkust. Afrikaanse en Europese systemen van erfrecht in Elmina, 1760-1860." In Geld & Goed. *Jaarboek voor Vrouwengeschiedenis* 17. Amsterdam: Stichting beheer IISG 1997), 114-130. ['Women, family and Property on the Gold Coast. African Women and European Systems of inheritance in Elmina, 1760-1860'].

Du Bois, W.E.B. *The Souls of Black Folk.* Ed., with an introduction by David W. Blight and Robert Gooding-Williams. Boston: Bedford/St. Martins, 1997.

Elkins, Stanley. Slavery: A Problem in American Institutional and Intellectual Life. Chicago: University of Chicago Press, 1969.

Eltis, David and Richardson, David (eds.). *Extending the Frontiers: Essays on the New Transatlantic Slave Trade Database.* New Haven, CT: Yale University Press, 2008.

Feelings, Tom and John Henrik Clark, *The Middle Passage: White Ships / Black Cargo.* New York: Dial Books, 1995.

Feinberg, H.M. Data on Europeans Mortality in West Africa: The Dutch on the Gold Coast, 1719-1760," in Anthony Disney (ed.), *An Expanding World. The European Impact on World History 1450-1800. Vol. 4. Historiography of Europeans in Africa and Asia, 1450-1800.* Aldershot: Variorum, 1995.

Floyd Jr., Samuel A. *The Power of Black Music. Interpreting its History from Africa to the United States.* New York: O.U.P., 1996.

Gaines, Kevin K. *American Africans in Ghana. Black Expatriates and the Civil Rights Era* (Chapel Hill: The University of North Carolina Press, 2006.

Garrard, Timothy F. *Akan Gold Weights and the Gold Trade.* London: Longman 1980.

Garvey, Amy Jacques (ed.). *The Philosophy and Opinions of Marcus Garvey,* repr. New York: Humanities Press, 1968.

Gemery, Henry A and Jan S, Hogendorn, "The Economic Costs of West African participation in the Atlantic Slave Trade: A Preliminary Sampling for the Eighteenth Century," in Henry A. Gemery and Jan S. Hogendorn (eds.), *The Uncommon market. Essays in the Economic History of the Atlantic Slave Trade.* New York: Academic Press, 1979

Gerard, Charley. *Jazz in Black and White. Race, Culture, and Identity in the Jazz Community.* Wesport, Conn.: Praeger, 1998.

Gilroy, Paul. *The Black Atlantic. Modernity and Double Consciousness.* Cambridge, Mass.: Harvard University Press, 1993.

Gomez, Michael. *Black Crescent: The Experience and Legacy of African Muslims in the Americas.* Cambridge, New York: Cambridge University Press, 2005.

Gomez, Michael A. *Exchanging Our Country Marks. The Transformation of African Identities in the Colonial and Antebellum South.* Chapel Hill: The University of North Carolina Press, 1998.

Gonzalez-Wippler, Migene. *Santeria. The Religion.* St Paul, Minn.: Llewellyn Publications, 1999.

Goslinga, C. C. *The Dutch in the Caribbean and on the Wild Coast, 1580-1680.* Assen, 1971.

Grace, John. *Domestic Slavery in West Africa: With Reference to the Sierra Leone Protectorate.* New York: Barnes and Noble, 1975.

Gutman, Herbert. *The Black Family in Slavery and Freedom, 1750-1925.* New York: Pantheon Books, 1976.

Hair, P.E.H. *The Founding of the Castelo de São Jorge da Mina. An Analysis of the Sources.* Madison: University of Wisconsin African Studies Program, 1994.

Hansen, Thorkild. *Coast of Slaves.* Kari Dako (trans). Accra: Sub-Saharan Publishers, 2002.

Harris, Eddy L. *Native Stranger: A Black American's Journey Into the Heart of Africa.* New York: Vintage Books, 1992.

Harlan, Louis R. "Introduction," *Up From Slavery.* East Rutherford, NJ: Viking Penguin, 1985.

Hartman, Saidiya V. *Lose Your Mother: a Journey Along the Atlantic Slave Route.* New York: Farrar, Straus & Giroux, 2007.

Hay, Vice-Admiral Sir John Dalrymple. *Ashanti and the Gold Coast: What We Know of It.* London: Edward Stanford, 6, 7, & 8, Charing Cross, 1874.

Herbert S. Klein, *The Atlantic Slave Trade:* Cambridge: Cambridge University Press, 1999.

Hernaes, Per. *Slaves, Danes and the African Coast Society.* Trondheim, Norway, 1995.

Hibbert, Christopher. *Africa Explored. Europeans in the Dark Continent, 1769-1889.* London: W.W. Norton & Co., 1982.

Hunwick, J.O. "African Slaves in The Mediterranean World: A Neglected Aspect of the African Diaspora." In Joseph E. Harris, *Global Dimensions of the African Diaspora.* 2nd. Edn., Washington D.C.: Howard University Press, 1993, 289-324.

Hyatt, Vera. *Ghana: The Chronicle of a Museum Development Project in the Central Region.* Washington, D.C.: The Smithsonian Institution, 1997.

Israel, Jonathan. *The Dutch Republic: its Rise, Greatness and Fall, 1477-1806.* Oxford: Clarendon Press, 1998.

Jones, Adam. "Brandenburg-Prussia and the Atlantic Slave Trade," in *De la Traite á L'Esclavage. Actes du Colloque International sur la Traite des Noirs,* édités par Serge Daget, Tomes I: Ve-XVIIIe Siècles, Nantes, 1985.

Karenga, Maulana . *Introduction to Black Studies.* 3rd edn. Los Angeles: University of Sankore Press, 2002.

Kessel, Ineke van. *Merchants Missionaries & Migrants. 300 Years of Dutch-Ghanaian Relations.* Legon, Accra: Sub-Saharan Publishers, 2002.

Klein, Herbert S. *The Atlantic Slave Trade.* Cambridge: Cambridge University Press, 1999.

Lawrence, A. W. *Trade Castles & Forts of West Africa.* London: Jonathan Cape, 1963.

Lewis, David Levering. *W.E.B. Du Bois. Biography of a Race 1869-1919.* New York: Henry Holt & Co., 1993.

Lovejoy, Paul E. *Transformations in Slavery. A History of Slavery in Africa.* Cambridge: C.U.P., 2011.

Lugard, Lord. *The Dual Mandate for Tropical Africa*, Cass, 1965.

Majozo, Estelle Conwill *Middle Passage: 105 Days.* Trenton, NJ.: Africa World Press, June 2003.

Manning, Patrick (ed.), *Slave Trades, 1500-1800*, Aldershot, 1966.

Manning, Patrick. "The Slave Trade in the Bight of Benin, 1640-1890," in Henry A. Gemery and Jan S. Hogendorn (eds.), *The Uncommon market. Essays in the Economic History of the Atlantic Slave Trade.* New York: Academic Press, 1979, 140.

Martin, Eveline C. *The British West African Settlements 1750-1821. A Study in Local Administration*, London: Longmans, Green & Co. Ltd., 1927.

Masselman, George. *The Cradle of Colonialism.* New Haven, 1963.

Maurice Peress, *Dvořák to Duke Ellington. A Conductor Explores America's Music and its African Roots.* New York: Oxford University Press, 2004.

Matibag, Eugenio. *Afro-Cuban Religious Experience: Cultural Reflections in Narrative.* Gainesville: University Press of Florida, 1996.

Miller, Ivor. *Voice of the Leopard.* Mississippi: University Press of Mississippi, 2008

Norregard, Georg. *Danish Settlements in West Africa 1658-1850*, trans., Sigurd Mammen. Boston: Boston University Press, 1966.

Miller, Joseph. *Way of Death: Merchant Capitalism and the Angolan Slave Trade.* Madison, WI.: University of Wisconsin Press, 1988.

Osei-Tutu, John Kwadwo. *The Asafoi (Socio-Military Groups) in the History and Politics of Accra (Ghana) From the 17th to the 20th Century.* Africa Series No.3 Trondheim: Norwegian University of Science and Technology, 2000.

Park, Maarten. *The Dutch Republic in the Seventeenth Century: The Golden Age.* Trans., Diana Webb. Cambridge, UK: Cambridge University Press, 2005.

Palmer, Colin. "Afro-Mexican Culture and Consciousness During the Sixteenth and Seventeenth Century." In Joseph E. Harris (ed.), *Global Dimensions of the African Diaspora.* 2nd. edn., Washington D.C.: Howard University Press, 1993, 125-136.

Parker, Geoffrey. *The Dutch Revolt.* Ithaca, N.Y. rev. edn. Cornell University Press, 1988.

Patterson, Orlando. *Slavery and Social Death: a Comparative Study.* Cambridge, Mass.: Harvard University Press, 1982.

Perbi, Akosua Adoma. *A History of Indigenous Slavery in Ghana From the 15th Century to the 19th Century.* Accra: Sub-Saharan Publishers, 2004.

Peress, Maurice. *Dvořák to Duke Ellington. A Conductor Explores America's Music and its African Roots.* New York: Oxford University Press, 2004.

Pollitzer, William S. *The Gullah People and Their African Heritage.* Athens: University of Georgia Press, 1999.

Postma, Johannes Menne. *The Dutch in the Atlantic Slave Trade 1600-1815.* Cambridge: Cambridge University Press, 1990.

Postma, Johannes. "Mortality in the Dutch Slave Trade, 1675-1795," in Henry A. Gemery and Jan S. Hogendorn, *The Uncommon market. Essays in the Economic History of the Atlantic Slave Trade.* New York: Academic Press, 1979.

Postma, Johannes. "The origin of African Slaves: The Dutch Activities on the Guinea Coast, 1675-1795." In Stanley L. Engerman and Eugene D. Genevese (eds.), *Race and Slavery in the Western Hemisphere: Quantitative Studies.* Princeton: Princeton University Press, 1975.

Redkey, Edwin S. *Black Exodus: Black Nationalism and Back-to-Africa Movements, 1890-1910.* New Haven, CT: Yale University Press, 1969.

Redmayne, Paul. *The Gold Coast Yesterday and Today* (Cape Coast: Methodist Book Depot, 1941.

Reis, Joao José. *Slave Rebellion in Brazil: The Muslim Uprising of 1835 in Bahia.* Baltimore: The John Hopkins University Press, 1993.

Rollin, Frank A. *The Life and Public Service of Martin Delaney.* New York: Kraus Reprint Co., 1969.

Schomp, Virginia and S. Pearl Sharp (eds.), *The Slave Trade and the Middle Passage,* Marshall Cavendish Corp, 2006.

Sertima, Ivan van. *They Came Before Columbus: The African Presence in Ancient America.* New York: Random House, 1976.

Simawe, Saadi A. *Black Orpheus: Music in African American Fiction From the Harlem Renaissance to Toni Morrison.* New York: Garland Publishing Inc., 2000.

Skinner, Elliott. "The Dialectic Between Diasporas and Homelands," in *The Global Dimensions of the African Diaspora,* 2nd ed., Joseph Harris (ed.). Washington D.C.: Howard University Press, 1982.

Stephens, H. Morse. "Introduction," in Waldemar Westergaard, *The Danish West Indies Under Company Rule 1671-1754.* New York: Macmillan, 1917.

Sterling, Dorothy. *The Making of an Afro-American: Martin Robinson Delaney, 1812-1885.* Garden City, New York: Doubleday, 1971.

Stuckey, Sterling. *Slave Culture: Nationalist Theory and the Foundations of Black America.* New York: Oxford University Press, 1987.

Svalesen, Leif. *The Slave Ship Fredensborg.* Trans. Pat Shaw and Selena Winsnes. Accra: Sub-Saharan Publishers, 2000.

Taylor, J.B. *Biography of the Elder Lott Carey, Late Missionary to Africa.* Baltimore: Armstrong & Berry, 1838.

Thomas, Lamont D. *Paul Cuffe: Black Enterpreneur and Pan-Africanist.* Urbana & Chicago: University of Illinois Press, 1988.

Thomas, Velma Maia. *Lest We Forget: The Passage from Africa to Slavery and Emancipation: A Three-Dimensional Interactive Book with Photographs and Documents from the Black Holocaust Exhibit.* New York: Crown, 1997.

Turner, D. Lorenzo. *Africanisms in the Gullah Dialect.* Chicago: University of Chicago Press, 1949.

Uya, Okon Edet. "The Middle Passage and Personality Change Among Diaspora Africans." In Joseph E. Harris (ed.), *Global Dimensions of the African Diaspora.* 2nd. Edn., Washington D.C.: Howard University Press, 1988, 83-98.

Vandenbosch, Amry. *Dutch Foreign Policy Since 1815. A Study in Small Power Politics.* Martinus Nijhoff: The Hague, 1959.

Vogt, John. *Portuguese Rule On The Gold Coast 1469-1682.* Athens: The University of Georgia Press, 1979.

Webster, J. B. and A. A. Boahen with H.O. Idowu, *The Growth of African Civilisation. The Revolutionary Years: West Africa Since 1800.* London: Longmans, 1967.

Wiggins, Rosalind Cobbs. *Captain Cuffe's Logs and Letters, 1808-1817.* Washington D.C., 1996.

Walvin, James. *Atlas of Slavery.* Edinburgh Gate: Pearson-Longman, 2006.

Williams, Eric. *Capitalism and Slavery. With a New Introduction by Colin A. Palmer.* Chapel Hill: University of North Carolina Press, 1994.

Wright, Richard. *Black Power. A Record of Reaction in a Land of Pathos.* New York: Harper, 1954.

Wyse, Akintola J.G. "The Sierra Leone Krios: A Reappraisal From the Perspective of the African Diaspora," in *The Global Dimensions of the African Diaspora,* 2nd ed., Joseph Harris (ed.). Washington D.C.: Howard University Press, 1982.

Yarak, Larry. *Asante and the Dutch, 1744-1873.* Oxford: Clarendon Press, 1990.

Yasema, Allan E. *American Colonization Society: an Avenue to Freedom?* University Press of America, 2006.

Journal articles

Adams, C. D. Activities of Danish Botanists in Guinea," *Transactions of the Historical Society of Ghana,* 3, 1957, 30-46.

Bartels, F. L. "Philip Quacoe 1741-1816," *Transactions of the Historical Society of Ghana*, 1952-5, 153-177.

Bean, Richard. "A Note on the Relative Importance of Slaves and Gold on West African Exports," *Journal of African History* XV, 3 (1974), 351-356.

Birmingham, David. "The Regimento da Mina," *Transactions of the Historical Society of Ghana* XI

Blakely, Allison. "The Negro in Imperial Russia: A Preliminary Sketch," *The Journal of Negro History*, 61 4 (October 1976), 351-361.

Boogart, Ernst van den. "The Trade Between Western Africa and the Atlantic World, 1600-90. Estimates of Trends in Composition and Value," *Journal of African History*, 33 (1992): 369-385.

Bredwa-Mensah, Yaw. "Slavery and Plantation Life at the Danish Plantation Site at Bibease, Gold Coast (Ghana) *EAZ, Ethnogr. Archäol. Z.* 38 (1996): 455-458.

Brooks Jr., George E. "The Letter Book of Captain Edward Harrington," *Transactions of the Historical Society of Ghana*, VI (1962), 74. Extract from the Letter Book dated June 15th (1840).

Bruner, Edward M. "Tourism in Ghana. The Representation of Slavery and the Return of the Black Diaspora," *American Anthropologist* 98, 2 (1996), 290-304.

Carpenter, Rhys. "A Trans-Saharan Caravan Route in Herodutus," *American Journal of Archaeology*, 60, 3 (July 1956), 231-242.

Datta, Ansu K and R. Porter, "The Asafo System in a Historical Perspective," *Journal of African History* 12, 2 (1971): 279-297;

Eltis, David. "The Volume and Structure of the Transatlantic Slave Trade: A Reassessment," *William and Mary Quarterly*, 3rd series, 58, 1 (2001) 17-40.

Eltis, David. "The Volume, Age/Sex Ratios, and the African Impact of the Slave Trade: Some Refinement of Paul Lovejoy's Review of the Literature," *Journal of African History*, 31, 3 (1990): 485-492.

Fage, John D. "Some Remarks on Beads and Trade in Lower Guinea in the Sixteenth and Seventeenth centuries," *Journal of African History*, 3 (1962), 343-7.

Fage, John D. "More About Aggrey and Akori Beads,"in Le sol, la parole et l'écrit (Mélanges en hommage à Raymond Mauny), Paris, 1981, 205-211.

Feinberg, H.M. "Who are the Elmina?" *Ghana Notes and Queries* 11 (June 1970): 20-26.

Green-Pedersen, "The History of the Danish Negro Slave Trade, 1733-1807. An Interim Survey Relating in Particular to its Volume, Structure, Profitability and Abolition," *Revue Français d'Histoire d'Outre-Mer* LXII, 226-227 (1975): 197-220.

Hyland, Anthony. "Monuments Conservation Practice in Ghana: Issues of Policy and Management," *Journal of Architectural Conservation*, 2 (1995), 45-62.

Johnson-Odim, Cheryl. "Review of Allison Blakely, Russia and the Negro: Blacks in Russian History and Thought. Washington D.C.: Howard University Press, 1986," in *African Studies Review*, 34, 3 (December 1991), 123-124.

Inikori, J.E. "Measuring the Atlantic Slave Trade; an Assessment of Curtin and Anstey," *Journal of African History* XVII, II (1976): 197-223.

Inikori, J.E. Measuring the Atlantic Slave Trade: a Rejoinder, *Journal of African History*, XVII, IV (1976), 607-627.

Kelley, Robin D.G. "How the West Was One: On the Uses and Limitations of Diaspora," *The Black Scholar* 30 (Fall 2000-Winter 2001): 31-35.

Lovejoy, Paul E. "The Volume of the Atlantic Slave Trade: A Synthesis," *Journal of African History*, XXIII (1982), 473-501.

Miller, Ivor. "Cuba Abaku á Chants: Examining New Evidence for the African Diaspora," *African Studies Review* 48, 1 (April 2005), 23-58.

n.a. "Autobiography of Omar ibn Said, Slave in North Carolina, 1831," *American Historical Review*, 30 (1924), 787-795.

Osei-Tutu, Brempong. "The African-American Factor in the Commodification of Ghana's Slave Castles," *Transactions of the Historical Society of Ghana* 6 (2002).

Palmer, Colin. "The African Diaspora," *The Black Scholar* 30, 3-4 (2000): 56-59.

Perbi Akosua, "The Relationship Between the Domestic Slave Trade and the External Slave Trade in Pre-Colonial Ghana," *Research Review*, 8, 1 (1992).

Prorok, Count Byron Khun de. "Ancient Trade Routes From Carthage into the Sahara," *Geographical Review*, 15, 2 (April 1925), 190-2005.

Siefman, Eli. "The United Colonization Societies of New York and New York and Pennsylvania and the Establishment of the African Colony of Bassa Cove," *Pennsylvania History* 35 (1968): 33-44.

Shaloff, Stanley. "The Cape Coast Asafo Company Riot of 1932." *International Journal of African Historical Studies* 7, 4 (1974): 591-607.

Simensen, Jarle. "Rural Mass Action in the Context of Anti-Colonial Protest: The Asafo Movement of Akim Abuakwa, Ghana." *Canadian Journal of African Studies* 8, 1 (1974): 25-41.

Sweet, James, "Teaching the Modern African Diaspora: A Case Study of the Atlantic Slave Trade," *Radical History Review* 77 (2000): 106-122.

The African Intelligencer 1, 1 (July 1820): 1-31.

The African Repository and Colonial Journal 1, 4 (June 1985): 129.

Tillet, Salamishah. "In the Shadow of the Castle: (Trans)Nationalism, African American Tourism, and Gorée island," *Research in African Literatures* 40, 4 (Winter, 2009)

Varley, W.J. "The Castles and Forts of the Gold Coast," *Transactions of the Gold Coast and Togoland Society*," 1 ... 1-20.

Vogt, John. "Portuguese Gold Trade: An Account Ledger From Elmina, 1529-1531," *Transactions of the Historical Society of Ghana* 14, 1 (June 1973): 96-97.

Vogt, John L. "The Early São Tomé-Principé Slave Trade with Mina, 1500-1540," *International Journal of African Historical Studies* 6, 3 (1973): 453-467.

Newspapers

Deku, Afrikadzata. "The Truth About Castles in Ghana and Africa," *Ghanaian Weekly Spectator*, May 8 (1993), 5, and May 15 (1993), 14.

Kilpatrick, James J. "So it Don't Make no Never Mind With Dialects, *Chicago Sun-Times*, January 30, 2000.

Dissertation

Feinberg, Michael Harvey. *Elmina, Ghana: A History of Its Development and Relationship With the Dutch in the Eighteenth Century.* Ph.D. Dissertation, Boston University, 1969.

✦ Index